A D Saunders
2/97

CHINA AT WAR

34.95
4.00

1-415-
723-1593
Order Fullment Dept.

MODERN WARS IN PERSPECTIVE

General Editors: *B.W. Collins and H.M. Scott*

ALREADY PUBLISHED

Mexico and the Spanish Conquest
Ross Hassig

The Wars of French Decolonization
Anthony Clayton

The Spanish-American War: Conflict in the Caribbean and the Pacific 1895–1902
Joseph Smith

The War of the Austrian Succession, 1740–1748
M.S. Anderson

China at War, 1901–1949
Edward L. Dreyer

CHINA AT WAR, 1901–1949

EDWARD L. DREYER

LONGMAN
London and New York

Longman Group Limited,
Longman House, Burnt Mill,
Harlow, Essex CM20 2JE, England
and Associated Companies throughout the world.

*Published in the United States of America
by Longman Publishing, New York*

First published 1995

ISBN 0 582 05125 8 CSD
ISBN 0 582 05123 1 PPR

British Library Cataloguing-in-Publication Data

A catalogue record for this book is
available from the British Library

Library of Congress Cataloging-in-Publication Data

Dreyer, Edward L.
China at war, 1901–1949 / Edward L. Dreyer.
p. cm. -- (Modern wars in perspective)
Includes bibliographical references and index.
ISBN 0-582-05125-8 (csd). -- ISBN 0-582-05123-1 (ppr)
1. China--History, Military. 2. China--History--20th century.
I. Title. II. Series.
DS775.4.D74 1995
951.05-dc20 94-32357
CIP

Set by 7 in 10/12 Sabon
Produced by Longman Singapore Publishers (Pte) Ltd.
Printed in Singapore

CONTENTS

LIST OF MAPS

This one is for Sor Chad, who
tells me that history is
boring because it has already
happened

INTRODUCTION

This volume describes the military history of China from 1901 to 1949. The century opened with a broad reform of China's institutions, including her military system. Revolution was the result of these reforms, followed by the breakup of China as the leaders ('warlords') of autonomous armies fought for power. The Northern Expedition of 1926–7 had the elimination of warlordism as its stated goal, but in fact civil war continued afterwards, and Japanese aggression from 1931 on dragged China into the wider tragedy of the Second World War. Civil war resumed soon after 1945, ending only with the communist victory on the mainland in 1949.

The themes of the 1901–49 period are military modernization coupled with political disunity. From 1901 on modernization of Chinese military forces along Western-Japanese lines was a priority goal of the Chinese elite, and the fighting of the 1911 revolution and the subsequent warlord period demonstrated that victory went to the armies most convincingly organized, trained, armed and equipped along modern lines. Military modernization began, however, at a time when China was financially decentralized and poor, and when faith in the old Confucian imperial order was eroding. After the 1911 revolution, incompletely modernized military forces had to compete with each other for exiguous local sources of revenue. Their leaders and soldiers shared the dilemma of the broader Chinese society: the old political order was defeated, discredited and gone, but there was nothing like consensus on what could replace it.

As it turned out, the search for a new order was carried out on the battlefield as well as in other places, and all the leaders who offered a vision of China's future understood that military power would be necessary to enforce their vision. Yuan Shih-k'ai offered a modernized imperial system as his solution, but he was called the Father of the Warlords and his power while it lasted rested on the fact that he commanded the Peiyang Army, the best of the modernized armies. Sun Yat-sen offered US-style progressive democracy, but by the time of his death he understood that military unification, carried out by an army loyal to the principles of his party, was a necessary precondition to political reform. Chiang Kai-shek claimed to be Sun's heir, but he was also the generalissimo, and his power rested on his Central Army and on the Whampoa clique of generals and officers. Mao Tse-tung and his fellow communists said frankly that political power grows out of the barrel of a gun. Analysts of the communist victory have tended to emphasize communist political and social mobilization contrasted to Nationalist corruption and demoralization, or to echo the claim that 'People's War' marks a radical conceptual advance in military science. In fact the communist triumph depended on victories in Manchuria and North China that are best understood as skilled applications of the standard military science that the various Chinese armies had been learning, with varying degrees of success, since 1901. Military victory might make possible some general social or political programme. But military victory first had to be won.

China has been at war for much of a well-recorded history over three thousand years long, so for most Chinese the internal civil wars of the first half of the twentieth century and the Sino-Japanese War of 1937–45 suggested historical parallels. And, indeed, Chinese often compared the events of the twentieth century to previous periods of division such as the Warring States (453–221 BC) or the Three Kingdoms (*c.* AD 190–280), periods whose rulers, statesmen and generals had grown to legendary stature with the passage of time. If the Japanese were brutal and destructive, ordinary propagandistic motives would make the Chinese compare them to previous barbarian invaders such as the thirteenth-century Mongols.

Historical comparisons by themselves, however, could not provide an adequate interpretation of China's twentieth-century experience, either for the people who endured it or for historians analyzing it afterwards. The first half of the twentieth-century includes the critical decades of the longer process variously described as China's response to the West, struggle for modernization, or ongoing revolution. This has led to strong emotional responses from those, scholars included, who have concerned themselves with China's destiny, and has led to much polemical literature. What is clear to all sides in these disputes, however, is that in the early years of the twentieth century the old imperial and Confucian order, consolidated in the Western Han period (206 BC to AD 9) and preserved or restored with variations ever since, finally collapsed. All Chinese who counted realized the inevitable necessity of transforming Chinese society radically and in all sectors. But there was no agreement on what should replace the old order. Radicals like Sun Yat-sen and Ch'en Tu-hsiu hoped to replace traditional institutions with imports from the USA or the USSR; the Soviet model appealed to idealists for a while after 1918. But even conservative modernizers like Yuan Shih-k'ai could see that traditional institutions would have to adapt in order to survive; their model was the Meiji modernization of Japan under imperial auspices, rather than the repudiation of change that was dominant in China until 1900.

Lacking the common intellectual and cultural assumptions that were essentially unchallenged prior to 1895, and lacking a legitimate and generally agreed upon political order after 1911, it seems natural in retrospect that Chinese leaders would turn to force to resolve their disputes. Cultural change and intellectual ferment went on in a context punctuated and disrupted by civil war, and civil war did not cease even when the Japanese invaded. The military history of China from 1901 to 1949 is thus inseparable from the general Chinese history of the period.

Defining the period requires some justification. The year 1949 is a clear break-point: since then the People's Republic of China (PRC) on the mainland and the Republic of China (ROC) on Taiwan have developed without internal civil war in either regime. Taiwan has become a major economic power despite high armament levels and the need to garrison Quemoy. The PRC has also boomed economically in recent years, and its earlier economic problems were due more to failed communist policies than to its foreign wars (Korea 1950–3, India 1961, Vietnam 1979) or to civil war. Since 1949 both Chinese states have produced political systems that are integrated by more than military means, and their economic development has not been frustrated by endless civil warfare.

For many scholars the period that ended in 1949 obviously began in 1927, when the split between the Chinese Communist Party (CCP) and the more conservative elements in the Kuomintang or Nationalist Party (KMT) who rallied around Chiang Kai-shek took place. This, so the argument goes, disrupted the First KMT–CCP United Front originally formed to defeat the (backward and reactionary) northern warlords, with the KMT becoming a reactionary force itself due to its betrayal of the revolution. The

CCP, driven to the countryside, remained true to the revolution and, under the leadership of Mao Tse-tung, created 'People's War' – a theoretically different type of war, wageable only by a mass party such as the CCP, in which rural land reform and guerrilla warfare waged by peasant auxiliaries gave the regulars of the Red Army the winning edge.

As with the historical parallels previously mentioned, the paradigm presented in the previous paragraph is not totally false, but it obscures more than it explains. In fact, the communists won the 1945–9 civil war in a series of set-piece conventional campaigns that reflect mastery of imported Western military science; the Nationalists lost because they overreached in reoccupying North China and Manchuria immediately after the Second World War, and then threw good money after bad by reinforcing exposed armies that were later lost. Foreign involvement – the long Japanese occupation, the Russian conquest of Manchuria in 1945, and US airlift and sealift that encouraged Nationalist command errors – greatly affected the outcome of the civil war, as did the demoralization and corruption of the Nationalist regime. None of this was caused by People's War, which both the Japanese and the Nationalists had earlier dealt with successfully. Indeed, it is now understood that communist rural radicalism in Kiangsi in the 1930s had the effect of mobilizing a hitherto indifferent rural elite behind the KMT.

Looking beyond KMT–CCP rivalry allows us to see more clearly that in 1927–37 (the 'Nanking Decade') Chiang Kai-shek actually had three different wars in hand: against the communists, which he nearly won; against the hydra-headed phenomenon of 'residual warlordism', which requires more discussion; and against the Japanese, whom he could not have defeated and against whom he was understandably reluctant to fight. Chiang's hopes for Great Power assistance against Japan were to be disappointed until it was too late. Obviously it was in the interests of the communists to call, from 1931 on, for a new United Front to resist Japan, but Chiang was still able to uproot them and force them on to the Long March. The real danger for Chiang in the calls to resist Japan was their appeal to all the nominally KMT elements that were in fact opposed to or uncomfortable with Chiang. These included not only Wang Ching-wei and the KMT political left, but also the military forces associated with Chang Hsueh-liang's Manchurians, Feng Yü-hsiang's Kuominchün, Yen Hsi-shan's Shansi forces, the Fukien rebels, the Kwangsi clique and the Canton opposition. While all of these elements had in the end joined the Northern Expedition, they retained much military autonomy. Chiang had to manoeuvre carefully against them. In effect he was the most powerful warlord, but, as with previous incumbents of that position (Chang Tso-lin, Wu P'ei-fu, Tuan Ch'i-jui, and Yuan Shih-k'ai himself), his hegemonic status encouraged the lesser fry to combine against him. Warlordism survived under new colours after 1927, and this implies that we must go back well before 1927 if we hope to understand the military history of the 1927–49 period.

Both the Chinese Communist People's Liberation Army (PLA, born on 1 August 1927) and Chiang Kai-shek's Central Army were conceived initially as 'Party Armies' whose indoctrination with the ideals of a revolutionary political party would help them transcend the limitations (mercenary attitudes, betrayal) perceived in the warlord armies. These armies would be under political control. Mao's injunction that the party must control the gun, and never must the gun control the party, seems to parallel the purely instrumental role for the military that is supposed to be the rule in modern democracies. In fact both armies depended on officers whose initial training and experience had been in the warlord armies. Their military science (what Whitson calls the 'warlord model') was that common to the warlord armies of the 1920s.[1] Given these continuities, it is worth pointing out that certain of the warlords (notably Feng Yü-hsiang and Yen Hsi-shan) considered themselves economic and social reformers, and that certain of the warlord armies (notably the Peiyang Army and the Yunnan Army in the period around 1911) attained a rather high level of professional development. Both reforms and professionalism were in the end thwarted by the basic disunity that led to warlordism, and this disunity lasted until 1949.

To understand the genesis and outcome of the Chinese Civil War that ended in 1949 we thus need to understand the wars and armies of the earlier warlord period, and to understand them we need to go back to the beginning of systematic military modernization in the Manchu reform movement that began in 1901. In that year the Manchu government, fresh from defeat and humiliation in the so-called Boxer Rebellion, committed itself – belatedly but irrevocably – to a comprehensive modernization of its institutions. Previous efforts at modernization in the late 1800s had

1 William W. Whitson, *The Chinese High Command: A History of Chinese Communist Military Politics, 1927–71* (New York, 1973), pp. 7–13.

created a few modern-inspired installations that coexisted uncomfortably with an established system that was extremely hostile to change. Military modernization was an important part of this process. While cutting their own throats, the Manchu rulers of the Ch'ing dynasty created the modernized armies that later contended for power under the warlords, and from which the Nationalist and communist armies of the 1945–9 Civil War emerged.

With the beginning and the ending both defined, we shall proceed chronologically in the body of the book. Chapter 1 gives some historical background and then describes the Manchu reform movement, the creation of the Peiyang Army and the other modernized armies, and the crucial role played by these armies in the revolution of 1911. Chapter 2 covers the period (1911–19) of the ascendancy of the unified Peiyang Army and the effort of its leader and founder, Yuan Shih-k'ai, to subvert the new Republic of China. Yuan was opposed by the leaders of other military factions, and ultimately by his own generals, including the leaders of the competing cliques into which the Peiyang Army broke up after Yuan's death in 1916. Chapter 3 deals with the period (1919–25) of most intense conflict among the warlords. The succession of major wars among the Peiyang Army factions not only failed to reunify the Peiyang Army, but also left China even more disunited, due to the rise of non-Peiyang regional armies, of which Chang Tso-lin's Fengtien (Manchurian) Army was only the most important.

Chapter 4 covers the background of the 1926–7 Northern Expedition, the Northern Expedition itself, the KMT–CCP split, the beginnings of the Maoist peasant strategy, and Chiang Kai-shek's efforts to complete the reunification of China under his rule, down until the Japanese seizure of Manchuria in 1931. Frustrated by the repeated betrayals of his minor-warlord armies, Sun Yat-sen had introduced a new element into the warlord world: the National Revolutionary Army that carried out the Northern Expedition was in principle a party army that was both professionally capable and indoctrinated with zeal for Sun's programme. Afterwards it was the communists who best understood and practised political indoctrination as a means of enhancing the cohesion of their own army. For Chiang, however, it was not the communists so much as the 'residual warlords' who most threatened his power after 1927. Chapter 5 shows more of this. Between the Manchurian Incident (1931) and the outbreak of full-scale hostilities with Japan (1937), Chiang came near to destroying the communists while using the anti-communist campaigns to uproot warlord rivals. He correctly interpreted calls for a United Front against Japan as ploys by his domestic enemies, and his strategy of internal pacification was eventually undone by the warlord–communist conspiracy against him at Sian (1936). Residual warlordism remained important until 1949, and it is not possible to view the post-1927 years solely in terms of KMT–CCP conflict.

Chapters 6 and 7 both deal with the Sino-Japanese War of 1937–45. Breaking in 1941 emphasizes a major point: almost all of the Chinese fighting against Japan was done before the United States' entry into the war in December 1941, and the Chinese were almost always defeated. By 1941 the Nationalists had lost the coastal and other treaty port cities that once had been their bases of power, while the equally battered communists survived mostly behind Japanese lines in North China, in the interstices of the railway network that was itself under tight Japanese control. From December 1941 to August 1945, the China theatre was a story of US hopes and dreams, given a limited reality due to such resources as the United States were willing to commit. The Chinese waited for the Americans to beat Japan, so that they could resume their civil war.

With all the past as prologue, Chapter 8 describes the Civil War of 1945–9 itself. Despite all that has been said about the clash of ideologies, the underlying political and social agendas, the corruption and decay of the Nationalist regime, the significance of communist China for the Third World or for US politics, or even about the claim that People's War marks a conceptual advance in military science, the outcome of the civil war is readily explainable in conventional military-historical terms. The Nationalists sent their best formations into a series of traps in Manchuria and North China, lost them, and afterwards never had a chance. Mao's revolution was a consequence, rather than a cause, of the communist victory on the mainland.

Chinese proper names are given in the modified Wade-Giles system used in most English-language writing on China until fairly recently. Despite the contemporary tendency to use the phonetically better Hanyu pinyin to transcribe names, I felt that using the older system would facilitate reference to the specialized studies on which this work is based. Calling the Old Marshal Zhang Zuolin might deter the reader from recognizing that Gavan McCormack's *Chang Tso-lin* refers to the same person. Strict Wade-Giles is modified by

Chinese Post Office or other standard usage, especially in place names: Nanking rather than Nan-ching, Canton rather than Kuang-chou, etc., but sometimes in personal names too: Chiang Kai-shek rather than Chiang Chieh-shih.

This book is based on the research of scholars of modern China and Japan, mostly done in the last few decades, but going back as far as Thomas F. Wade's 1851 study of the Chinese army. I wish to acknowledge my indebtedness to the authors of these studies, without which a work of synthesis such as this work would not be possible. Of course, the errors and other shortcomings of this work are solely the responsibility of the author.

1 MILITARY REFORM AND REVOLUTION, 1901–11

Empress Dowager Tz'u-hsi, who had been the de facto ruler of China since 1862, concluded in 1901 that comprehensive reform and modernization were necessary to preserve Manchu-ruled China from partition. This belated conclusion followed her return to Peking in 1901, after her forced flight from the expeditionary force sent by the Great Powers to suppress the Boxer Rebellion, a nativist attack on foreign influence that she had originally supported. The moment was not propitious; among other things, the Boxer Rebellion had resulted in a huge reparations debt to the Great Powers, so that funding for any new projects was precarious. Nevertheless, the years down to the death of Tz'u-hsi in 1908 saw the creation of a powerful and Western-appearing military force, the Peiyang Army, which in turn was the centrepiece of a general reconstruction of China's military system. The price of reform, however, was the destruction of the traditional institutions that had maintained the Manchu Ch'ing dynasty for over two centuries. In the revolution of 1911, the modern army turned against the dynasty, while the remnants of the old-style forces fought in its defence. By turning against its creators the modern army made the 1911 revolution possible, and by dividing into warring factions the army caused the failure of the republican experiment. The civil wars that lasted until 1949 were thus an unforeseen legacy of military modernization.

TRADITIONAL MILITARY FORCES AND NINETEENTH-CENTURY REGIONALISM

In 1644 the native Chinese Ming dynasty, which had ruled since 1368, was overthrown by the Manchus, whose pretensions to empire dated to 1616 and who had adopted the Chinese-style dynastic name Ta Ch'ing (Great Pure). The Manchus were a people related to the Mongols, like them nomadic and speaking a language of the Ural-Altaic group, with no affinities to Chinese. They were native to the region now constituting the three northeastern provinces of China, known to the Chinese simply as the northeast (tung-pei), but often called Manchuria by foreigners. The first two Manchu emperors created a state in Manchuria in which Mongol and Chinese collaborators participated on equal terms with the Manchus. In 1644 Manchu rule seemed preferable, to many in the Ming dynasty elite, to the rule of the peasant rebels who had undermined the Ming. In the following decades the Ch'ing dynasty conquered all of the rest of China, and imposed the Manchu hairstyle ('queue': the front of the head is shaved, and the hair grows long in the back and is braided into a pigtail) on the Chinese as a visible symbol of submission.[1]

In the mature Ch'ing dynasty system, Manchu and Chinese personnel and civil and military elements checked and balanced one another, leaving all important initiative to the throne. Coupled with the general acceptance of the Manchu claim to be the legitimate protectors of Chinese civilization, the resulting system proved highly durable.[2] Its military expression was a dual army: the Eight Banners (pa-ch'i) and the Army of the Green Standard (lü-ying).

The Eight Banners were the descendants of the original Manchu conquerors, and of certain Mongols and Chinese who had joined the Manchus before 1644. Each of the twenty-four Banner units (eight for each of the three national divisions) was divided into regiments and companies. Membership in each company was

1. The extensive literature on the founding of the Manchu empire includes Franz Michael, *The Origins of Manchu Rule in China* (Baltimore, 1942); Lynn A. Struve, *The Southern Ming, 1644–1662* (New Haven, 1984); Robert B. Oxnam, *Ruling from Horseback: Manchu Politics in the Oboi Regency, 1661–1669*, (Chicago, 1975); Lawrence D. Kessler, *K'ang-hsi and the Consolidation of Ch'ing Rule, 1661–1684* (Chicago, 1976); and Jonathan D. Spence, *Ts'ao Yin and the K'ang-hsi Emperor: Bondservant and Master* (New Haven, 1966). Arthur W. Hummel and Fang Chao-ying, *Eminent Chinese of the Ch'ing Period* (Washington, 1943–4); cited afterwards as ECCP) has excellent short biographies of the most important personalities involved.

2. Ch'ing institutions are described in detail in H.S. Brunnert and V.V. Hagelstrom, *Present Day Political Organization of China* (English translation; Shanghai, 1912; cited as BH) and in Pao Chao Hsieh, *The Government of China, 1644–1911* (Baltimore, 1925), and are analyzed in Thomas A. Metzger, *The Internal Organization of Ch'ing Bureaucracy: Legal, Normative and Communication Aspects* (Cambridge, MA, 1973). See also T'ung-tsu Ch'ü, *Local Government in China under the Ch'ing* (Cambridge, MA, 1962), and Kung-ch'uan Hsiao, *Rural China: Imperial Control in the Nineteenth Century* (Seattle, 1957).

hereditary, with fathers required to serve until their sons were grown, and expeditionary forces were often constituted by drafting a stated number of men from each company. In the earlier phase of the dynasty, Banner forces usually fought on horseback, with artillerists coming from the Chinese bannermen. However, after the fall of Peking, most of the Banner forces were moved there, to constitute the dynasty's ultimate military reserve. Small Banner garrisons were also placed in a few important cities, most of which were also capitals of governors-general. Despite imperial exhortations, the fighting qualities of the Banner forces gradually deteriorated, and by the time of the White Lotus rebellion (1796–1804) the Banner forces no longer had much fighting value.[3]

The original Green Standard troops were the soldiers of the Chinese military commanders who surrendered to the Ch'ing in 1644 and after. Their troops enlisted voluntarily and for long terms of service; they usually came from the socially disadvantaged, and remained segregated from Chinese society, partly because of the latter's deep anti-military bias, and partly because they were paid too poorly and irregularly to marry and support a family. The contempt in which soldiers were held, expressed in the often repeated ditty 'good iron is not made into nails, good men are not made into soldiers', extended to their officers as well, since most Green Standard officers were promoted from the ranks, and this attitude has greatly hindered China's efforts at military modernization. Typically, Green Standard troops outnumbered bannermen by about two to one (approximately 600,000 to 300,000), but from the eighteenth century on the Green Standard army was divided into garrisons of battalion size, reporting through regional brigade generals (tsung-ping) to commanders-in-chief (t'i-tu) in each province, who nominally were on the same level of authority as the Banner generals and the civilian governors-general and governors.

3 Thomas F. Wade, "The army of the Chinese Empire : its two great divisions, the bannermen of National Guard, and the Green Standard of provincial troops", in *Chinese Repository*, vol. 20 (May, June and July 1851), pp.250–80, 300–40 and 362–422, has detailed lists of units and their deployment. Chao-ying Fang, "A technique for estimating the numerical strength of the early Manchu military forces", in *Harvard Journal of Asiatic Studies* 13 (1950), pp.192–215, explains the working of the Banner system at its peak. Ralph A. Powell, *The Rise of Chinese Military Power, 1895–1912* (Princeton, 1955), pp.3–19, gives a general overview.

During most of the Ch'ing dynasty, the eighteen provinces of China proper were ruled over by sixteen governors (hsun-fu), most of whom were subordinated in pairs to one of the eight governors-general (tsung-tu). These high officials represented the civilian element in the system of checks and balances, and originally most governorships went to Chinese and most governor-generalships to Manchus, thus preserving the ethnic balance also found in the two armies and in the major organs of government in Peking. Governors-general and governors each had a battalion of Green Standard troops under their personal command, but their primary duties as civil administrators lay in the judicial and revenue areas; coping with invasion or rebellion was the duty of Banner generals and Green Standard commanders-in-chief.

By 1800 both the Banner forces and the Green Standard armies had declined to a low level of military effectiveness, as was shown in both the Opium War (1839–42) and the Taiping rebellion (1851–66).

The Opium War was provoked by Britain in order to open China to trade. It inaugurated the period of the Unequal Treaties (lasting in law until 1943), during which China lost her tariff autonomy and submitted to the creation of numerous enclaves (treaty ports, of which Shanghai was the most important) characterized by foreign legal jurisdiction (extraterritoriality) and military control. The Opium War also indicated the extreme vulnerability of China to sea power, since China gave up when the British fleet sailed up the Yangtze to Nanking, thus interdicting the Grand Canal route from the lower Yangtze on which Peking depended. Nevertheless, and in stark contrast to Japan, defeat by a much more advanced foreign power actually had little impact on Chinese society prior to 1900. The technology of steamships, rifled cannon and exploding shells was so advanced and alien that it seemed like magic. Chinese modernizers afterwards viewed such things essentially as icons, whose mere possession was a guarantee of efficacy. As Chinese officials came to understand the rivalries among the Western powers, the venerable Chinese diplomatic tradition of 'using barbarians to control barbarians' (yi-yi chih-yi) came into play. The combination of purchasing advanced technology and 'barbarian management', in other words, kept the impact of the West decisively marginalized until 1900. This was so despite Chinese defeats in the Arrow War (1856–60, including the Anglo-French occupation of Peking and destruction of the Summer Palace in 1860), the Sino-French War (1884–5) and the First

Sino-Japanese War (1894–5).[4]

The Taiping rebellion, on the other hand, mobilized millions of Chinese in opposition to the Ch'ing dynasty and to the Confucian intellectual foundations of Chinese civilization. Such a profound threat to Manchu rule, affecting the most heavily populated areas of China, obviously had to be suppressed, even if the price was institutional reform. The solution that ultimately emerged was the creation of the so-called 'militia armies'. Unlike the Green Standard forces, these were recruited from the more prosperous peasantry by means of clan and family ties. They were officered by the lower ranks of the degree holding 'gentry' (shen-shih) – a class that normally held aloof from military service – and commanded at the higher levels by governors and governors-general who in turn had been appointed because of their ability to raise and lead troops. The most important militia armies were the Hunan Army of Tseng Kuo-fan (d. 1872), the Fukien Army of Tso Tsung-t'ang (d. 1885) and the Anhwei Army of Li Hung-chang (d. 1901). Funding of these armies was precarious, depending heavily on the internal transit duties (likin) that had sprung up in the wake of the rebellion.[5]

The militia armies remained in existence after the effective end of the Taiping rebellion (1864). Parts of them were sent elsewhere in the empire to suppress other rebellions. Since the chain of command in the militia armies depended heavily on personal, rather than institutional, loyalties, transferring an army to a new area effectively ceded civil authority there to the army's commander. The militia armies were equipped with a mixture of traditional and modern weapons, and their commanders advocated military modernization.

4 Hsin-pao Chang, *Commissioner Lin and the Opium War* (Cambridge, MA, 1964); John K. Fairbank, *Trade and Diplomacy on the China Coast: The Opening of the Treaty Ports, 1842–1854* (2 vols, Cambridge, MA, 1953); Mary C. Wright. *The Last Stand of Chinese Conservatism: The T'ung-chih Restoration, 1862–1874* (Stanford, 1957); John K. Fairbank and Teng Ssu-yu, *China's Response to the West: A Documentary Survey, 1839–1923* (Cambridge, MA, 1954); and Lloyd E. Eastmann, *Throne and Mandarins: China's Search for a Policy during the Sino-French Controversy, 1880–1885* (Cambridge, MA, 1967) are some of the major works on these topics.

5 Powell, *Rise*, pp.19–50. See also Stanley Spector, *Li Hung-chang and the Huai Army: A Study in Nineteenth Century Chinese Regionalism* (Seattle, 1964); W.L. Bales, *Tso Tsungt'ang: Soldier and Statesman of Old China*, (Shanghai, 1937); and William James Hail, *Tseng Kuo-fan and the Taiping Rebellion* (New Haven, 1927) on the principal regional leaders. Yu-wen Jen, *Taiping Revolutionary Movement* (New Haven, 1973), is excellent but strongly pro-Taiping; see also Franz Michael and Chang Chung-li, *The Taiping Rebellion: History and Documents* (3 vols, Seattle, 1966–7).

During the 'self-strengthening' period of the 1860s, the militia army leaders had some success, sponsoring the translation of Western works, the purchase of foreign steamships and weapons, and the creation of two major installations – the Kiangnan Arsenal and the Foochow Shipyard – with military importance. The self-strengtheners were able to suppress the other local rebellions, essentially through traditional techniques of Chinese statecraft. Tso Tsung-t'ang reconquered Sinkiang and bluffed Russia into withdrawing in the 1880s. In the Sino-French War the Chinese actually won the land battles, even though her naval defeat in Foochow harbour meant the loss of the war.

In effect, the Taiping rebellion had demonstrated the obsolescence of the traditional military forces and had placed effective military authority in the provinces in the hands of the civil governors. This meant the destruction of the traditional checks and balances, which was acceptable since the official class headed by those governors had demonstrated its loyalty to the dynasty during the rebellion. The resulting pattern of political-military power is usually called 'regionalism'. Anhwei Army creator Li Hung-chang was its most important exemplar. At the height of his influence in the 1880s and 1890s he usually controlled five major provinces: Chihli (later renamed Hopei) directly as governor-general, Shantung through a colleague, and the three Yangtze provinces of Kiangsu, Anhwei and Kiangsi often through his brother Li Han-chang as governor-general at Nanking. Li used the customs and tax revenues of the provinces under his control to modernize segments of the Anhwei Army, and to build a modern navy (the Peiyang Fleet), which was destroyed in the course of the first Sino-Japanese War (Peiyang, meaning literally 'Northern Ocean', refers to the customs revenues collected in North China, which were used to fund first the Peiyang Fleet and later the Peiyang Army).

Devolution of military power to the provinces, military authority resting on personal loyalties, and irregular local funding of military forces all were characteristics of the warlord period (and of periods of dynastic breakdown in previous Chinese history). Regionalism was thus in a certain sense the precursor of warlordism. The important difference was that the regionalist governors remained civil officials, no matter how much military authority they wielded, or for how long. For over two thousand years Chinese civil officials had been the products of an educational system based on the classical books of Confucianism. In both the Ming and the Ch'ing, civil official status depended on written examinations that tested not only knowledge of the classics but also the composition of poetry and prose. The regional leaders remained products of this education and examination system, which internalized the Confucian values, including both loyalty to the throne and disdain for soldiers. The throne itself was manipulated by the Empress Dowager, who had seized power in 1862 as regent for her son Emperor T'ung-chih (r. 1862–74) following the death of her husband Emperor Hsien-feng (r. 1851–61). She was embittered all her life against the West and its works because of the sack of Peking and the burning of the Summer Palace that followed the Ch'ing defeat in the Arrow War (1856–60). For her, regionalism was a way of adopting what was absolutely needed from the West while keeping the West at a distance.

Unfortunately, regionalism prevented the systematic modernization of China's military and naval forces. Instead of a single army and a single navy, China entered the Sino-Japanese War with four navies, of which only the Peiyang Fleet had modern ships, and numerous different armies. The war was fought by Li Hung-chang's forces, unsupported by the forces of other provinces, just as Li Hung-chang had kept his forces out of the Sino-French War. In the war the Peiyang Fleet, which included two pre-Dreadnought battleships, was overwhelmed by the well-served quick-firing guns of a lighter Japanese fleet that included no battleships.[6] On land similarly Japan's German-inspired conscript army, led by academy-trained professional officers, defeated China's best regionalist troops.[7] China's defeat surprised the world and suggested that China was ripe for partitioning, which the Japanese inaugurated by annexing Taiwan. From 1895 on, the creation of a modern, unified national state as the basis for military power was high on the agenda of Chinese political reformers. In fact the legacy of regionalism prevented this before 1949, and the Empress Dowager was not converted to the necessity of reform until 1901.

Between 1895 and 1901, the pattern of regionalism persisted, despite growing pressures for reform from the Confucian literati

6 Edwin A. Falk, *Togo and the Rise of Japanese Seapower* (New York, 1936), pp.152–220; Bruce Swanson, *Eighth Voyage of the Dragon: A History of China's Quest for Seapower* (Annapolis, 1982), pp.85–112; John L. Rawlinson, *China's Struggle for Naval Development, 1839–1895* (Cambridge, MA, 1967), pp.63–197, is the best account of nineteenth-century naval development, but Herbert W. Wilson, *Ironclads in Action* (2 vols, Boston, 1898) and *Battleships in Action* (2 vols, Boston, 1926) gives the flavour of contemporary Western reactions to Chinese efforts.

7 Roger Hackett, *Yamagata Aritomo and the Rise of Modern Japan, 1838–1922* (Cambridge, MA, 1971), pp.54–89, 156–1.

class. K'ang Yu-wei (d. 1927), a brilliant intellectual who attempted to create a revisionist Confucianism to serve as the basis for the systematic reform of Chinese society, emerged as the leader of the reform movement. He and his followers were briefly in power in the summer of 1898, with the support of Emperor Kuang-hsu (r. 1875–1908), the cousin of T'ung-chih whom the Empress Dowager had adopted as her son. They envisaged a comprehensive overhaul of Ch'ing institutions, modelled on the career of Peter the Great of Russia (1689–1725). The Empress Dowager's coup (22 September 1898) against the Emperor ended these plans. The reformers fled or were executed, and regionalism once again became the order of the day. Tz'u-hsi's unwillingness to cope intellectually with the challenge of Western military and naval power found its symbolic expression in her use of naval funds to rebuild the Summer Palace. Her embrace of the Boxer movement, essentially a traditional sort of peasant-based rebel movement, whose leaders hoped to eliminate the Western presence in China, and who claimed to have magical powers to render themselves and their followers invulnerable to weapons, was an act of desperation; imperial governments for two millennia had suppressed such movements as a matter of principle. In 1900 the combined expeditionary force of the eight Great Powers took Peking to rescue the foreign legations from the Boxers, and for the second time in forty years, Tz'u-hsi and the rest of the Chinese court fled Peking because China lacked the military power to resist a Western (or Westernized: in 1900 the Japanese were present) expeditionary force of only moderate size.[8]

Regionalism now contributed greatly to saving China from partition. Almost all of the governors-general and governors had been unconvinced by the Boxer claims to invincibility, and had ignored the Empress Dowager's declaration of war against all the powers. Since they had made local arrangements with foreign consuls to keep peace in their provinces, it became possible to describe the Boxers as a 'rebellion' for face-saving purposes. The Empress Dowager therefore was able to return to Peking. She consented to execute various scapegoats, and to receive (and be

8 Jung-pang Lo, ed., *K'ang Yu-wei: A Biography and a Symposium* (Tucson, 1967); Victor Purcell, *The Boxer Uprising: A Background Study* (Cambridge, MA, 1963); Chester Tan, *The Boxer Catastrophe* (New York, 1955). In the end K'ang's disciple Liang Ch'i-ch'ao became politically more important than K'ang; Hao Chang, *Liang Ch'i-ch'ao and Intellectual Transition in China, 1890–1907* (Cambridge, MA, 1964), and Joseph W. Levenson, *Liang Ch'i-ch'ao and the Mind of Modern China* (London, 1959).

photographed with) the foreign diplomatic community that she had previously attempted to kill off. Most importantly, she finally became convinced of the necessity for serious military reform.

Unfortunately, part of the price for this was the 450 million tael Boxer Indemnity, a form of punitive damages imposed on China by the victorious powers. Compared to China's ordinary revenues (officially reported as 105 million taels for 1902), it was very large; paying it required a substantial surcharge on the ordinary land taxes, a tax rise that further eroded the dynasty's prestige.[9] By this time the reliable revenues from the foreign-run Imperial Maritime Customs Service were mostly pledged for foreign loans, and likin and other new (post-Taiping) sources of domestic revenue also were fully committed.[10] Military reforms had to rest on fragmented and localized sources of revenue, and this made the creation of a centralized army impossible, despite the intentions of the reformers.

THE MANCHU MILITARY REFORMS, 1901–8

Li Hung-chang, the leading reformer of the nineteenth century, died in 1901, and Jung-lu, the long-time Manchu confidant and supporter of the Empress Dowager, in 1903. Chang Chih-tung, Liu K'un-yi and Yuan Shih-k'ai were the leading provincial officials in these years. All had opposed the Boxer movement. They recommended, in essence, that China adopt a Japanese model of military modernization. In 1901 the obsolete military examination system was abolished, and provincial authorities were ordered to establish military academies. These steps were part of a comprehensive reform movement, which included the abolition of the much more important civil examinations (1905) and the complete restructuring of the agencies of government. Later revolutionaries felt that the Manchu reforms were piecemeal, insincere and self-serving. The reality was more subtle: to reform, the government had to destroy the institutions, and the balance among them, on which its own power rested.[11]

9 Yeh-chien Wang, *Land Taxation in Imperial China, 1750–1911* (Cambridge, MA, 1973), pp.62, 74.

10 Stanley F. Wright, *Hart and the Chinese Customs* (Belfast, 1950), on the organization and role of the Imperial Chinese Maritime Customs Service.

11 Wolfgang Franke, *The Reform and Abolition of the Traditional Chinese Examination System* (Cambridge, MA, 1960) on the examination system; Meribeth E. Cameron, *The Reform Movement in China, 1898–1912* (Stanford, 1931) on the reform process in general.

Yuan Shih-k'ai emerged as the leading figure of the post-1901 reforms. After a career as Li Hung-chang's troubleshooter in Korea, Yuan had been given command in 1895 of the brigade-sized Newly Created Army. He drilled and trained it, personally selecting the recruits and cultivating the officers. The latter included Chang Hsun (who 'restored' the Manchu dynasty for a week in 1917), Hsu Shih-ch'ang (president of the republic 1918–22), Ts'ao K'un (president 1922–4 and leader of the Chihli military clique), Tuan Ch'i-jui ('prime minister' during much of 1916–20 and leader of the Anhwei military clique) and Feng Kuo-chang (president 1917–18 and founder of the Chihli clique); they rose with Yuan Shih-k'ai and later occupied the leading positions in the Peiyang military clique. Yuan definitely belonged in the camp of those regional officials who recognized the necessity of military reform. When opponents of reform in 1898 coalesced around the Empress Dowager, the reformers approached Yuan, hoping to use his Newly Created Army to remove her permanently from political life. Instead, Yuan betrayed the reformers, which permitted the Empress Dowager's return to power. His reward was the governorship of Shantung. He used his authority to kill or expel the local Boxers, and thus emerged from the Boxer Rebellion in the good graces of the foreigners. He was thus a natural successor to Li Hung-chang, and in 1901 was appointed to the governor-generalship of Chihli and the other offices attached thereto, including that of Superintendent of Trade for the Northern Ocean (Peiyang ta-ch'en) responsible for collection of the customs revenues and relations with foreigners in North China. Yuan may be described as a traditional Chinese would-be emperor who nevertheless understood better than most of his contemporaries the importance of the military and other challenges posed by the West. Personally ruthless, he could often use honesty and loyalty to achieve his purposes. In 1902 Yuan organized a Military Administration Department (chün-cheng-szu) divided into staff, organization and training sections. He proposed organizing his modern forces in Western-style divisions, and by the end of the year the court had ordered the provinces generally to organize their modern forces in a uniform manner.[12]

12 Powell, *Rise*, pp.71–82, 137–46; updated by Steven R. MacKinnon, *Power and Politics in Late Imperial China: Yuan Shikai in Beijing and Tianjin* (Berkeley, 1980), pp.90–116; Jerome Ch'en, *Yuan Shih-k'ai (1858–1916): Brutus Assumes the Purple* (2nd edn, Stanford, 1972).

Chang Chih-tung (d. 1908) was the other provincial leader most affected by this. He had emerged in the 1870s as one of the 'Purification Clique' of brilliant young literary officials who opposed dealing with the West. The experience of the Sino-French and Sino-Japanese wars had changed his mind, and in his mature writings he advocated the adoption of Western technology in order

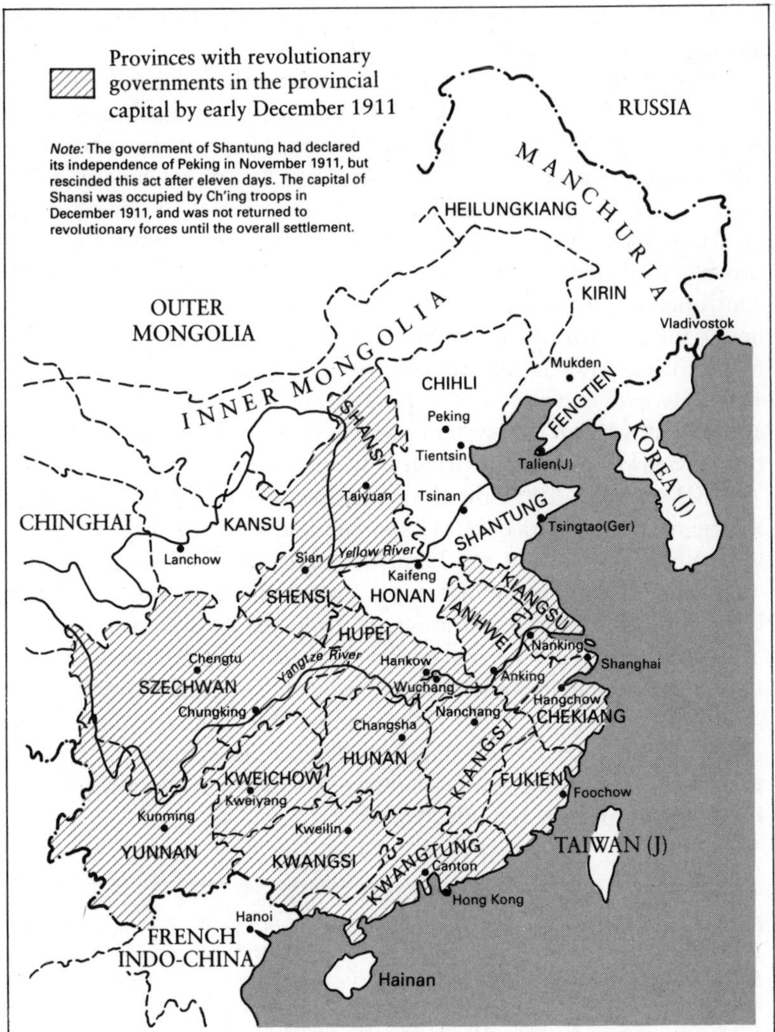

1. China in 1911 (After: Young, *The Presidency of Yuan Shih-k'ai*)

to preserve Chinese cultural values. His famous slogan 'Chinese learning as the foundation, Western learning for practical application' (Chung-hsueh wei t'i, Hsi-hsueh wei yung) suggests the limits of Confucian willingness to accommodate the West. The peak of his career had been as governor-general of Hupei and Hunan, where he had promoted various modern institutions. The military aspect of this activity had been a force called the Self-Strengthening Army, which he had organized and drilled from 1895 on, more or less on the German model.[13]

Most other provincial leaders were well behind Yuan and Chang in military modernization, but most established military academies. Japanese predominated among instructors. They were nearer, came cheaper, and were more likely to know Chinese; in any event, they knew the written language, which was often an insurmountable hurdle for Europeans. Hoping for rapid reform, the court permitted, as it had before, the growth of many provincially controlled modernizing armies, instead of a single modern army under the control of the central government. Creating the latter, as Inspector-General of Maritime Customs Sir Robert Hart advised in 1904, would have required a comprehensive overhaul of the antiquated Ch'ing tax system, which in turn implied much more central control over the provinces.

In December 1903 the court created a Commission for Army Reorganization, headed by Yuan Shih-k'ai's patron Prince Ch'ing, with Yuan himself and the Manchu nobleman T'ieh-liang as junior members. The composition of the commission, as well as Yuan's leadership as a military reformer, foretold the recommendation that Yuan's army should be the model on which the military forces of the other provinces should be standardized. The commission's report (approved 12 September 1904) called for the creation of an uniformly organized army (Lu-chün: literally land army, as opposed to Hai-chün, meaning navy) of thirty-six divisions and a supporting hierarchy of military schools.[14]

13 Powell, *Rise*, pp.60–71, 146–56; Thomas L. Kennedy, 'Chang Chih-tung and the struggle for strategic industrialization: the establishment of the Hanyang Arsenal, 1884–1895', in *Harvard Journal of Asiatic Studies* 33 (1973), pp.154–82; William Aryes, *Chang Chih-tung and Educational Reform in China* (Cambridge, MA, 1971); and Daniel H. Bays, *China Enters the Twentieth Century: Chang Chih-tung and the Issues of a New Age, 1895–1909* (Ann Arbor, 1978) for general background on Chang.

14 Powell, *Rise*, pp.166–87.

Under the thirty-six division plan, each division was to have two infantry brigades (each of two regiments of three battalions of four companies), a single artillery regiment (fifty-four guns in nine batteries), a cavalry regiment (three squadrons totalling twelve troops), an engineer battalion and a supply battalion (both of the latter in four companies). Each division was to have 12,512 personnel in peacetime, rising in wartime to 21,000 through the doubling of the size of the infantry companies. Japanese influence showed in that the division, rather than the corps, was the basis of combined arms organization and allocation of engineer and supply battalions, and in the reduced scale of artillery support. Despite this, the plan called for the sort of 'square' divisions with which most armies began the First World War. In practice, Chinese armies were never supplied with artillery and technical services in anything like the amounts prescribed, and counted themselves lucky if all their infantry had rifles.[15]

The report called for enlisted men to be carefully recruited, and to serve for three years followed by three years in the first line reserves and four years in the second line; in effect this adopted the idea of a short service army backed by a trained reserve, but without the idea of universal conscription, which would have been wildly unrealistic given the size and poverty of China's population.

Position titles and duties of officers were carefully specified, and a modern table of ranks was created, with each officer position declared precisely equal to a prestigious civil position at the same level. While much of the elaborate terminology was scrapped in the wake of the 1911 revolution, the basic pattern remained.

The thirty-six division plan carefully avoided the questions of reform in the tax structure and changes in the relationship between the provinces and the central government, and did not recommend the abolition of the old-style military forces. The new divisions, then, would be cut from the same template but responsive to different masters, as shown by the course of events after 1911.

The commission also recommended creation of a comprehensive system of military schools. Past efforts at military institutional reform had always foundered due to the continued existence of the traditional civil service examinations: since these led to the greatest prizes Chinese society had to offer, the best students refused to

15 H.S. Brunnert and V.V. Hagelstrom, *Present Day Political Organization of China* (Shanghai, 1912) gives the new regulations in great detail; also Powell, *Rise*, pp.166–87, and Mackinnon, *Power*, pp.91–103.

study anything but the traditional classical curriculum. The abolition of the civil service examinations on 2 September 1905 cleared the way for a more modern military personnel system. In November 1906 the old Board of War and various other agencies were abolished, and replaced by a Ministry of War divided into bureaux on modern lines.

Soon after his appointment as governor-general of Chihli, Yuan Shih-k'ai had founded specialized military schools at the provincial capital at Paoting. These eventually merged into the Paoting Military Academy, which remained the most important centre of military education in China throughout the warlord period. The Paoting system served as the model for the commission's recommendations regarding military schools, and also provided the trained personnel for the expansion of Yuan Shih-k'ai's own military forces. As governor-general, Yuan was also Superintendent of Trade for the Northern Ocean (Peiyang ta-ch'en); the army under his control thus was known as the Peiyang Army. Chihli had long served as the keystone of Li Hung-chang's regional power and the location of his efforts at military modernization. To some extent, therefore, Yuan was continuing an ongoing concern. For Yuan as for Li, to be governor-general of the province containing the capital was ideal: it permitted both command of troops as a regional official and access to the throne as a central official.

By 1905 Yuan had increased the Peiyang Army to six divisions. In October he held manoeuvres near Hokien in central Chihli. Anticipating developments during the warlord wars, the newly completed Peking–Hankow railway was used to move the troops to the battlefield. Foreign observers, well lubricated by Yuan's hospitality, returned generally favourable reports, noting nevertheless that the cavalry seemed poorly mounted and that the artillery, though well drilled, seemed to be led by officers who were not familiar with the abilities of their weapons. Nevertheless, Yuan's province was the only one in which the recommendations of the commission were more or less carried out.[16]

Chang Chih-tung in Hupei had the second best modernized army. He also organized and trained his forces along modern lines after the Boxer Rebellion. After the commission report was issued, he increased the strengths of his units in conformity with it, and his troops were designated the 8th Division and the 21st Brigade of the Lu-chün. In October 1906 manoeuvres were held at Changte

16 Powell, *Rise*, pp.200–10.

(Honan) between Chang's and Yuan's modernized troops. It was the unanimous opinion of the observers that Yuan's Peiyang Army was larger, better equipped and better trained than its rival in Central China.[17]

This was not a comfortable realization. Yuan was now in the recognizable historical category of the overmighty subject on whom the dynasty is unwillingly dependent; he was likely to be murdered if he did not seize the throne himself. The central government reforms already undertaken had eliminated the even division of offices between Chinese and Manchus, and had led to a scramble between the two ethnic groups. Yuan's Manchu colleague on the commission, T'ieh-liang, once a friend, was now a bitter enemy, and was Minister of War. The Empress Dowager still supported him, but she could not live forever. On 18 November 1906 Yuan recommended that his 1st, 3rd, 5th and 6th divisions – two-thirds of his army – be transferred to the direct command of the Ministry of War. This was an effort to lower his profile, as Yuan continued his long-cultivated personal connections with the officers of these formations, who were mostly his protégés.

Early 1907 marked the high point of the military aspects of the Manchu reform movement. The new armies certainly looked impressive and modern compared to their predecessors. However, in fact only Yuan and Chang had made serious and sustained efforts, and the overall achievement nationwide was far short of the objectives of the thirty-six division plan. More serious were the deficiencies within both Yuan's and Chang's forces. The most thoughtful scholar to treat the period concluded:

> The adoption of Western arms, tables of organization, schools and military techniques were important external modifications, but beneath the surface the largely unchanged Chinese society exerted tremendous influence on the Chinese armies. . . . The senior provincial officials rendered polite recognition to the authority of the throne and the central military organs, but since they recruited, paid, and trained their own troops, they continued to exercise a high degree of control over what were still semi-private armies. . . . Moreover, it was this decentralization of control which more than any other factor prevented greater uniformity among China's divisions.[18]

17 Powell, *Rise*, pp.210–24.
18 Powell, *Rise*, pp.239–40.

THE COLLAPSE OF THE CH'ING DYNASTY, 1907–11

The Ch'ing dynasty had been plagued by what amounted to Chinese nationalism since its foundation. From 1907 on, it very rapidly alienated the 'hearts and minds' of the Chinese population in general. The reforms aggravated this process, by severing the links between the dynasty and the traditional educated class, and by fomenting Manchu–Chinese rivalry in the upper ranks of the governing elite.[19] The personnel, especially the officers, of the Lu-chün, were affected by the same tendencies, and proved unwilling to die for the dynasty in the crisis of 1911. As in the contemporary Ottoman Empire, the militarily proficient modernized army proved to be a source of political instability.[20]

The disintegration of the Ch'ing governing elite coincided with the solidification of the revolutionary movement of Sun Yat-sen (1866–1925). Sun had grown up in Hong Kong and Hawaii; his political thought at this time was most strongly influenced by the US constitution and by contemporary American political theory. As yet there was little place in his thinking for military matters; the concepts of military unification, political tutelage and his own title 'generalissimo' (ta yuan-shuai) would come only many years and many setbacks later. Sun also was imperfectly informed about Chinese history and the Chinese political tradition. Nevertheless, his impassioned appeals to shake off Manchu rule fell on responsive ears, especially on Chinese students in Japan, who grew more ashamed of their pigtails (the 'queue' was originally the Manchu hairstyle; after 1644 it was imposed on the Chinese population as a sign of submission) the more they learned about the modern world.

19. Powell, *Rise*, pp.243–68, summarizes this period; see also Frederic Wakeman, jr, *The Fall of Imperial China* (New York, 1975), pp.199–256, and Jonathan D. Spence, *The Search for Modern China* (New York, 1990), pp.245–68 for more recent views. The essays collected in Mary C. Wright, *China in Revolution: The First Phase, 1900–1913* (New Haven, 1968), examine the Ch'ing–Republic transition from a number of viewpoints, and Li Chien-nung, *The Political History of China, 1840–1928* (English translation, Princeton, 1956), pp.200–44, is still worth reading.

20 Lord Kinross, *The Ottoman Centuries: The Rise and Fall of the Turkish Empire* (New York, 1977), pp.517–81, and Bernard Lewis, *The Emergence of Modern Turkey* (Oxford, 1958), pp.77–81 and 192–222 for general Ottoman background; Morris Janowitz, *The Military in the Political Development of New Nations: An Essay in Comparative Analysis* (Chicago, 1964), John J. Johnson, *The Role of the Military in Underdeveloped Countries* (Princeton, 1962) and P.J. Vatikiotis, *The Egyptian Army in Politics: Pattern for New Nations* (Bloomington, 1961) for analyses of the strains of military development in 'traditional' societies.

Sun's power as a speaker, and the force of his nationalist and republican convictions, had gained him organizational and financial support among the overseas Chinese communities in North America and Southeast Asia. After 1898 Sun had to contend with efforts by K'ang Yu-wei and Liang Ch'i-ch'ao, the exiled leaders of the 1898 reforms who were still loyal to Emperor Kuang-hsu, to tap the same constituency in support of the monarchical principle. On the whole Sun prevailed among the overseas Chinese, but he was much less successful in turning his external support into political impact within China. Before 1905, he had established contact with secret societies that had always used anti-Manchu slogans but were in fact more oriented to ordinary criminal activity than to revolution. In 1905, making a major change in strategy, he dissolved his Revive China Society (Hsing-chung hui), replacing it with the Alliance Society (T'ung-meng hui). Chinese students abroad were targeted as members of the new organization; they could be expected to return to positions of some responsibility in the reformed institutions, including the Lu-chün, and thus would be better placed to advance the revolution than typical secret society members. In its obedience to Sun as leader, its cellular organization, and its sense of its members as a professional revolutionary vanguard, the Alliance Society seems distinctly Leninist, but Lenin was then not widely known, and Sun's ideas were his own. Moreover, Sun's aims always remained democratic, however much they were compromised by his willingness to grasp whatever means came to hand.[21]

The expansion of the Lu-chün meant that prospective officers were often sent abroad for education, often to the Japanese army's military academy (Rikugun shikan gakkō). Especially in Japan, they formed part of a community of Chinese students who were cutting off their queues, aping Japanese styles, and becoming evermore convinced that the overthrow of the Manchus was a necessary precondition for China's recovery of independence and international respect.

Meanwhile within China revolutionary violence increased in scale, and frightened conservative officials into opposing all reforms. The Empress Dowager attempted to hold the balance, but the

21 Lyon Sharman, *Sun Yat-sen: His Life and its Meaning* (Stanford, 1934); Harold Z. Schiffrin, *Sun Yat-sen and the Origins of the Chinese Revolution* (Berkeley, 1968); and Marius B. Jansen, *The Japanese and Sun Yat-sen* (Cambridge, MA, 1954), remain the classic studies of Sun Yat-sen, who may be the only figure to inspire post-1949 hagiography on both sides of the Taiwan Strait.

Ch'ing consensus was visibly unravelling in the last two years of her life. In the summer of 1907 she publicly promised a constitution, and also ordered that the thirty-six division plan for the Lu-chün be accelerated to completion in 1912, ten years ahead of the original schedule.[22] Since the central government could not fund the divisions it ordered created, this measure put more pressure on the provinces. The reorganization of the government of the three Manchurian provinces placed them under Yuan Shih-k'ai's protégé Hsu Shih-ch'ang, with a garrison drawn from the Peiyang divisions that was intended to serve as the cadre for the Lu-chün in that region.[23] In September 1907 the Empress Dowager promoted both Yuan and Chang Chih-tung to the Grand Council, still the highest advisory and policy-making body under the throne; this step removed both from direct command of the best developed Lu-chün formations. In August 1908 a draft constitution was announced; it was essentially a copy of the very conservative Japanese constitution of 1889. On 14 November Emperor Kuang-hsu died, and the Empress Dowager died the following day; the circumstances suggest that she murdered her nephew when she knew her own end was near.

The Empress Dowager had ordered the succession of the 3-year-old P'u-yi, who became Emperor Hsuan-t'ung (r. 1909–12) under the regency of his own father, Prince Ch'un, a brother of the late emperor. The new regent hated Yuan Shih-k'ai because of the latter's role in the events of 1898, and on 2 January 1909 he dismissed Yuan. Chang Chih-tung died that October. Afterwards, the regent relied chiefly on the advice of a narrow coterie of Manchus, mostly close relatives in the imperial family. Yuan bided his time in retirement, carefully maintaining his network of personal contacts with the many serving officers and officials of the Peiyang clique.

In both military and financial matters, the regent pursued a policy of centralization that offended vested interests and contributed to the crisis of 1911. In 1909–10 the navy was separated from the Ministry of War and placed under a new ministry headed by the regent's brother Tsai-hsun, aided by the British-trained Rear-Admiral Sa Chen-ping. The same treatment was given to the General Staff under another brother, Tsai-t'ao, which

22 Powell, *Rise*, p.249.

23 Robert H.G. Lee, *The Manchurian Frontier in Ch'ing History* (Cambridge, MA, 1970), discusses the reorganization of local government in Manchuria.

received not only institutional independence but also the right to nominate generals and admirals and control over military education, including the schools at Paoting. Minister of War T'ieh-liang, who opposed these steps, was dismissed and replaced by another Manchu, Yin-ch'ang, a former protégé of Yuan Shih-k'ai.[24]

Yin-ch'ang, who was serving as Chinese minister to Berlin at the time of his appointment as Minister of War, made every effort to graft the militarism of his Japanese training and German experiences on to the body of the Lu-chün. He wore his uniform, complete with boots and sabre, to the office, and expected his subordinates to do likewise. He reduced the number of his subordinates and reorganized the bureau structure of his ministry, in each case with incomplete success. He rejected grandiose ideas of expanding the Lu-chün to fifty-five divisions, concentrating instead on forming twenty-five of the original thirty-six division plan. He suppressed firmly a number of mutinies in newly forming Lu-chün units in Central and South China. These mutinies shared certain factors. Members of Sun Yat-sen's Alliance Society (T'ung-meng hui) were more successful in infiltrating new units in those areas than in the original Peiyang divisions, and the abuses traditional to the Chinese military system, especially embezzlement of pay, were more prevalent therein. The old-style troops – the Green Standard and militia armies and the patrol and defence forces that had originally been recruited as a backup for the Lu-chün – turned out to be more reliable than main force Lu-chün units when forcible suppression was required. The six original Peiyang divisions were free from these problems, and gave at least the appearance of loyalty. In 1911 Yin-ch'ang placed all of them under his direct command. At this time, only four Peiyang divisions were located in Chihli, the 3rd Division being in Manchuria and the 5th Division in Shantung. This was a reorganization only on paper. Yuan Shih-k'ai retained the ability to manipulate the Peiyang Army, due to the loyalties of its officers to him personally.[25]

Military centralization was only one aspect of the revolutionary situation that existed in China in 1911. The government also attempted to centralize the financial system under the new Ministry of Finance, an unrealistic scheme that failed due to the objections of the provinces.

24 Powell, *Rise*, pp.260–5; Swanson, *Dragon*, pp.120–3 on the navy.
25 Powell, *Rise*, pp.266–78.

The traditionally educated Chinese literati (ju) or gentry (shen-shih) class had been deprived of its vocation, its prospects for office, and to some extent of its emotional bearing by the abolition of the civil service examinations in 1905. This class nevertheless remained the basis of social organization in the provinces. The Empress Dowager had promised a constitution shortly before her death in 1908, to be implemented according to a nine-year plan for the formation of local and then provincial assemblies, followed by a national assembly with advisory powers, culminating in fully constitutional government in 1917. The provincial assemblies came into existence early in Prince Ch'un's regency, and naturally were dominated by members of the gentry class. With some justice, the assemblies viewed the regent's centralizing measures as a grab for a political monopoly by a narrow Manchu clique, and opposition to the court grew, particularly in the south. In November 1910 the regent agreed to full constitutional government by 1913. This concession did no good, and in May 1911 the court further undermined its credibility when it abolished both the Grand Secretariat and the Grand Council, replacing both by a Cabinet composed of the heads of ministries on the Western model. Unfortunately most of the Cabinet members were Manchus, including Prime Minister Prince Ch'ing and the regent's brother, Navy Minister Tsai-hsun. The star of the new Cabinet, however, was one of its Chinese members, Minister of Communications Sheng Hsuan-huai, whose effort to centralize the railway system contributed greatly to the 1911 crisis.[26]

Since the 1880s railway construction had been the most visible sign of modernization in China, and by 1911 the major trunk lines (Peking–Hankow and Tientsin–Pukow) and various branch lines in China proper were in operation. In Manchuria two major lines, the South Manchurian Railway Company and the Chinese Eastern Railway, were owned by Japan and Russia respectively. Railway construction required large inputs of capital, and foreign loans were still available for this purpose (and indeed were strongly pressed upon the Chinese authorities). Despite the pledging of most of China's dependable sources of revenue against foreign obligations, railway loans could still be raised abroad, since they could be

26 Albert Feuerwerker, *China's Early Industrialization: Sheng Hsuan-huai (1845–1916) and Mandarin Enterprise* (Cambridge, MA, 1958), on Sheng's earlier career. Spence, *Search*, pp.245–68 is a recent summary of the pre-revolutionary period.

secured by the anticipated earnings of the railway itself, and by concessions in the area of the railway line. Here the model was the Chinese Eastern Railway, whose officials had police powers along the right of way, and whose financial arm was the Russo-Chinese Bank, which was the depository for railway earnings and the source of capital for numerous satellite enterprises. This whole apparatus was run by Russians, and after 1905 the Japanese essentially duplicated the pattern in the sphere of the South Manchurian Railway Company. Chinese nationalist sentiment thus understandably felt that building railways with foreign loans strengthened imperialism and promoted the partition of China that had been talked up in foreign circles ever since 1895.[27]

In Szechwan and other southern provinces, gentry associations formed corporations and issued bonds to fund railway construction: a novel activity for the gentry. The slogan of railway recovery was explicitly anti-foreign, and the provincial basis of the gentry companies reflected the growing alienation of provincial society from the imperial government. Shortly before his death, Chang Chih-tung, fearing that the provincial companies would inhibit the growth of a unified railway network, opened negotiations with a foreign banking consortium for funding to buy out the provincial companies. Sheng Hsuan-huai continued the negotiations. The shareholders in the companies mobilized public opinion against the consortium loan, another sign of the changes taking place in the Chinese political process. The government backed down and refused to ratify the already negotiated loan. Unfortunately, the consortium consisted of German, French, British and US bankers, and the Ch'ing government could not resist the diplomatic pressure of these four Great Powers. On 10 May 1911 the government ordered the provincial companies disbanded; the bondholders were given rather vague promises of future compensation. Protest and riot followed quickly in Szechwan.[28]

The revolutionary movement, meanwhile, had failed in its efforts to overthrow the dynasty prior to 1911. Minor mutinies at

27 Chang Kia-ngau, *China's Struggle for Railway Development* (New York, 1943), and more recently Ralph Huenemann, *The Dragon and the Iron Horse: The Economics of Railroads in China, 1876–1937* (Cambridge, MA, 1984), cover railway development.

28 Li, *Political History*, pp.240–4.

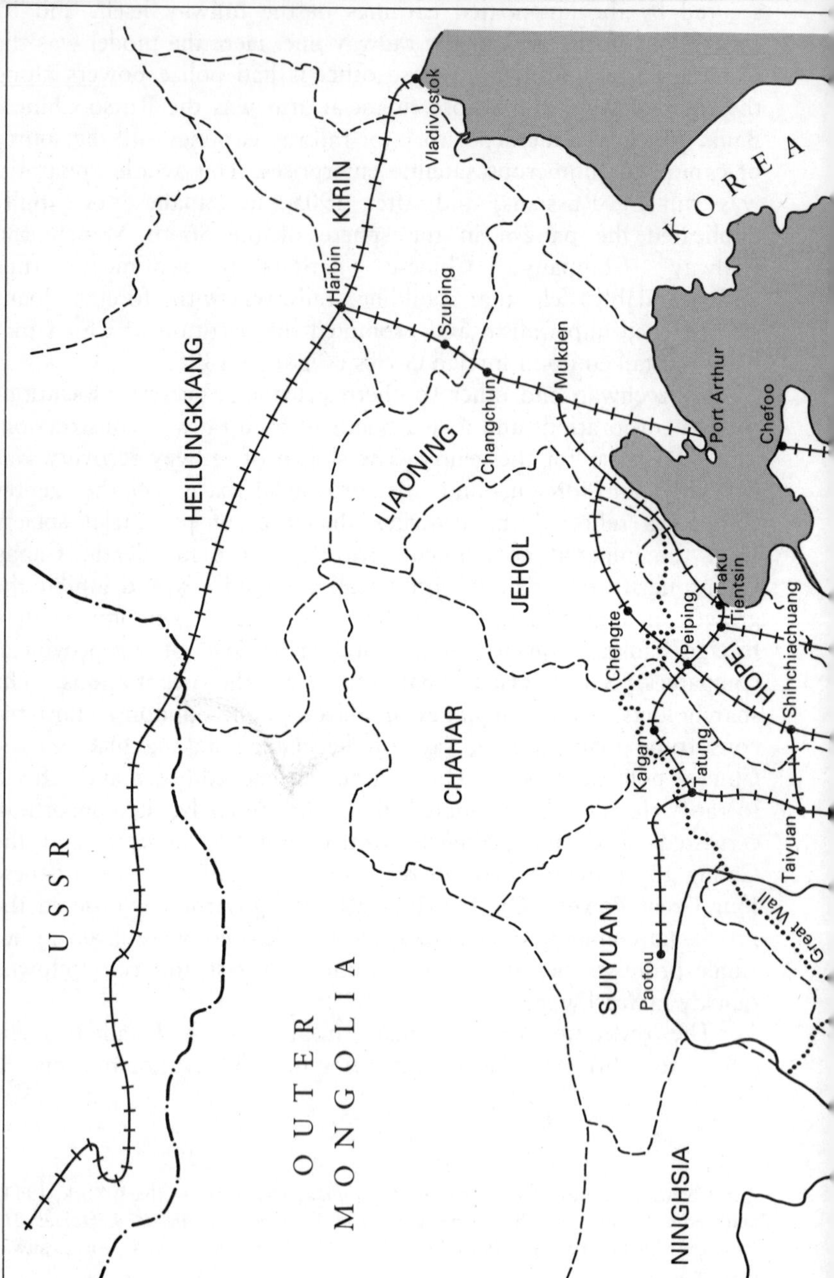
USSR
OUTER MONGOLIA
HEILUNGKIANG
KIRIN
LIAONING
JEHOL
CHAHAR
HOPEI
SUIYUAN
NINGHSIA
KOREA
Vladivostok
Harbin
Szuping
Changchun
Mukden
Port Arthur
Chefoo
Taku
Tientsin
Peiping
Chengte
Shihchiachuang
Kalgan
Tatung
Taiyuan
Paotou
Great Wall

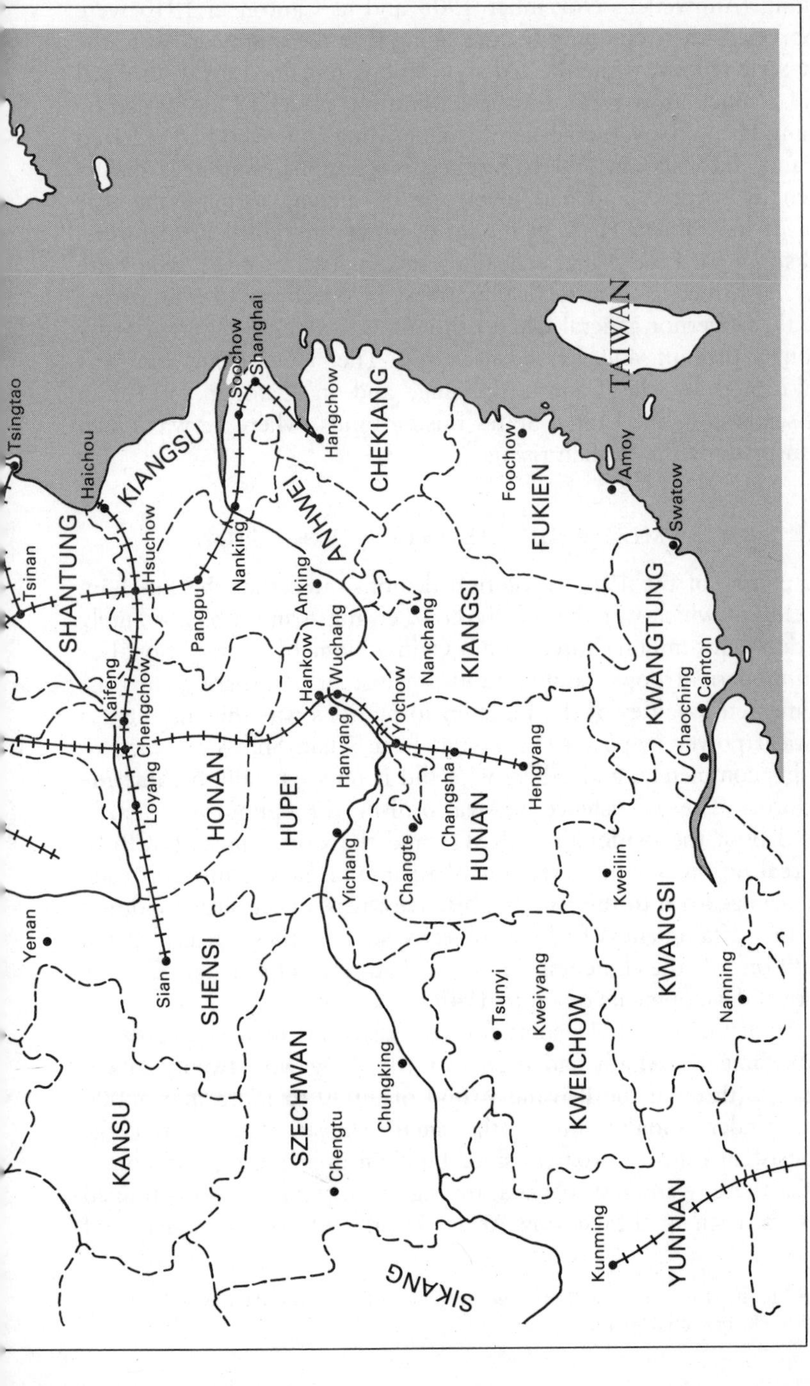

2. Provinces and principal railways of China

Anking (Anhwei) in November 1908 and at Canton in 1910 were suppressed, their common feature being that the mutineers were the new-style troops, while the old-style troops remained loyal. In April 1911 a much more serious insurrection took place at Canton, led by Huang Hsing. Governor-general Chang Ming-ch'i, who had received advance information and had taken precautions, was nevertheless taken by surprise and had to escape by digging through the rear wall of his yamen. He kept his head, however, rallied loyal forces, and suppressed the rising, beheading seventy-two captives, who were later enshrined as Nationalist martyrs. In Szechwan the following month, Governor-general Chao Erh-feng was able to maintain order through prompt and harsh measures. The T'ung-meng hui was bankrupted by the Canton uprising, and in October 1911 Sun Yat-sen was in the United States raising funds, where he was taken by surprise by the Wuhan rising.[29]

THE NEW ARMIES AND THE 1911 REVOLUTION

The course of the 1911 revolution demonstrated that the Lu-chün, the elite of which was the six-division Peiyang Army, was absolutely the dominant military force within China. None of the traditional or semi-modern troops could stand against it. Gathering up the fragmented loyalties of the Lu-chün formations was thus the key to political power in post-1911 China. Even Yuan Shih-k'ai failed to do this completely, and others who did it only partially became the warlords. The persistence of warlordism throughout the 1920s forced both the Nationalists (KMT) and the Communists (CCP) to the realization that the creation of their own new armies, in each case armies loyal to the party's objectives, was a necessary condition for the attainment of these objectives. For these reasons, the condition of the Lu-chün in 1911 had an impact on Chinese political developments down to 1949.

As of October 1911 some fourteen divisions of over two-thirds establishment strength had been formed, along with twenty mixed brigades (three in the Peiyang Army) of 2,000 to more than 6,000 men. Understandably, given the small elapse of time and the inconsistent rates of progress since Lu-chün units started forming in 1902, these were not backed by significant numbers of trained reserves, even in the Peiyang Army. From 1908 on, a sequence of

29 Chun-tu Hsueh, *Huang Hsing and the Chinese Revolution* (Stanford, 1961); Li, *Political History*, pp.238–40.

French, British and US military attaché reports evaluated the trained and combat-ready strength of the Lu-chün, their estimates ranging from a low of 152,000 to a high of 266,000 men; the average estimate was 190,000 throughout these years, an indication of how greatly the rate of Lu-chün growth had slowed after the death of the Empress Dowager.[30]

Territorial recruiting had been a key feature of the thirty-six division plan. Each province was assigned at least one division, and each regiment recruited its soldiers from a defined area. This led to some problems, since men from certain areas were less likely to enlist or were felt to be less capable soldiers, but the potential gains in unit cohesion made territorial recruiting worth keeping. Despite efforts to attract a better class of recruit, the average enlisted man remained an illiterate peasant, recruited by economic hardship. Most armies can deal with such material, and the Lu-chün troops continued to impress foreign observers as clean, well drilled and well disciplined. In fact discipline within the Lu-chün was deteriorating. This was mostly due to the permeation of the officer corps with revolutionary and republican sentiments, but the discontents of the non-commissioned officers (NCOs) contributed to it. Sergeants and corporals were paid very little more than privates, but such partially educated men as were recruited usually ended up in those positions, and their resentments of the officers were growing. Since the NCOs were responsible for the direct leadership of the troops, their radicalism had an effect on the Wuhan rising.[31]

Almost all of the officers were ethnically Chinese, a fact that aggravated the pre-revolutionary situation. Manchu efforts to form an elite Guard division, in addition to the thirty-six division plan, had foundered on the utter unwillingness of the effete bannerman population to consider military service. Meanwhile the top Manchu princes and leaders were often seen in public wearing German-style military uniforms, and were seen as trying to monopolize political power and military command. Most officers were graduates of some military course in one of the provincial military schools. As of 1911 about 800 were returned students from Japan, who, as the best educated of China's officers, often themselves taught in these

30 Powell, *Rise*, pp.268–94; Jerome Ch'en, "Defining Chinese warlords and their factions", in *Bulletin of the School of Oriental and African Studies* 31 (1968), pp.563–600, lists on pp.587–9 the divisions and brigades created as of late 1911.

31 Powell, *Rise*, pp.291–2; Wakeman, *Fall*, p.248.

schools. They were the main means for the propagation of revolutionary attitudes throughout the Lu-chün.[32]

Armament was not standardized, but was better in that respect than either before or later. Most of the infantry were armed with either the standard 1896 Japanese rifle or the Mauser 7.9mm. Artillery still had a variety of guns, despite the efforts of the Ministry of War to impose order, and cavalry continued to ride poorly. Medical and other supporting technical services continued to be weak, despite elaborate paper prescriptions.

The new armies, as noted, received officers from the graduates of about seventy military schools nationwide, of which the Paoting complex remained the most important. The supporting system of military education had grown greatly since 1901. This was not true of the system of arsenals (primarily Tientsin, Wuhan and Kiangnan, the latter at Shanghai) which had not changed greatly since 1899 and which still continued to manufacture obsolete weapons for obsolete forces, as well as inferior copies of modern weapons for the new armies.[33]

On the night of 9 October 1911, an explosion occurred in a building in the Russian concession of Wuchang being used as a revolutionary bomb factory. The police arrested some of the plotters and seized their membership lists. The following day an altercation arose between a sergeant of the 8th Engineer Battalion and some officers of the same unit, who suspected that materials from the 8th Division ammunition dump were being diverted to the revolutionaries. Tensions were running high in the 8th Division on 10 October, since the police were arresting soldiers suspected of revolutionary sympathies. The sergeant shot the officers, and the revolution was on.[34]

It should not have succeeded. Similar outbreaks in Canton and Szechwan had been suppressed by prompt action on the part of the authorities. In Wuchang, Governor-general Jui-ch'eng, a Manchu, panicked and fled, and most of the other authorities followed his example. Mutinous troops of the 8th Division now controlled the city, and they made Li Yuan-hung, one of the brigade commanders, their leader. The story that the troops pulled a frightened Li by the boots from his hiding place under his wife's bed is now,

32 Ch'en, "Chinese warlords", pp.589–600 details the backgrounds of Japanese- and Paoting-trained officers.

33 Powell, *Rise*, pp.298–302.

34 Wakeman, *Fall*, p.249.

unfortunately, discredited, but it suggests the extent to which he often presided over events he did not control. Both Sun Yat-sen, then in the United States, and the Ch'ing government were taken by surprise by the success of the Wuchang rising.[35]

Subsequent developments indicated the extent to which modern developments, themselves limited, had transformed the realities of Chinese politics. The provincial capitals were now linked by telegraph, and so could transmit news and negotiate among themselves much more rapidly than before. The provincial assemblies were another new element. In South China their membership was very hostile to the central government, because of rising Han Chinese nationalism and growing anti-Manchu revolutionary sentiment; in recent years the railway recovery movement had become the catalyst for these sentiments. Li Yuan-hung over the years had cultivated close personal relationships with certain of the assembly leaders. Within a month, assemblies met in thirteen provinces and passed resolutions of secession. Except in Shantung, the new armies everywhere supported the revolutionaries, and were easily able to defeat the old-style forces, who remained loyal.

On 12 October the regent ordered Minister of War Yin-ch'ang to take two Peiyang Army divisions down the Peking–Hankow railway to suppress the rising. Rear-Admiral Sa Chen-ping was ordered to lead the small squadron of protected cruisers and gunboats that constituted China's battle fleet upstream to Hankow, to cover the army's crossing of the Yangtze.

Yin-ch'ang's troops were in action against the revolutionaries at Hankow by 27 October. Meanwhile, Li Yuan-hung had undertaken with enthusiasm his duties as military commander of the emerging revolutionary regime. He wrote to Sa Chen-ping, successfully exhorting him to join the revolution with the fleet. Sa and his officers were vulnerable to the same revolutionary urgings as the new armies, and the fleet's defection made it very difficult to suppress the revolution south of the Yangtze, even had the new armies remained loyal. They were not loyal, however. Before the end of the month elements of the 20th Division in northeast Chihli were refusing to entrain for Hankow. By this time the court's

35 Powell, *Rise*, p.308 cites T'ang Leang-Li for the bed story; Li, *Political History*, pp.246–9, cites Li Yuan-hung's own explanation: 'I was quickly arrested and asked to become the commander of this revolutionary army. I was surrounded by guns at the time, and I might have been killed instantly if I had not complied with their request.'

negotiations with Yuan Shih-k'ai had overtaken in importance all the rest of the events of October.[36]

THE EMERGENCE OF YUAN SHIH-K'AI

Soon after 11 October Prime Minister Prince Ch'ing and the new Empress Dowager Lung-yü (Tz'u-hsi's niece) had urged the Prince Regent (whom she cordially disliked) to recall Yuan Shih-k'ai. The foreign diplomatic community in Peking joined in this recommendation. All of these felt that Yuan was the only man who could rally the new armies in defence of the throne. On 14 October the Prince Regent appointed Yuan governor-general of Hupei and Hunan, with orders to suppress the Wuhan rising. Yuan refused to accept this appointment, and replied with a set of conditions which included the calling of a parliament, the establishment of a responsible Cabinet system, as well as full authority for himself over the armed forces, with adequate funding. Yuan's conditions, which also called for amnesty for the revolutionaries, foreshadowed his later programme of playing the revolutionaries off against the court.

Rumblings within the Peiyang Army added to the pressures on the court. Chang Shao-tseng, commander of the 20th Division, and 2nd Brigade commander Lan T'ien-wei, two Japanese-trained generals, submitted a programme of constitutional demands. Their troops refused to entrain to join Yin-ch'ang's army, and remained at Luanchow in Chihli. Chang and Lan were in communication with Wu Lu-chen, commander of the 6th Division at Paoting, who was also trained in Japan and sympathetic to the revolution. When Wuchang rose in rebellion, Wu had asked the court to send his division against them, which led the court to suspect him. However, when Shansi passed a resolution of secession, the court did appoint Wu governor of Shansi, and directed him to suppress the revolutionaries with his division. Wu moved his troops to the critical railway junction at Shihchiachuang, thus interdicting rail communication between Peking and Hankow, and began negotiating with both the Shansi revolutionaries and the 20th Division leaders. A move against Peking by disaffected Peiyang elements seemed briefly possible, but in the end the 20th Division remained conditionally loyal. Wu was murdered on 7 November – probably at the instigation of the court, though Yuan Shih-k'ai has also been

36 Powell, *Rise*, pp.308–12; Swanson, *Dragon*, pp.123–5.

blamed – and Lan fled to Shanghai to join the revolution.[37]

Yuan Shih-k'ai assumed the premiership on 13 November, after all his conditions had been accepted. The revolutionary assembly at Nanking had also offered him the premiership. The actual fighting during the revolution demonstrated that, whatever their failures of internal cohesion, the modernized forces of the Peiyang Army were dominant on the battlefield.

MILITARY ACTIONS AT HANKOW AND NANKING

Yin-ch'ang's First Army was composed of the 4th Division, one mixed brigade each from the 2nd and 6th divisions, and a personal guard for Yin-ch'ang drawn from the 1st Division. The General Staff at Peking arranged for the rail transport of this force to Hupei with a speed and efficiency that earned the surprised admiration of the foreign military attachés. After rendezvous with the disaffected fleet of Admiral Sa, Yin-ch'ang attacked the revolutionary army commanded by Huang Hsing in the vicinity of Hankow on 27 October.

Covered by their own field artillery and the guns of the fleet, the imperial infantry attacked with a cloud of skirmishers followed by a line of close order company fronts. These textbook tactics were soon to be discredited in the intense fighting of the First World War, but against an undisciplined revolutionary army with no particular doctrine and no machine guns, they worked perfectly. Many revolutionary soldiers evacuated Hankow during the next two days, despite desultory and inaccurate fire from the fleet.[38]

Politics then intervened. On the 27th the court had ordered Yuan Shih-k'ai to take command in Hupei of the forces being gathered to suppress the rebellion. Yuan had refused these orders, but secured high commands for his two most trusted associates. Feng Kuo-chang was ordered to replace Yin-ch'ang in command of the 1st Army, while Tuan Ch'i-jui took command of a new 2nd Army (built around the 3rd Division) whose mission was to secure the Peking–Hankow railway line that even then was being threatened by Wu Lu-chen. Feng and Tuan, respectively, were the founders of the Chihli and Anhwei cliques into which the Peiyang military clique fractured after Yuan's death. Feng arrived at Hankow and announced he would take command on the 31st;

37 Li, *Political History*, pp.249–55; Powell, *Rise*, p.311.
38 Powell, *Rise*, pp.321–5.

Yin-ch'ang then ordered an attack for the 30th which Feng countermanded.

The fighting then stalled while Yuan increased his pressure on the court. On 12 November Admiral Sa took the fleet over to the revolution. On the 17th the rebels tried to dislodge the imperial position with a flank attack from Hanyang. Finally, on the 20th Yuan permitted Feng to launch an all-out assault on Hanyang. The rebel forces were still qualitatively inferior to the imperial, but by now had had time to dig in and prepare, and it took Feng's army seven days to evict them from Hanyang. During the battle the bravery of the imperial troops was noted by foreign observers. Yuan ordered Feng not to carry the fight to Wuchang. Whether he could have taken it must remain speculative. The gunnery of the fleet had not been improved by their defection, but the imperial army, with its field guns and horses, paradoxically was less able to improvise a river crossing than the less well organized rebels. Yuan's restraint, of course, was politically motivated, as he was also negotiating with the revolutionaries.[39]

The only other place where serious combat took place during the revolution was Nanking. There the Lu-chün troops (principally the 9th Division) joined the revolution, and the defence rallied around Chang Hsun, who remained a sincere monarchist to the end of his life; this was exceptional among the commanders of modern forces. Chang proved himself an inept general, even considering the limitations of his old-style troops. After some false starts, revolutionary troops took the Purple Mountain on 1 December. This elevation, later the site of Sun Yat-sen's tomb, adjoins the wall of Nanking to the east of the city, and has been considered the key to the Nanking area ever since the third century AD. Chang should have known these historical precedents, but nevertheless failed to defend Purple Mountain, and had to evacuate in unseemly haste when it fell.[40]

The military actions of the 1911 revolution had shown that Lu-chün forces could defeat old-style troops or untrained revolutionary levies without much difficulty, and that the Peiyang divisions were the best of the Lu-chün. Politically, however, the officers and men of the Lu-chün ranged from hostile to at best indifferent to the dynasty. Had Yuan Shih-k'ai sincerely attempted to suppress the revolution with the Peiyang Army, the chaotic state

39 Powell, *Rise*, pp.325–7.
40 Powell, *Rise*, pp.327–8.

of imperial finances would soon have led to irregularities in pay that would have played into the hands of the many Peiyang officers with revolutionary and republican sympathies. While Yuan was the creator of the Peiyang Army, his great personal power before 1909 rested primarily on the old Empress Dowager's support.[41] In 1911 he was certainly the official with the best chance of holding the Peiyang Army together for some purpose, but due in large part to Yuan's own insistence on Westernized education and training, the army had many minds of its own. It was not a mere instrument of Yuan's ambitions, and Yuan eventually fell from power when he forgot that simple truth.

Over the next ten weeks Yuan threatened the revolutionaries with the Peiyang Army and threatened the court with the revolution. The end result was that the revolutionary national assembly, meeting at Nanking, elected Yuan as provisional president of the Republic of China. Sun Yat-sen, the idealistic leader of the T'ung-meng hui, yielded his natural claims in the hope of smoothing the transition to the republic. The Manchu leaders were paid off with a treaty that gave them sovereign rights within the Forbidden City of Peking and a subsidy from the new government. The 6-year-old Manchu Emperor formally abdicated on 12 February 1912.[42]

41 MacKinnon, *Power*, pp.117–36 and throughout, stresses the contingent nature of Yuan's power.

42 Powell, *Rise*, pp.329–37; Li, *Political History*, pp.256–67.

2 PEIYANG ARMY ASCENDANCY, 1911–19

The years 1911–19 form a bridge between the centralized imperial regime of the Ch'ing and the provincial warlordism of the 1920s. During this period the Peiyang Army remained the most powerful native military force in China, and Yuan Shih-k'ai remained the only man in China who could hold the Peiyang Army together. However, Yuan's control over the Peiyang Army eroded to the vanishing point because of his ill-judged monarchical movement, and only his well-timed death in 1916 saved him from overthrow. Afterwards the Peiyang Army split into cliques led by Yuan's principal protégés. Tuan Ch'i-jui's Anhwei clique and the Chihli clique founded by Feng Kuo-chang, but led after Feng's death by Ts'ao K'un and Wu P'ei-fu, were the principal Peiyang cliques. In certain provinces, the Peiyang Army's ascendancy was challenged by the rise of provincial armies organized on Western patterns and sometimes supported by local arsenals and military academies. The Yunnan Army, Yen Hsi-shan's regime in Shansi, and the Fengtien clique, the latter controlling Manchuria under Chang Tso-lin's leadership, were the most important provincial armies. The qualitative level of the provincial armies rose as that of the Peiyang Army and its fragments declined. Also, by 1919 Sun Yat-sen had concluded that his Nationalist movement needed a territorial military base of its own in order to compete with the warlords. These centrifugal forces collectively destroyed all but the pretence of unity by 1919.

YUAN SHIH-K'AI AS PRESIDENT

Sun Yat-sen had offered, during the late 1911 negotiations between the revolutionaries and the court, to resign the presidency in favour of Yuan Shih-k'ai. Sun's reasoning was an uneasy mixture of idealism and pragmatism. Forcing Yuan to fight for the dynasty might cause the failure of the revolution; the Hankow–Hanyang operations in October–November had shown the strength of the Peiyang Army. On the other hand, placing Yuan at the head of the new government might coopt him, and create the republic without protracted civil war and bloodshed. So Sun hoped, but he attached three conditions to his resignation: Nanking was to be the capital of the republic, Yuan was to come to Nanking for his inauguration as president, and Yuan was to agree to abide by the constitution to be drafted by the revolutionary Senate assembled at Nanking.

Yuan indicated that he would accept these conditions, and in late February 1912 a delegation including Peking University president Ts'ai Yuan-p'ei and veteran revolutionaries Wang Ching-wei and Sung Chiao-jen arrived in Peking to escort Yuan to Nanking. But on the night of 29 February troops of Ts'ao K'un's 3rd Division mutinied and went on a rampage in Peking, and other outbreaks of military violence occurred in Paoting and Tientsin. Ultimately Yuan was blamed for these developments, but he achieved his immediate purpose, which was to create a climate of uncertainty in North China that would lead to threats of foreign intervention. The ruse worked; in response to appeals by his own delegation, Sun agreed to permit Yuan to be inaugurated in Peking if first he would submit his Cabinet to Nanking for approval. Yuan was formally inaugurated in Peking on 10 March. His prime minister designate was T'ang Shao-yi, who had been his chief negotiator in 1911. T'ang secured the approval of the Cabinet, which included Peiyang Army general Feng Kuo-chang as Minister of War. Sun Yat-sen then resigned on 1 April.[1]

Meanwhile the revolutionary Senate had drafted a provisional constitution that served briefly as the formal basis of national politics. The constitution gave the president the usual executive powers, including the command of the army and navy, provided for the separation of legislative, executive and judicial powers at the central level, and also gave a strong measure of autonomy to the provincial governments. Many of the features of the provisional constitution suggested the political system of the United States, which was of course greatly admired by Sun Yat-sen and much talked of as a model in China at this time. The provision for legislative consent to Cabinet appointments was designed specifically to restrain Yuan Shih-k'ai. Considering the late development of representative institutions in China and the short time they actually

1 Li Chien-nung, *The Political History of China, 1840–1928* (English translation, Princeton, 1956), pp.263–73.

functioned in the early republic, it has seemed naive to most historians that anyone felt that Yuan and the other Peiyang warlords could be restrained by constitutions or other scraps of paper. But in fact optimism was widespread in April 1912. The revolutionary Alliance Society (T'ung-meng hui) changed its name to the more familiar Nationalist Party (Kuomintang) in anticipation of an open politics of elections and parliaments.

Even though the 1911 revolution had not involved much outright warfare between well organized armies, in every province there had been conflict and revolutionary forces had been organized. Usually the provincial assembly appointed one of the recognized leaders as military governor (tu-tu). In certain provinces, notably Sinkiang, Shansi and Yunnan at this stage, the armies created by military governors made the provincial regimes in fact autonomous.[2] In Chihli the Nationalists, as part of their strategy of hemming Yuan Shih-k'ai in with constitutional restrictions, secured the election of Wang Chih-hsiang as military governor. The insertion of an outsider into the chain of command between Yuan and the Peiyang Army was a clear challenge to Yuan's power. The commanders of the five Peiyang divisions in Chihli sent a circular telegram objecting to Wang's appointment.

Yuan then proposed to send Wang on a face-saving inspection tour to Nanking. Prime minister T'ang Shao-yi objected; Yuan sent the order to Wang without the prime minister's countersignature, and T'ang then resigned, citing the violation of the constitution. For the rest of 1912 Yuan governed through a succession of pliable prime ministers, and insinuated his creatures into the Cabinet.[3] The revolutionary leaders continued to hope that cooperation with Yuan would remain possible. Sun Yat-sen had withdrawn from active politics, and was gestating a fantastic plan for railway

2 Jerome Ch'en, 'Defining Chinese warlords and their factions', in *Bulletin of the School of Oriental and African Studies* 31 (1968), pp.563–600, has lists of military governors on pp.599–600. For individual regions, Gavan McCormack, *Chang Tso-lin in Northeast China, 1911–1928: China, Japan and the Manchurian Idea* (Stanford, 1977), pp.21–45; Donald S. Sutton, *Provincial Militarism and the Chinese Republic: The Yunnan Army, 1905–1925* (Ann Arbor, 1980), pp.77–113; Robert A. Kapp, *Szechwan and the Chinese Republic: Provincial Militarism and Central Power, 1911–1938* (New Haven, 1973), passim; Andrew D.W. Forbes, *Warlords and Muslims in Chinese Central Asia: A Political History of Republican Sinkiang, 1911–1949* (Cambridge, UK, 1986), passim; and Donald G. Gillin, *Warlord: Yen Hsi-shan in Shansi Province, 1911–1949* (Princeton, 1967), pp.16–18.

3 Li, *Political History*, pp.279–85.

development,[4] and other Nationalist leaders were preparing for the nationwide elections scheduled for early 1913.

The election results were somewhat ambiguous, since many candidates were willing to claim affiliation with more than one party. The Nationalists nevertheless claimed over 360 of the approximately 500 seats in the new House of Representatives, and were undoubtedly the strongest of the parties. Sung Chiao-jen, who had been the pre-eminent Nationalist politician in the election campaign, continued afterwards to address political meetings in several provinces, arguing that the constitution mandated a Cabinet responsible to the legislature; Yuan's ministers should therefore be dismissed, and a new Cabinet formed, headed by Sung. The argument was debatable, but the debate took the form of the murder of Sung at the railway station in Shanghai on 20 March 1913. Yuan Shih-k'ai was implicated almost immediately, and his guilt has never been seriously questioned. Sung's murder deprived the Nationalists of their best political leader; the survivors were unable to agree on a programme of resistance to Yuan.[5]

The next major political issue was the so-called Reorganization Loan. Great Power recognition of the Republic of China had been contingent on the republic's assumption of the obligations of the Ch'ing Empire. Hence China's customs and all other sources of revenue that could be pledged as security for loans continued to be so pledged; the revolution did not improve, or significantly change, the financial situation of the Chinese government. Yuan therefore needed money to pay the Peiyang Army, which as the largest and most powerful was also the most expensive of the several Chinese armies. Negotiations for a large foreign loan therefore began when T'ang Shao-yi was still prime minister. The ultimate package was a £25 million (sterling) loan from a five-power banking consortium, secured against the salt revenues, which were to be placed under foreign operation. Another smaller loan was secretly negotiated with Austria-Hungary. In presenting the loans to the legislature Yuan's supporters admitted that they had been negotiated irregularly, but asked for their approval anyway. Despite an uproar from the Nationalists, the loans were signed, money flowed in to pay the Peiyang Army, and Yuan was ready for an armed confrontation. Early in May 1913 Yuan publicly repudiated the KMT.[6]

4 Sun's railway plan is preserved as the endpaper of Chang Ch'i-yun, *Chung-hua Min-kuo Ti-t'u Chi* (Atlas of the Republic of China) (Taipei, 1962).

5 Li, *Political History*, pp.285–8.

6 Li, *Political History*, pp.288–90, 292.

Sun Yat-sen now returned from Japan, and the KMT leaders tried to organize armed resistance to Yuan. Their military means were limited. In Kiangsi the military governor was Li Lieh-chün, a long-time revolutionary with impeccable KMT credentials, and his army was probably the best at the KMT's disposal. In Hupei troops who might have had Nationalist sympathies were commanded by Li Yuan-hung, who had sold out to Yuan Shih-k'ai. In Hunan the military governor was T'an Yen-k'ai, pro-KMT but irresolute on this occasion. In Kiangsu also the troops might have sided with the KMT but the (civilian) military governor, Ch'eng Te-ch'uan, was two faced. Ts'ai O's Yunnan Army, the best of the non-Peiyang military forces, sat this one out.

The fighting phase of the 'Second Revolution' began on 12 July 1913. On 25 July Li Lieh-chün's forces were decisively beaten and on 1 August Nanchang fell, ending resistance in Kiangsi. Resistance in Kiangsu was stimulated by Huang Hsing, a revolutionary intellectual of limited military experience who had gained a great reputation as a result of his role in the 1911 revolution. At Hsuchow, Nanking and Shanghai the fighting went badly for the KMT from the start, and on 1 September Chang Hsun's troops captured Nanking. Chang had been forced to surrender Nanking to the revolutionaries in 1911, and now gained revenge for his humiliation; even though he was now working for Yuan Shih-k'ai, he remained loyal to the Manchus in his heart and made his troops retain their Ch'ing dynasty queues. Yuan now appointed four of his loyal lieutenants as military governors in the conquered Yangtze provinces: Tuan Ch'i-jui in Anhwei, Feng Kuo-chang in Kiangsu, Li Shun in Kiangsi and T'ang Hsiang-ming in Hunan.[7] Li Yuan-hung remained in Hupei. The unified Peiyang military clique now attained its maximum extent of territorial control.

From 1911 to 1913 Yuan Shih-k'ai had used the Peiyang Army to lever the Ch'ing dynasty from office and then to subvert the embryonic political system of the republic. These years have fixed in the imagination of historians the idea that the Peiyang Army was always the personal instrument of Yuan Shih-k'ai, who thus deserves his title as 'Father of the Warlords'. As noted above, (pp.38–9), even though Yuan certainly was the creator of the Peiyang Army, his power down to 1908 depended on his relationship to the old Empress Dowager. He probably would not have been recalled to office had it not been for the outbreak of the

7 Li, *Political History*, pp.290–4.

revolution in 1911. In the following years Yuan seems to have been always aware that the army would remain loyal to him only if he kept it paid. Yuan also attempted to build ties of personal loyalty to himself among his officers. His career as president shows how well he succeeded in this, but their loyalty had limits: they refused to follow him from president to emperor.

YUAN SHIH-K'AI AS EMPEROR

The defeat of the Second Revolution was followed by the formal election of Yuan Shih-k'ai as president and by the drafting of what was planned as a permanent constitution. Li Yuan-hung was chosen vice-president. Yuan objected strongly to restraints placed on presidential power and interfered repeatedly during the drafting process. On 25 October he issued a circular telegram to the governors and provincial military commanders, in which he accused the KMT of trying to ruin the government of the republic. Most of these officials, appointed by Yuan, responded by urging publicly that the parliamentary memberships and immunities of the KMT be revoked. The circular telegram – theoretically a communication from one important personage to another, but simultaneously sent to other parties and published in the newspapers – became a standard pressure tactic of the warlord period.

The Progressive Party (Chin-pu-tang) was the second most important bloc in the legislature. Many of its members were supporters of the reforming constitutional monarchist movement of 1898 and afterwards, whose leaders in opposition had been K'ang Yu-wei and Liang Ch'i-ch'ao. Before 1911 they had often been in conflict with Sun Yat-sen's movement over influence within the overseas Chinese community, and now the Progressives were more willing than the Nationalists to cooperate with Yuan. The Cabinet headed by Hsiung Hsi-ling was supported by the Progressives; its members included Liang Ch'i-ch'ao – one of the major leaders of the 1898 reforms and the exiled proponent of constitutional monarchy down to 1911 – as Minister of Justice and Chang Chien – an industrialist and financier who had been prominent in the Manchu reforms – in the agriculture and commerce portfolio. But despite their differences with the KMT, the Progressives also favoured republicanism and constitutional government.

On 4 November Yuan issued an order, countersigned by prime minister Hsiung, dissolving the KMT and revoking the parliamentary status of KMT members. The legislature met the next day cordoned off by troops, who expelled the KMT representatives. By February 1914 the Hsiung Cabinet had resigned, and many of the Progressives began to cooperate with the now outlawed Nationalists.[8] Public politics, however, now revolved around Yuan's efforts to amend the constitution so that he could become emperor. A Constitutional Conference opened in January, composed of members handpicked by Yuan. Yuan proposed revisions in the constitution that placed all appointments and the treaty- and war-making powers in the hands of the president, and gave him substantial emergency powers. All of these changes had been accomplished by June 1914.[9] The Peiyang Army, in firm control of North China and the Yangtze provinces, supported Yuan every step of the way; the non-Peiyang provinces remained divided and were in any case collectively weaker.

The outbreak of the First World War affected the political and military situation in China in subtle ways that grew in importance. Japan, on the basis of the Anglo-Japanese Alliance, at once declared war on Germany and conquered her colony at Tsingtao.[10] China had, in effect, been preserved from partition ever since 1900 by the conflicting interests of the Great Powers, all of which except Austria-Hungary and the United States were looking for some territorial share when the Chinese melon was finally carved up. The European war precluded the European powers from contemplating further commitments in China. Japan, on the other hand, was only marginally involved in the war after the fall of Tsingtao, and only the United States was effectively able to restrain Japanese ambitions in China. The United States was already estranged from and unfriendly towards Japan, but demonstrated repeatedly between 1914 and 1941 that she was not going to go to war with Japan over any cause originating in China.[11] The First World War also stimulated the textile industry worldwide. The textile industry in the Chinese treaty port cities grew, and Japanese investment in this industry grew proportionately. By the end of the war the Japanese were second only to the British as the largest foreign investors in

8 Li, *Political History*, pp.294–303.

9 Li, *Political History*, pp.304–9.

10 John E. Schrecker, *Imperialism and Chinese Nationalism; Germany in Shantung* (Cambridge, MA, 1971), on the Tsingtao colony and Germany's role in Shantung; Charles B. Burdick, *The Japanese Siege of Tsingtau: World War I in Asia* (Hamden, 1976), on Japan's capture of Tsingtao in 1914.

11 A. Whitney Griswold, *The Far Eastern Policy of the United States* (New York, 1938), is the classic exposition of this viewpoint; more recently Tang Tsou, *America's Failure in China, 1941–1950* (Chicago, 1963), pp.7–11.

China. Since postwar Britain had other domestic and imperial concerns, Japan in fact was the Great Power with the greatest vested interest in maintaining the existing system of unequal treaties, extraterritoriality and gunboat diplomacy, which Britain had taken the initiative in creating.[12]

On 18 January 1915 the Japanese government of Count Ōkuma Shigenobu presented China with the notorious Twenty-One Demands. These were divided into five groups, of which the first four called for Japanese succession to Germany's former rights in Shantung, extension of the Japanese leases in southern Manchuria to ninety-nine years, half-ownership in the Han-yeh-p'ing Company (the iron and steel complex at Hanyang) and other state enterprises, and the non-alienation of any part of China's coastline to any third power. These were the sorts of demands that China had suffered ever since the revelation of her extreme military weakness in the war of 1894–5. Yuan Shih-k'ai's regime, always near bankruptcy, was receiving diminishing percentages of provincial revenues. Japan was now the only likely source of foreign loans, since the European powers were at war and the United States was bankrolling Britain and France, and already felt that she had done enough for China by remitting her share of the Boxer Indemnity. Japan was also well armed and nearby. The first four groups of the Twenty-One Demands could not have been refused by any conceivable Chinese government in 1915.

The fifth group was another matter. The Japanese had deliberately made them unacceptable in order to provide some face-saving negotiating leeway for the Chinese. They called for the appointment of Japanese 'advisers' to the key positions in Chinese ministries and provincial governments, and for railway leases in the Yangtze Valley. The latter of course violated the non-alienation agreement that the Ch'ing court had previously concluded with Britain, Japan's ally. Yuan Shih-k'ai's government agreed to the first four groups and refused the fifth on 9 May. Yuan's supporters represented this outcome as a great triumph, but Sun Yat-sen, now in open opposition, denounced Yuan for betraying the nation, and certainly won the battle of public opinion.[13]

12 Chi-ming Hou, *Foreign Investment and Economic Development in China, 1840–1937* (Cambridge, MA, 1965), especially pp.17–19. In 1914 Britain had 37.7% of the total foreign investment in China, and Japan ranked fourth with 13.6%. By 1931 Britain had 36.7% and Japan 35.1%. In 1930 63% of Japanese investment was concentrated in Manchuria and 25% in Shanghai.

13 Li, *Political History*, pp.310–12.

Despite this setback, the monarchical movement continued, and public advocacy of the idea of monarchy was voiced by Yuan's supporters, only to be publicly rejected by Yuan himself. In the spring Peiyang Army general Feng Kuo-chang and Liang Ch'i-ch'ao (who had been an advocate of constitutional monarchy in his intellectual career) visited Yuan privately, and Yuan again denied his monarchical ambitions. All educated Chinese could see that Yuan was playing the ancient game of the Three Refusals (san-jang), the polite rejection of the offered throne that made the throne legitimate when finally accepted. In August Yuan's US legal adviser, Dr Frank J. Goodnow, produced his famous memorandum advocating constitutional monarchy as the form of government best suited to China's conditions. Goodnow was an expert on administrative law and an admirer of the constitutional arrangements of Hohenzollern Germany; by constitutional monarchy he meant a system in which the emperor, within a constitutional framework, would be the effective political head of the government, rather than a ceremonial or symbolic figure.

Due to previous constitutional revisions, Yuan was already president for ten years with the right of indefinite re-election. From September on, he arranged an elaborate charade of telegrams from the provinces urging first a fundamental change in the political system and later that Yuan should become emperor. On 12 December, after declining repeated requests from the Political Council (ts'an-cheng-yuan) that was serving as the standing committee of the legislature, Yuan accepted the throne, proclaiming the regnal era Hung-hsien or Overflowing Constitutionality.[14]

Yuan's imperial proclamation was like the shock that crystallizes an oversaturated solution. China had changed faster than Yuan realized, and the change had been fastest in the unquantifiable realm of language and symbols. Yuan had usurped the throne in accordance with all the appropriate historical precedents, but the imperial terminology he employed to enhance his legitimacy actually destroyed it. From Tuan Ch'i-jui and Feng Kuo-chang down, the Peiyang generals who would have been, at least briefly, the highest titled nobility of a new imperial dynasty resented and opposed Yuan's imperial pretensions, even though – one might argue – these did not involve any increase in Yuan's actual power. Even more important in the short run, non-Peiyang provinces were willing to oppose Yuan by force, even before the alienation and division of the

14 Li, *Political History*, pp.304–10, 312–24.

Peiyang military clique became evident. Yunnan was the most important such province.[15]

3. Yunnan army influence during the Early Republic (After: Sutton, *Provincial Militarism and the Chinese Republic*)

15 Li, *Political History*, pp.324–34, for the general unravelling of Yuan's position; cf. Ernest B. Young, *The Presidency of Yuan Shih-k'ai: Liberalism and Dictatorship in Early Republican China* (Ann Arbor, 1977), p.231: 'The monarchical movement, with its awkward pretensions, was a catalyst to a situation already on the verge of crystallization.'

YUNNAN AND THE NATIONAL PROTECTION ARMY

Yunnan had been designated to have two divisions under the thirty-six division plan, but prior to 1911 only the 19th Division had been activated. Yunnan was far outside the purview of the main military reform efforts that created the Peiyang Army, central government funds were not available, and the local authorities therefore complied only nominally with the plans to create the New Army. By 1907 military reform consisted of the creation of two new military schools and the recruitment of about 3,000 soldiers described by foreigners as even more slovenly and less disciplined than the old-style troops, who were still continued on the rolls.[16]

The reforming Mongol Hsi-liang became governor-general in 1907, and the following year suppressed (with old-style troops) a revolutionary rising at Hokou, where the French-owned railway crossed into French Indo-China. The sensitivity of this rising convinced the court to give more priority and funding to military reform in Yunnan, which continued even after Hsi-liang left in 1909. By 1911, exceptionally for the non-Peiyang portions of the New Army, the 19th Division was near its full peacetime strength of 12,500 men. Its infantry were armed with 6.8mm Mauser rifles and supported by a unit with twenty-four 8mm Maxim machine guns, and its artillery had the full prescribed number of fifty-four 75mm Krupp mountain howitzers. Foreign observers were somewhat effusive regarding the unit's parade ground appearance and evolutions; one Frenchman noted that the only fault he could find was that the band could not play the 'Marseillaise'.[17]

Most of the officers of the 19th Division were Yunnanese who had received good military educations. This level of educational attainment was in contrast to the post-Taiping militia armies, in which family and local connections had determined original appointments of officers. The degree of local attachment contrasted with the Peiyang Army, where first Yuan Shih-k'ai and then the Manchu ministers of war tried before 1911 to enforce a more modern system of officer assignments, partly in order to inhibit the development of unit cliques and local ties. Most of the Yunnanese who had attended the Japanese Military Academy, however, went back to Yunnan for their military careers. In Yunnan itself, the military reformer and provincial native Li Ken-yuan had won

16 Sutton, *Provincial Militarism*, pp.53–8. Roger Des Forges, *Hsi-liang and the Chinese National Revolution* (New Haven, 1973), for the Yunnan background.

17 Sutton, *Provincial Militarism*, pp.66–8.

Hsi-liang's confidence and had greatly expanded the scale and improved the quality of the provincial military schools. Peking's efforts to bring the 19th Division under stronger central control were frustrated by governor-general Li Ching-hsi, who before 1911 deliberately promoted non-Peiyang men to high positions. One beneficiary was the Hunanese Ts'ai O (1882–1916), who by 1911 was a major-general in command of the 37th Brigade.[18]

While the cadre of Yunnanese officers gave the 19th Division a strong provincial cast, most of the officers with modern military educations, regardless of their provincial origin, supported revolutionary goals. They were angered and frustrated by the apparent succcess of the Ch'ing in repressing the revolutionary movement from 1909 to 1911. When the October 1911 revolution broke out, however, the 37th Brigade and the other 19th Division forces at Kunming (Yunnanfu) rallied for the revolution and captured the thickly walled governor-general's yamen in a battle that was more bloody than the fighting in Wuchang. Ts'ai O then became military governor, establishing an administration staffed by New Army officers. The new regime spent the following months bringing the other 19th Division forces (principally the 76th Regiment at Tali and the 75th Regiment at Linan) under its control and in getting its authority recognized by the rapidly proliferating gentry-led paramilitary organizations. The latter, known by a variety of names including t'uan-lien (militia) and min-chün (people's army), filled the void at the local level caused by the collapse of Ch'ing institutions. In most provinces, such bodies became important sources of both troops and officers as Chinese armies evolved in the direction of warlordism.[19]

In 1912 the Yunnan Army intervened in the affairs of both Szechwan and Kweichow. Szechwan, where the revolutionary movement had been successfully suppressed by the Ch'ing, was thrown into great disorder by the 1911 revolution, and never attained provincial unification throughout the warlord period. Yunnan forces occupied southern Szechwan, partly to pacify this disorder, but mostly in order to pay their army with Szechwan salt revenues. Pressures from within Szechwan and from the central

18 Sutton, *Provincial Militarism*, pp.27–52, 62–6, 80–3.

19 Sutton, *Provincial Militarism*, pp.83–96, 101–13. Philip A. Kuhn, *Rebellion and its Enemies in Late Imperial China: Militarization and Social Structure, 1796–1864* (Cambridge, MA, 1970), though dealing with an earlier period, offers important and broadly applicable general insights on the social bases of local militarization in China.

government eventually forced their withdrawal. In Kweichow it was different. Kweichow was a much more backward province, and the New Army regiment forming there collapsed promptly in October 1911. Yunnan forces under T'ang Chi-yao had some hard fighting against local bandits, but their presence was supported by the Peking government and not challenged by local elites or strong forces from neighbouring provinces. T'ang's success in Kweichow in the end propelled him to the leadership of the entire Yunnan Army.[20]

As a Hunanese, Ts'ai O's leadership position was resented by the Yunnanese majority of the army. Nevertheless, the corporate sense of the army was strong in this period. Foreign reports attested that troop training continued to be rigorous, though perhaps less exacting than before 1911. Officers were rotated regularly, which exemplified modern personnel management and inhibited the formation of cliques. Ts'ai O, T'ang Chi-yao and the other leading Yunnan commanders all favoured the kind of nationalist, centralized and republican regime they thought Yuan Shih-k'ai was working for after the overthrow of the Manchus, and the Yunnan Army gave no support to the Second Revolution. Afterwards, Yuan felt strong enough to accept the frequently offered resignation of Ts'ai O, who was brought to Peking and given a civil position with high status but no military power. T'ang Chi-yao became military governor of Yunnan. Yuan thought he could rely on T'ang and on Lu Jung-t'ing, T'ang's opposite number in Kwangsi, but neither was a Peiyang general, unlike the new governors appointed in the Yangtze provinces in the aftermath of the Second Revolution.[21]

Despite Yuan Shih-k'ai's efforts to orchestrate popular demand for his accession to the throne, this step alienated many of his supporters and enraged his enemies all the more. Sun Yat-sen had reorganized his followers as the Revolutionary Party (Ko-ming-tang) in 1914. On 10 November 1915 Ch'en Ch'i-mei – most famous as the early patron of Chiang Kai-shek, whose nephews led the CC clique in later KMT politics – acting on Sun's behalf engineered the assassination of Yuan's Shanghai commander, Cheng Ju-ch'eng. Ex-Kiangsi military governor Li Lieh-chün was already in Yunnan trying, also on Sun's behalf, to persuade T'ang Chi-yao to rebel against Yuan. T'ang stalled; the Yunnan Army was no match for the Peiyang Army. However, both Feng Kuo-chang and Tuan Ch'i-jui,

20 Sutton, *Provincial Militarism*, pp.114–38.
21 Sutton, *Provincial Militarism*, pp.141–83.

the future leaders of the already coalescing Chihli and Anhwei cliques within the Peiyang Army, were gravely discontent with Yuan's imperial project, whose success would have meant that Yuan's eldest son Yuan K'o-ting would succeed Yuan Shih-k'ai, rather than either of them. Liang Ch'i-ch'ao and his Progressive Party, men who had supported constitutional monarchy before 1911, also turned against Yuan. At this stage Ts'ai O, who considered Liang his mentor, escaped from his position in Peking and after many dramatic adventures returned to Yunnan. Four days later, on 23 December, T'ang Chi-yao, Ts'ai O, Li Lieh-chün and others signed a circular telegram calling on Yuan to renounce the monarchy forever. Yunnan declared independence, with T'ang as military governor (tu-tu), and renamed its army the National Protection Army (hu-kuo-chün).[22]

At first Yunnan was isolated, though ultimately the anti-monarchical cause prevailed. Yunnan troops invading Szechwan were successfully opposed by Peiyang forces under Ts'ao K'un. But Yuan was unable to make his commanders move vigorously against Yunnan. Feng Kuo-chang at Nanking pleaded illness. Lu Jung-t'ing in Kwangsi eventually proclaimed his own independence. By March 1916 Yuan had been pointedly asked by the foreign diplomatic community in Peking how he planned to suppress the rebellion against his rule, and had received advice to terminate his monarchical ambitions from, among others, vice-president Li Yuan-hung, Feng Kuo-chang, Tuan Ch'i-jui and Peiyang clique elder statesman and future president Hsu Shih-ch'ang. On 22 March Yuan, in a great loss of face, publicly repudiated monarchy and began to negotiate a settlement with the southern provinces.[23]

Tuan Ch'i-jui, alienated from Yuan since the beginning of the monarchical scheme, now became his former patron's chief hope. Yuan had attempted to engage Tuan's active support by offering him the position of Chief of Staff. Tuan now played with Yuan a game similar to that which Yuan had played with the Ch'ing in 1911–12, escalating his demands while the situation ripened. The men who had forced Yuan to relinquish his empire were no longer willing to accept him as president. On 22 April Yuan appointed Tuan prime minister, issuing a proclamation implying that the prime minister and Cabinet now had full authority and that his presidency was henceforth nominal.

22 Li, *Political History*, pp.325–30.
23 Li, *Political History*, pp.330–4.

Meanwhile the National Protection Army created a national government at Chaoching in Kwangtung. Kwangsi, Kweichow and of course Yunnan were already affiliated with the anti-Yuan movement, and troops from these provinces had moved into Kwangtung, whose military units often were sympathetic. Lung Chi-kuang, the military governor of Kwangtung who had been appointed by Yuan, declared independence on 6 April, but the continued erosion of his authority outside Canton proper eventually forced him into closer association with the Yunnan-based movement. The government created at Chaoching on 8 May included the military governors of the four provinces and other notables including Ts'ai O and Liang Ch'i-ch'ao. It issued a proclamation declaring Yuan Shih-k'ai deposed and Li Yuan-hung the legal president in accordance with the 1912 constitution. Since Li was not free to act on his own, the Chaoching regime would take charge until normal constitutional procedures could be restored.

At Peking, Tuan Ch'i-jui was trying to collect on the promises of real authority that Yuan had made. In telegrams to the southern authorities he tried to make the case that the Yuan problem had been solved by the transfer of executive authority to the Cabinet. When the southerners replied that nothing but the resignation of Yuan would do, Tuan began to support them. Yuan had no intention of fulfilling his promises to Tuan, much less of resigning. He now tried to use Feng Kuo-chang, in command at Nanking, to rally the Peiyang generals in the northern provinces to demand that Yuan continue in power. Feng, however, played the same game as Tuan, which both had learned from Yuan. He kept his own position ambiguous and convened a conference of provincial representatives, which met on 18 May. While this was going on Yuan offered Feng the premiership, to get him out of Nanking and to get rid of Tuan, but Feng did not accept. After 18 May most of the northern provinces declared their independence also, and demanded the resignation of Yuan Shih-k'ai. Even though outright civil war seemed inevitable, Yuan did not have much to fight it with. The only prominent Peiyang general to remain loyal to Yuan and eager to fight for him was the irrepressible Chang Hsun, who had defended Nanking for the Manchus in 1911–12 and would try to restore them in 1917.[24]

Yuan had long suffered from kidney disease, and contemplation of his own mortality had intensified both his own desire and the

24 Li, *Political History*, pp.334–44.

pressures from his family to become emperor while he still lived. He died of his illness on 6 June 1916, as if he had chosen the most dramatic possible moment. Yuan is usually called the Father of the Warlords, simply because the leading warlords of the 1916–28 period were his former protégés and subordinates in the Peiyang Army. It is not really correct to attribute the other characteristics of warlordism, such as quasi-independent provincial armies and fragile military coalitions held together by personal loyalties and relationships, to his own preferences, since in his career as a military reformer down to 1909 he had attempted to create a modern army on the Japanese model. He demonstrated then that he understood how staff work, military education, and regular transfers of officer personnel fitted together to make a modern military organization. After his return to power in 1911, however, he seemed willing to sacrifice everything to his imperial ambitions, and ruled, as Liang Ch'i-ch'ao noted, by a combination of violence and bribery that destroyed the idealism of the early Republican movement. Since those who opposed Yuan could do so only from a territorial military base, Yuan's career as president and emperor contributed greatly to China's subsequent political division.[25]

WARLORDISM AFTER THE DEATH OF YUAN SHIH-K'AI

Yuan's death punctuated the already evident disintegration of the Peiyang Army. Feng Kuo-chang and Tuan Ch'i-jui quickly emerged as heads of the two most important factions, the Chihli and Anhwei cliques, respectively, but there were others. Disunited, the Peiyang generals could no longer repress lesser fry, so local warlords ruling a group of adjoining provinces, a single province, or only a part of a province, proliferated. The Yunnan and Kwangsi (Lu Jung-t'ing) cliques in South China were already prominent by 1916, but one consequence of Yuan's fall was to permit the ex-bandit Chang Tso-lin to consolidate his control over the three provinces of Manchuria. Some provinces neither fell under the control of a multi-province ruler nor produced a unifying warlord of their own, and therefore spent the warlord period divided among several weak

25 Li, *Political History*, pp.344–5.

but still predatory generals: Szechwan after the withdrawal of the Yunnan forces was the outstanding example.[26]

Weak or strong, a warlord had to have an army that was 'personal' in the sense of being willing to follow him into rebellion whenever the warlord fell out with the other warlords who had custody of the national government in Peking. The requirement of personal loyalty of course had to be transmitted all the way down the chain of command, which meant that despite their modern terminology and uniforms the warlord armies had an essentially feudal organizational structure. If, for example, a regiment commander were killed in battle, he usually could not be replaced with any other colonel, as in a modern army. Instead, the new regimental commander would have to be someone usually from within the same regiment whom the troops would follow, and who also was acceptable to the warlord. While such personal loyalties can be as strong as the national and institutional loyalties found in modern societies, any commander who could be subverted could usually bring over all of his subordinates. Warlords therefore went into battle haunted by fears of betrayal. And an organizational structure built on personal loyalties could not adapt to the modern (both Western and Japanese) system of rotating officers systematically on the basis of rank, service record and education. This feature of Chinese military practice lasted well beyond the end of the warlord period proper, and made US assistance to the Chinese army extremely difficult in the Second World War.[27]

Warlord soldiers typically came from the landless, economically marginal class of the large Chinese population. For centuries Chinese social prejudice against soldiers had been very strong, extending to generals and lower officers as well. Once recruited,

26 The major studies of individual warlords and their regions are James E. Sheridan, *Chinese Warlord: The Career of Feng Yu-hsiang* (Stanford, 1966); Gillin, *Warlord*; Sutton, *Provincial Militarism*; Diana Lary, *Region and Nation: The Kwangsi Clique in Chinese Politics, 1925–1937* (Cambridge, UK, 1974); McCormack, *Chang Tso-lin*; Kapp, *Szechwan*; Odoric Y.K. Wou, *Militarism in Modern China: The Career of Wu P'ei-fu, 1916–1939* (Canberra, 1978); and Forbes, *Warlords and Muslims*. Overall analyses of warlordism include Lucien Pye, *Warlord Politics: Conflict and Coalition in the Modernization of Republican China* (New York, 1971) and Hsi-sheng Ch'i, *Warlord Politics in China, 1916–1928* (Stanford, 1976).

27 Sheridan, *Chinese Warlord*, pp.20–2, and Ch'i, *Warlord Politics*, pp.36–42 on the importance of personal relations. Sutton, *Provincial Militarism*, has the Yunnan Army going from a high standard of professionalism before 1911 to resembling 'the lowest common denominator of warlord armies' (p.258) in the 1920s.

soldiers were difficult to demobilize; they might stay together and use their military skills to survive as bandits. Pay was poor and irregular in the lower ranks, and a soldier was not a good marriage prospect, which hurt even more in China's family-oriented Confucian society.[28] Soldiers nevertheless needed to be paid as regularly as possible if the warlord was to count on them. Central government subventions depended on the current state of warlord politics, and the central government continued financially very weak: even though it nominally controlled the customs and other foreign-administered revenues, most of these continued to go right out again for debt service and other payments to foreigners. Subsidies from foreign governments existed, but obviously compromised a warlord's independence, and his reputation, as Chinese nationalism grew. For the most part, then, warlords had to maintain their armies by savagely predatory taxation of the territories they controlled.[29]

In general, who the warlords and their soldiers were, and how they ruled, made it difficult for even long-established local warlords to establish an effective political system in their territories. Those who made efforts to do so were thwarted by the realities of warlord politics, under which the civilian population had to be sacrificed to maintain the army. Beyond that was the fact that the warlord enterprise was fundamentally illegitimate: it contradicted both the old imperial ideal of the unity of All under Heaven and the newer nationalist ideal of a unified China resisting foreign imperialism. Since warlordism was in principle transitional, warlords had to fight each other in pursuit of national unification.

THE SOUTH AND THE PERIPHERY AFTER 1916

No Peiyang warlord ever achieved the degree of control over the Peiyang military clique that Yuan Shih-k'ai possessed at the peak of his power. Nevertheless, for almost a decade after Yuan's death, the agenda of the leading Peiyang warlords was to reunify China by first reuniting the Peiyang Army and then conquering the lesser provincial armies. The history of the major warlord wars down to 1925 recounts the failure to carry out this agenda. Meanwhile regional regimes developed in Manchuria, Shansi and Sinkiang;

28 Diana Lary, *Warlord Soldiers: Chinese Common Soldiers, 1911–1937* (Cambridge, UK, 1985), pp.13–35; Ch'i, *Warlord Politics*, pp.77–90.

29 Numerous examples in Sheridan, *Chinese Warlord*, pp.23–9.

Mongolia and Tibet seceded; and most of South China remained beyond Peiyang Army control, to become the incubator for both the Nationalist and Communist movements. The situation greatly resembled the period of the Five Dynasties and Ten Kingdoms (907–59),[30] in which conflicts within the central armies permitted local regimes to prosper, but it did not last as long. We shall survey the periphery before describing the disintegration of the Peiyang military clique.

The word Manchuria, though derived from the word Manchu adopted by Ch'ing dynasty founders as the official designation of their people, was often used by nineteenth- and twentieth-century imperialists to emphasize the non-Chinese character of the three northeastern provinces (Fengtien, later renamed Liaoning; Kirin and Heilungkiang). Chinese usually call the area the northeast, and even at the beginning of the Ch'ing the Chinese component of the population outnumbered the non-Chinese (chiefly Manchu, Mongol and Korean). Japanese and Russian railway imperialism stimulated industrial development in these provinces, and the last decades of the Ch'ing saw the extension of regular Chinese provincial administration to the northeast, as well as Sinkiang and Taiwan, partly in the attempt to forestall annexation. After the Russo-Japanese War Japan was solidly entrenched in Port Arthur and along the South Manchurian Railway Company, while imperial Russia survived in the north at Harbin and along the line of the Chinese Eastern Railway. Industrialization and gold mining both created a proletariat, with the usual connotations of social displacement, and banditry was rife in the sparsely settled rural regions.[31]

Chang Tso-lin (d. 1928) was born sometime in the 1870s, raised in poverty, and became a bandit in 1894. By 1903 he was leader of a gang of several hundred, and a Ch'ing local official legitimized his position by designating him a garrison commander, with his gang as

30 Wang Gungwu, *The Structure of Power in North China during the Five Dynasties* (Kuala Lumpur, 1963), and Edward H. Schafer, *The Empire of Min* (Rutland, 1954), remain the most accessible accounts of this period in English, but Edmund H. Worthy, 'The founding of Sung China, 950–1000: integrative changes in military and political institutions' (PhD diss., Princeton, 1976) adds a lot to these older accounts. As in the 1920s, in the tenth century also the reunification of China required political legitimacy in addition to military force.

31 Robert H.G. Lee, *The Manchurian Frontier in Ch'ing History* (Cambridge, MA, 1970), for general background; McCormack, *Chang Tso-lin*, pp.1–14.

the garrison. The rapid expansion of the new armies led to promotion for Chang; by 1911 he led a force of several battalions. The regular New Army forces in the northeast (10th Division, Wu Lu-chen's 6th Division, Lan T'ien-wei's 2nd Mixed Brigade) were drawn into the fighting in 1911, and in 1912 the troops of Chang and his colleagues were expanded into two new divisions (27th and 28th). Chang was now second in command; when the military governor died in 1915, Yuan Shih-k'ai attempted to install Tuan Chih-kuei, a long-time Peiyang officer, as his successor. Chang, with his local power base, prevailed, and in April 1916 Tuan fled to Peking. Yuan, whose power was slipping away in the last months of his life, confirmed Chang as military governor of Fengtien. In 1917 Chang's remaining rivals in Fengtien, and the military commanders of Kirin and Heilungkiang, made the mistake of supporting Chang Hsun's Manchu restoration move. Chang Tso-lin was then able to lever them out of office and take over their troops and territories. In the same year the Russian revolutions removed the Russian imperialist threat, if not the presence of Russians, while leaving China more exposed to Japanese imperialist ambitions.[32]

By 1920 Chang Tso-lin's Fengtien clique had expanded beyond its bandit base to incorporate professionally trained New Army officers and civilians of varying educational backgrounds. Chang himself remained a mah-jongg playing illiterate all his life. His control over Chinese affairs in the northeast entailed some sort of working relationship with the Japanese. Chinese nationalists came to denounce him as a Japanese puppet; the Japanese in the end considered him an obstacle and contrived his murder. Chang, like the other warlords, was no one's puppet, but had to take financial and other assistance where he could get it, which in his case usually meant the Japanese.

In contrast to Chang Tso-lin, Yen Hsi-shan (b. 1883) in Shansi was a well-educated product of the Manchu reform movement. While studying in Japan (Imperial Military Academy, class of 1909) he met Sun Yat-sen and joined the Alliance Society. By 1911 he commanded a regiment at Taiyuan and led the attack on the Manchu garrison there in October. Revolutionary forces took over the province, declared secession, and chose Yen as military governor. Yen then attempted to interdict Yuan Shih-k'ai's Hankow campaign (described on pp.35–8) by capturing the critical railway junction at Shihchiachuang. Yuan's troops defeated the much

32 McCormack, *Chang Tso-lin*, pp.15–44.

weaker Shansi forces and drove Yen from Taiyuan. Yen made his peace with Yuan, who permitted him to remain as military governor. Yen afterwards kept Shansi out of the Second Revolution, supported Yuan's monarchical movement, and kept some of Yuan's henchmen in office in Shansi until 1917. Yen's attempts to expand outside of Shansi were unsuccessful, and until the end of his power in 1949 he concentrated on maintaining control of Shansi and governing it as effectively as possible.[33]

The Yunnan Army reached the peak of its influence in the anti-monarchical movement, during which its leading general, the Hunanese Ts'ai O, had led Yunnan troops into Szechwan. On Yuan's death the militarily powerless Li Yuan-hung had succeeded to the presidency and appointed Ts'ai as both civil and military governor of Szechwan. Ts'ai unfortunately died of long untreated tuberculosis on 8 November 1916. He had been the idealistic heart of the Yunnan Army; his death left the pragmatic T'ang Chi-yao as the leading Yunnan general. T'ang remained in Yunnan. Other Yunnan troops under Tsai K'an remained in occupation in Kweichow. In Szechwan Lo P'ei-chin succeeded, as acting military governor, to command of two Yunnanese divisions.[34]

The Yunnan Army by now had expanded to a larger size than the resources of Yunnan could support, so that the withdrawal of the troops in Kweichow, Szechwan and Kwangtung would have been a disaster for the province. Lo P'ei-chin attempted to solve this problem by designating the Yunnan troops in Szechwan as national forces, which would be supported by, and monopolize, the military appropriations provided by the disintegrating central government. The Szechwan troops also under Lo's nominal command would be supported by provincial revenues. This discrimination, coupled with Lo's personal corruption and abrasive command style, led to civil war in Szechwan. In June and July of 1917, Szechwan troops under Liu Ts'un-hou drove Lo from the province, captured Chengtu (killing Lo's successor in the process), and then defeated Lo again when he tried to reconquer Szechwan. T'ang Chi-yao then dismissed Lo, and from December 1917 to early 1918 reconquered Szechwan with the main force of the Yunnan Army. T'ang was successful for a while in reconciling Szechwan provincial sentiment to occupation by an army from another province, but in 1920 a Szechwan coalition

33 Gillin, *Warlord*, pp.9–22.
34 Sutton, *Provincial Militarism*, pp.184–213.

drove the Yunnan Army from the province.[35]

By then the expansion of the Yunnan Army and the territory under its control had both diluted its professional level and destroyed its internal cohesion. In September 1918 T'ang Chi-yao was escorted into Chungking by a magnificently uniformed bodyguard (commanded by future Yunnan warlord Lung Yun). A 101-gun salute climaxed the ceremonies, and T'ang was nicknamed King of the Southwest from then on. T'ang allegedly commanded 200,000 troops; some of these were of other armies of highly contingent allegiance, but they included 30,000 to 40,000 thousand Yunnan troops in Szechwan as well as the Yunnan troops in Kwangtung, Kweichow and Yunnan itself.[36]

In Kwangtung, troops of Lu Jung-t'ing's Kwangsi Army jostled for position with Yunnan and local forces. Since Sun Yat-sen chose to make his next bid for national authority from Canton, events in Canton became part of national politics.

PEKING AND PEIYANG POLITICS AFTER YUAN SHIH-K'AI

By general agreement Vice-President Li Yuan-hung succeeded to the presidency when Yuan Shih-k'ai died. That was as far as agreement went. Anhwei clique chieftain Tuan Ch'i-jui and most of the other Peiyang militarists, who did not agree among themselves on a successor to Yuan's military power, nevertheless wanted to maintain the strong executive presidency provided under Yuan's 1914 constitution. The politicians and leaders of the Yunnan and other southern armies, working under the banner of the Chaoching military government, wanted to restore the provisional constitution of 1912, and its parliament, which had had the right to control the executive through approval (or disapproval) of Cabinet appointments. The Chinese navy, which was dominated throughout this period by a clique of officers from Fukien who were considerably more liberal than most of the militarists, supported the 1912 constitution. Chihli clique leader Feng Kuo-chang was then in control of the Peiyang troops in the Shanghai area, and thus was relatively vulnerable to such pressures as the navy could bring to bear. He was also Tuan Ch'i-jui's main potential rival within the Peiyang Army. Feng's support enabled Li Yuan-hung to proclaim

35 Sutton, *Provincial Militarism*, pp.217–37.
36 Sutton, *Provincial Militarism*, pp.229–30.

the restoration of the 1912 constitution. On 14 July 1916 the Chaoching military government dissolved itself.[37]

On 1 August a new Cabinet was announced, in which Tuan Ch'i-jui held the key portfolios of Prime Minister and Minister of War, while T'ang Shao-yi, Yuan Shih-k'ai's first prime minister, was Minister of Foreign Affairs and other ministries were given to members of or men acceptable to the KMT. However, pressure from Peiyang commanders forced T'ang Shao-yi and everyone to the political left of him to resign or to refuse to take up office. In place of the revival of constitutionalism desired by both the KMT (still designated Ko-ming-tang or Chinese Revolutionary Party) and the Progressives, a politics of military factions emerged, with no player as strong as Yuan Shih-k'ai had been. Liang Ch'i-ch'ao's Progressives eventually emerged as the Research clique, whose members placed their hopes in a succession of northern militarists.[38] Sun Yat-sen spent the rest of his life from 1917 on trying to organize an alternative military government at Canton, as the basis for a military reunification of China; this involved him in a succession of deals with weaker, but equally untrustworthy, southern militarists.

CHANG HSUN RESTORES THE MANCHU DYNASTY

On 9 June 1916, shortly after Yuan Shih-k'ai's death, the ultraconservative Peiyang general Chang Hsun, commanding at the critical railway junction at Hsuchow in northern Kiangsu, greeted other Peiyang generals from seven northern provinces whom he had summoned to a conference. The eccentric Chang and his pigtailed troops did not fit into either the Anhwei coalition forming around Tuan Ch'i-jui or the still equally loose Chihli grouping around Feng Kuo-chang. Tuan Ch'i-jui relied on the advice of his chief Cabinet secretary and subordinate general Hsu Shu-cheng (called 'Little Hsu' to distinguish him from senior Peiyang statesman and future president Hsu Shih-ch'ang, known as 'Big Hsu'). Little Hsu decided to support Chang Hsun as a counterweight to Feng Kuo-chang. As a result of this decision, a second Hsuchow conference in September 1916 elected Chang as generalissimo of an Interprovincial Association which most prominent military leaders eventually

37 Li, *Political History*, pp.352–7.

38 Li, *Political History*, pp.356–8; Joseph W. Levenson, *Liang Ch'i-ch'ao and the Mind of Modern China* (London, 1959), pp.181–92.

joined, even Feng Kuo-chang. The charter of the association gave Chang the right to take military action against vaguely defined threats to the political order. Little Hsu used the pressure from the association to threaten the non-military members of the Cabinet. When Li Lieh-chün and Lung Chi-kuang moved toward civil war in Kwangtung, Interior Minister Sun Hung-yi wanted them to negotiate their differences; Hsu insisted that the Cabinet authorize Lung to suppress Li, and prevailed. In December military leaders from twenty-two provinces, headed by Vice-President (since October 1916) Feng Kuo-chang, signed a circular telegram that essentially ordered President Li Yuan-hung to leave the government of the country to Prime Minister Tuan Ch'i-jui, with no interference from the parliament. Chang Hsun called a third Hsuchow conference in January 1917, which reiterated these demands. In other words, as 1917 opened, the Peiyang Army seemed to be maintaining its unity through collegial contacts and negotiation, despite Yuan Shih-k'ai's death; and, as during Yuan's presidency, military force inhibited the development of normal constitutional politics.[39]

When Germany announced the resumption of unrestricted submarine warfare in early 1917, the United States invited China to join her in formal protests. For the Chinese military elite, association with the war against Germany then became very attractive, opening the prospect of foreign subsidies and, conceivably, the renegotiation of the unequal treaty system. These hopes were shared by the civilian parliament, which overwhelmingly voted a declaration of war on 10 March. However, the details of the communication of the declaration of war to Chinese diplomatic representatives led to a serious quarrel between Prime Minister Tuan Ch'i-jui and president Li Yuan-hung. When Tuan in fury offered his resignation, Feng Kuo-chang mediated between him and the president. Most of the parliament, including Liang Ch'i-ch'ao's supporters, were alienated from Tuan as a result. In May Tuan tried, in the true Yuan Shih-k'ai tradition, to intimidate the parliament into passing the implementing legislation for China's participation in the war. On 18 May an English language newspaper in Peking published the details of the large loan Tuan had just negotiated with the Japanese. It could be argued that this was just normal First World War financing; many countries had, after all, borrowed substantial sums to go on fighting against Germany. But it looked like Yuan Shih-k'ai's Reorganization Loan all over again,

39 Li, *Political History*, pp.359–63.

and for Li Yuan-hung, who already had the parliament on his side, it seemed the ideal issue for mobilizing military force against Tuan. Li dismissed Tuan as prime minister on 23 May.[40]

President Li, who had no military support of his own, was gambling that except for Tuan's supporters most of the Peiyang generals would support the 'constitutional' president and parliament. Tuan's supporters, as expected, declared the independence of their provinces, and gathered at Tientsin where they planned to create yet another government under the nominal leadership of Hsu Shih-ch'ang. However, most of the other Peiyang generals also declared independence, and those who did not declare independence also did not support Li Yuan-hung. Chang Hsun, a pivotal figure because of his control of the Interprovincial Association, issued a call for the resignation of Li and the dissolution of the parliament. Hsu Shih-ch'ang, who had no troops of his own despite his high standing in the Peiyang clique and long association with Yuan Shih-k'ai, refused to mediate between Li and the generals, and Liang Ch'i-ch'ao not only refused but also withdrew his followers from parliament, so that there was no quorum. Li then accepted an offer to mediate from Chang Hsun, who meanwhile was negotiating with Tuan, and demanding Tuan's support for a restored Manchu monarchy as the price for Chang's support of Tuan. Tuan pretended to agree, and on 13 June Li, yielding to Chang's pressure, ordered the dissolution of parliament.

Chang Hsun then occupied Peking with his army, and on 1 July shocked the Chinese political world by proclaiming the restoration of the Manchu dynasty. For Chang this was an end, not a means. Despite his prominence in the Peiyang Army, Chang had fought hard for the dynasty in 1911, and had made his troops keep their queues ever afterwards. The leading monarchist reformer of 1898, K'ang Yu-wei, who remained a Manchu loyalist until his death, was Chang's intellectual mentor, and drafted the decrees issued by the new imperial government during its week in office. Liang Ch'i-ch'ao, on the other hand, who had been K'ang's right-hand man in the pre-revolutionary Emperor Protection Society, denounced the restoration immediately as a 'farce', and military leaders of all factions – except of course Chang Hsun – condemned it strongly. Tuan Ch'i-jui reneged on his promise of support, leaving Chang Hsun, whose colleagues in the Interprovincial Association were also opposed to the restoration, out on a limb. Li Yuan-hung fled to the

40 Li, *Political History*, pp.363–7.

Japanese legation, first sending by a trusted courier the presidential seal and other regalia to Vice-President Feng Kuo-chang at Nanking. K'ang Yu-wei also fled to the Japanese legation as the restoration collapsed.[41]

Historians of the period have tended to dwell on the comical aspects of the 1917 Manchu restoration, but it is an important historical milestone nevertheless. The elimination of Chang Hsun left the Peiyang Army divided into two major military groupings: the Chihli clique of President Feng Kuo-chang, who got his seals and called on his supporters to form a government under him at his Nanking headquarters, and the Anhwei clique of Prime Minister Tuan Ch'i-jui, whose title was now of uncertain provenance but who nonetheless re-entered Peking in triumph on 14 July. Since Chang Hsun had eliminated the remnants of the weak but lingering constitution dating from the 1911 revolution, the collapse of the restoration inaugurated a decade of high warlordism, during which China failed to attain unity by either political or military means.

TUAN CH'I-JUI IN POWER, 1917–19

Feng Kuo-chang went to Peking to assume the presidency after securing general consent to the appointment of his protégés as military commanders in Kiangsi, Hupei and Kiangsu. These three provinces now became the bases of the strength of the Chihli military clique (so named after Feng's province of origin). Feng was therefore not as helpless as Li Yuan-hung had been, but was nevertheless weaker than Tuan Ch'i-jui, particularly if Manchurian warlord Chang Tso-lin was willing to support Tuan. Tuan resumed office as prime minister, his military followers (the Anhwei, sometimes called Anfu, clique) dominated the Peking area, and he reorganized the parliament with Research clique (Liang Ch'i-ch'ao's party) members who were willing to support him. On 6 August 1917 Tuan appointed Anhwei clique general Fu Liang-tso as military governor of Hunan and Wu Kuang-hsin as defence commissioner of Szechwan.[42] Both provinces were under the divided leadership of local militarists; conquering them would set the Anhwei clique on the way to conquest of the south while avoiding confrontation with either the Chihli or the Manchurian Fengtien clique.

41 Li, *Political History*, pp.367–73.
42 Li, *Political History*, pp.378–80.

Admiral Ch'eng Pi-kuang had been appointed Minister of the Navy by President Li Yuan-hung, a classmate at the Foochow Naval Academy. Ch'eng had long been a disciple of Sun Yat-sen; he resigned from Tuan's Cabinet and went to Woosung, whence on 22 July 1917 he led the cruisers of the navy's 1st Squadron to Canton to join Sun Yat-sen. After much deal-making, Sun proclaimed a military government at Canton on 3 September, with himself as generalissimo or grand marshal (ta-yuan-shuai), aided by two marshals: Yunnan Army supremo T'ang Chi-yao and Kwangsi clique head Lu Jung-t'ing. The Yunnan Army still contained some idealists among its leadership, notably Li Ken-yuan and Li Lieh-chün, even after the death of Ts'ai O; however, T'ang was utterly pragmatic, and joined Sun only because of the threat from Tuan. Lu would have liked nothing better than a deal with Tuan putting him in charge of Kwangtung and Kwangsi, so his loyalty to Sun was always very conditional. This was also true of Kwangtung's own local militarists, the most important of whom was Ch'en Chiung-ming. The navy remained the military force most consistently supportive of Sun's efforts, but its rather motley collection of obsolete cruisers and gunboats was no substitute for troops on land, and its leadership declined after the murder of Admiral Ch'eng in February 1918.[43]

Meanwhile Tuan Ch'i-jui's war in Hunan and Szechwan was unravelling. Neither of Tuan's designated provincial commanders had great ability, and the division commanders of the 8th and 20th Peiyang divisions, that were supposed to do the actual fighting in Hunan, both were affiliated with the Chihli faction, and in conversation with Feng Kuo-chang had come to understand that he did not wish the campaign to succeed. Feng meanwhile had engineered the appointment of Ts'ao K'un, his eventual successor as leader of the Chihli military clique, as military governor of Chihli itself. After various setbacks in both Hunan and Szechwan the commanders of the 8th and 20th divisions recommended a negotiated settlement, which idea was publicly endorsed by Ts'ao K'un and the military governors of the Chihli-controlled provinces of Hupei, Kiangsi and Kiangsu. Bowing to the inevitable, Tuan resigned on 20 November.

43 Bruce Swanson, *Eighth Voyage of the Dragon: A History of China's Quest for Seapower* (Annapolis, 1982), pp.132–5; Li, *Political History*, pp.376–8. For Ch'en Chiung-ming, see Howard L. Boorman, ed., *Biographical Dictionary of Republican China* (4 vols, New York, 1967–71), I, pp.173–80.

Tuan's resignation did not deprive him either of his personal ascendancy over the Anhwei faction of the Peiyang Army or of the Japanese sources of funding and weapons which both he and Chang Tso-lin had cultivated. In December Tuan's subordinate Ni Tz'u-ch'ung, who had loudly advocated monarchy in Yuan Shih-k'ai's day and later had encouraged Chang Hsun, called a conference of northern warlords at Tientsin. Feng tried to get rid of Tuan by designating him commander-in-chief of the War Participation Army, supposedly intended to fight in the First World War, but this merely permitted Tuan to get more loans (these were loans in name only, since they were unsecured) from the Japanese. As 1918 opened, Ts'ao K'un urged the military conquest of Hunan, whose provincial forces were now on the border of Hupei and threatening the conquest of that Chihli-held province. Feng ordered Ts'ao's 3rd Division, under the command of the cultivated poet and strategist Wu P'ei-fu, to go to Hunan. Despite this, Chang Tso-lin sent some of his own Manchurian troops to the Peking area and 'advised' the reappointment of Tuan Ch'i-jui, who duly became prime minister again on 23 March 1918.[44]

Meanwhile Wu P'ei-fu was conquering Hunan from its local forces. Though an outsider, Wu evidently made some good local contacts, since he was able to survive in Hunan for several years after his catastrophic fall from power in 1924. By April his troops had reached Hengyang in the mountainous southern half of the province. They were worn out, and Wu was angry. The position of military governor of Hunan, which Wu felt he had earned, had been given instead to Anhwei clique stalwart Chang Ching-yao. Ts'ao K'un shared Wu's disaffection and fear of Tuan's power. Behind Tuan stood the much hated Hsu Shu-cheng. On 15 June Little Hsu invited Lu Chien-chang to dinner at his house in Tientsin and summarily executed him. Lu was a long-time member of the Peiyang Army and a supporter of Feng Kuo-chang; at the time of his murder he was lining up support for Feng's peace policy and allegedly was planning a surprise attack on Ni Tz'u-ch'ung. Lu's murder seemed to reveal a policy of eliminating all non-Anhwei military formations in order to unify China by force.[45] On 20 June Tuan offered Ts'ao K'un and Wu P'ei-fu supreme command over Hunan, Kiangsi, Kwangtung and Szechwan, an obvious attempt to get them out of Chihli without giving them even the military governorship of Hunan

44 Li, *Political History*, pp.378–84.
45 Ch'i, *Warlord Politics*, pp.25–7.

itself. Ts'ao and Wu rejected this and in August issued a circular telegram calling for the cessation of inter-provincial war.[46]

Since returning as prime minister in 1918, Tuan Ch'i-jui had borrowed about $120 million (Chinese) from Japan in the so-called Nishihara loans. Nishihara, the special representative of the Japanese prime minister, Count Terauchi, had facilitated the extension of these unsecured credits to Tuan's government, ostensibly as investments in the industrial development of Manchuria. The Japanese certainly understood that the loans would be diverted to Tuan's army; they also made repeated demands for repayment, even after Tuan had fallen from power. Tuan of course used these funds to develop the War Participation Army into a powerful force of three divisions and four mixed brigades. Its higher standard of armament obviously made it a threat to the forces of other generals, none of whom expected Tuan's new army ever to sail to Europe. Hsu Shu-cheng, Tuan's most powerful subordinate, commanded this force (under successive designations) until the disintegration of the Anhwei clique after 1920. Liang Ch'i-ch'ao participated in the negotiations for the loans, some of the proceeds of which were used to create a new parliament which convened in August 1918. Not surprisingly, its members overwhelmingly supported Tuan, and its agenda was the election of a new president. Feng Kuo-chang's hold on the office had depended on Ts'ao K'un's military support in Chihli province, but Ts'ao had abandoned Feng on the question of the war in the southwest, and Tuan had promised Ts'ao the vice-presidency. But when the elections were held in September, instead of Tuan Ch'i-jui the Peiyang elder statesman Hsu Shih-ch'ang, who was respected by all the factions of the Peiyang Army, was chosen president. This effectively eliminated Feng Kuo-chang from political life, and he died in December 1919. Ts'ao K'un, however, inherited his leadership of the Chihli faction. To Ts'ao's fury, however, the vice-presidency was left vacant, so that it could be offered to the leading personality in the south.[47]

At Canton, Sun Yat-sen's position crumbled rapidly after the murder of Admiral Ch'eng Pi-kuang on 26 February 1918. Sun's position as generalissimo at Canton had always been slightly unreal, since the two strongest militarists nominally supporting him – old Kwangsi clique leader Lu Jung-t'ing and Yunnan chieftain T'ang Chi-yao – were in fact pursuing their own power agendas, which

46 Li, *Political History*, p.383.

47 Li, *Political History*, pp.383–4; Ch'i, *Warlord Politics*, pp.27–30.

Sun was reluctant to admit. The situation was complicated by the fact that many of the Peking parliamentarians who had gone south and thrown in their lot with the Canton government were members of the Political Study clique and other groups more conservative than Sun Yat-sen; their inclusion made the Canton government both more representative and harder to control. But the Canton regime looked impressive as 1918 opened: on 20 January a Union for the Protection of the Constitution was proclaimed by six southern provinces (Kwangtung, Kwangsi, Yunnan, Kweichow, Hunan and Szechwan). Sun attempted to consolidate his position by installing Admiral Ch'eng as governor of Kwangtung. Lu Jung-t'ing, who wanted the position himself, pretended to agree, but Ch'eng's murder followed soon after. Lu, the Political Study clique parliamentarians, and others began to agitate for the replacement of Sun's supreme command by a collective leadership. In April the leading elements at Canton moved to replace Sun Yat-sen's unitary command with a governing committee. Sun then resigned and went to Shanghai, and the Canton government was reorganized as a junta dominated by Lu Jung-t'ing and his Kwangsi clique generals, despite the nominal inclusion of absentee members such as Sun Yat-sen himself and T'ang Chi-yao of Yunnan.[48]

Faced with the mounting pressures for peace from all the non-Anhwei generals and the bitter enmity of Ts'ao K'un and Wu P'ei-fu, Tuan Ch'i-jui resigned as prime minister on 10 October 1918, the day of Hsu Shih-ch'ang's inauguration as president. Tuan retained his Japanese connections and his behind-the-scenes political and military influence, and the nominal Peking government continued to be composed of his creatures. Meanwhile, the end of the First World War permitted Britain and the United States to take a greater interest in Chinese affairs, and both countries urged a general peace settlement in China. In response to all of these pressures a peace conference convened in Shanghai in February 1919. It soon broke down over Tuan's Japanese loans and the growing power of the army funded by them. Also, the worldwide impact of Wilsonian idealism meant that the end of the First World War raised nationalist expectations to a new height.[49]

48 Li, *Political History*, pp.384–8.
49 Li, *Political History*, pp.388–94.

THE MAY FOURTH MOVEMENT

China participated only marginally in the First World War, sending a force of labourers for rear-area duty in France. Her declaration of war arose partly because of internal politics and partly in order to give China a voice at the peace conference. China was nevertheless greatly affected by the war, in two ways. First and most dramatically, the outbreak of the war ended the balance of power among the imperialist nations in China that had both threatened China with partition and preserved her from takeover. Germany henceforth was cut off from China by British sea power, and lost her colony in Shantung to the Japanese in November 1914. While Britain, France and Russia all had forces available for use outside the main European theatres, none could or would challenge Japan, whose large and capable conscript army was not involved in the European war and was within easy striking distance of China. Quite naturally, Japan viewed the First World War as an opportunity to expand its influence in China. From this perspective the Twenty-One Demands were entirely logical. And while the United States, the only other Great Power not involved (until 1917) in the European war, was hostile to Japanese aspirations and tried to maintain her (by now) traditional Open Door policy, US efforts were confined to diplomacy. For most Americans, China was a marginal concern, and the existence (from 1902 to 1922) of the Anglo-Japanese Alliance certainly complicated matters.[50]

Second, the war caused dramatic changes in the worldwide economy. As the European economies went over to a war footing, the United States and other countries became the suppliers of consumer goods. In the case of China this meant a dramatic expansion of the textile industry to fill the need for uniform cloth. Capital for this expansion came largely from Japan. Britain and the other European powers were spending their capital at home, and borrowing as much as they could in the process. US capital for the most part could find better uses than investment in China. The result of these trends was that, by the end of the First World War, China possessed an expanded industrial sector, much of it Japanese

50 Ian H. Nish, *The Anglo-Japanese Alliance: The Diplomacy of Two Island Empires, 1884–1907* (London, 1966) and *Alliance in Decline: A study in Anglo-Japanese Relations, 1908–1923* (London, 1972), together constitute the standard recent account, but William L. Langer, *The Diplomacy of Imperialism, 1890–1902* (2nd edn, New York, 1951), pp.746–86, must still be read for its truly global context.

owned, in her economy, and Japan had surpassed Britain as the foreign power with the greatest stake in the imperialist system of extraterritoriality and unequal treaties.

Parallel to these developments, though not caused by the war, was the intellectual revolution sweeping China. Like those who thought of themselves as intellectuals, military leaders had for the most part rejected the Confucian political and intellectual system whose institutional expression had been the monarchy and the old-style civil service examinations. Like intellectuals, military leaders were strongly nationalistic but had failed to agree on a new standard of legitimacy. Officers with Western or Westernized educations, who had refused to fight for the Manchus in 1911 or 1917 because of a nationalist or republican ideology, were going to be affected by intellectual debates even if they did not lead them. To the extent that they were affected, such officers were likely to affect their superiors. As 1919 opened, the Chinese intellectual world, which for years had been debating the question of Chinese literary culture versus Western science and democracy, was in effect handed two new challenges from the West. The first was the October Revolution in Russia, which seemed to make communism a viable, and even more modern, alternative to liberal democracy. The second was the Versailles peace conference and the ideals of Woodrow Wilson, which seemed to offer the hope that the Great Powers would voluntarily dismantle the unequal treaty system in China.

The Tuan Ch'i-jui dominated government of China had representatives at Versailles, as did the many other minor powers that had joined the winning side at the last moment. The main decision-making bodies at Versailles, however, were conferences of the heads of government and foreign ministers of the five victorious Great Powers, among whom the Japanese were the only non-whites. Japanese efforts to introduce a declaration of racial equality into the peace settlement were firmly rejected by the British and French out of concern for their own colonial empires. Japan's relations with the United States also were not good; the two countries were engaged in a battleship–building race that the Japanese, at least, could not afford. Even if Japan had had more clout at Versailles, she could not have been expected to pursue a fully anti-colonial agenda, which would have conflicted with her own colonial empire and her aspirations in China. At Versailles, therefore, Japan took a rather low profile, insisting only that the former German position in Shantung, which she had conquered in 1914, be confirmed to her. The European powers supported this demand as part of their general insistence that the secret agreements made among the Allies during the war be honoured.

Tuan Ch'i-jui meanwhile was attempting to use the Shanghai peace conference that had opened in February 1919 to bring pressure on the militarists supporting the Canton government. These non-Anhwei (indeed, non-Peiyang) militarists should disarm, while Tuan continued to use Japanese funding to build up the War Participation Army, now renamed the National Defence Army. Japan's price for the continued funding of Tuan was the 'happy concurrence' of China, as represented by Tuan's underlings, to Japan's legal succession to the German rights in Shantung. When word of China's agreement to the draft Treaty of Versailles incorporating these provisions reached Peking, the result was the May Fourth Movement, which began with massive student demonstrations in Peking on 4 May 1919 and soon spread beyond the capital to China's other major cities.[51] The initial demands of the protesters were for the removal and punishment of the three officials identified as responsible. While the protests were going on, the southern delegates to the Shanghai peace conference, headed by T'ang Shao-yi, presented a programme calling for refusal to accept the Japanese takeover of the former German position in Shantung, the cancellation of all secret agreements between China and Japan, and the disbanding of the National Defence Army. Significantly, the southern militarists were not on the Japanese payroll. Tuan used these demands as the pretext for withdrawing from the peace conference. His forces suppressed the demonstrations in Peking. On 24 June the National Defence Army was renamed the Frontier Defence Army, and Hsu Shu-cheng was publicly designated as its commander.[52]

Tuan seemed to be unbeatable, but the steps he had taken to build up his military power had badly eroded his political legitimacy, and his acquiescence to Japanese demands had destroyed any claims he might have made to be a nationalist. In 1917 Tuan had been supported by Chang Tso-lin, and the Chihli leaders had at least acquiesced in Tuan's recapture of Peking from Chang Hsun. By 1919 Anhwei power threatened both the Fengtien militarists under Chang Tso-lin and the Chihli militarists under Ts'ao K'un. In the south the Yunnan Army was losing its ability to influence events

51 Chow Tse-tsung, *The May Fourth Movement: Intellectual Revolution in Modern China* (Cambridge, MA, 1960), pp.41–116, including general background.

52 Li, *Political History*, pp.390–4.

outside of Yunnan, and even combined with the Kwangsi clique it was no match for any of the three major northern factions. Such as it was, the influence of Sun Yat-sen and the southern leaders was anti-Tuan until Tuan's fall.

China remained in the state of high warlordism. Before May–June 1919, some combination of fighting and negotiation among the major military leaders was expected to lead to military unification, which in turn would permit the restoration of the constitutional political processes that Yuan Shih-k'ai had disrupted. By 1919 the three major northern military factions had emerged, two of them – Anhwei and Chihli – directly from the Peiyang Army and the third – Fengtien – from an amalgamation of Peiyang and local troops. They and their imitators on a smaller scale were willing to get money and arms from any source in order to survive, and the weaker factions would combine against the stronger. Warlordism, in other words, had become a self-sustaining system that was an obstacle to national unification.

3 HIGH WARLORDISM, 1919–25

During the years 1919–25 three major wars among the northern warlords left China more divided than before. The An–Chih War of 1920 resulted from a combination of Tuan Ch'i-jui's enemies against him, and it finished Tuan as a major warlord, even though Anhwei clique warlords remained in power in Fukien and Chekiang. While Chang Tso-lin and his Fengtien clique maintained and consolidated their hold over the Manchurian provinces and added Inner Mongolia, Ts'ao K'un and Wu P'ei-fu of the Chihli clique were the principal beneficiaries, adding the former Anhwei clique base in Peking and northern Chihli province to the original Chihli clique heartland in the Yangtze Valley. In 1922 they challenged Chang Tso-lin in the First Chih–Feng War. Chihli victory, while not total, nevertheless permitted Ts'ao K'un to elevate himself to the presidency in a manner that most intellectuals considered scandalous. Feng Yü-hsiang's betrayal of the Chihli leadership in the Second Chih–Feng War of 1924 eliminated Ts'ao K'un and reduced Wu P'ei-fu to the status of warlord of Hupei and Hunan. From then until the Northern Expedition China was a collection of regional warlord regimes. Chang Tso-lin of Manchuria was the most powerful of these, and, since he also controlled Peking, he received foreign recognition as the government of China. Chang and the other warlords were increasingly repugnant and suspect to intellectual and nationalist opinion, which turned more and more to Sun Yat-sen, who hung on precariously at Canton.

WARLORDISM AS A SYSTEM

Despite the phenomena of regionalism and local power, China under the Manchus had definitely had a national political system, in which imperial recognition and Confucian values conferred legitimacy on the holders of power. Yuan Shih-k'ai's machinations and other developments had made it impossible for the president of the republic to replace the emperor as the source of legitimacy, and Western democratic and constitutional values, imperfectly understood and incompletely accepted, similarly could not replace Confucianism as a validating ideology, even though Confucianism itself was moribund. While the intellectuals wrestled with these problems, the warlords wrestled with one another in a vacuum of political legitimacy. Had a single warlord emerged as dominant in a reasonable time, he might have contributed creatively to the making of a new political order. In reality, however, the vacuum of legitimacy introduced systemic weaknesses into the various warlord armies, making it unlikely that any one of them could conquer all the rest.

One needs warlords to have warlordism, and by 1919 the term 'warlord' (chün-fa) and its derivatives had come into common use. A warlord may be defined as a troop commander in effective, autonomous control of a territory that provides the revenues in cash and kind needed to support his troops. It was important for the warlord to remain the personal link between his army and his territory; a warlord who divided his army into separate garrisons for sustenance purposes might find the commanders of the separate garrisons turning into independent warlords. Warlords therefore usually kept their armies concentrated near their headquarters, and drew off the best of their subordinates' soldiers into better paid and better fed elite units whose uses included keeping the other units in line.

A warlord typically was either military governor (tu-tu, tu-chün, tu-li, or tu-pan) of a single province or defence (or other) commissioner of part of a province or several provinces. These titles were solemnly conferred by presidential mandates of the Peking regime or equivalent orders from whichever other 'national' government the warlord claimed to obey. Enforcing these orders was the warlord's own responsibility; he had to lead his army in person to drive out the forces of his predecessor and establish his own effective rule. Once this was accomplished, the warlord would usually discover that his new province had been bled white by his predecessor's taxes and had been looted by both the departing and the arriving army. Regardless of this, the new province had to yield revenues immediately. While the various national governments often provided subventions to certain warlords, they did this as part of their own political manoeuvring, and any warlord dependent on such financing would, by definition, cease to be independent. Warlords therefore became adept at devising new taxes, at collecting the land taxes many years in advance, at promoting the cultivation and sale of opium, and in extorting voluntary contributions that really amounted to protection money. These abuses were ameliorated to some extent in warlord regimes, outstandingly that of Yen Hsi-shan in Shansi, that remained in the same province or region for a long time, though even these warlords had to match increases in other provincial armies by increasing their own forces and raising their revenues accordingly. The Ch'ing inability to modernize and centralize its fiscal system had now come full circle, leading to the creation of locally financed warlord armies whose existence inhibited national unification and modernization.

The warlord exercised control through a chain of command whose officers bore Western-style titles of rank (major-general, lieutenant-colonel, etc.), and the formations and units of warlord armies were designated by the accepted Chinese equivalents of Western military terms (shih = division, t'uan = regiment, ying = battalion, etc.). Military rank by itself, at least at the higher levels, ceased to have much meaning after Ts'ao K'un in his quest for the presidency promoted most of the division and higher commanders to the rank of marshal.[1] But even the position designations are misleading, since in the warlord armies appointment as a unit commander depended, and had to depend, on personal relationships and loyalties to one's superiors. A general who became a warlord would promote his relatives and subordinates who had aided him in his rise to power. Command positions that became vacant usually had to be filled by subordinate officers within the same unit, who fitted into the existing structure of relationships. Better educated outsiders, such as graduates of the Paoting Military Academy that functioned throughout this period, were valued as staff officers but usually would not be given command of troops because of their educational qualifications alone.

The divergence between the modern terminology and the premodern social structure of the warlord armies requires emphasis. By the time of the First World War, modern armies had adopted, or at least were in the process of creating, personnel systems in which officers' postings were determined, or at least heavily influenced, by objective factors including rank and seniority, educational background, and service record. Officers being groomed for generalships would have a career in which staff and command time

1 James E. Sheridan, *Chinese Warlord: The Career of Feng Yü-hsiang* (Stanford, 1966), p.129.

were carefully balanced, and in which service in various units and areas gave a sense of the army as a whole. But behind such modern armies stood modern nations with legitimate political systems that could validate officers' qualifications and enforce such personnel policies in the interests of generally agreed concepts of military effectiveness. Elements of such a personnel system were present in the Peiyang Army before the 1911 revolution, and in the Yunnan Army down to 1916. But by 1919 China lacked such a legitimate political system, just as she lacked a centralized financial system, and in its place, personal loyalties were the chain that held the warlord armies together. And the chain could be broken through bribery ('silver bullets' in the slang of the period) or other means at any link.[2]

At the bottom of the military pyramid were the ordinary soldiers. These continued to be recruited by poverty, and to be poorly treated and poorly paid, a generalization that also applied to their sergeants and corporals. To the extent that the Manchu thirty-six division plan had contemplated common standards of recruitment, these had vanished after 1911 as many local armies had expanded, each in its own way. Bandits had joined as individuals, and, as in the case of Chang Tso-lin (who favoured his ex-bandit associates even when the Fengtien clique was at the height of its power), whole bandit gangs had joined some armies as units, whose designations would depend approximately on their size. Both the Nationalists and the communists later would expand their armies from the same source, and indeed one may discern the same process of army formation in the many inter-dynastic periods of previous Chinese history, which the warlord period resembles. Since bandits also were the dregs of society, they were not much different from ordinary military recruits. Soldiers' pay was at or below subsistence level, and was usually not on time. Medical services ranged from poor to nonexistent, so that a soldier wounded even superficially (and the warlord wars in fact were bloodier than condescending foreign opinion liked to believe) had a good chance of a painful death.[3] While almost all numbers are suspect for China in this

2 Most of the studies of individual warlords cited elsewhere have some definition of warlordism; in general Hsi-sheng Ch'i, *Warlord Politics in China, 1916–1928* (Stanford, 1976), pp.36–76; and Lucien Pye, *Warlord Politics; Conflict and Coalition in the Modernization of Republican China* (New York, 1971), passim.

3 Diana Lary, *Warlord Soldiers: Chinese Common Soldiers, 1911–1937* (Cambridge, UK, 1985), and Ch'i, *Warlord Politics*, pp.77–91, for the soldiers of the warlord armies.

period, one source estimates total strength on both sides at 225,000 in the First Chih–Feng War and 320,000 in the Second, with total casualties estimated as high as 30,000 and as low as 10,000.[4]

Bad as the soldier's lot was, it was the only lot he had. Desertion and return to peasant life was not an option for a man who had become a soldier because he had been forced out of peasant life. The soldier's world thus became his immediate unit, which he would go along with if it transferred its allegiance to another warlord. Attempts to demobilize such an army would usually convert its primary units to bandit gangs. Past imperial dynasties usually had managed demobilization by creating military colonies for the demobilized troops, and some of the warlords – notably Feng Yü-hsiang and Yen Hsi-shan – experimented with the same idea, as did the CCP after taking power. But most inter-warlord demobilization conferences foundered on their participants' yearning to gain relative advantage by forcing asymmetric reductions on their rivals. For most soldiers, demobilization meant leaving the fragile security provided by their unit, wherein, if pay was late, there were usually opportunities to loot.

Standards of training and armament had dropped since 1911. In theory the tables of organization adopted for the thirty-six division plan remained in force throughout the warlord period. In practice most divisions were under 10,000 men, well short of the 12,512 listed as the theoretical peace establishment of a division. Warlords recruited more troops, and the total numbers in the major warlord armies may have increased from about 500,000 in 1916 to about 2 million in 1928.[5] Beginning in that year, censuses carried out by the Nanking government reported total population figures ranging from 441 million to 479 million, probably underestimates given the 583 million reported in the benchmark communist census of 1953.[6] While peacetime standing armies of under 0.5 per cent of the population are easily maintained by developed economies, numbers on this scale were a great burden on China's subsistence economy. Increase in numbers was matched by the creation of new divisions and lower units, to provide the numbers of command billets called for by the evolution of military politics. Once recruited, whether and how a soldier was trained depended on the policy of his

4 Ch'i, *Warlord Politics*, p.138.

5 Ch'i, *Warlord Politics*, p.78, Lary, *Warlord Soldiers*, p.3.

6 Ho Ping-ti, *Studies on the Population of China, 1368–1953* (Cambridge, 1959), p.86.

warlord. Some warlords feared defection if they made too many demands on their troops, while a minority – again Feng Yü-hsiang and Yen Hsi-shan are notable – understood the morale-building and unit-bonding potential of a rigorous training programme.[7] Published pay scales from the warlord period show monthly rates of $7 (Chinese) to $10.5 for first-class privates and $9 to $16 for sergeants. Due to the extortions of the higher levels in the chain of command and uncertainty of payment, these wages were not too far from subsistence, but even subsistence had its attractions in China's poor peasant society, in which landless labourers in civil life typically earned $20–30 per year.[8] The only important research survey of a large Chinese military unit surviving from this period showed that the majority of a 5,000-man brigade were illiterate and considered themselves poor. The majority also remitted some of their pay to family members in their home villages, in the manner made more familiar by the overseas Chinese.[9]

Warlord armies consisted mostly of infantry armed with rifles, if armed at all. Especially in poorer armies, a new recruit often had to wait to inherit a rifle from a deceased fellow soldier. Machine guns, mortars and artillery pieces were rare and proportionately valuable. In 1918 there were allegedly 1,480 field guns and 46 heavy guns in China. In 1920 1,394 machine guns were reported for the entire country.[10] These numbers work out to about one artillery piece and one machine gun per thousand men, which may be compared with the German 1913 standard of 16 machine guns and 6.4 artillery pieces per thousand infantry. Cavalry, while less obsolete in a battlefield with few machine guns, was also less available due to the low profile of the horse in Chinese agriculture. Nevertheless, cavalry units were the mainstay of the forces of the Tungan Muslim warlords of Kansu, and were important in the Manchurian Fengtien army of Chang Tso-lin. Airplanes, armoured cars and armoured trains were military exotica, prestige items cherished to the point of fetishism by the warlords who had them, but too rare to have decisive importance in battle.

Supply of armaments depended upon domestic manufacture and foreign purchase. Domestic manufacture depended on the half-dozen arsenals that actually produced weapons (there were other facilities

7 Ch'i, *Warlord Politics*, pp.91–115.
8 Lary, *Warlord Soldiers*, pp.42–6.
9 Ch'i, *Warlord Politics*, pp.79–80.
10 Ch'i, *Warlord Politics*, p.117.

called arsenals that stored and repaired weapons but did not manufacture them). Two of the best of these, at Mukden and Taiyuan, produced exclusively for the armies of Chang Tso-lin and Yen Hsi-shan, respectively. Hanyang, the largest and most modern, usually produced a surplus for sale or distribution within the Chihli faction. Shanghai's famous Kiangnan Arsenal was now technically behind the more recent establishments, and the other arsenals also were inadequate to supply the needs of the armies dependent on them. The arsenals produced mortars in increasing numbers in the 1920s, but most of their product was Chinese copies of standard bolt action repeating rifles. Aggregate monthly output of Chinese arsenals rose from an estimated 7,000 rifles and 5.5 million cartridges in 1923 to 16,000 rifles and 18.5 million cartridges in 1928;[11] the figures look large but are modest compared to rates of ammunition expenditure in Europe in the First World War.

Foreign supply was complicated by the signature, ironically on 5 May 1919 (the day after the beginning of the May Fourth Movement), of the Arms Embargo Agreement. In the United States and Britain international arms sales (promoted by 'merchants of death') were now being cited as a cause of the First World War; Wilsonian idealism therefore demanded their abolition. France and Japan also signed, though somewhat reluctantly, and continued to supply their clients (in Japan's case both Chang Tso-lin and Tuan Ch'i-jui, despite the rivalry of the Fengtien and Anhwei cliques) covertly. The agreement and the atmosphere that led to it made the arms trade rather disreputable, so that statistics on it are exiguous even by the standards of China in the 1920s. But there is no doubt that the volume of arms imports increased steadily during the decade. The agreement did not apply to private citizens, even if they were citizens of the contracting powers, so sales through front men were always possible. Also, some of the leading arms producers in the world (Germany, Austria, Czechoslovakia, Switzerland, the Scandinavian countries, and the newly renamed Soviet Union) were not parties to the agreement. Warlords heavily dependent on arms from a particular foreign power were popularly regarded as puppets of that power, but this assumption was generally false, as the cases (see Chapter 4) of Japanese puppet Chang Tso-lin and Soviet puppet Feng Yü-hsiang were to show. In the end, the greatest consequence of the Arms Embargo Agreement may have been to provide a

11 Ch'i, *Warlord Politics*, pp.118–20.

convenient pretext for the United States and Britain not to provide assistance to Sun Yat-sen, who turned reluctantly to the Soviet Union in the last year of his life.[12]

Armies armed with rifles, with heavier weapons present but only in small numbers, meant that even though the warlord wars occurred after the First World War, they were unevenly influenced by the military experience of that war (this was true of the Russian Civil War and the Russo-Polish War as well). Since machine guns were rare, and rifle cartridges in short enough supply to be conserved, close order infantry attacks and even an occasional cavalry charge were tactically feasible. On the other hand, the presence among the besiegers of even a few mortars or field guns made the defence of a traditionally fortified city impossible. Mud brick walls were easily demolished by explosive shells, and the tightly packed houses behind them burned easily. The larger cities were equally vulnerable, and in any case tearing down walls and replacing them with ring roads was part of the progress of the 1920s. Down until 1949 China's civil wars could be fought with an obsolete and essentially early-nineteenth-century (by Western standards) infantry tactics. A strategy of unification, on the other hand, required the rethinking, and perhaps the reversal or abandonment, of two millennia of historical precedents, well known to educated Chinese, that enjoined taking the walled cities first, and using them as the secure bases for extending one's authority into the countryside.

Foreigners, looking at the warlord period from the privileged and relatively safe vantage of the treaty ports, often viewed the warlord wars as less than serious. Battles preceded by endless political manoeuvrings and utterly mendacious public statements, and decided by betrayal, and armies whose umbrella-wielding soldiers might break off the fighting because of rain, lunch or nightfall, seemed to invite an analysis based on condescending anecdotes. 'China's wars are always civil', as a Chinese admiral of the period allegedly remarked,[13] seemed to sum it up. The anecdotes are certainly diverting. According to admittedly hostile rumour, Feng Yü-hsiang in his Christian phase baptized his entire brigade by spraying them with holy water through a fire hose; in his communist phase, after his break with the rest of the Chihli clique,

12 Ch'i, *Warlord Politics*, pp.120–6, on the effects of the arms embargo.

13 Cited in Sheridan, *Chinese Warlord*, p.23.

he would change, just before leaving his train, from his normal ornately gold braided and bemedalled marshal's uniform to the quilted cotton worn by the common soldiers.[14] The equally physically imposing Chang Tsung-ch'ang of Shantung was always accompanied by his harem of White Russian concubines, but earned the nickname 'Dog Meat General' from his culinary appetites. As military governor of Shantung, he was also called 'three don't knows' since he did not know how much money, how many troops or how many women he had.[15] His diminutive superior Chang Tso-lin survived the Fengtien clique defeat of 1922 by meeting his defeated and desertion-prone troops with trunks full of money, and bribing them individually.[16] Classically educated Wu P'ei-fu could be seen on the battlefield in a scholar's gown, with brush and inkstone, composing poetry.[17] He was the favourite of the British, who also admired Yen Hsi-shan, the 'model governor' of Shansi, who, like his contemporary Benito Mussolini, made the trains run on time.[18] Even a local warlord whose chief assets were a fancy uniform and a few thousand scruffy troops might seem diverting to foreigners who did not need to suffer under his rule.

In fact the warlord wars were more serious than they appeared. By 1919 the pattern of military allegiances had crystallized, and the fighting that ensued between the factions was on a much larger scale than what had gone on before. The always history-conscious Chinese understood that the fall of the Manchus had introduced a period of inter-dynastic instability, like that described in the novel

14 Harold R. Isaacs, *The Tragedy of the Chinese Revolution* (2nd edn, Stanford, 1961), p.255, which is not an objective source, at least for Feng. I have heard this anecdote personally on several occasions. Sheridan, *Chinese Warlord*, takes Feng's Christianity and his simplicity of dress at face value.

15 Howard L. Boorman, *Biographical Dictionary of Republican China* (4 vols, New York, 1967–71), I, pp.122–7, for all of these anecdotes.

16 Gavan McCormack, *Chang Tso-lin in Northeast China, 1911–1928: China, Japan and the Manchurian Idea* (Stanford, 1977), p.72.

17 See pp.569–71 of Jerome Ch'en, "Defining Chinese warlords and their factions", in *Bulletin of the School of Oriental and African Studies*, 31 (London, 1968), pp.563–600. Wu published many works under his own name and liked to be photographed holding a writing brush, but, as Ch'en notes, his writings exhibited 'a marked difference of style' after the death of his secretary Chang Ch'i-huang in 1927.

18 Donald G. Gillin, *Warlord: Yen Hsi-shan in Shansi Province, 1911–1949* (Princeton, 1967), p.22, on Shansi as the 'Model province'.

The Romance of the Three Kingdoms[19] and in the numerous operas and other popular entertainments deriving therefrom. The political rules for such periods, though well understood, could not be admitted for public (and especially foreign) consumption. Under these rules, a warlord's army constituted his political capital, and if his troops were expendable, they nonetheless had to be spent carefully. Whatever their Westernized educations, the warlords remained disciples of Sun Tzu rather than Clausewitz, and may be forgiven for imagining that 'those skilled in war subdue the enemy's army without battle'.[20] Unfortunately Clausewitz's famous analogy remains the last word: like cash settlement in business, battle cannot be entirely avoided.[21]

THE AN–CHIH WAR, 1920

As of late 1919 military forces of the Anhwei clique controlled Peking and the northern part of Chihli. Hsu Shu-cheng's Frontier Defence Army, the best equipped and most impressive Anhwei military force, and generally regarded as the basis of Tuan Ch'i-jui's military power, controlled the Special Administrative Areas (later provinces) of Jehol, Chahar and Suiyuan. Five other provinces – Shantung, Shensi, Fukien, Chekiang and Anhwei itself – were under the command of Anhwei clique military governors. In Peking itself, the new parliament created by Tuan was under his control, and on 24 September the premiership was given to Anhwei clique member Chin Yun-p'eng. Hsu Shu-cheng demonstrated the power of his army with forays into Outer Mongolia, which in November led the

19 Chinese title *San Kuo Chih Yen Yi*; the authorship of this work, often attributed to Lo Kuan-chung, is uncertain but published versions have been circulating since the late sixteenth century. It is based on the history and legends of the period AD 180–263, and, like the equally picaresque *Outlaws of the Marsh* (Chinese title *Shui Hu Chuan*; authorship attributed to Shih Nai-an and Lo Kuan-chung; excellent English translation by Sidney Shapiro in 2 vols, Bloomington, 1981) is a collection of tales featuring battle and intrigue that are widely known in China and provide the basis for operas and other popular entertainments. Andrew H. Plaks, *The Four Masterworks of the Ming Novel: Ssu Ta Ch'i Shu* (Princeton, 1987), concludes that, whatever earlier material these novels may incorporate, the form in which they exist now reflects the efforts of sixteenth-century Ming literary culture.

20 Samuel B. Griffiths, ed. and trans., *Sun Tzu: The Art of War* (Oxford, 1963), p.79.

21 Peter Paret is the leading contemporary translator and interpreter of Clausewitz. For a fine short introduction to Clausewitz's ideas, see the essay by Hans Rothfels in Edward M. Earle, ed., *Makers of Modern Strategy: Military Thought from Machiavelli to Hitler* (Princeton, 1941), pp.93–113.

4. Chinese provinces during the warlord era

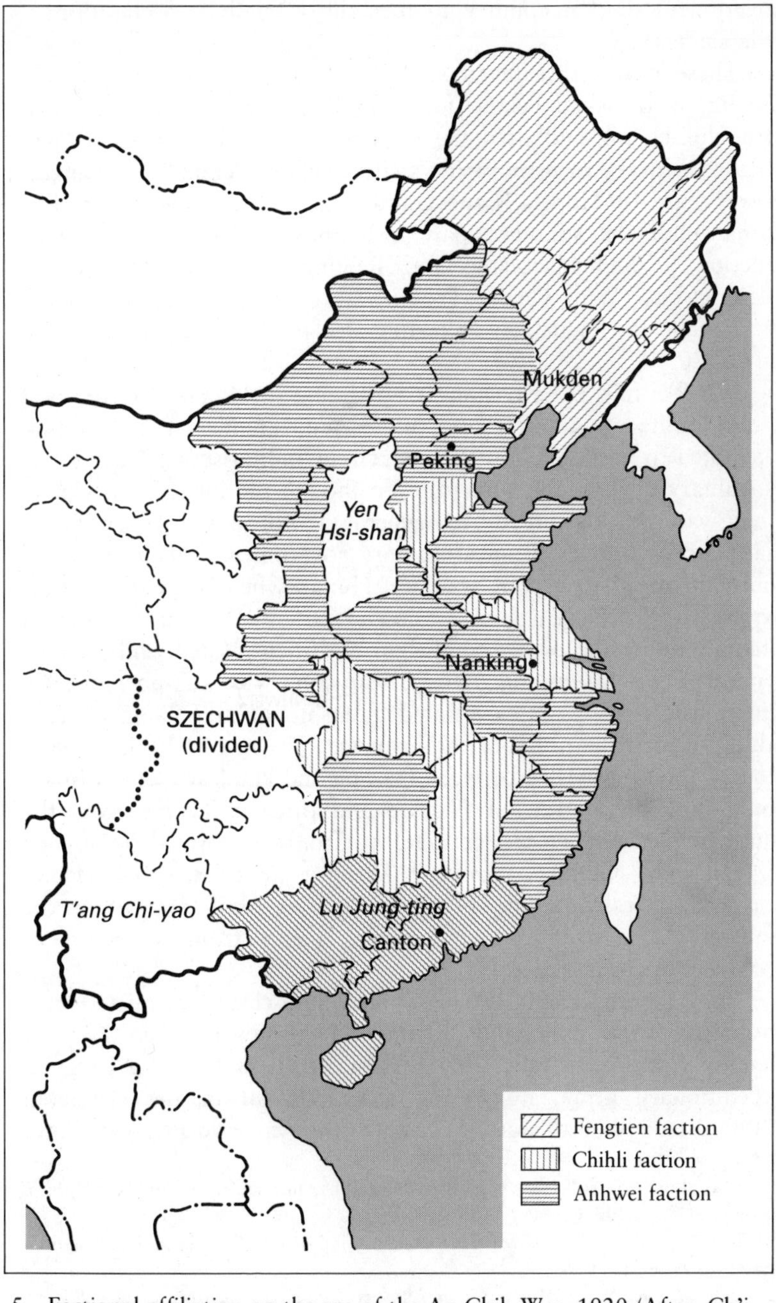

5. Factional affiliation on the eve of the An-Chih War, 1920 (After: Ch'i, Hsi-sheng, *Warlord Politics in China*)

government of that country to formally rescind its declaration of independence.[22]

These moves threatened and alienated Fengtien leader Chang Tso-lin, who visited Peking for formal conferences with President Hsu Shih-ch'ang and used the opportunity to make an anti-Tuan alliance with Ts'ao K'un. Ts'ao's Chihli clique retained its Yangtze power base of Hupei, Kiangsi and Kiangsu, and also controlled Honan and the southern part of Chihli, including the railway junction at Shihchiachuang and Paoting, where Ts'ao had his headquarters. With Chang Tso-lin's three Manchurian provinces, these made the Eight Provinces that declared war against Tuan in July 1920.[23]

Wu P'ei-fu's 3rd Division at Hengyang in Hunan was the best Chihli military unit. To undermine Wu, Premier Tuan Ch'i-jui attempted to impose fellow Anhwei clique militarist Wu Kuang-hsin as military governor of Hunan, even though the incumbent, Chang Ching-yao, was also an Anhwei general. To forestall this, Wu P'ei-fu made a deal with the Canton military government, which permitted southern troops to occupy southern Hunan when Wu withdrew his troops to Wuchang (by 31 May 1920). Wu left a brigade at Changte under the highly competent and then trusted Chihli clique general Feng Yü-hsiang, whose mission was to prevent Wu Kuang-hsin's troops (concentrated at Hsinti on the Yangtze) from taking over in the north of the province. The rest of Wu's division secured the railway line between Paoting and Hankow. Chihli forces could now concentrate at Paoting and threaten Peking from the south, while Fengtien troops marched from the east, also supplied by rail. The Chihli control of Kiangsu interdicted the second north–south railway line (Tientsin–Pukow), thus preventing the Anhwei clique from drawing reinforcements from the southern provinces under its control.[24]

By prearrangement, President Hsu Shih-ch'ang dismissed Hsu Shu-cheng from command of the elite Anhwei clique Frontier Defence Army on 4 July. Chang Tso-lin then mobilized a Fengtien expeditionary army, numbering some 70,000 of the estimated 120,000 troops of all sides involved in the war, and invaded Chihli

22 Hsu Shu-cheng still lacks a modern biography, but see Boorman, *Biographical Dictionary*, II, pp.143–6.

23 Li Chien-nung, *The Political History of China, 1840–1928* (English translation, Princeton, 1956), pp.394–7.

24 Odoric Y.K. Wou, *Militarism in Modern China: The Career of Wu P'ei-fu, 1916–1939* (Canberra, 1978), pp.30–2; Sheridan, *Chinese Warlord*, pp.96–9.

through Shanhaikuan. Japanese government agencies, including their military intelligence, were caught completely by surprise, having assumed until the last minute that their two clients, Tuan and Chang, would settle their differences by negotiation. Tuan's actual response was to hold Peking with the Frontier Defence Army, which he now renamed the Nation-Securing Army (ting-kuo-chün) and took command of himself. Hapless Hsu Shih-ch'ang, now functioning as Tuan's puppet, rescinded his previous dismissal of Hsu Shu-cheng. Tuan gave the larger half of the army to Little Hsu to resist Chang Tso-lin's invasion from the north and east; Hsu managed to avoid major defeats but was forced back on Peking by Chang's greatly superior forces. Tuan Chih-kuei, with the remainder of the Nation-Securing Army, faced the assault from the south of the Chihli troops, who advanced directly from Paoting north to Peking under the battlefield leadership of Wu P'ei-fu. Between 14 and 18 July Wu defeated Tuan Chih-kuei at Chochow and then at Liuliho (both near Peking). These defeats destroyed Tuan Chih-kuei's army and made Peking untenable. On 19 July Tuan Ch'i-jui and the other leading Anhwei personalities resigned and took refuge with the Japanese, and by early August the Anhwei clique was eliminated as a factor in politics. Despite three years of special treatment, the Nation-Securing Army was a failure in actual combat.[25] Chang Tso-lin's men inherited its much envied weapons and equipment. Chang's prestige rose, but Wu P'ei-fu had fought the hardest battles, and gained his reputation as a military genius from them. Already respected for his campaigns in Hunan, he henceforth was viewed as the indispensable prop for Ts'ao K'un.

The An–Chih War had been fought and won by a coalition whose sole unifying principle was hostility to Tuan Ch'i-jui and his Anhwei clique. Their victory did not produce stability in either north or south. The Peking government itself was a delicate compromise. Premier Chin Yun-p'eng, though himself an Anhwei general, had been forced out of office during Hsu Shu-cheng's period of greatest influence. He was also a relative by marriage of Chang Tso-lin, and an early patron of Wu P'ei-fu. He was therefore acceptable to all sides as premier.[26] The Ministry of Communications, the Chinese foreign service, and the other national institutions shifted their allegiance to the Chihli faction. Chihli clique leader Ts'ao K'un, faced by the public hostility of Sun

25 McCormack, *Chang Tso-lin*, pp.49–55.
26 Li, *Political History*, pp.409–10.

Yat-sen and his supporters at Canton, and the covert opposition of military leaders who counted, postponed his desire to ascend to the presidency, but remained dominant in Peking. The Chihli clique also took over Anhwei province, leaving Anhwei warlords in control only in Fukien (Li Hou-chi) and Chekiang (Lu Yung-hsiang).

Immediately after the An–Chih War, Chang Tso-lin left some 30,000 troops in the Peking area under one of his trusted deputies. Chang's real reward, however, in addition to the arms and equipment of Little Hsu's army, was its former territorial base in Chahar, Jehol and Suiyuan. Chang also inherited Little Hsu's policy of reconquering Outer Mongolia. That area was now under the shaky rule of White Russian General Baron von Ungern-Sternberg, who dreamed of reviving the empire of Chinggis Khan under his own leadership. Ungern-Sternberg was defeated and killed in July 1921 as the communist revolution came to Mongolia.[27] Meanwhile, growing tensions with the Chihli clique diverted Chang Tso-lin's attention southward.

Wu P'ei-fu, as related, had contrived to abandon Hunan as part of his manoeuvres prior to the An–Chih War. Provincial sentiment remained strong throughout the south, and the vacuum had been filled by Hunanese troops under T'an Yen-k'ai, a KMT hero associated with Sun Yat-sen. The Anhwei clique generals Wu Kuang-hsin and Chang Ching-yao were left without territory as a result of the war, and the military governor of Shensi, Ch'en Shu-fan (also Anhwei), was threatened. All three controlled cash savings from their years of government, safely deposited in banks in the foreign concessions of Hankow. Chihli clique general Wang Chan-yuan, who had been nominally military governor of Hupei since 1916, gained in actual power, though he was far from the ablest or strongest member of the clique, and was very unpopular in the province.

The Hunan military was supported by a coalition of civilian leaders in the province, who were drawing up a provincial constitution calling for, among other things, an elected civilian governor. They hoped for a reconstruction of China along federal lines. The aforementioned Anhwei clique generals made contact with them, and arranged to finance a Hunan invasion of Hupei. This took place in July 1921. Wang Chan-yuan was defeated, and fled from Wuchang on 7 August. In response Ts'ao K'un appointed Wu P'ei-fu to lead an army to reconquer Hupei, aided by Wu's protégé

27 McCormack, *Chang Tso-lin*, pp.53–6.

Hsiao Yao-nan and Wang Chan-yuan's former subordinate Sun Ch'uan-fang. Wu moved with his customary speed and decisiveness, coming down by rail from Loyang. The Hunan Army abandoned the Wuhan area and retired southward up the Yangtze toward Hunan. Wu had ordered naval units up to Wuhan, and these pursued the retiring Hunan Army. Wu meanwhile marched his own army overland, and on 27 August took Yochow, the river port where the Tungting Lake flows into the Yangtze, and also a station on the Wuhan–Changsha railway. He thus cut off the Hunan army's line of retreat. Trapped, the Hunan Army agreed to return to Hunan and stay there. Wu kept Yochow, and turned his attentions to the Szechwan warlords, who had come through the Yangtze Gorges and were attacking Yichang, upstream on the Yangtze from Yochow. Though the desultory fighting lasted another month, the result was another truce under which the Szechwan army evacuated Hupei. The historian Li Chien-nung analyzed the outcome with the proverb 'when a cat upsets a jar, the dogs get a good meal'.[28] Wu P'ei-fu was content for now to be Ts'ao K'un's running dog, and his victories enhanced Ts'ao's power.

The Chihli clique as of late 1921 controlled the provinces containing the two north–south railway lines (Peking–Hankow and Tientsin–Pukow) and the two principal east–west lines of communication (the Lunghai railway and the Yangtze River downstream from the Gorges). Chihli's principal rival remained the Fengtien clique with its compact territorial bloc of six Manchurian and Inner Mongolian provinces. Yen Hsi-shan of Shansi was strong enough to remain independent, which was his goal. The south, once strong and unified enough to bring down Yuan Shih-k'ai, had disintegrated into a motley assemblage of provinces, some of which were badly disunited internally.

SOUTH CHINA AND SUN YAT-SEN, 1920–2

In most general histories of modern China, the struggles of the southern Chinese warlords serve as the backdrop for Sun Yat-sen's struggles to create a regime at Canton strong enough to bring down the northern warlords. During his last years, Sun gave the final shape to his political theory, and came to realize that military unification was a necessary precondition for the democratic development that he had struggled for all his life. His efforts to

28 Li, *Political History*, pp.404–8; Wou, *Militarism*, pp.42–6.

forge a unified south were repeatedly wrecked by the treachery of the local militarists, and this has obscured the question of whether success in the south would have mattered very much. In fact it is difficult to imagine any southern coalition prevailing against Ts'ao K'un and Wu P'ei-fu prior to 1924. In that year Feng Yü-hsiang's famous betrayal (described on pp.110–12) shattered the Chihli faction and postponed, in the event permanently, the unification of China that might have resulted from Chihli victory in the Second Chih–Feng War. But even after 1924 the various northern armies seem to have been more effective militarily than the southern, and they were certainly larger.

Provincial loyalties remained strong in the south, and inhibited the formation of political units embracing more than one province. The best of the southern armies, the Yunnan Army, came to be resented as 'foreigners' when operating outside of Yunnan.[29] In Szechwan, Hunan, Kwangtung and Kwangsi armies based on local military men came to power, and maintained their power by intermarrying with the local elite, whose sons entered the local army as officers.[30] The surviving Anhwei military governors, Li Hou-chi in Fukien and Lu Yung-hsiang in Chekiang, seem to have played the same game, though Lu in particular became more involved in national politics after 1924. Such armies were bound to be less attractive to, and less interested in, the Paoting Military Academy or Japanese Military Academy trained officers who continued to provide an edge of military professionalism to the northern armies. The southern armies were also less well served with arsenals and major treaty ports, which both generated foreign exchange and provided the commercial facilities for the import of weapons; these factors contributed to their lesser military effectiveness.

Given the circumstances, the southern provincial regimes had a degree of 'legitimacy', though the idea should not be pressed too far, given the even greater importance of the ideal of national unification against the imperialists. Federalism might possibly have reconciled these conflicting imperatives. Even though Hunan in 1922 was the only province actually to write a constitution assuming a federal

29 Donald S. Sutton, *Provincial Militarism and the Chinese Republic: The Yunnan Army, 1905–1925* (Ann Arbor, 1980), pp. 217–61. The argument of these two chapters is that the occupation of other provinces destroyed the professionalism of the Yunnan Army, even in Yunnan.

30 Robert A. Kapp, *Szechwan and the Chinese Republic: Provincial Militarism and Central Power, 1911–1938* (New Haven, 1973), pp.38–55, analyzes this process.

framework, many other provinces expressed intentions of doing so. What made locally based armies attractive at a more mundane level was the fact that changes of garrison could be avoided; these were always the worst times for military violence, as both the departing and the arriving army could be expected to loot, rape and kill in an uninhibited manner. The other side of the coin was that the southern regimes tended to splinter into parts of provinces, as in Szechwan. A province-by-province survey may add some perspective to Sun Yat-sen's story.

After the death of Ts'ai O, T'ang Chi-yao had taken over the Yunnan Army, but many officers resented this, and resented T'ang's efforts to take all the credit for the antimonarchical movement. The Yunnan Army lost prestige (as related on pp.60–1) when driven from Szechwan in 1920. In the same year, a rift in the Yunnan Army contingent in Kwangtung, between T'ang and Li Ken-yuan, permitted the Kwangsi generals dominant in Kwangtung to drive the Yunnan forces to the periphery of Kwangtung and cut off their funding. In Yunnan itself, demoralization had set in; though a relatively poor province, Yunnan was supporting a large army, much of which was away from the province, and opium sales had come to constitute the main revenue source for both army and province. On 8 February 1921 T'ang was overthrown by long-time Yunnan clique member Ku P'in-chen. T'ang escaped, protected by a bodyguard under his eventual successor Lung Yun, a soldier from the Yi minority nationality (often referred to in English by the Chinese pejorative Lolo). The following year T'ang returned to power, and remained at the head of Yunnan affairs until his death in 1927. Financed by opium and staffed by nepotism, the Yunnan Army within Yunnan from 1920 to 1949 was almost a caricature of warlordism, as noted by Stilwell and other foreign observers during the Second World War. The situation in Kweichow after the 1923 expulsion of Liu Hsien-shih, the local warlord who had collaborated with the Yunnan Army, was similar if more obscure.[31] In Szechwan, after the expulsion of the Yunnan Army, various generals of local origin carved out spheres of influence for themselves. The mature system in which Szechwan was divided into several 'garrison areas' – each a weak warlord regime in its own right – stabilized only after the KMT Northern Expedition of 1926–7, and extraprovincial

31 Sutton, *Provincial Militarism*, pp.252–7.

influence on Szechwan developments was minimal until the mid-1930s.[32]

Chao Heng-t'i became governor of Hunan in 1921. T'an Yen-k'ai and Ch'eng Ch'ien, the province's two other leading local military men, took their armies into Kwangtung and supported Sun Yat-sen in his efforts there. Despite the sincere KMT affinities of all three, Chao was willing to enlist the help of Wu P'ei-fu to block the return of T'an and Ch'eng to Hunan. This permitted Wu to survive as warlord of Hunan and Hupei after the débâcle of 1924, with Chao as governor of Hunan under him until 1926.[33]

The Canton regime created by Sun Yat-sen in 1917 had figured peripherally in the events of the next four years, but Sun Yat-sen had failed to weld together its disparate elements. This was not due to lack of effort or ability on Sun's part; centrifugal forces were powerful throughout the south. Sun's supporters may be summarized as most of the navy (based on a Fukien clique whose officers were mostly trained at the much-analyzed Foochow Naval Academy);[34] the Kwangtung branch of the Yunnan Army (discussed on pp.60–1) the so-called First Kwangsi clique, centred on Lu Jung-t'ing; and KMT-orientated leaders from Kwangtung (including Ch'en Chiung-ming) and elsewhere. These elements were willing to rally against Yuan Shih-k'ai's hated henchman Lung Chi-kuang, but power in the military government quickly tilted toward Lu Jung-t'ing.

Lu's career resembled Chang Tso-lin's in some respects. He was a successful Kwangsi bandit who had been coopted into the Green Standard Army, and had risen to the rank of brigade general by 1911. Unlike most old-style commanders, he joined the revolution, and afterwards gained Yuan Shih-k'ai's confidence. Though related by marriage to Lung Chi-kuang, he broke with Yuan and Lung and joined the Constitution Protection Movement in 1916. Chang Hsun appointed him 'imperial' governor-general of Kwangtung and Kwangsi in 1917, but he did not rise to the bait. Despite squalid origins, Lu had been on the right side from 1911, and Sun was willing to pay for his support by naming him one of his two marshals, the other being Yunnan clique chieftain T'ang Chi-yao.

32 Kapp, *Szechuan*, pp.24–38, on the garrison areas, and pp.87–101 on the collapse of the system.

33 For Chao Heng-t'i, Boorman, *Biographical Dictionary*, I, pp.143–4.

34 Bruce Swanson, *Eighth Voyage of the Dragon: A History of China's Quest for Seapower* (Annapolis, 1982), pp.127–31.

Lu, however, was not easy to control. T'ang's main forces and concerns lay in Yunnan, and the navy and the KMT militarists collectively were unable to check the expansion of Lu's influence in Canton. In May 1918 Sun Yat-sen left Canton for Shanghai, and in August 1919 he formally resigned from the military government. Lu, who was not personally much respected, ruled a rump military government at Canton; he succeeded in forcing the Yunnan Army out of Kwangtung, but was not able to prevent Kwangtung native Ch'en Chiung-ming's creation of a power base in the eastern half of the province.[35]

Ch'en Chiung-ming (1878–1933) came from an old gentry family of Haifeng in eastern Kwangtung. His early career exemplifies the radicalization of the Chinese literati class after 1895: from holding a sheng-yuan (the lowest of the traditional literary degrees), he became a follower of the constitutional monarchist doctrines of K'ang Yu-wei and Liang Ch'i-ch'ao; by 1908 he had earned a modern law degree, and a year later joined Sun Yat-sen's Alliance Society. He participated in the April 1911 Canton uprising, and then in the successful revolution later that year. His career had placed him in close association with the major KMT leaders Huang Hsing and Hu Han-min. In June 1913 Yuan Shih-k'ai appointed Ch'en to succeed Hu as governor of Kwangtung. Despite Yuan's favour, Ch'en opposed Yuan's monarchical ambitions, and led troops in 1916 in an unsuccessful attempt to capture Huichow from Lung Chi-kuang. In July 1917 Ch'en accompanied Sun Yat-sen and Admiral Ch'eng Pi-kuang on the expedition to Canton that set up the military government. Ch'en's place as the archetypal treacherous warlord is so fixed in the demonology of early KMT history that it may not be redundant to stress that, until 1918, Ch'en was much more the archetypal revolutionary intellectual. Even in his years as a regional warlord he extended his patronage to the leftist intellectuals Ch'en Tu-hsiu, whose accomplishments included founding the Chinese Communist Party, and P'eng P'ai, whose ideas on land reform and organization of the peasantry for revolutionary purposes were later adapted (or stolen) by Mao Tse-tung.[36]

Despite Sun Yat-sen's title as grand marshal of the military government, the actual military forces affiliated with the regime were those of the two marshals, Lu Jung-t'ing and T'ang Chi-yao,

35 Li, *Political History*, pp.397–8; and Boorman, *Biographical Dictionary*, II, pp.447–9, for Lu Jung-t'ing's career.

36 For Ch'en Chiung-ming, see Boorman, *Biographical Dictionary*, I, pp.173–80.

the respective heads of the Kwangsi and Yunnan military cliques. Neither was willing to squander their military capital in a premature Northern Expedition (pei-fa), as favoured by Sun, against the powerful warlord armies of the north. Sun pushed; Lu and T'ang stalled. Sun finally succeeded in getting Ch'en appointed commander of the garrison battalions in Canton itself. In January 1918 Sun sent Ch'en to invade Fukien. Passing through his home territory in eastern Kwangtung, Ch'en Chiung-ming turned into a warlord.

He dallied in the treaty port city of Swatow several months, making contacts and reorganizing the local administration. After further admonitions from Sun, Ch'en invaded Fukien in August 1918 and took Changchow (near Amoy), where he remained two years, despite the wishes of Sun, who remained in Shanghai in these years. During this period he strengthened his network of local contacts, promoted education and land reform, and corresponded with Chinese and international leaders (including Lenin).

Tuan Ch'i-jui's defeat and the fall of the Anhwei clique in the 1920 An–Chih War changed the alignment of political forces. Soon afterwards Li Hou-chi, military governor of Fukien and one of the few surviving Anhwei warlords, was persuaded to provide funds to help Ch'en Chiung-ming invade Kwangtung; this of course meant removing Ch'en's army from Fukien. Ch'en invaded in August and by the end of October had forced Lu Jung-t'ing to dissolve the military government, evacuate Canton and withdraw his army into Kwangsi. Ch'en, in other words, had enhanced his military effectiveness in the last two years, and until 1925 his military power would rest on a solid base of local contacts in the Huichow-Haifeng-Swatow region of eastern Kwangtung. His position resembled that of Chao Heng-t'i in Hunan, whose ideas on federal government he professed to share.

Sun Yat-sen had a much higher political profile and other ideas. He convened a parliament at Canton, which in May 1921 elected him president. The provincial leaders advocating federal government considered this step premature, and the democratic foreign powers disappointed Sun by continuing to recognize Peiyang clique elder statesman Hsu Shih-ch'ang in Peking, despite – or because of – the latter's figurehead status and lack of real power. Ch'en Chiung-ming, already governor of Kwangtung and commander in chief of the Kwangtung Army, accepted appointment as Minister of War and Minister of the Interior under Sun. Leading his army west from Canton up the West River, Ch'en captured Wuchow, the gateway to Kwangsi, on 21 June. Subsequent operations eliminated

Lu Jung-t'ing's military power by September. Some of Lu's officers (Li Tsung-jen and Pai Ch'ung-hsi were the most important) survived to lead the so-called Second Kwangsi military clique, which was much more under KMT influence than Lu had ever been.[37]

The conquest of Kwangsi naturally encouraged Sun, who directly afterwards resumed his advocacy of a Northern Expedition. As with his revolutionary plans before 1911, Sun seems to have assumed that, once launched, a Northern Expedition would have a momentum of its own, and that the northern warlords would not be able to prevent their own soldiers and people in general from flocking to Sun's banner. Implicit in this view was a devaluation of specifically military factors and the military professionalism that, however attenuated, still informed the leadership of China's various armies. Sun also did not give enough weight to the fact that his main military force was Ch'en Chiung-ming's army, and that Ch'en, like Chao Heng-t'i in Hunan, did not wish to jeopardize his provincial standing by gambling on the uncertain outcome of a major war. As 1921 progressed, Ch'en and Chao corresponded, and both did all they could behind the scenes to delay the Northern Expedition.

Meanwhile the rift widened between the major northern factions, adding to Sun's sense of urgency regarding a Northern Expedition. In a sense Ch'en Chiung-ming's relationship to the Kwangtung Army resembled Yuan Shih-k'ai's to the Peiyang Army: the warlord's ascendancy rested on personal loyalties and personal ties, but many of the officers were susceptible to Sun Yat-sen's revolutionary and nationalist agenda. Those so susceptible included T'an Yen-k'ai and Vice-Minister of War Ch'eng Ch'ien,[38] who both resented being excluded from their native Hunan, and chief of staff Teng K'eng, whose assassination in March 1922 was credited by informed opinion to Ch'en Chiung-ming. This provided a pretext for Sun to remove Ch'en as commander-in-chief of the Kwangtung Army and governor of Kwangtung. Sun then proclaimed 4 May 1922 as the launch date of the Northern Expedition. Meanwhile in the north, the First Chih–Feng War had already entered its shooting phase.

37 Li, *Political History*, pp.414–17; Diana Lary, *Region and Nation: The Kwangsi Clique in Chinese Politics, 1925–1937* (Cambridge, UK, 1974), passim, on the origins and development of the Second Kwangsi military clique.

38 Boorman, *Biographical Dictionary*, I, pp.280–4.

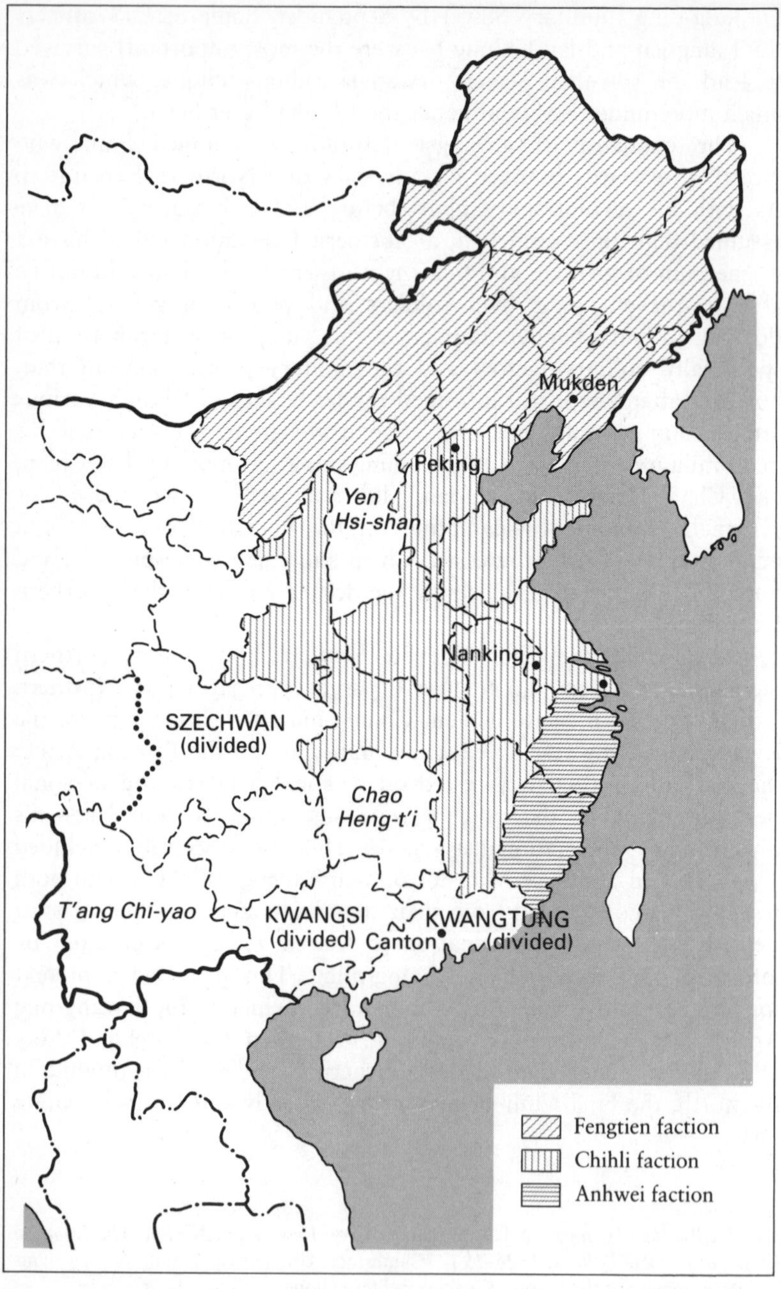

6. Factional affiliation on the eve of the First Chih-Feng War, 1922 (After: Ch'i, Hsi-sheng, *Warlord Politics in China*)

THE FIRST CHIH–FENG WAR, 1922

In the outcome of the An–Chih War, it seemed that Wu P'ei-fu had done most of the fighting, on Ts'ao K'un's behalf to be sure, while Chang Tso-lin had gained most of the spoils. The latter included the armament of Little Hsu's supposedly elite Frontier Defence Army (later Nation-Securing Army) and his control over Inner Mongolia, but went beyond that. Chang had left troops in northern Chihli and had great influence over the central government headed by ex-Anhwei clique figure Chin Yun-p'eng. With the fall of Tuan Ch'i-jui, Chang had also become the only important warlord still on the Japanese payroll, and his Manchuria and Mongolia realm was the part of China of most interest to the Japanese (despite the Japanese designs on Shantung). Japanese policy itself was in some turmoil; they had lost their investment in Tuan Ch'i-jui, and in a broader sense Japan had failed to find her bearings in a postwar world in which Anglo-American cooperation and Chinese nationalism both seemed directed against Japan. Generally the Japanese supported Chang in maintaining his position in northeast China, and resisted his efforts to create a strong central government headed by himself. Chang for his part denounced the Chihli clique leadership of Ts'ao K'un and Wu P'ei-fu, publicly and to the Japanese, as puppets of Anglo-American interests, and as allies of the dangerous radical Sun Yat-sen, whose KMT movement then did include a left-wing element that overlapped with the still-small Chinese Communist Party (CCP). Relations between Chang and Wu were very bitter; allegedly this stemmed from the Aftermath Conference at Peking after the An–Chih War, during which Chang denied Wu, whom he called a mere division commander, ceremonial status equal to himself and Ts'ao K'un.

Chang hoped to extend his territory southward, and to win some adherents from the imperfectly united Chihli clique. At a conference in Tientsin in April 1921, whose main purpose was to force the reorganization of the Chin Yun-p'eng Cabinet, Chang went out of his way to treat Wang Chan-yuan, military governor of Hupei and Hunan, as equal to himself and Ts'ao.[39] The effort to subvert Wang led to nothing, since Wu P'ei-fu kept Wang's provinces for himself after the so-called War to Rescue Hupei (discussed on pp.88–9). Part of the fallout from this was the rise of

39 McCormack, *Chang Tso-lin*, pp.49–62; Li, *Political History*, pp.409–11.

Christian General Feng Yü-hsiang – still a Chihli stalwart – to military governor of Shensi.

Feng since 1918 had commanded the 16th Mixed Brigade, in garrison at Changte, and in effect maintaining Wu P'ei-fu's interest in Hunan. During this time Feng led his troops in Christian observances, including hymn-singing, and maintained good standards of training and discipline. His local administration was, by warlord standards, fair and somewhat progressive, and his reputation away from Changte was good enough that Shensi opinion welcomed the prospect of Feng coming into authority over them. Feng, whose father was a soldier in the Huai Army of Li Hung-chang, was no doubt sincere in his professed desire to reform China, though he lacked the educational background to offer an ideological alternative to the plans of the major intellectuals. And, however sincere his intentions (which his contemporaries came to doubt), the nature of warlord politics was such that any reforms he might achieve were going to be partial and temporary.

After the Tientsin conference, on 25 May 1921, the Peking government appointed Yen Hsiang-wen, commander of the 20th Division and an associate of Wu P'ei-fu, as military governor of Shensi. Anhwei clique incumbent Ch'en Shu-fan stalled for time, hoping to get the opium crop harvested in order to fill his war chest. This led Wu P'ei-fu to add the 7th Division and Feng Yu-hsiang's 16th Mixed Brigade to Yen's army, which conquered Shensi in early July. Feng's brigade performed well, and in reward was increased in size and status, becoming the 11th Division. When Yen Hsiang-wen committed suicide, for reasons unknown, on 23 August, Feng succeeded him as military governor.[40]

Meanwhile Peking politics revolved around the issue of money. The consortium of the usual lenders to China had agreed that a unified Chinese government should be a condition of further loans. While Premier Chin Yun-p'eng secured the dissolution of the Anhwei-dominated parliament at Peking, Sun Yat-sen remained adamantly oppositional at Canton. As the prospect of further foreign loans evaporated, the domestic Chinese banking system became more of a political factor. The banking system was dominated by the so-called Communications clique, composed mostly of men with backgrounds in the Ministry of Communications, who controlled the Bank of China and the Bank of Communications, the banks that issued currency, and were

40 Sheridan, *Chinese Warlord*, pp.96–106.

influential in the Treasury Bureau of the Finance Ministry as well. Finance Minister Chou Tzu-ch'i and Communications Minister Yeh Kung-cho were the leaders of the Communications clique in the Cabinet. Neither got along with Chin Yun-p'eng. When Chin dismissed Chou and Yeh, the Communications clique promptly aligned itself with Chang Tso-lin. On 24 December 1921 President Hsu Shih-ch'ang appointed Liang Shih-yi, the generally recognized head of the Communications clique, as prime minister. In the next few days leading figures of the Anhwei clique were formally pardoned, and central government funding for Wu P'ei-fu's troops in Hupei and Hunan was cut off. Wu now faced a coalition of Fengtien, Anhwei and Communications clique enemies, aided by disloyalty within the Chihli clique; even Ts'ao K'un's behaviour was ambiguous. Hunan and Hupei were not the sum of Wu's power, but his position there was too important to be risked.

Wu struck back shrewdly and swiftly, publishing a telegram accusing Liang Shih-yi of treason because of his actions regarding the Washington conference.[41] While naval limitation was the main agenda item for the conference, Secretary of State Charles Evans Hughes, its American host, hoped to end the rivalry between the United States and Japan that had led to the battleship-building race in the first place. To this end the conference also adopted (in addition to the Five Power Treaty on naval limitations) the Nine Power Treaty guaranteeing the territorial integrity of China. While this was going on Liang had cabled the Chinese delegation to go easy on the Japanese, hoping, as usual, that they would reciprocate with a loan. Wu had evidence for his accusations, and, despite Chang Tso-lin's public support, public opinion forced Liang from office. War resulted. Wu P'ei-fu seemed the weaker party, and was deserted by some of the lesser Chihli generals and not strongly backed by Ts'ao K'un. Chang Tso-lin, on the other hand, in addition to the financiers of the Communications clique, had received assurances of support from Tuan Ch'i-jui ('retired' but still influential leader of the defeated Anhwei military clique), Chang Hsun (Peiyang general, Ch'ing dynasty loyalist and mastermind of the Manchu restoration of 1917) and Sun Yat-sen (founder of the Republic of China and long-time enemy of the two preceding) – surely as strange an assortment of bedfellows as any nation's politics has ever produced.

41 Li, *Political History*, pp.409–11; Wou, *Militarism*, pp.50–1.

Liang Shih-yi left office, on the pretext of sick leave, on 19 January 1922. Chang Tso-lin considered this a personal attack, and resolved to separate Wu P'ei-fu from the rest of the Chihli faction, and crush him. At first this strategy seemed successful. Ts'ao K'un and his brothers were related through marriage ties to Chang Tso-lin, and during February and March emissaries went between Chang's headquarters at Mukden and Ts'ao's headquarters at Paoting, which Ts'ao controlled with his personal army of about 10,000 men. Ts'ao refused to sign any of the public statements issued by Wu during this period. In March all the anti-Wu elements conferred at Tientsin, and agreed on the following programme: Sun Yat-sen was to become president, Liang Shih-yi to return as premier, Chang Hsun to become inspector-general of Kiangsu, Anhwei and Kiangsi, while Anhwei warlord Tuan Chih-kuei became military governor of Chihli. To accomplish these goals, Sun Yat-sen and the Anhwei warlords of Chekiang (Lu Yung-hsiang) and Fukien (Li Hou-chi) were to attack Wu P'ei-fu from the south while the Fengtien Army came down from the north. Wu would then be confined to his position as inspector-general of Hunan and Hupei, and the victorious coalition would govern China in happy harmony. On 22 March Chang Tso-lin began moving his main forces through Shanhaikuan into northern Chihli.[42]

Chang Tso-lin's imposing coalition collapsed immediately. Chang had been counting on Japanese support, which did not materialize, even though his Japanese connections made him suspect in nationalist eyes. From its Shanghai headquarters, the 2nd Squadron of the navy, whose river gunboats had been important in Wu P'ei-fu's victory in the war for Hupei the previous year, issued a statement of support for Wu. Despite its small size, the navy was run by a well-educated clique of officers, mostly from Fukien, with nationalist sympathies and fairly broad political contacts. The stand of the navy made it unlikely that the Anhwei warlords of Chekiang or Fukien (in which the navy's training squadron was based) would in fact move against Wu. The 1st Squadron of the navy was at Canton,[43] where Ch'en Chiung-ming had broken with Sun Yat-sen, thus aborting the latter's Northern Expedition (these events are treated at greater length on pp.103–5). Chang Hsun's monarchist restoration of 1917 had not been forgiven, and public protests caused him to withdraw from active participation. Tuan Ch'i-jui

42 McCormack, *Chang Tso-lin*, pp.62–70.

43 Swanson, *Dragon*, pp.127–38, on the role of the navy in this period.

and Tuan Chih-kuei also remained inactive, so that Chang Tso-lin had to crush Wu P'ei-fu on his own.

As in 1920, Wu P'ei-fu's axis of power was the Peking to Hankow north–south railway line. As the 1922 crisis opened, he did not control all of it. Ts'ao K'un held Paoting, important in its own right as the capital of Chihli province and site of the Paoting Military Academy, and Ts'ao's flirtation with Chang Tso-lin has already been noted. The military governor of Honan, Chao T'i, a Chihli militarist loosely connected to Ts'ao K'un, was openly hostile, though his numerous (allegedly 25,000 men) army was composed chiefly of poorly disciplined Honan bandits. Wu's best units were his own 3rd Division and Feng Yü-hsiang's growing Shensi forces. Feng himself was showing signs of independence, ominously (in view of his later betrayal of Wu in 1924) calling publicly for a negotiated settlement of the differences between the warlords. Chang's troop movements obviously pre-empted negotiations, and brought Feng and Ts'ao into alignment with Wu. Feng's army came east by rail from Shensi, and Wu left Feng to hold the critical railway junction of Chengchow in Honan (where the east–west Lunghai line from Shensi crosses the north–south Peking–Hankow line), while, with units including one of Feng's brigades, he joined forces with Ts'ao K'un at Paoting. By the lowest of the common estimates, Wu had concentrated 64,000 men against the 84,000 Fengtien troops in Peking.[44] Contemporary observers felt that Wu's troops were better trained and disciplined, and possibly better armed, though some were impressed by the weapons and equipment of Chang's forces.

Wu moved north to take Peking, and major fighting began around 28 April at Changhsintien, on the railway line very near Marco Polo Bridge (Lukouchiao). The Fengtien Army at Changhsintien was under the overall command of Chang Ching-hui. The right wing was composed of the 16th Division under Chang's protégé Tsou Fen, and the army also included the 27th Division under Chang Tso-hsiang. Both Changs were sworn brothers of Chang Tso-lin from bandit days, though not actually related to him. The two armies held out against each other for several days, but during the night of 3–4 May the brigade of Feng Yü-hsiang's 11th Division included in Wu's army marched around the Fengtien right wing. The 16th Division collapsed and fled, and at this news Chang Tso-hsiang led his division in panic to the rear. Wu P'ei-fu was able

44 Wou, *Militarism*, pp.52–4.

to move on and occupy Peking. Casualties may have aggregated 10,000 to 30,000; in any event, the intensity of the fighting had sharpened noticeably since 1920.

Chang Tso-lin met his fleeing troops at Luanchow, between Tientsin and Shanhaikuan on the railway line to Manchuria. He gave every soldier a $10 tip from supplies of banknotes brought along for that purpose. Since a soldier's nominal monthly wage was unchanged from the pre-revolutionary $4.20, this was no doubt welcome. Naturally the Changhsintien defeat produced rumours. Tsou Fen before the battle had been suspected of collusion with Wu P'ei-fu; he and Chang Ching-hui now disappear from Fengtien service. It was also said that President Hsu Shih-ch'ang had threatened to attack the Fengtien Army from the rear with three neutral divisions in the capital, which in fact did not move.[45] Chang Tso-lin's postmortem concluded that trained staff officers were in subordinate positions where their advice was ignored, and that the generals of bandit background commanding the divisions were not equal to their duties. Chang subsequently pursued a programme of reorganization and professionalization that prolonged the power of the Fengtien Army.[46]

Meanwhile in Honan, Chao T'i rebelled, spreading the rumour that Wu P'ei-fu had been defeated and killed in the north. Feng Yu-hsiang moved east from Chengchow, took the provincial capital at Kaifeng, and as a result could hardly be denied the title of military governor of Honan as well. He immediately started recruiting more troops and instructing them in the doctrines of Christianity.[47]

Despite the Changhsintien victory, Wu P'ei-fu was not strong enough, nor was his army unified enough, to follow Chang Tso-lin into Manchuria and finish him off. Instead, a politics of public poses and private intrigues followed the battle. Liang Shih-yi had to go, and went. On 14 May Sun Ch'uan-fang (later the warlord of the five lower Yangtze provinces who was destroyed by the KMT Northern Expedition of 1926–7; he fitted into the Chihli clique as a protégé of defeated Hupei military governor Wang Chan-yuan) issued a call for the resignation of the presidents in both Peking and Canton, and the revival of the old constitution. Hsu Shih-ch'ang got the message and resigned on 2 June. The Chihli militarists then

45 McCormack, *Chang Tso-lin*, pp.69–73.
46 McCormack, *Chang Tso-lin*, pp.100–10.
47 Sheridan, *Chinese Warlord*, pp.110–12.

persuaded Li Yuan-hung (reluctant leader of the Wuhan rising in 1911, and Yuan Shih-k'ai's vice-president and ill-fated successor) to come back, and he did so, not realizing that his mission was to keep the presidential seat warm for Ts'ao K'un.[48]

SOUTH CHINA AFTER THE FIRST CHIH–FENG WAR

While the First Chih–Feng War was being fought out in the north, Sun Yat-sen's southern government collapsed. In planning his 1922 Northern Expedition, Sun made Yunnan clique militarist (and long-term KMT supporter) Li Lieh-chün his chief of staff. When Ch'en Chiung-ming's opposition became evident, Sun (as previously related) removed him as governor of Kwangtung and commander of the Kwangtung Army. Sun was able to do this by marching from Wuchow on the Kwangtung–Kwangsi border to Canton with the troops he considered loyal and intended to use to attack the north. Most of Ch'en's troops were still at Nanning in Kwangsi as a result of the Kwangsi war. Ch'en fled to Huichow in order to preserve his eastern Kwangtung base. Sun was advised by some, including the still very low-ranking Chiang Kai-shek, to postpone the Northern Expedition and first crush Ch'en Chiung-ming. Sun wanted to keep his promise to support Chang Tso-lin against the Chihli clique, and felt that the war in the north gave an expedition from the south a chance of success. Sun also believed that Ch'en had learned his lesson, and could be trusted to remain as Minister of War; clearly, Sun could not imagine that an old revolutionary figure like Ch'en could betray the leader of the revolution. While all of these assumptions turned out to be wrong, they show Sun close up as anything but an impractical idealist: he was more like a gambler taking excessive risks in order to get the most out of a weak hand.

Sun formally began the Northern Expedition on 6 May with an invasion of southern Kiangsi from Shaochow in northern Kwangtung. While the invasion was in progress, Ch'en Chiung-ming's troops occupied Canton and, feigning mutiny, demanded the restoration of Ch'en to his former offices. When Sun's troops captured Kanhsien in southern Kiangsi on 13 June, they discovered telegraphic communications between Ch'en and the Chihli clique military governor, who had already fled from Kiangsi. Sun meanwhile had returned to Canton to reason with Ch'en Chiung-ming. When he ordered the continuation of the Northern

48 Li, *Political History*, pp.419–22.

Expedition on 15 June, Ch'en's troops surrounded his office building and threatened his life. Sun escaped to the cruiser *Hai-ch'i*, later transferring his flag to the gunboat *Yung-feng*. From then until his departure in August, such power as he exercised in the Canton area rested on the 1st Squadron of the Navy.

Sun was now out of step with most political and intellectual opinion in China. Chihli clique strongman Wu P'ei-fu had skilfully portrayed both Fengtien clique leader Chang Tso-lin and Communications clique leader Liang Shih-yi as pro-Japanese traitors. Sun Yat-sen's alliance with Chang therefore called Sun's own sincerity and judgement into question, since Sun could not very well explain publicly that he intended to betray Chang Tso-lin whenever he could. Ts'ao K'un and Wu P'ei-fu were now demanding the restoration of the old constitution and the old parliament elected in 1913, along with the old president Li Yuan-hung. While the terms for which these people had been elected had expired in 1919 at the latest, the desire for peace and order was understandable, and led to a consensus to treat the warlord years so far as a kind of aberration from the path of normal constitutional government. Sun received telegrams from Peking University president Ts'ai Yuan-p'ei and other leading intellectuals urging his resignation in the interest of unity.

The representatives of the major foreign powers at Canton agreed. Sun's warships were bombarding his enemies in Canton, incidentally endangering foreign lives and property, and business-orientated foreign opinion was further alienated when Canton's small but growing labour union movement proclaimed a general strike to force Sun's restoration. Ch'en Chiung-ming meanwhile accused Sun of responsibility for the 1918 murder of Admiral Ch'eng Pi-kuang (unsolved, but certainly perpetrated by Sun's enemies). On 14 July the dockyard at Whampoa fell to Ch'en; Sun's increasingly disaffected ships thus lost their port facility. On 9 August Sun escaped from Canton on a British vessel. The 1st Squadron fell under the command of Admiral Wen Shu-te, who in 1923 took it to Tsingtao and placed it under Wu P'ei-fu.

Sun Yat-sen was out but not down, and some more political and military manoeuvres permitted the restoration of the Canton government in March 1923. Sun's Northern Expeditionary Army of 1922 had consisted, basically, of a Yunnan force of about 10,000 troops under Chu P'ei-te (the remnant of the once much larger Yunnan Army in Kwangtung) and a Kwangtung force under Li Fu-lin and Hsu Ch'ung-chih. After Ch'en Chiung-ming's coup, the

Yunnan troops had retired to Kwangsi. There they cooperated with Kwangsi soldiers to resist the efforts of Wu P'ei-fu's military governor designate, Shen Hung-ying, to take over the province.

Li Fu-lin and Hsu Ch'ung-chih took their troops to the Kwangtung–Fukien border, where Hsu made contact with the southern Fukien garrison commander Wang Yung-ch'üan. Both Wang and Fukien military governor Li Hou-chi originally had been protégés of Hsu Shu-cheng in the Anhwei clique, but Li Hou-chi was now trying to cuddle up to Wu P'ei-fu in order to maintain his rule, while Wang favoured alliance with Sun and a northern expedition. Anhwei clique founder Tuan Ch'i-jui not surprisingly favoured Wang in this disagreement, and urged him to take action in support of Sun. On 12 October Wang took Foochow and ousted Li Hou-chi, with the help of the Kwangtung troops. Wang of course retained military authority in his own hands, but KMT stalwart Lin Sen, a Fukien native, became civil governor.

Attacked now by Hsu Ch'ung-chih's Kwangtung troops from the east and Chu P'ei-te's Yunnanese from the west, Ch'en Chiung-ming could not hold Canton. He fell back first to Huichow and announced his retirement on 15 January 1923. Later he was able to re-establish and hold his position in eastern Kwangtung as far as Swatow until 1925. Sun Yat-sen returned to Canton, resumed his title of grand marshal, and appointed the Hunanese revolutionary T'an Yen-k'ai as Minister of the Interior and long-time KMT loyalist Liao Chung-k'ai as Minister of Finance. Government headquarters were now located at the fortified Honam Cement Works, on an island in the Pearl River, so that they would be less accessible to mutinous troops. Shen Hung-ying's effort to take control of Kwangtung and Kwangsi for Wu P'ei-fu was disposed of by May.[49]

By this time Ts'ao K'un's efforts to usurp the presidency were already tarnishing the bright image Wu P'ei-fu had created, and Chang Tso-lin had survived and was recovering his power in the northeast. Hopes for national unity had evaporated in Sun's absence, which made his return to local power seem less subversive. Sun's third effort at Canton rested on firmer foundations than the first two, but as 1924 opened informed observers of the China scene felt it most likely that national unification would be achieved by Wu P'ei-fu's final defeat of the other northern warlords.

49 Li, *Political History*, pp.414–19, 425–8, remains the liveliest account of these events. Swanson, *Dragon*, pp.135–8, on the role of the navy.

THE SECOND CHIH–FENG WAR, 1924

Wu P'ei-fu, born of poor parents in 1874, had earned the lowest degree in the traditional examination system before deciding that he wanted a military career in the Peiyang Army. By 1905 he was a junior officer in Ts'ao K'un's 3rd Division. Wu had evidently internalized his Confucian upbringing, since he remained loyal to Ts'ao K'un despite the latter's failings, which included the willingness (in 1922) to save his own hide at Wu's expense.[50] Chihli victory in 1922 caused Ts'ao's ambitions to swell. Ts'ao's henchmen now took over the major positions of authority in Chihli province, and Ts'ao began a campaign of bribery and intimidation reminiscent of Yuan Shih-k'ai.

Wu P'ei-fu returned to Honan, where his deteriorating relations with Feng Yü-hsiang were presumably behind the latter's transfer to Peking as inspector-general of the army (31 October 1922). The leading elements of the civil population of Honan petitioned against Feng's transfer, since Feng now had an excellent reputation as a civil administrator, while under Wu banditry and extortion had flourished. Wu nonetheless needed Feng's departure to re-establish his authority in his own base area. Feng therefore concentrated his army at Nanyuan, south of the capital. Training and Christian indoctrination continued. Feng's army at this time (one division and three mixed brigades) was probably the most powerful in Chihli, and Feng maintained good relations with Ts'ao K'un and his brothers and with Wang Huai-ch'ing, an officer long associated with Ts'ao K'un and now commander of the Peking police.[51]

In June 1923 Feng Yü-hsiang and Wang Huai-ch'ing jointly presented their resignations to President Li Yuan-hung, saying that unless their men were paid, they could no longer be responsible for maintaining order in the capital. Finances were indeed in bad shape. Chinese diplomats and consuls abroad were resigning for lack of pay, and Wu P'ei-fu was not receiving anything from the central government. After several days of standoff, Li Yuan-hung physically left Peking on 13 June, taking the presidential seals and stationery, and continuing to issue orders countersigned by the one Cabinet member who stood by him in the crisis, Agriculture Minister and

50 Wou, *Militarism*, is the standard modern study of Wu P'ei-fu.

51 Sheridan, *Chinese Warlord*, pp.112–24. In addition to Feng's 11th Division, the three mixed brigades were the 7th of Chang Chih-chiang, the 8th of Li Ming-chung, and the 25th of Sung Che-yuan, afterwards kingpin of the Hopei–Chahar Political Council in the period of Japanese expansion in North China in the early 1930s.

Yunnan Army figure Li Ken-yuan. It was to no avail. Ts'ao K'un's minions forcibly deprived Li of office and over the next few months bribed the reassembled legislators of the old parliament to elect their leader president. Ts'ao was inaugurated on the symbolically important date of 10 October, proclaimed a constitution incorporating the ideas of the federal government movement, and soon afterwards promoted Feng Yü-hsiang and numerous other generals to the rank of marshal.[52]

The brazenness of Ts'ao's usurpation offended informed opinion, and this mattered a lot, even in the warlord era. Prior to the First Chih–Feng War in 1922, Wu P'ei-fu had effectively orchestrated opinion against the Fengtien clique. Ts'ao's behaviour now diminished Wu, since Wu's loyalty to Ts'ao was known, even though Wu had not favoured the tactics Ts'ao employed. Revulsion with Ts'ao aided Sun Yat-sen's continuing efforts in the south. Even in the context of a politics resting solely on force, Ts'ao's presidency was narrowly based, really depending on the troop units in Chihli province alone. While Ts'ao intrigued his way to the presidency, Chang Tso-lin rebuilt his power in the northeast.

After patching his army back together in the wake of the Changhsintien defeat, Chang Tso-lin had declared the independence of the three northeastern provinces. The Peking government, now of course controlled by Ts'ao K'un and the Chihli clique, attempted to induce defections among Chang's key subordinates by appointing them to governorships and other important positions in the northeast, but Kao Shih-pin was the only Fengtien general to rebel, and loyal Fengtien forces under Chang Tsung-ch'ang defeated him in early June. Maintaining de facto Fengtien independence meant arguing using the rhetoric of the federal government movement, but Chang Tso-lin firmly repressed the efforts of his provincial assemblies to create civil governments independent of military control, one of the major goals of that movement. Government position in the northeast thus remained 'highly traditional', and dependent on position in the Fengtien clique. On the other hand, mutual hostility to Ts'ao K'un made for polite relations between Chang Tso-lin and Sun Yat-sen in this period. This meant that Chang's regime too talked the language of national unification, rights recovery and anti-imperialism. Chang's economic programme included railway development and a new seaport at Hulutao, both of which competed with the well-established and Japanese-owned

52 Sheridan, *Chinese Warlord*, pp.124–30.

South Manchurian Railway Company and its seaport at Dairen. Chang, widely regarded as a Japanese puppet, was in fact pursuing a calculated policy of distancing himself from Japanese imperialism, which, it may be recalled, had failed to support him in the 1922 war.[53]

The point, of course, of holding and governing the three provinces was to make them contribute to Chang Tso-lin's military strength, and military reform was clearly needed after the 1922 defeat. In 1922 Chang's forces had been organized in five divisions, of which the 16th and 28th disintegrated and were allowed to lapse. The 27th and 29th, along with a totally reorganized 1st, were retained at the divisional level, and the rest of Chang's numerous troops were formed into the 1st to 27th Mixed Brigades and the 1st to 5th Cavalry Brigades. Unit organization was standardized, 150 men formed a company, three companies a battalion, three battalions a regiment, and three regiments a brigade of over 4,000 men. In practice there were variations, both authorized and unauthorized, but the reorganization did mean an enumeration of the army and a reshuffling of its commanders, and Chang used the opportunity to promote officers with professional education at the expense of the opium-smoking bandit types whose company he personally preferred. Other efforts included the purchase of new machinery to expand the output of the Mukden arsenal, the purchase of four small gunboats as the nucleus of a naval force on the Gulf of Chihli, and the development of an air force. The last was a personal project of Chang's eldest son and eventual heir, Chang Hsueh-liang. By the summer of 1923 some forty French Breguet aircraft were being operated by fewer than twenty mostly foreign pilots.

By late 1923 Chang's reorganized army of nearly 200,000 men was certainly as formidable as any in China, but it had its internal weaknesses. A year of intense training had greatly improved the strictly military abilities of the Fengtien troops, but Chang Tso-lin was well behind Sun Yat-sen and even Feng Yü-hsiang and Wu P'ei-fu in trying to infuse the training with ideology. And the enhanced status of professional officers was paralleled by the rise of Chang Tsung-ch'ang. Chang, who was not related to Chang Tso-lin, grew up on the wharves and in the brothels of Harbin, and was

53 Summarized from McCormack, *Chang Tso-lin*, pp.75–100. For the cronyism and nepotism in the Fengtien clique, indicating a 'highly traditional' concept of office, p.86.

both physically imposing and fluent in Russian. He had entered the new army before 1911 and rose as a protégé of Feng Kuo-chang to the status of division commander. In 1922 he returned to his native Manchuria and joined Chang Tso-lin, whose confidence he gained by crushing the Kao Shih-pin rebellion. He then built up great personal wealth through extortion, violence and encouragement of opium cultivation. Chang Tsung-ch'ang was a capable military commander, but he represented in an exaggerated form the vices associated, by the Kuomintang and others, with the northern warlords.[54]

Chang Tso-lin still received Japanese assistance, but still differed with the Japanese concerning his own future role in Chinese politics. For Chang 'autonomy was merely a tactical retreat in the course of the drive for absolute power over China as a whole', while for the Japanese support of Chang was merely a means to the end of maintaining Japanese hegemony in Manchuria. This was spelled out in an unofficial memorandum for Chang in August 1923 by Honjō Shigeru, then Chang's principal Japanese military adviser and in 1931 commander-in-chief of the Japanese Kwantung Army during the Mukden Incident. Chang had asked for more Japanese arms in anticipation of a second war with Chihli. Honjō responded by denying this request, criticizing the Fengtien Army's level of training and readiness, implying that Japan would continue to support Chang's rule in Manchuria, and telling him not to invade China proper; 'the Empire always demands that you exercise circumspection so that order may be maintained in the Eastern Provinces'. Japanese policy was not unified, Honjō being regarded as too partial to Chang, but no Japanese element favoured bankrolling Chang in a bid for supreme power in China.[55]

Whatever the Japanese wished, Chang Tso-lin, with his reorganized and more powerful Fengtien Army, was too powerful to be left alone by the Chihli leaders, who also confronted a revived KMT at Canton. War might have come sooner, and thus before the military revival of the Fengtien forces, had it not been for the much publicized train robbery at Lincheng (Shantung) in April 1923, in which several foreigners were kidnapped. Loud calls for Great Power intervention to restore order led Chihli and Fengtien to sign a peace agreement in June.[56]

54 McCormack, *Chang Tso-lin*, pp.100–10.

55 McCormack, *Chang Tso-lin*, pp.111–28 treats the Japanese connection at length. The quotation is on p.126.

56 McCormack, *Chang Tso-lin*, pp.128–9.

Meanwhile Chihli was taking strong action against the Anhwei remnants in Fukien and Chekiang. In March 1923 Sun Ch'uan-fang was appointed military governor of Fukien. Sun, the former protégé of the previous Hupei military governor Wang Chan-yuan, was a rapidly rising star in the internal politics of the Chihli clique, who had the support of Ts'ao K'un. He drove Anhwei clique military governor Wang Yung-ch'üan out of Foochow and had the province of Fukien under firm Chihli control by early 1924. Wu P'ei-fu intended that Fukien should be the springboard for the conquest of Kwangtung. This development obviously jeopardized the remaining Anhwei warlord, Lu Yung-hsiang of Chekiang. In addition to Chekiang, Lu since 1917 had controlled Shanghai, with its arsenal and its extensive revenues from opium, foreign trade and foreign contacts, and he had carefully maintained his alliances with both Sun Yat-sen and Chang Tso-lin after the Anhwei defeat in 1920. On 10 November 1923 the police chief of the Shanghai area, a Lu subordinate, was assassinated, and both Lu and Ch'i Hsieh-yuan, the Chihli-appointed military governor of Kiangsu, attempted to appoint a successor. Lu won, and compounded the insult by giving refuge to Anhwei troops evacuating Fukien. By August 1924 Sun Ch'uan-fang had moved his forces to the Fukien–Chekiang border and fighting had also broken out on the railway line between Shanghai and Nanking. Lu appealed for help to Sun Yat-sen, who was not able to give it, and to Chang Tso-lin, who was. Feng Yü-hsiang, ominously, refused Wu's order to take his army to Ch'i Hsieh-yuan's assistance, but Lu was defeated anyway, by a combination of battlefield setbacks and internal treachery. Lu fled to Mukden on 13 October, as the Second Chih–Feng War raged.[57]

The war for Chekiang provided Wu P'ei-fu with the occasion for the showdown with Chang Tso-lin. Wu was confident of the outcome. He had mobilized over a quarter of a million troops, divided into three armies, of which the 1st Army under P'eng Shou-hsin, a member of Wu P'ei-fu's group within the overall Chihli faction, would invade Manchuria through Shanhaikuan, supported by the 2nd under Wang Huai-ch'ing, the former Peking police commandant, advancing from Hsifengkou. The 3rd under Christian General Feng Yü-hsiang meanwhile would advance from Peking into Jehol. Wu trusted his own military abilities, and seems to have felt that the loyalty of his principal subordinates was adequate. Here he was wrong. Feng's grievances ran very deep; he had already been

57 Li, *Political History*, pp.468–70; McCormack, *Chang Tso-lin*, pp.129–30.

insubordinate regarding the war against Lu Yung-hsiang, and he had woven others, including Wang Huai-ch'ing, Peking garrison commandant Sun Yueh, and Hu Ching-yi (whom Wu was counting on to kill Feng if necessary) into his web of disaffection. Feng complained bitterly that his army had been slighted in the distribution of munitions and supplies, and moved his troops very slowly out of Peking. By 24 September Feng's vanguard was at Luanping (Jehol) and his main body at Kupeikou; these were supported by a force at Miyun and another 10,000 men who 'needed further training' due north of Peking.[58]

By this time secret negotiations, with Anhwei clique patriarch Tuan Ch'i-jui serving as intermediary from his residence in the Japanese quarter of Tientsin, had resulted in a bribe of between 1.0 million and 2.5 million Japanese Yen (then about two to the US$) for Feng Yü-hsiang from Chang Tso-lin's Japanese-supplied war chest. Since Chang had reason to believe that Feng would betray Wu, he concentrated his own forces around Shanhaikuan. Most of the Fengtien Army was thus concentrated to oppose the advance of the Chihli 1st Army of P'eng Shou-hsin, the only one of the three Chihli army commanders truly loyal to Wu P'ei-fu. Even after Wu personally took command, the Chihli troops suffered a sequence of setbacks, and by mid-October the Shanhaikuan front was stalemated. Wu then ordered Feng to advance from Luanping against Chang's rear, and diverted three divisions from the Shanhaikuan front to reinforce Feng.

Feng instead made a local truce with the Fengtien commander, Li Ching-lin (who then sent some of his forces as reinforcements to Shanhaikuan), and on the night of 20 October marched his army back to Peking. The coup was very carefully thought out. Hu Ching-yi, a long-term subordinate of Feng Yü-hsiang whom Wu P'ei-fu had failed to subvert, led a division to Luanchow (Chihli), interdicting the railway line between Tientsin and Shanhaikuan, and one of Feng's brigades seized Changhsintien, cutting the railway line south of Peking. Soon after midnight on the morning of the 23rd Sun Yueh admitted Feng's concentrated army to Peking. The following day President Ts'ao K'un was persuaded to dismiss Wu P'ei-fu from his military positions. Feng issued a public statement deploring civil war and urging the warlords to settle their differences by negotiation. Feng Yü-hsiang the Christian General had long

58 Wou, *Militarism*, p.85; Sheridan, *Chinese Warlord*, pp.130–4; McCormack, *Chang Tso-lin*, pp.130–3.

provided comic relief for the treaty port press, but from 1924 on Chinese tended to refer to him as the Betraying General.[59]

On the more mundane level of ensuring the success of the anti-Wu P'ei-fu conspiracy, Yen Hsi-shan sent a force from Shansi to seize the railway junction at Shihchiachuang, thus blocking a movement north from Honan along the Peking–Hankow railway by Hsiao Yao-nan, who remained supportive of Wu. Ch'i Hsieh-yuan and Sun Ch'uan-fang also continued to support Wu P'ei-fu, but their movement north up the Tientsin–Pukow line from their base area in the Shanghai and lower Yangtze region was interdicted by the Chihli military governor of Shantung, who was trying unsuccessfully to switch sides. Wu himself had immediately assessed Feng's betrayal as the main threat to his position, and had hurried to Tientsin with a few thousand picked troops, before Hu Ching-yi closed off Luanchow. Wu's hopes of raising an army from the south to suppress Feng were destroyed by the Shansi and Shantung actions, and meanwhile his best army at Shanhaikuan disintegrated, being attacked frontally by Chang Tso-lin while simultaneously threatened from the rear. Wu evacuated his entourage by sea and, after failing to land in Shantung, returned to his Honan–Hupei base area after various adventures.[60]

THE NORTHERN WARLORDS AFTER THE SECOND CHIH–FENG WAR

The Second Chih–Feng War was the most impressive warlord conflict to date. Some 450,000 troops had been involved on all sides, and in the main theatre of operations large armies had opposed one another for nearly a month along the Great Wall line from Shanhaikuan to the vicinity of Peking. Casualty estimates ranged from 20,000 to 30,000.[61] Yet in the end Feng Yü-hsiang's betrayal caused Wu P'ei-fu's defeat, and, despite Feng's pre-existing dislike of Wu, bribery made Feng's betrayal possible. Military unification now seemed more remote than ever, and military politics more chaotic.

Immediately after seizing Peking, Feng Yü-hsiang reorganized his forces as the 1st National Army (Kuominchün); his co-conspirators Hu Ching-yi and Sun Yueh became commanders of

59 Sheridan, *Chinese Warlord*, pp.134–7.

60 Li, *Political History*, pp.471–3; Gillin, *Warlord*, p.23.

61 Ch'i, *Warlord Politics*, pp.137–8.

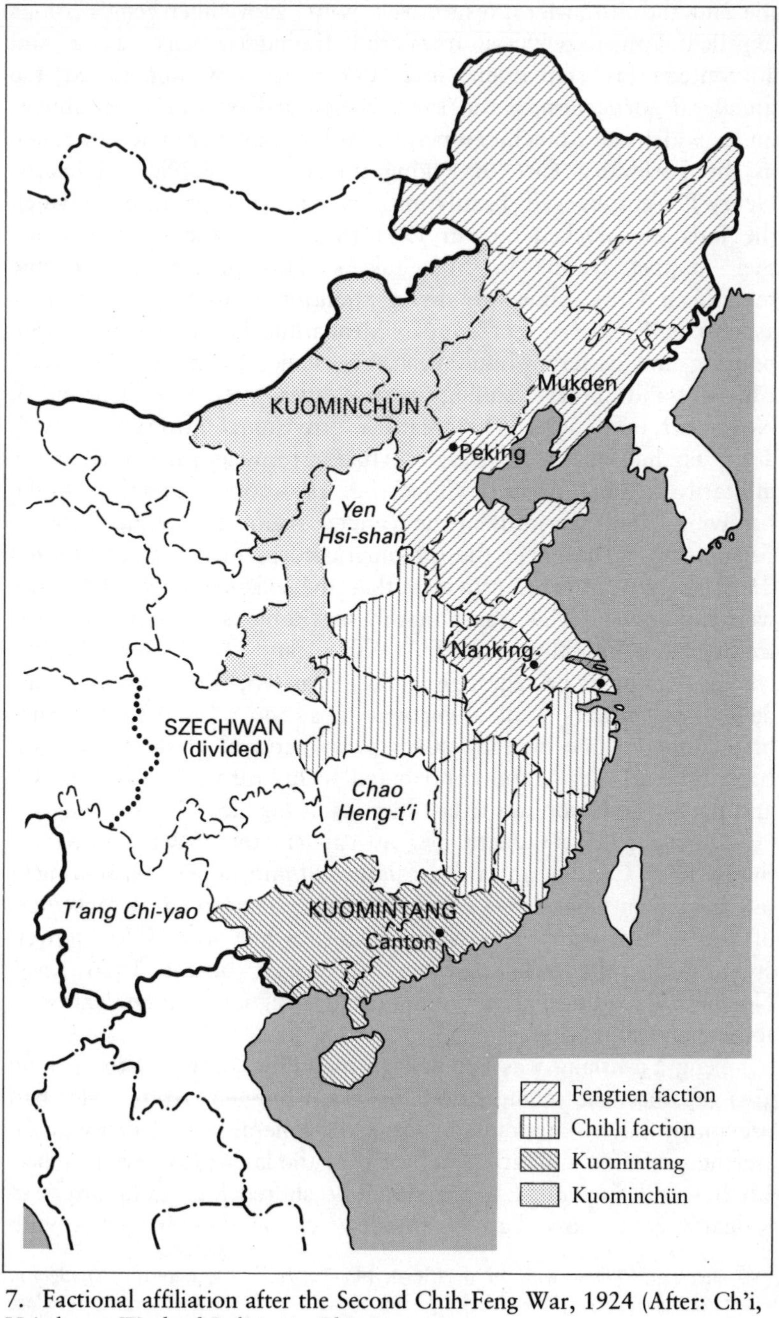

7. Factional affiliation after the Second Chih-Feng War, 1924 (After: Ch'i, Hsi-sheng, *Warlord Politics in China*)

the 2nd and 3rd armies, respectively. On 5 November Feng's troops expelled Emperor P'u-yi from the Forbidden City. Feng had advocated this step ever since 1917; he now announced the unilateral abrogation of the 1912 Treaty of Favourable Treatment, under which the Manchu emperor and his court continued to reside in the Forbidden City of Peking under the republic.[62] Emperor Henry P'u-yi thus went hastily into his exile in Tientsin, from which the Japanese plucked him in 1931 to serve as the figurehead for their puppet regime in Manchukuo. This posture of extreme republican virtue aimed to divert attention from the less savoury aspects of Feng's current course. Meanwhile Fengtien troops were pouring into eastern Chihli. Feng Yü-hsiang, Chang Tso-lin, Tuan Ch'i-jui and other leading personalities met in Tientsin in November, and agreed to create a provisional government with Tuan as chief executive. Despite Tuan's status as the leader of the militarily defunct Anhwei clique, he was more acceptable to the surviving Chihli warlords in the Yangtze region than either Feng or Chang. On 9 December the diplomatic corps in Peking recognized the Tuan government, provided that the existing unequal treaties were maintained. This was probably inevitable, since Japan was the leading imperialist power, and Chang and Tuan were Japan's leading Chinese protégés. For Sun Yat-sen, the fact that the democratic powers went along with this, and refused to recognize his Canton regime instead, was a great betrayal of their professed constitutional ideals, and contributed to his turn towards the CCP and the Soviet Union in the last months of his life.

During 1925 the death of Sun Yat-sen, the growing power of the KMT at Canton, and the escalation of anti-imperialist sentiment (all treated in Chapter 4) occupied centre stage for most observers of the China scene. The warlords meanwhile jostled for power, creating the alignment that was the target of the 1926 KMT Northern Expedition. Their complicated intrigues must be dealt with somewhat summarily.

Feng Yü-hsiang was not able to maintain control of the Peking area against the competition of the Fengtien Army. He had previously been appointed inspector-general of Northwestern Defence, in effect military governor over the later provinces of Jehol, Chahar and Suiyuan. Early in 1925 he shifted his headquarters to Kalgan. Feng now had a military clique of his own, with

62 Sheridan, *Chinese Warlord*, pp.136–8, 145–7. Reginald F. Johnston, *Twilight in the Forbidden City*, (New York, 1934), describes these years from a palace viewpoint.

subordinates controlling Honan, Shensi and Kansu. His armies grew in size and declined in quality, though Feng continued to interest himself in the training and discipline of the core of his army. Feng continued to profess sympathy for KMT aspirations, and accepted Russian assistance when it was offered beginning in April 1925. Both of these steps distanced himself from Chang Tso-lin; neither was permitted to compromise Feng's control of his troops and territory.[63]

Yen Hsi-shan continued to rule Shansi and play the balance of power game among the stronger warlords. In 1925 he capitalized on his good relations with Tuan Ch'i-jui, and he also maintained contacts with the Canton regime.

Chang Tso-lin was able to appoint Li Ching-lin as military governor of Chihli and Chang Tsung-ch'ang to the equivalent position in Shantung. As the growth of the labour movement led to unrest among factory workers in Tsingtao, Chang Tsung-ch'ang suppressed this vigorously. Strident anti-labour and anti-communist attitudes continued to be a trademark of the Fengtien leaders, as of those Chihli leaders who survived.[64] Chang Tsung-ch'ang also spearheaded the effort to destroy Chihli influence in the Yangtze Valley. By the summer of 1925 the Chihli warlord Ch'i Hsieh-yuan was out as military governor of Kiangsu, replaced by the familiar Anhwei clique figure Lu Yung-hsiang, who, however, was militarily dependent upon Fengtien. In August Lu was replaced by Yang Yü-t'ing, one of the leading Fengtien generals.

Yang's appointment portended an effort to extend Fengtien power to Chekiang and Fukien. In October the powerful Chihli clique warlord Sun Ch'uan-fang struck back, proclaiming himself commander-in-chief of the five provinces of Chekiang, Fukien, Anhwei, Kiangsi and Kiangsu. Sun defeated Yang, forcing him to evacuate Shanghai and then Nanking, and retire on Hsuchow. Chang Tsung-ch'ang and the other Fengtien leaders reconciled themselves to Sun Ch'uan-fang as a neighbour.

Meanwhile Wu P'ei-fu resurfaced in Hankow on 21 October. He succeeded in re-establishing his authority in Hupei, but for the time being had to accept that Honan remained under Feng Yü-hsiang's control. Wu was now a player again, however, and his relative position rose as a consequence of the rivalry between Feng and Chang Tso-lin. But Wu never regained the leadership of the

63 For Feng Yü-hsiang in the northwest, Sheridan, *Chinese Warlord*, pp.149–76.
64 cf. McCormack, *Chang Tso-lin*, pp.142–58.

now hopelessly ruptured Chihli clique, and meanwhile the First KMT–CCP United Front had transformed the appearance (if not the substance) of Chinese politics.[65]

65 McCormack, *Chang Tso-lin*, pp.159–62.

4 THE NORTHERN EXPEDITION, 1925–31

On the eve of the death of Sun Yat-sen, the idealistic revolutionary and founder of the Republic of China, his Nationalist Party (KMT) was reorganized and entered into a formal United Front with the Communist Party of China (CCP). At the newly founded Whampoa Military Academy near Canton a cadre of officers trained for a new party army, in principle animated by a devotion to the ideology of the party and thus not vulnerable to the betrayals that had been so important in the warlord wars. In 1926 the KMT–CCP combination carried out the Northern Expedition, resulting in the elimination of two major Chihli clique warlords (Sun Ch'uan-fang in the lower Yangtze region and Wu P'ei-fu in Hupei) and the confinement of Chang Tso-lin's Fengtien clique to Manchuria.

While the purpose of the northern expedition was the destruction of the power of the northern warlords, in fact the elimination of warlordism was more apparent than real. Model Governor Yen Hsi-shan in Shansi and Christian/Betraying General Feng Yü-hsiang in the northwest raised the Nationalist flag while manoeuvring with their usual skill to retain their regional power. The new Kwangsi clique led by Li Tsung-jen and Pai Ch'ung-hsi did the same in the south. For Chiang Kai-shek the communists posed a greater threat, and in 1927 he led the KMT right wing in a drastic attack on the CCP, in which most of the communists were killed and Chiang himself took over the Nationalist Party and the national government. Afterwards Chiang was able to eliminate the military power of both Feng Yü-hsiang and the Kwangsi clique, keep Yen Hsi-shan confined to Shansi, and win acknowledgement of his paramountcy from Chang Hsueh-liang, son and successor of Chang Tso-lin as head of the Fengtien militarists. Despite his later ineptitude as a commander-in-chief in the more narrowly military sense, Chiang Kai-shek in these years demonstrated a subtle mastery of the realities of Chinese politics in the unacknowledged or 'residual' warlord period that followed the Northern Expedition.

By coming to terms with so many of the northern warlords, the KMT had, in the opinion of many Chinese, betrayed its original principles and demonstrated its fundamental hypocrisy; demoralization and disenchantment with the national government set in almost immediately. The KMT–CCP split had driven the surviving communists into the countryside, where they demonstrated a surprising ability to organize rural discontents into effective guerrilla warfare. Finally there was the problem of Japan: a recognized Great Power estranged from the Anglo-Saxon victors of the First World War, feeling herself the main target of Chinese nationalism, and battered by the world depression. When Japan struck in 1931, the Manchurian Incident ended the prospect that the KMT could both complete the military unification of China and get on with national reconstruction.

THE CHINESE COMMUNIST PARTY AND THE FIRST UNITED FRONT

Chinese politics from the 1911 revolution to the Second Chih–Feng War in 1924 may be understood almost without reference to foreign powers or foreign ideas, as the above account (Chapters 2 and 3) demonstrates. This was not because of lack of Great Power interest, even though the endless speculation that certain warlords represented the interests of certain powers had little factual basis. Rather was it due to the fact that Yuan Shih-k'ai and his successors were both socially and diplomatically conservative, and took pains to assure foreign owners that their property would be respected and foreign officials that the unequal treaty system would be maintained. Abuses committed by soldiers were usually settled at a higher level.

The warlord wars were also fought without much reference to the Chinese intellectual community, despite that community's revulsion with Tuan Ch'i-jui in the May Fourth movement and despite the occasional adherence of certain intellectuals to certain warlords. Chinese intellectuals now generally accepted that it was impossible to reject Western civilization and culture entirely. This realization raised the greatest problem for Chinese culture since the rise of Neo-Confucianism, and Chinese intellectuals in the first two decades of the twentieth century therefore eagerly debated the nature and extent of the Chinese and Western contributions to the amalgamated culture that would have to arise. Eventually one of the warlords would conquer his rivals, and intellectuals needed to be ready then to advise him. Sun Yat-sen had a different perspective, derived essentially from a US model, but he lacked the stature as a Chinese intellectual to dominate the debate. Modernizing intellectuals who did have stature in traditional terms remained opponents of Sun. Liang Ch'i-ch'ao and K'ang Yu-wei, the principal surviving leaders of the 1898 reform movement, continued their pre-1911 rivalry with Sun into the 1920s. Liang Ch'i-ch'ao's Progressive Party (chin-pu-tang) generally opposed Sun's KMT and supported warlord governments whenever the Peking parliament was allowed to assemble. K'ang Yu-wei was somewhat of a laughing-stock after his association with the abortive Manchu restoration of 1917. After 1918, ironically like many Westerners in China, K'ang became convinced that Sun was a Soviet stooge, and spent much effort rallying educated opinion in support of the classically educated and poetry-writing General Wu P'ei-fu, in order to preserve Chinese culture by stopping Sun.[1] K'ang's efforts had little practical result. Many of the most significant intellectuals of this period confined themselves largely to aesthetic and cultural pursuits, broken by political protest, but without firm commitment to a particular warlord faction or political ideology. This withdrawal was itself part of the Confucian pattern that most of them (but not K'ang) now rejected on the conscious level. It was as though they expected a legitimate ruler to arise, without their efforts, around whom they could rally.

In fact intellectual issues were also issues of immediate practical import. In past periods of division, a warlord who beat his rivals could win over the intellectuals and thereby create political legitimacy for his rule by using the long-established Confucian Mandate of Heaven theory. Yuan Shih-k'ai's 1912–16 career at least proved that the old way was dead, but it remained the case that getting out of warlordism required a political ideology that could transcend warlordism. As a contemporary student of the problem notes:[2]

> The worst burden of regional militarism on China was that it was self-perpetuating, that it induced stagnation, that it could not fill the ideological vacuum left by the collapse of the old order. Soldiers could not provide a stable and prosperous

1 Jonathan D. Spence, *The Gate of Heavenly Peace: The Chinese and their Revolution, 1895–1980* (New York, 1981), passim, but especially pp.204–5.

2 Diana Lary, *Region and Nation: The Kwangsi Clique in Chinese Politics, 1925–1937* (Cambridge, UK 1974), p.13.

> administration for China, but they could prevent anyone else from doing so. Militarism had the strength to crush the development of any new political force which might unite China and give its people a workable administration. China had to wait for some military force to unite it before militarism could be crushed. . . . This had to be a militarism committed to some higher ideological goal. Most existing militarists, committed to the status quo, would go to great lengths to prevent this from developing.

Sun Yat-sen had come to realize this, hence the importance of military unification in his *Outline of National Reconstruction* (*Chien-kuo ta-kang*, 1924). But, lacking adequate military forces of his own, his position in Canton through 1923 remained uncertain and subject to the constraints described above.

In 1921 Ch'en Tu-hsiu – Dean of Letters at Peking University and long a famous and outspoken advocate of the radical transformation of Chinese society along modern and Western lines – and a small group of sympathizers including the youthful Mao Tse-tung met in Shanghai and founded the Chinese Communist Party. The May Fourth Movement had shown the disappointment of the Chinese intellectual community with the democratic powers that had ignored Chinese aspirations, while the new Soviet regime had (temporarily) renounced Russian rights under the unequal treaties. For Ch'en Tu-hsiu, founding the CCP meant that he could maintain his position as the fountainhead of advanced Western thinking in China. In military terms, he had outflanked Hu Shih – John Dewey's student and the leading spokesman in China for US-style progressive democracy – on the left.[3]

In the period of the Alliance Society, Sun Yat-sen had independently evolved many of the features of Leninist party organization (a small corps of professional revolutionaries supported by a larger body of dues-paying members, all obeying the party leader through a cellular organization). Communism used the same structure to serve an entirely different theory of history – whose pretensions to scientific status were taken more seriously than they would be today – according to which a Chinese Communist Party

3 Jonathan D. Spence, *The Search for Modern China* (New York, 1990), pp.300–3, summarizes a lot of earlier work on Chinese Marxism. Benjamin Schwartz, *Chinese Communism and the Rise of Mao* (Cambridge, 1958), remains the best analysis of the resonance between Communism and the earlier Confucian political tradition.

might be considered premature. Excited debates raged over whether Chinese society was feudal, but no one thought it bourgeois. As Ch'en, Li Ta-chao[4] and others explained Marxist doctrine and translated its scriptures, it seemed evident that the duty of Chinese communists was to cooperate with other progressive forces to carry out the bourgeois revolution (against Chinese warlords and foreign imperialists), whose success would begin the process of class differentiation objectively necessary for the eventual (if distant) triumph of the socialist revolution. They would do this by organizing the proletariat. A 1927 estimate credited China with about 1.5 million factory workers and 1.75 other industrial workers (miners, seamen, railway workers) out of a total population of over 300 million.[5] A small percentage, but factory workers lived in cities, physically if not socially close to intellectuals, and they lived in conditions of Dickensian squalor with real, exploitable grievances that were often aggravated by the foreign identity of the factory owners.

Communist achievements before and during the Northern Expedition were much less than their adversaries imagined, but these imaginings were exaggerated enough to have a historical importance of their own. By 1923 the Rice Riots in Japan and the red flags that fluttered briefly in Germany, Italy, Austria and Hungary had been suppressed, but Soviet Russia remained in frightening existence, and the real atrocities of the Russian Revolution lost none of their gruesomeness when related abroad by émigrés. Organized labour in many advanced countries, including Britain and Germany, remained loyal to socialist parties whose inspiration was Marxist, if not necessarily Leninist. Worldwide fears of communism translated themselves to China, where warlords, compradors and foreign devils all could see labour unrest and related political activity as leading directly to Bolshevization, whether or not China's peasant population was involved.

These factors helped to drive Sun Yat-sen toward the First United Front with the communists. Sun had received Japanese support on earlier occasions, and had derived most of his political theory from US sources. He hoped for recognition from either or both of these powers, but was disappointed. Maintaining the unequal treaty system required the fiction that China was a united

4 Maurice Meisner, *Li Ta-chao and the Origins of Chinese Marxism* (Cambridge, MA, 1967), is the major study of this important figure.

5 Harold R. Isaacs, *The Tragedy of the Chinese Revolution* (2nd edn, Stanford, 1961), p.33.

nation governed from Peking, which city was now held by Japan's clients (Fengtien clique leader Chang Tso-lin, with guest appearances from Anhwei clique founder Tuan Ch'i-jui) after their victory in the Second Chih–Feng War. Even before the war, at the Kuomintang Party Congress in January 1924, Sun had accepted the United Front, with communists joining the KMT as individuals. Chiang Kai-shek, Sun's military adviser and eventual successor, had visited Russia in the summer of 1923. Canton under the KMT became host during 1924 to numerous Russian advisers and agents, which aggravated left–right tensions within the party and led foreigners and warlords to regard the whole party as Red. In May 1924 Sun inaugurated the Whampoa Military Academy, whose curriculum aimed at developing an officer corps loyal to KMT principles and whose political commissar system was obviously of Russian origin. Chiang Kai-shek, by now Sun's most trusted military adviser, became its first superintendent.[6]

Sun's military position in 1923–4 rested on an unsteady coalition of small armies: militarily capable Yunnanese under Yang Hsi-min, who was less loyal to Sun than his predecessor Chu P'ei-te had been, a Kwangsi contingent under Liu Chen-huan, and less capable but politically more reliable Cantonese under Hsu Ch'ung-chih and Hunanese under T'an Yen-k'ai. Sun's authority was in fact confined to Canton and the central part of Kwangtung province, and strongly contested by Ch'en Chiung-ming in the eastern part. Sun failed in his attempt to launch a Northern Expedition in 1924. In the summer and autumn he contended with the Canton Merchants Association, who had formed an armed militia of their own and staged a protest strike in August when Sun's government tried to cut off their arms supplies. In October the Merchants Association attempted to seize Canton in collusion with Ch'en Chiung-ming, and Chiang Kai-shek personally led the Whampoa cadets to defeat and dissolve their militia.[7]

In November 1924 Sun left Canton, hoping to use the inter-warlord conferences in the aftermath of the Second Chih–Feng War to enhance the position of his regime. He travelled by way of Shanghai, Japan and Tientsin; by the time he reached Peking in

6 F.F. Liu, *A Military History of Modern China, 1924–1949* (Princeton, 1956), pp.3–24, and Li Chien-hung, *The Political History of China, 1840–1928* (English translation, Princeton, 1956), pp.436–58, both of which are pro-KMT sources.

7 Li, *Political History*, pp.458–66; Donald A. Jordan, *The Northern Expedition: China's National Revolution of 1926–1928* (Honolulu, 1976), pp.22–7.

December he was already ill. Sun Yat-sen died in Peking on 12 March 1925. He has been derided as a naive idealist by some, and there can be no doubt that the confidence he expressed in such characters as Yuan Shih-k'ai and Ch'en Chiung-ming was misplaced. Yet one should note that Sun kept his revolutionary organization going for a quarter of a century and that he was instrumental in bringing down the Manchu dynasty and later seized Canton on three occasions. Doing this required fund raising and other pragmatic skills, which most of his intellectual contemporaries lacked. He was also ahead of them in realizing that a political ideology, as opposed to a cultural agenda, was needed to turn the Chinese people from a 'sheet of loose sand' into a modern nation.

CHIANG KAI-SHEK AND THE WHAMPOA MILITARY CLIQUE

Sun Yat-sen's long-time associate Hu Han-min[8] succeeded to nominal authority at Canton, but his power was challenged by the continued existence of Ch'en Chiung-ming at Huichow and by T'ang Chi-yao in Yunnan assuming the title of deputy grand marshal that he had consistently refused to accept while Sun was alive. In fact Sun's military successor was Whampoa superintendent Chiang Kai-shek, whom Sun had also appointed Canton garrison commandant.

Chiang (1887–1975), from the Ningpo region of Chekiang, had attended both Paoting and the Japanese Military Academy before the 1911 revolution. In his early career he benefited from the patronage of Ch'en Ch'i-mei, whose murder at Yuan Shih-k'ai's instigation kept Chiang firmly in the anti-Yuan camp. After the May Fourth Movement, Chiang attached himself to Sun Yat-sen's organization. He served as an operations officer on Ch'en Chiung-ming's staff, but abandoned Ch'en when the latter turned against Sun. In these years he formed his long-enduring and still controversial ties with the Green Gang (ch'ing-pang), the controlling force of the Chinese underworld in Shanghai and the lower Yangtze Valley. By mid-1921 he had won Sun Yat-sen's confidence, and other assignments followed, including the 1923 trip to the Soviet

8 Howard L. Boorman, ed., *Biographical Dictionary of Republican China* (4 vols, New York, 1967–71) I, pp.159–66. Hu would later head the Canton opposition to Chiang Kai-shek's rule.

Union that prepared the way for the founding of the Whampoa Military Academy the following year.[9]

Whampoa was created to produce officers quickly, and the military education given there was a diluted form of the Japanese-derived curricula of the Yunnan and Paoting Military Academies, whose graduates, including Ch'en Ch'eng,[10] Chang Chih-chung[11] and Chiang Kai-shek himself, figured prominently among the military faculty. This explains the elements of the bushido mentality that found their way into the elite units of the KMT – defending untenable positions to the last man, attacking regardless of losses, obeying orders without question – as the leaders of the Whampoa clique had absorbed the values appropriate to Japanese lieutenants and captains, without the staff procedures and trained staff officers at higher levels that might have directed such spirits more usefully. Chiang himself remained very much a traditional Chinese, who adopted Tseng Kuo-fan – the nineteenth-century soldier-statesman, opponent of the Taiping rebellion, and founder of the militia armies – as his role model. He remained devoted to the idea of collective responsibility (lien-tso-fa), under which all the members of a unit were punished for the failure of any one of them. Of course, collective responsibility was bad for morale and individual initiative, but Chiang could never see the value of the latter in his years of power.

Sun Yat-sen called the first class of Whampoa graduates the Party Army (tang-chün), and it is difficult to quarrel with his insight that an army animated by some transcendental political loyalty was needed to carry out the military unification of China. This was to be the first of the three stages outlined in Sun's *Outline of National Reconstruction* (*Chien-kuo ta-kang*), followed by stages of political tutelage and full democracy. The adoption of the Soviet commander-commissar system followed logically from the First United Front. Chou En-lai, already a prominent communist, became chief political commissar of Whampoa, and the Russian advisers Michael Borodin[12] and 'General Galen' (V. K. Blykher, or Blücher,

9 More dust needs to settle before a satisfactory scholarly study of Chiang Kai-shek can be written. Boorman, *Biographical Dictionary*, I, pp.319–38, is now old, and most of the biographies cited there are relentlessly polemical. The often-cited Keiji Furuya *Chiang Kai-shek: His Life and Times* (New York, 1991), is essentially a compilation.

10 Boorman, *Biographical Dictionary*, I, pp.152–60.

11 Boorman, *Biographical Dictionary*, I, pp.41–6.

12 Dan Jacobs, *Borodin: Stalin's Man in China* (Cambridge, 1981), is the modern study of this interesting figure.

later one of the first five Marshals of the Soviet Union) became very visible at Canton. The prominence of CCP organizers in the Hong Kong strike in the summer of 1925 convinced both foreigners and right-wing KMT members that Sun's movement had been taken over by its communist wing.

Meanwhile, Ch'en Chiung-ming had strengthened his power in eastern Kwangtung after Sun's departure for Peking, and Sun's illness and death gave him an opportunity to seize Canton. In collusion with Yunnan warlord T'ang Chi-yao, he suborned Yang Hsi-min and Liu Chen-huan, whose Yunnan and Kwangsi troops remained inactive as Ch'en moved on Canton in January and February 1925. The Cantonese and Hunanese contingents of the KMT army remained loyal, but the crisis was severe enough to commit the first two Whampoa classes immediately to battle. Their enthusiasm spread to the other units, and KMT forces proceeded to conquer Swatow and the other major places in eastern Kwangtung. Documents found at Hsingning positively incriminated Yang and Liu, whose forces were overwhelmed and disbanded on 13 June. Ch'en remained a threat from his main stronghold at Huichow, but a second Eastern Expedition in October resulted in the siege and capture of Huichow and Ch'en's flight to a powerless exile in Hong Kong. These events solidified Chiang Kai-shek's connection with the Whampoa clique, whose members henceforth were forgiven their other failings because of their presumed loyalty to Chiang personally and to the ideals of the KMT.[13]

While these events were going on, the so-called New Kwangsi clique built around Li Tsung-jen, Pai Ch'ung-hsi and Huang Shao-hsiung took control of Kwangsi. Shen Hung-ying, the leading Kwangsi militarist and an opponent of Sun Yat-sen, rather unwisely allied himself with these three to oppose a comeback attempt of the old Kwangsi leader Lu Jung-t'ing. After dumping Shen, the Kwangsi leaders fought off T'ang Chi-yao's attempt to impose Liu Chen-huan as governor. By mid-July the Yunnan troops had withdrawn from the province. The Li–Pai–Huang alliance endured with a firmness unusual in Chinese politics. Usually Huang governed the province while Li and Pai led Kwangsi troops in alliance with the KMT. Despite Kwangsi's poverty, relatively honest administration (including opium transit taxes) permitted Kwangsi to field an impressive army. However, the genuine loyalty of the Kwangsi

13 Li, *Political History*, pp.495–6; Jordan, *Northern Expedition*, pp.12, 29–30.

leaders to Sun Yat-sen did not transfer to Chiang Kai-shek.[14]

On 1 July 1925 the KMT proclaimed a national government at Canton. A sixteen-member political committee included Wang Ching-wei as chairman and Liao Chung-k'ai as Minister of Finance, representing the left wing of the party, and Hsu Ch'ung-chih as Minister of War and Hu Han-min as Communications Minister representing the right. Despite the effort at balance, the KMT regime seemed too radical to both Westerners and Chinese conservatives. Borodin, then nicknamed 'Emperor of Canton',[15] and Galen were very visible, and Chou En-lai's position as commissar of Whampoa obscured the extent to which Chiang Kai-shek was turning the academy into his personal instrument. In the military reorganization accompanying the proclamation of the national government, the Whampoa-dominated Party Army was designated the 1st Army, while T'an Yen-k'ai's 15,000 Hunanese became the 2nd and Chu P'ei-te's Yunnanese the 3rd. The 4th Army was a force of Cantonese under Li Chi-shen, then invading Fukien, while the 5th Army consisted of Fukienese in Kwangtung under Li Fu-lin. In November another force of Hunanese under Ch'eng Ch'ien became the 6th Army, and in February 1926 the 30,000 troops of the new Kwangsi clique were designated the 7th Army. While all of these units had demonstrated loyalty to KMT ideals, they varied in size and in their levels of training and readiness, and were – like the warlord armies they opposed – divided by their provincial origins and loyalties to different commanders.[16]

Liao Chung-k'ai had become the principal spokesman for Sun Yat-sen's policies of cooperation with the Russians and Chinese communists. When he was gunned down on 20 August, suspicion naturally fell on the KMT right, and in the end both Hu Han-min and Hsu Ch'ung-chih were implicated and had to leave Canton. Chiang Kai-shek rose to the position of leadership in the KMT military vacated by Hsu. Chiang, then called 'the Red general' by foreigners,[17] remained outwardly cordial to the Russian advisers. His prestige and Whampoa's rose with the final suppression of Ch'en Chiung-ming in October, and he associated himself with Sun Yat-sen's legacy by repeatedly calling for a Northern Expedition

14 Summarized from Lary, *Region and Nation*; also Li, *Political History*, pp.496–8, and Donald S. Sutton, *Provincial Militarism and the Chinese Republic: The Yunnan Army, 1905–1925* (Ann Arbor, 1980), pp.282–9.

15 Liu, *Military History*, p.21.

16 Li, *Political History*, pp.498–500; Jordan, *Northern Expedition*, pp.22–7.

17 Jordan, *Northern Expedition*, p.33.

against the warlords. Meanwhile, he retained his Shanghai contacts, which permitted him to negotiate and propose a deal with Chihli clique warlord Sun Ch'uan-fang, his classmate from the Japanese military academy, who was now consolidating his rule over the five provinces of Kiangsu, Anhwei, Kiangsi, Chekiang and Fukien. As Chiang rose within the KMT military, the departure of KMT conservatives tilted the civil government at Canton to the left.[18]

In November 1925 the right-wing members of the KMT Central Executive Committee met in the presence of Sun Yat-sen's coffin at the Western Hills (Hsi-shan) near Peking, and passed resolutions calling for the end of the party's alliance with the CCP and the Russians. Wang Ching-wei – after Liao's murder the unchallenged leader of the KMT left – declared these resolutions null and void, and called a counter-meeting at Canton in January 1926. The Western Hills faction then set up an alternative party organization at Shanghai. Meanwhile at Canton an undercover struggle for the KMT's destiny continued. Chiang Kai-shek continued to call for a Northern Expedition, while the KMT left, CCP, and Russian advisers advocated greater social revolution at Canton and support for the continuing Canton strike. Chiang now was formally Canton garrison commander and inspector-general of the National Revolutionary Army (NRA) for the preparation of the Northern Expedition. His authority was threatened by the growth of a hierarchy of communist political commissars in the separate armies of the NRA and in the navy. During February 1926 Chiang on several occasions approached Wang Ching-wei and demanded the removal of the Russian advisers, whom he accused of inciting mutiny among his subordinates.[19]

In March a combination of left-wing and Russian pressures placed a communist, Li Chih-lung, in command of the Canton navy. Li started cracking down on the navy's smuggling activities and replacing ship captains with communists. On 18 March the fleet flagship, the gunboat *Chung-shan*, moved without Chiang's knowledge or approval from Canton to Whampoa. Chiang later alleged a plot to kidnap him and remove him to Vladivostok. Chiang's explanations have not won universal acceptance, but his fears seem to have been genuine; in the highly charged atmosphere of the time a coup from either left or right was expected. Chiang ordered the *Chung-shan* back to Canton, and she moored in front

18 Li, *Political History*, pp.500–3; Jordan, *Northern Expedition*, pp.28–33.
19 Jordan, *Northern Expedition*, pp.34–9.

of the officer's club the next day, her crew apparently at general quarters.[20] At 4:00 a.m. on 21 March Chiang placed Canton under martial law, and arrested all known communists holding positions of authority. The KMT Political Council held a few days later approved Chiang's actions. Those arrested were removed from their positions and left Canton. Chiang carefully explained that this action was taken against uncooperative individuals, and was not a repudiation of the KMT–CCP alliance as such.[21]

Wang Ching-wei left Canton in May. On 4 June Chiang was chosen as commander-in-chief of the Northern Expedition, whose formal order to begin was issued on 1 July. Chiang's authority, and the generally rightward tilt of the KMT, might still be challenged by the Canton–Hong Kong strike organization and the communist-dominated peasants of eastern Kwangtung (the latter were organized according to the ideas of P'eng P'ai, a radical theorist felt by some to be the source of Mao Tse-tung's ideas on rural revolution,[22] who had been supported by Ch'en Chiung-ming). The Northern Expedition, launched from an uncertain base, was a gamble at long odds.[23]

THE NORTHERN WARLORDS ON THE EVE OF THE NORTHERN EXPEDITION

As noted in Chapter 3, by 1925 five principal warlord regimes had emerged in Central and North China, of which the Fengtien clique was the strongest and Yen Hsi-shan's the most territorially compact. The Chihli militarists Wu P'ei-fu and Sun Ch'uan-fang between them controlled the Yangtze Valley east of Szechwan and Feng Yü-hsiang controlled the northwest. This balance was shaken but not altered by the Kuo Sung-ling affair and the defeat of Feng Yü-hsiang that followed.

By September 1925 the Fengtien clique mustered some 350,000 soldiers,[24] nearly double its strength before the Second Chih–Feng

20 Bruce Swanson, *Eighth Voyage of the Dragon: A History of China's Quest for Seapower* (Annapolis, 1982), pp.156–7.

21 Jordan, *Northern Expedition*, pp.39–40.

22 Roy Hofheinz, *The Broken Wave: The Chinese Communist Peasant Movement, 1922–1928* (Cambridge, MA, 1977), develops this argument at length.

23 Jordan, *Northern Expedition*, pp.41–64, explains the complicated internal politics of this period.

24 Gavan McCormack, *Chang Tso-lin in Northeast China, 1911–1928: China, Japan and the Manchurian Idea* (Stanford, 1977), p.147.

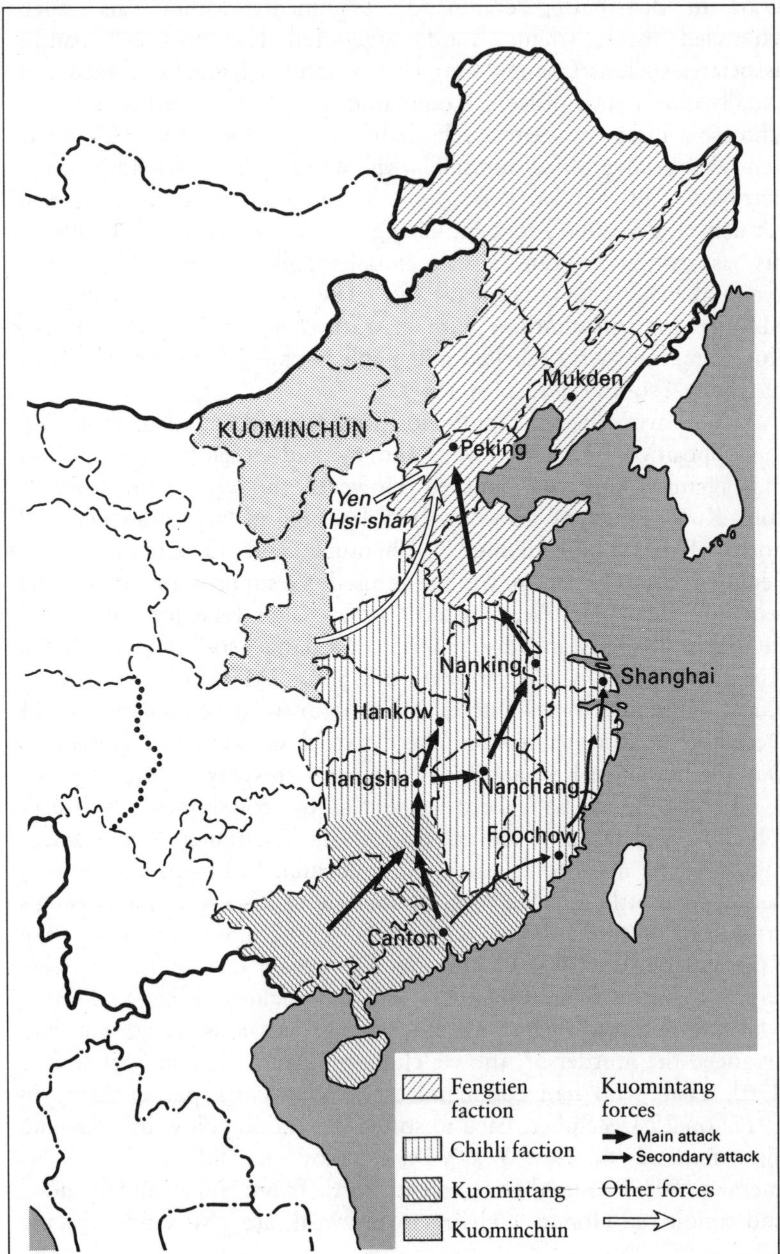

8. The Northern Expedition, 1926–8 (After: Ch'i, Hsi-sheng, *Warlord Politics in China*)

War. In distributing command assignments within this much expanded force, Chang Tso-lin favoured both his old bandit associates such as Chang Tsung-ch'ang and his Japanese-trained and usually junior staff officers. Commanders who were graduates of the Chinese military academies felt slighted. As of October 1925, while Feng Yü-hsiang allied himself with Wu P'ei-fu – whom he had betrayed and almost destroyed the previous year – and Sun Ch'uan-fang against Fengtien, Chang Tso-lin concentrated 70,000 of his best troops between Tientsin and Shanhaikuan under his son and eventual heir Chang Hsueh-liang. The latter then returned to Mukden for consultations with his father, leaving the army under Kuo Sung-ling, who rebelled and publicly called for the resignation of Chang Tso-lin on 22 November.

Kuo's army moved rapidly northeast toward Mukden, shredding the opposition along the way, and by mid-December it appeared that Chang Tso-lin was finished. However, the weather turned very cold, Kuo's reluctant troops started deserting in large numbers, and both Chang Tsung-ch'ang in Shantung and Li Ching-lin, the Fengtien commander in Chihli, refused to support or supply the rebellion. The Japanese, concluding that Kuo's rebellion threatened their position in Manchuria, supported Chang Tso-lin and excluded Kuo's troops from the area of the South Manchurian Railway. Kuo's dwindling forces entered Hsinmintun west of Mukden on 21 December and were crushed there two days later. On Christmas Day the bodies of Kuo and his wife were on display in Mukden.[25]

Li Ching-lin had been expected to collaborate in Kuo's rebellion, and when he did not do so Feng Yü-hsiang moved against him with the main force of the Kuominchün. Li fought tenaciously, perhaps to settle any lingering doubts about his loyalty, and Feng's army took until 23 December to expel him from Tientsin. By then Kuo was out and Wu P'ei-fu and the revived Chang Tso-lin were happy to settle their differences and turn against Feng Yü-hsiang, who had betrayed them both on previous occasions. Feng, who had arranged the murder of Anhwei clique eminence Hsu Shu-cheng (the 'Little Hsu' who had commanded the War Participation Army in 1917) on 29 December, tried to soften the coming blow by resigning his commands on New Year's Day, a ploy that did not deceive his enemies. Wu P'ei-fu then marched north from Hupei and invaded and conquered Honan.[26] His relatively weak army was aided by the

25 McCormack, *Chang Tso-lin* pp.146–52, 182–3.

26 McCormack, *Chang Tso-lin*, pp.159–67; James E. Sheridan, *Chinese Warlord: The Career of Feng Yü-hsiang* (Stanford, 1966), pp.185–9.

Red Spears, an organization of peasants against warlord depredation, foreign influence, alcohol and opium. Though called bandits in the warlord-derived sources, the Red Spears seem to have been a spontaneous peasant mobilization, without the leadership of the large landowners, against the kind of misrule represented by Yueh Wei-chün, the representative of Feng Yü-hsiang and Kuominchün commander in Honan.[27]

In Chihli Feng's subordinate Lu Chung-lin faced an offensive from Li Ching-lin and Chang Tsung-ch'ang in Shantung and the main Fengtien Army in Manchuria. Li invaded in February 1926. After resisting for several weeks, Lu Chung-lin skilfully evacuated his 100,000-man army from Tientsin on 21 March. He held Peking for another month against enemies who now included Wu P'ei-fu, coming north from Honan. The arrest of Tuan Ch'i-jui and release of Ts'ao K'un on 9 April failed to sow the expected dissension between Wu P'ei-fu and Chang Tso-lin. On 16 April Lu evacuated Peking, again with a skill that excited comment, and retreated to Nankow Pass about thirty miles northwest of Peking, where about 90,000 Kuominchün troops resisted 450,000 opponents until 16 August. By then Shansi warlord Yen Hsi-shan had turned against the Kuominchün, and their evacuation was not as successful. Chahar fell to Chang Tso-lin's troops moving northwest from Peking and Suiyuan fell to Yen Hsi-shan's troops moving north from Shansi. The memory of the long defence of Nankow sustained the morale of the Kuominchün as it retreated west into Kansu.[28]

While the main Kuominchün held Nankow, other units had consolidated Feng's authority over Kansu, which previously had been held by a number of weak warlords whose areas of control were affected by the religious divisions in the province. Feng meanwhile took the trip to Russia that he had announced at the time of his 'resignation'. When he returned from Russia in August, he gave expression to numerous left-wing opinions that certainly added to the general confusion. He reorganized and re-established control over his army, winning back Han Fu-chü and Shih Yu-san, two of his leading generals who had temporarily defected to Yen Hsi-shan. Feng's next goal was to recover his position in Shensi, where only Sian held out for him; it had been under siege since April 1926 by Liu Chen-hua, the previous warlord of Shensi, whose forces were augmented by Red Spears from Honan. As the enemy of

27 Sheridan, *Chinese Warlord*, p.91, for discussion of the Red Spears.

28 Sheridan, *Chinese Warlord*, pp.188–91; McCormack, *Chang Tso-lin*, pp.204–8.

all the other northern warlords, and as the possessor of advanced ideas, Feng was well placed to make a deal with the KMT, and negotiations were under way as the Northern Expedition opened.[29]

THE NORTHERN EXPEDITION IN HUNAN AND KIANGSI

Both Wu P'ei-fu at Wuhan and Sun Ch'uan-fang at Nanking were Chihli faction warlords, but Sun was not a client of Wu; personal relations between the two were not good and cooperation was virtually nonexistent. Their long-term ability to hold out against Chang Tso-lin – whose Manchuria-based Fengtien clique, in control of Peking and the 'national' government, was clearly the strongest military group in China after 1924 – meant consolidating their authority in the Yangtze provinces they had seized in October 1925. Neither succeeded fully, as both were opposed by local elites with military connections. Sun Ch'uan-fang tried, clumsily, to publicize his idea of a five province (Kiangsu, Anhwei, Kiangsi, Fukien and Chekiang) union. This nebulous concept failed to override existing provincial loyalties, and Sun did not control the area long enough to persuade or intimidate the Chinese business class in the major treaty ports of these provinces to support him wholeheartedly. Long Anhwei clique rule in Fukien and Chekiang, and the presence of the naval clique – often aligned with the KMT – in Fukien complicated the picture for Sun Ch'uan-fang. Nevertheless the wealth of the five provinces permitted Sun to expand his army rapidly, and he put up a more sustained resistance than Wu. However, the KMT Northern Expedition struck both Sun and Wu before they were ready. National Revolutionary Army commander-in-chief Chiang Kai-shek attacked Wu P'ei-fu's forces in Hunan first, avoiding hostilities with Sun Ch'uan-fang until Hunan was conquered.

As previously, the axis of Wu P'ei-fu's power was the sector of the Peking–Hankow railway line in Honan and Hupei. Wu's urban base was the Wuhan city complex in Hupei which included Hankow, the second most important (after Shanghai) treaty port in China. His main fear was that Christian General Feng Yü-hsiang, his betrayer in 1924, would come east from Shensi (as he did in fact in 1927) to seize the railway junction at Chengchow and conquer Honan. The Red Spear peasant movement in Honan, one of Mao Tse-tung's models for the organization of peasant military power,

29 Sheridan, *Chinese Warlord*, pp.191–209.

hated Feng Yü-hsiang and the Kuominchün, and therefore ended up helping Wu P'ei-fu to maintain his hold on the province.

Between Hupei and Kwangtung lay the province of Hunan. Nativist sentiment was strong there, the movement for federal government had originated there, and the province had rebuffed Wu P'ei-fu's previous efforts to control it. However, Hunan continued to be vulnerable due to its internal political divisions. Governor Chao Heng-t'i[30] had joined forces with Wu P'ei-fu as the best defence against both the KMT and Sun Ch'uan-fang, but many Hunanese feared that dealing with Wu would lead to rule from outside the province. T'ang Sheng-chih, commander of the largest of the four divisions of the Hunan Army, resented Chao's patronage policies, and was negotiating secretly with the KMT, even though his father was a member of Chao's Cabinet. Hunan was also the home of a widespread and politically articulate peasant movement that could be exploited in opposition to warlord rule, as noted by Hunan native Mao Tse-tung, who found in the Hunan peasant movement the clearest model for his emerging concept of a rural and peasant-based revolutionary strategy. Mao's analysis[31] noted the articulate class nature of peasant opposition to the landlords, whose class provided the officer corps of the Hunan armies. In other words, the peasant movement might oppose warlordism of extraprovincial origins but it also was an obstacle to the provincial elite's desire for autonomy. Also, complicating the picture further, Hunan expatriaties were strongly represented in the KMT, in the form of T'an Yen-k'ai's 2nd Army of the NRA.

In February 1926 T'ang Sheng-chih rebelled against Wu P'ei-fu and Chao Heng-t'i, captured Changsha and temporarily installed himself as acting governor. Wu was involved in the war against Feng Yü-hsiang in North China until April, after which he struck back hard, driving T'ang in defeat into the southern part of the province. On 2 June T'ang accepted from Chiang Kai-shek the title of commander of the 8th Army of the NRA, whose 4th and 7th armies then entered Hunan in force. This was the beginning of the Northern Expedition against the northern warlords, long argued for and longed for in KMT circles, and the beginning of the process of military unification called for in Sun Yat-sen's political theory. By

30 Boorman, *Biographical Dictionary*, I, pp.143–4.

31 The often-cited 'Report of an investigation into the peasant movement in Hunan', in Mao Tse-tung, *Selected Works of Mao Tse-tung* (4 vols, Peking, 1961–5), I, pp.23–59.

accepting T'ang as front commander and as Hunan governor, the KMT had coopted provincial sentiment, and recruits and coolies flocked to their armies.[32]

Wu P'ei-fu's main forces were still north of the Yangtze, and his men in Hunan were holding the line of the Lien and Lu rivers south of Changsha. This position started to crumble on 5 July and collapsed totally on the 10th. T'ang Sheng-chih entered Changsha the next day and began to set up a provincial government. In this phase the sound money of the Canton government, and the KMT policy of paying for supplies and coolies, rather than requisitioning them, kept recruits coming and supplies moving. By mid-August there were over 100,000 KMT troops in Hunan. Chiang Kai-shek ordered the crossing of the Milo river line and a rapid advance to Wuhan, before Sun Ch'uan-fang could make up his mind to go to Wu P'ei-fu's assistance.

The 4th and 6th armies crossed the Milo on 17 August and advanced to besiege Yochow, the port from which Wu's small navy operated on the Tungting Lake, which fell on the 22nd. Railway workers sympathetic to the KMT–CCP cause effectively sabotaged the evacuation of Wu's troops from Yochow to Wuhan, but Wu's navy controlled the Yangtze in that vicinity.

The 4th and 7th armies now led the advance toward Wuchang along the railway line, which ran like an elevated isthmus through a low-lying country of lakes and flooded rice paddies and thus should have been easily defensible. Spearheaded by Chang Fa-k'uei's 12th Division, afterwards called the 'Ironsides' for its performance in these battles, the 4th Army broke through Tingszu Bridge on 26 August. Two days later it ran into Wu P'ei-fu himself further north at Hosheng Bridge. Wu's recent setbacks had been due to betrayal and had not diminished his reputation as a battlefield general, and he had brought along his Big Sword Corps for the summary beheading of subordinates considered cowardly. On 29 August he launched a frontal assault that was cut to pieces by well-aimed rifle fire and artillery support. This defeat, which demonstrated the relatively good military qualities of the NRA, had decisive consequences. Wu retreated the following day, breaching dikes to slow the enemy advance. He left 10,000 men in Wuchang, but took the bulk of his army across the Yangtze River, dividing them to defend the arsenal town of Hanyang and the commercial metropolis of Hankow, both of which were vital to his continued influence.

32 Jordan, *Northern Expedition*, pp.68–74.

Showing his desperation, he invited Sun Ch'uan-fang to enter his territory to fight the NRA.

Weakly supplied with artillery, Ch'en Ming-shu's 4th Army was unable to take Wuchang by assault, and the city held out another month. However, despite Wu's fleet patrolling off Hankow, other NRA units crossed the Yangtze in force upstream and besieged Hanyang, which fell quickly due to the defection of Wu's garrison commander. Before the NRA could cut the Peking–Hankow railway line, Wu P'ei-fu evacuated Hankow and prepared for a last stand in the hills along the Hupei–Honan border.[33] Wu was finally finished as a political-military force, just as Sun Ch'uan-fang, whose stance had been ambiguous enough to be considered pro-KMT in some rumours, decided to move against the Northern Expedition.

Sun, from Shantung, was part of the Chihli faction but was not close to Wu P'ei-fu and had profited from Wu's fall. His vacillation at the start of the Northern Expedition meant that he now faced an invasion of Kiangsi from both the west and the south, where his garrison commander at Kanhsien promptly defected, taking with him the southern half of the province. Sun's army, by rumour some 200,000 men, was poorly integrated and mostly not in Kiangsi. But once he decided to move Sun acted decisively, coming in person with his best troops to secure the Nanchang area. A large-scale roundup and execution of students, teachers, KMT and union members, and in general anyone with short hair followed; Sun and his fellow northern warlords were appealing to the imperialist powers whose gunboats sailed the Yangtze by highlighting the radical and communist affinities of the KMT. Chiang Kai-shek in response demanded and received the prompt settlement of the Canton–Hong Kong strike. Many of the strikers left to join the NRA.

Sun's forces advanced west from Nanchang, attempting to drive the NRA back into Hunan and to relieve Wu P'ei-fu's besieged garrison at Wuchang. The relief effort failed, and on 3 October the NRA 7th Army took Tean, cutting the railway line between Nanchang and Kiukiang on the Yangtze. Sun's forces soon retook the town, but meanwhile Wuchang surrendered on 10 October. In the next few days Sun crushed the rebellion of civil governor Hsia Ch'ao of Chekiang. Hsia had mobilized Chekiang provincial sentiment against Sun's northern officers and troops, but the latter easily dispersed the ill-trained police and local levies Hsia had raised.

33 For the Hunan–Hupei campaign, Jordan, *Northern Expedition*, pp.75–82.

In late October and early November the Kiangsi campaign was a bitter contest along the Kiukiang–Nanchang line. Chiang threw in every available man including the fourth class of Whampoa cadets, graduated in October. The decisive blow was a frontal assault on Tean that took the town, this time for good, in early November. The Yangtze River ports of Kiukiang and Hukou soon afterwards fell. Sun's troops at Nanchang were now demoralized and fearful of being cut off. They began to evacuate, and the NRA took the city on 9 November.

The Kiangsi campaign is the high water mark of Chiang Kai-shek's career as a military commander and certainly was decisive for the success of the Northern Expedition. Chiang correctly identified Tean, whose capture cut off the Kiangsi provincial capital of Nanchang from rail access to the Yangtze, as the key to the campaign and spent lives to take it – some 20,000 casualties in that phase of the campaign alone, and some 100,000 in the rest of the Kiangsi campaign.[34] The numbers are small in terms of the Chinese population, but represented the young elite of the KMT military system. Chiang's insistence on will and determination and his willingness to spend life won victory here, but later led to repeated disasters against the equally determined and much more professionally commanded Imperial Japanese Army.

THE NORTHERN EXPEDITION IN FUKIEN AND SHANGHAI

As the launch of the main Northern Expedition into Hunan was being prepared in the summer of 1926, Ho Ying-ch'in (one of Chiang Kai-shek's closest military associates and his Minister of War during the Second World War)[35] with the NRA 1st Army (the elite of the KMT army, with the largest concentration of Whampoa graduates among its officers) was stationed at Swatow against the possibility of an invasion by Sun Ch'uan-fang's commander in Fukien, Chou Ying-jen. Chou invaded in September; Ho stopped him before he reached Swatow, and then launched a counter-invasion through the hilly back country of Fukien.

Ho was aided politically by the good credit and good reputation that the KMT government had at that time, by defections among Chou's subordinates, and by the success of KMT political workers

34 For the Kiangsi campaign, Jordan, *Northern Expedition*, pp.83–92.
35 Boorman, *Biographical Dictionary*, II, pp.79–84.

in exploiting the resentment of Kwangtung and Fukien natives against 'foreign' (extraprovincial) militarist exploitation. The 1st Army broke into Fukien through the Sungkou Pass on 13 October, and grew swiftly through local recruitment. By the end of November all of Fukien south of the Min River, including Amoy, Changchow and Chuanchow, was in KMT hands. Foochow surrendered on 9 December, and Chou evacuated Fukien with only 2,000 of an army originally numbering 60,000, most of whom had defected.[36]

Meanwhile Sun Ch'uan-fang had gone to Tientsin to beg for help from the Fengtien clique leaders, the diminutive Marshal Chang Tso-lin and the physically imposing Dog Meat General Chang Tsung-ch'ang, of whom the latter was now in control of Shantung. The three warlords agreed to recognize Chang Tso-lin as commander-in-chief of the Ankuochün (National Pacification Army), to extend aid to Wu P'ei-fu whether he wanted it or not, and to move a 60,000-man army built around Chang Tsung-ch'ang's best units into the Shanghai area. Chang's army included White Russian cavalry formations as well as artillery carried on armoured trains; the Shantung troops, considered the most predatory in all of warlord China, would be paid for, reluctantly, by Sun from the resources of Shanghai. The move of Chang's army, which paid in worthless Shantung scrip for items requisitioned, created apprehensions and pro-KMT sentiment in the Yangtze Valley. At the same time, as the area under KMT rule grew, red flags waved and communist organizations spread behind the lines; fear of communism bound the northern warlords together to a limited extent, and anti-communist propaganda helped in the struggle for foreign recognition. For Chiang Kai-shek and the NRA field commanders, the wave of strikes and agitations that broke out again in November 1926 was hindering the military effort; a reaction from the KMT right was to be expected.

Late in October, Sun Ch'uan-fang reconstructed his regime in Chekiang by transferring thereto two divisions commanded by Chekiang men: Chou Feng-ch'i, who had been peripherally involved in Hsia Ch'ao's unsuccessful rebellion, and Ch'en Yi (not the future communist marshal and foreign minister). In December both defected to the KMT, becoming respectively commanders of the 26th and 19th armies of the NRA. In other words, in Chekiang as in Fukien – both provinces with long histories of rule by Anhwei clique warlords, whose local militarists had little attachment to Sun

36 Jordan, *Northern Expedition*, pp.93–6.

Ch'uan-fang – the Northern Expedition led its enemies to join the NRA en masse. While this snowballing effect contributed to the rapid success of the Northern Expedition, the instant transformation of unreconstructed warlords into NRA generals diluted the political quality of the new KMT government. When the communists faced similar problems at the close of the 1946–9 civil war, they were careful to reorganize surrendered troops under politically reliable officers. Sun, whose rear areas were now secured in a sense by the arrival of Chang Tsung-ch'ang's army, sent four reliable divisions under Meng Ch'ao-yueh to retake Chekiang. Meng captured Ch'en Yi and scattered his troops, but Chou Feng-ch'i held out at Chuhsien in the hilly southwestern part of the province.

Chiang Kai-shek then appointed Pai Ch'ung-hsi, with Li Tsung-jen the outstanding field commander of the new Kwangsi military clique, to the overall command of the NRA campaign in Chekiang. Pai relieved Chuhsien and then advanced straight down the Chientang River toward Hangchow, defeating Meng Ch'ao-yueh in a series of battles. On 17 February 1927 Meng's army evacuated Hangchow without a struggle and retired, looting as it went, to Kiangsu. Chou Feng-ch'i became provincial chairman for the KMT, while 1st NRA commander Ho Ying-ch'in concentrated the troops of the East Route Army of the NRA around Chiahsing, in preparation for an advance north into Kiangsu.[37]

By this time the civil government of the KMT had moved to Wuhan, where it had fallen more under the influence of Russian adviser Michael Borodin, the CCP and the KMT left. Foreign refugees from regions occupied by the NRA had congregated in Shanghai, where they spread atrocity stories, many of them true, regarding communist activities. On 19 February the CCP-dominated National General Labour Union called a general strike at Shanghai, a rare instance of CCP organizations coming out into the open before the physical conquest of a city by the NRA. This played into Sun Ch'uan-fang's hands; his sword-wielding executioners decapitated several hundred of the strike's leaders. Given the hostility to this radicalism among the established imperialist powers, there was reason to fear that a move on Shanghai by the NRA might provoke the unified opposition of the foreign powers using their armed forces.[38]

37 For the Fukien–Chekiang campaign, Jordan, *Northern Expedition*, pp.96–105.

38 Jordan, *Northern Expedition*, pp.106–10. Compare the older accounts in Liu, *Military History*, pp.36–40, and Isaacs, *Tragedy*, pp.111–29.

Chiang Kai-shek was already an enemy of the left, and had strongly opposed strike activities during the Northern Expedition. He was also complaining to the Wuhan government about their dilatory payments to his troops. He now faced a carefully orchestrated campaign of rumour and innuendo, supported by public speeches and mass meetings, accusing him of collusion with imperialists and warlords. The goal was to replace him as commander-in-chief with Hunan militarist T'ang Sheng-chih, presumed to be more controllable by the left. Hunan was one of several provinces (Yunnan, Kwangsi, Szechwan and Shansi being others) in which local militarists had family and other connections with local landlords and other elite class elements. This had led to a strong elite commitment to provincial autonomy, but T'ang was far from being a revolutionary and in fact felt threatened by the Hunan peasant movement so much admired by Mao Tse-tung. Belief in the revolutionary sentiments of T'ang Sheng-chih (and of Christian General Feng Yü-hsiang in his post-Moscow red phase) provided what humour there was in China in 1927. T'ang was supposed to rally an army built around the troops of Chang Fa-k'uei (whose 12th or Ironsides Division had earned its name in the recent conquest of Wuchang), Ch'en Ming-shu (4th NRA of Cantonese troops), Chu P'ei-te (3rd NRA of Yunnanese troops), and Li Tsung-jen (7th NRA of the New Kwangsi clique). All of these formations had participated in the Hunan–Hupei phase of the Northern Expedition and all were composed of non-Hunanese troops who had no particular reason to follow Hunan general T'ang Sheng-chih.[39]

Chiang's response was to remain physically distant from Wuhan, to invoke the memory of Sun Yat-sen, and to continue the campaign against the Shanghai area. He secured the defection of Ch'en T'iao-yuan, Sun Ch'uan-fang's commander of Anhwei province, and on 20 February 1927 NRA units from Kiangsi entered southern Anhwei through the Chimen Pass. By 17 March units of Ch'eng Ch'ien's 6th Army of Hunanese troops reached Wuhu only seventy miles from Nanking, with its large foreign community. Simultaneously NRA East Route Army units were advancing up the west coast of Lake Tai, while north of the Yangtze Li Tsung-jen's 7th Army took Hofei on 18 March. Sun Ch'uan-fang was being crushed between the NRA attacks from the south and the arrival of

39 Jordan, *Northern Expedition*, pp.110–13.

his Shantung 'allies' from the north. Fengtien clique General Chang Tsung-ch'ang, the commander of the Shantung army who had little interest in the political survival of Sun Ch'uan-fang, seems to have concluded at this point that Shanghai would have to be abandoned in order to hold Nanking; he ordered reinforcements bound for Shanghai and already east of Nanking at Changchow to return to Nanking.

Admiral Yang Shu-chuang, leader of the Fukien naval clique, now publicly defected to the KMT. The previous allegiance of the navy to Sun Yat-sen and its defection to Wu P'ei-fu has been described (Chapter 3); one squadron had rejoined Wu when he bounced back after the Second Chih–Feng War, but the rest under Yang had joined Sun Ch'uan-fang's five province union, which controlled their base areas. Nevertheless, Yang had been negotiating with the KMT since August 1926. His defection reunified the navy and made it impossible for the northern warlords to operate south of the Yangtze. Sun Ch'uan-fang's Shanghai garrison commander, Pi Shu-ch'eng, also defected to the KMT. Pai Ch'ung-hsi completed the NRA occupation of Shanghai on 22 March, and two days later Ch'eng Ch'ien's troops occupied Nanking.[40]

THE KMT-CCP SPLIT

In various locations, most notably in Hankow and Kiukiang with their large foreign enclaves, NRA occupation had been followed by communist-led mass action directed against foreigners. Kiukiang's concession area had been abandoned, and both there and at Hankow the British had, under duress, returned their authority over the concession area to the Chinese. Similar actions broke out in both Shanghai and Nanking in the wake of the NRA occupation; at Nanking the southern soldiers joined in.[41] Meanwhile the Wuhan regime passed numerous resolutions depriving Chiang of his authority to issue general regulations or control military administration from his field headquarters. Figures of the KMT centre and right, feeling increasingly uncomfortable at Wuhan, began to congregate around Chiang at Shanghai. Merchants at Wuhan began to complain of having their premises taken over by

40 Jordan, *Northern Expedition*, pp.113–17, for the rest of the Shanghai–Nanking campaign.

41 Jordan, *Northern Expedition*, pp.117–18 for the events at Shanghai, Nanking and Kiukiang. Compare Isaacs, *Tragedy*, pp.124, 144–50.

radicals. In Canton, Shanghai and in the Yangtze city of Chenchiang fights between CCP dominated and non-communist unions led to fatalities.

At this juncture Wang Ching-wei returned from Russia, conferring with Chiang before going to Wuhan. Chiang may have hoped briefly, and in any event stated publicly on 1 April, that Wang would provide a political leadership that the NRA and the KMT right could live with. At Wuhan, however, Wang tilted decisively against Chiang.

On 6 April Chang Tso-lin's men raided the Soviet embassy in Peking, seized documents, and arrested the CCP notable Li Ta-chao and others. Simultaneously concession police raided the Soviet consulates in Tientsin and Shanghai, and Chiang's troops closed down the NRA Political Department at Shanghai, headed by another CCP figure, Kuo Mo-jo. While the simultaneous raids tended to substantiate the charges of collusion between Chiang, the northern warlords, and the imperialist powers that controlled the concession police, the seized documents provided persuasive confirmation of the degree to which the CCP and the KMT left had been subverted and were now controlled from Moscow through Borodin. Chiang now received encouragement from the leaders of the Kwangsi clique (Li Tsung-jen, Pai Ch'ung-hsi and Huang Shao-hsiung), the KMT political and military leadership at Canton (Li Chi-shen and Ch'en Shu-jen), and the army leadership in Shanghai and Nanking, as well as business groups and already established rightist elements (such as the Western Hills faction and the Green Gang), to take action against the CCP. These events coincided with a reversal of the military situation that added to the pressures on Chiang. After advancing from Hofei north to Pangpu (on the Huai River and the Tientsin–Pukow railway), from 3 to 11 April the NRA fell back all the way to the Yangtze in the face of a well-mounted Ankuochün counter-offensive. The navy made the Yangtze into a moat, but the resumption of the offensive, and its continuation northward to destroy the Ankuochün and its Fengtien clique leadership, seemed to require the restoration of political unity in the KMT part of China.[42]

On 12 April Chiang Kai-shek and the military units under his leadership launched a massive purge of CCP elements at Shanghai. This soon spread to Nanking and most other areas in which the

42 Jordan, *Northern Expedition*, pp.118–28. Again, compare the older accounts of Isaacs, *Tragedy*, pp.142–74; and Liu, *Military History*, pp.30–47.

military commanders inclined to Chiang. CCP members, labour organizers and other suspected radicals were rounded up and summarily killed, grounds for suspicion being often no more than a short haircut or possession of some left-wing literature. Having previously done its best to undermine Chiang's position as commander-in-chief, the left government at Wuhan now reacted passively. They formally dismissed Chiang, but at the same time made efforts to come to terms with him, on the instructions of Stalin.

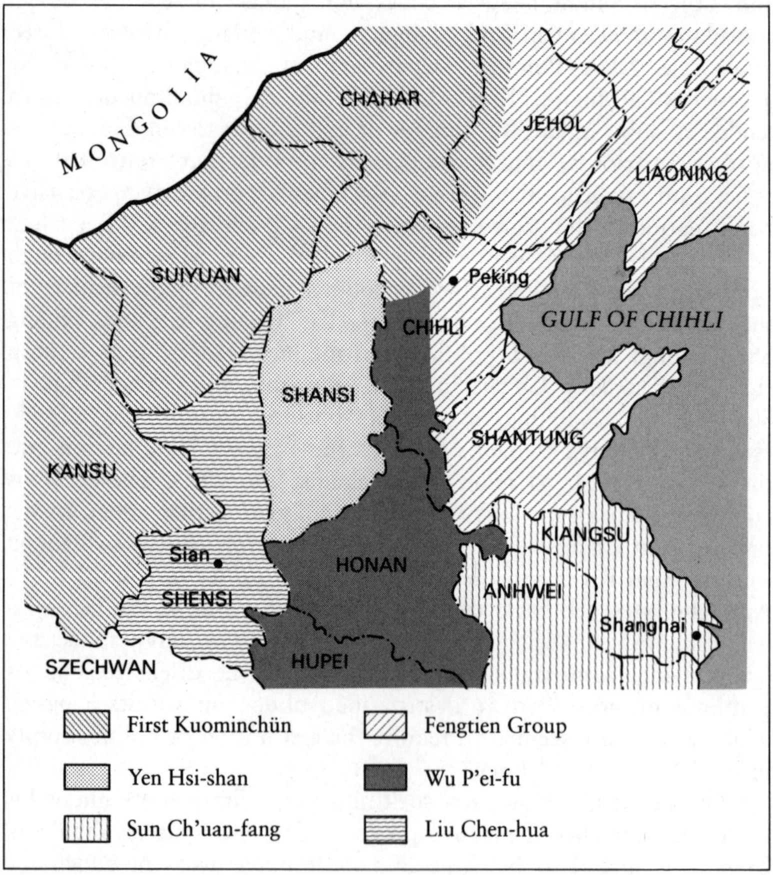

9. North China, May 1926 (After: Sheridan, *Chinese Warlord: The Career of Feng Yü-hsiang*)

Chiang had begun the purge in a sense of desperation,[43] but its outcome was greatly to his advantage. Chiang now became the paramount leader of the centre-right majority of the KMT, which now rejected the CCP and the United Front because of perceived communist outrages during the Northern Expedition. His military leadership position also improved. KMT soldiers blamed the communists for slowing down the momentum of the Northern

10. North China, January 1927 (After: Sheridan, *Chinese Warlord*)

43 Jordan, *Northern Expedition*, p.124.

Expedition, while warlord generals could see Chiang as a man with whom they could deal. The later acceptance of 'surrenders' from such people as Feng Yü-hsiang and Yen Hsi-shan has often been criticized, and certainly helped to preserve warlord patterns of military relations in the Nanking decade, but it was a major tactic of the Northern Expedition from the beginning. A Wuhan government might well have led to a firm alliance among the northern warlords that would have been difficult for the enthusiastic but still poorly armed and trained southern troops to defeat. Chiang's dramatic break with the left made this less likely, and a KMT government under his control was also more likely to win foreign recognition.

INTO NORTH CHINA

The (3 to 11 April 1927) offensive of the Fengtien military clique's National Pacification Army (Ankuochün) had reached south as far as the Yangtze. Lacking the naval means to cross the river, the Ankuochün under Shantung warlord Chang Tsung-ch'ang spent late April and early May shelling Nanking from the north bank. On 10 May units of the NRA 1st and 6th armies crossed the Yangtze. Linking up with the Kwangsi troops of Li Tsung-jen's 7th Army, they advanced and took Hofei, Pangpu and Suhsien in succession by 28 May. Chang Tsung-ch'ang then withdrew his 15,000-man expeditionary force north toward Shantung. Meanwhile troops under 1st NRA commander Ho Ying-ch'in advanced through northern Kiangsu against Sun Ch'uan-fang's remaining forces, and in early June took the railway junction at Hsuchow and Haichou, the eastern terminus of the Lunghai railway.

In Hupei an Ankuochün force commanded by Chang Hsueh-liang, son and heir of Fengtien clique leader Marshal Chang Tso-lin, was invading from the north parallel to Chang Tsung-ch'ang's invasion of Kiangsu. The Wuhan government dominated by the KMT left had appointed T'ang Sheng-chih, the Hunan warlord whose actions had precipitated the Northern Expedition the year before, as commander-in-chief. Britain and Japan were now in the process of withdrawing recognition from Wuhan and extending it to the counter-government created under Chiang Kai-shek's auspices at Nanking. Military action by Wuhan's troops thus was actually in competition if formally in cooperation with Nanking. After receiving some defections from Wu P'ei-fu's crumbling army, T'ang attacked the Ankuochün contingent and by a series of flank attacks forced it north along the Peking–Hankow railway line past Yencheng (in Honan, but south of the railway junction at Chengchow).

As in the earlier warlord wars, access to the Yangtze River from North China depended on controlling the two major north–south railway lines, the eastern Tientsin–Pukow to Nanking and the western Peking–Hankow to Wuhan. As of May 1927 the Ankuochün, having come south along both lines, was now retreating north along both lines. In the numerically stronger East Route Army of the NRA Chiang Kai-shek's close ally Ho Ying-ch'in and the Kwangsi generals Pai Ch'ung-hsi and Li Tsung-jen had gathered the military laurels; these troops of course were controlled by Chiang's alternative government at Nanking. The NRA in Hupei and Honan was under T'ang Sheng-chih, who had been appointed by the Wuhan government, and who had lost about a fifth of his originally 70,000-strong army in the campaign so far. Despite the massacre of communists and leftists in the regions under Nanking's control, open conflict between NRA units had yet to occur, and obviously had to be avoided if the Northern Expedition were to have any chance of unifying China politically.[44]

The northern warlords similarly lacked unity. Yen Hsi-shan continued to be chiefly concerned with maintaining his position in Shansi, and would make a deal with a winner if he could. He was also well placed to interdict the Peking–Hankow railway line, as he had done in 1924 by taking Shihchiachuang (Chihli) and thereby preventing Chihli clique forces in Hupei and Honan from going north by rail to aid Wu P'ei-fu. Christian General Feng Yü-hsiang was even more strategically placed. By early 1927 he had suppressed the challenges to his position in Shensi, and naturally was pleased to see the Northern Expedition going after his old rivals among the northern warlords. In Shensi Feng held the western end of the east–west Lunghai railway, which ran eastward to intersect the Peking–Hankow line at Chengchow (Honan) and the Tientsin–Pukow line at Hsuchow (Kiangsu) before reaching the East China Sea at Haichou. In other words, simply by moving east along the Lunghai line, Feng, depending on the evolution of the situation, could block the advance or retreat, or attack in the flank, either branch of either the Ankuochün or the NRA.

44 Jordan, *Northern Expedition*, pp.129–36.

Feng Yü-hsiang entered the fray in May, and Chang Hsueh-liang promptly abandoned the vital railway junction at Chengchow and retired north of the Yellow River. Feng had moved east through the Tungkuan Pass and captured Loyang from Wu P'ei-fu's troops on 26 May. Feng nominally was one of the deputy commanders of the Ankuochün, but of course had suffered a bitter defeat at Chang Tso-lin's hands in 1925–6. Now Feng's revived and reorganized National People's Army (Kuominchün) was once again a highly competitive force. It occupied Chengchow and then Kaifeng with no opposition from the much weaker army of T'ang Sheng-chih. As noted, Hsuchow and Haichou fell almost simultaneously to Chiang K'ai-shek's troops. Wang Ching-wei and the KMT left leadership hoped that Feng's recently professed radicalism was genuine, and that between Feng and T'ang Sheng-chih they could put together a military counterweight to the armies of Chiang Kai-shek. Feng was not encouraging when he met with the Wuhan leadership at Chengchow on 10–12 June. He insisted on recognition as KMT chairman of Honan, and advised T'ang Sheng-chih to return to Wuhan to restore order. Despite his hearty proletarian manner and his recent adoption of up-to-date Bolshevik slogans, Feng basically was a practised veteran of the warlord politics of the past decade. He was now well positioned to cut a deal, and Chiang was the man to deal with. Feng met Chiang at Hsuchow on 20 June, and was promised money, weapons, and recognition as KMT chairman of Honan. The following day he wired Wang Ching-wei, advising him to cut his ties to the CCP and send Borodin back to Russia, and soon after began shooting his own communists.[45]

Feng's betrayal kicked the military props from under the Wuhan government, and took the CCP and their foreign advisers by surprise. The Wuhan government's promotion of social revolution and land redistribution in Hunan had frightened and alienated the officers of most of the NRA armies. At this high point of communist influence in Wuhan, even such high-status leftists as Wang Ching-wei felt impotent in face of the CCP and their mass organizations.[46]

Meanwhile, Chang Tso-lin had reorganized the Peking government to enhance his personal control, and had reinforced Sun Ch'uan-fang's remaining army with heavy artillery. Sun and Chang

45 Sheridan, *Chinese Warlord*, pp.216–32.

46 Jordan, *Northern Expedition*, pp.136–7.

Tsung-ch'ang recaptured Hsuchow on 24 July and then divided, part heading west, where around Kueite Feng Yü-hsiang's army fought them off for several months in a successful defence of Honan. The main body headed south, recaptured Yangchow and Pukow, and subjected most of Anhwei and Kiangsu north of the Yangtze to the Ankuochün.

This latest Ankuochün counter-offensive harmed the prestige of Chiang Kai-shek, who was already under criticism from – among others – Ho Ying-ch'in and the Kwangsi generals Li Tsung-jen and Pai Ch'ung-hsi for splitting the KMT by his extreme anti-leftist policies. On 12 August Chiang resigned as commander-in-chief and went to Shanghai with an entourage of notables, expecting to be begged to return in the near term. When this failed to happen, he went to Japan, where his main accomplishment was negotiating his marriage to Soong Mayling, sister of both T.V. Soong and Mme Sun Yat-sen. The marriage was celebrated in Shanghai on 1 December, with both traditional and Christian ceremonies. Chiang's public profession of Christianity, a condition of the marriage, raised Chiang's reputation with the missionary lobby and (later) with US public opinion.

After shelling Nanking from across the river for several weeks, Sun Ch'uan-fang ferried his army to the south bank near Lungtan in the predawn hours of 26 August. In the fierce battle to contain and destroy the bridgehead that followed, the NRA 1st (Ho Ying-ch'in), 2nd (now Pai Ch'ung-hsi) and 3rd (now Li Tsung-jen) armies were well supported by Yang Shu-chuang's navy, and were joined by contingents from most of the territories flying the KMT flag, including those under Wuhan control. The bridgehead fell on 31 August. Sun Ch'uan-fang and a few thousand of his troops escaped, but 30,000 surrendered (along with 30 artillery pieces and 35,000 rifles) and some 10,000 had been killed. NRA losses were comparable in number, but included 500 Whampoa cadets, half of the 5th Class that had graduated in July 1926.[47]

While the Nanking NRA was fighting the Ankuochün, T'ang Sheng-chih's now 25,000-man army held Anking and other west Anhwei locations, apparently threatening Nanking. After his withdrawal from Chengchow in June, T'ang, still Wuhan's nominal commander-in-chief, had been instrumental in Wuhan's turn against the left. Surviving CCP insurgents seized Nanchang on 1 August (since celebrated as PLA day), but were soon driven out. In Hunan,

47 Jordan, *Northern Expedition*, pp.137–42.

Kiangsi and in Kwangtung the KMT leadership had come to see CCP social revolution as a critical problem, and Chiang's withdrawal from the Nanking regime made it possible for those who had opposed him personally to reunite with Nanking. Most of the Wuhan leaders did so, with the exception of Wang Ching-wei, who withdrew angrily in mid-September. Wang's withdrawal from central KMT politics left his protégé T'ang Sheng-chih isolated. After being surrounded by hostile KMT armies, T'ang resigned and left for Japan on 12 November.

This cleared the left flank and permitted an offensive on Hsuchow by NRA forces under Ho Ying-ch'in. On 14 December Sun Ch'uan-fang's 10,000 troops and 60,000 of Chang Tsung-ch'ang's 150,000-strong army counterattacked, supported by an armoured train and the Ankuochün air force. The NRA repelled them within two days, and drove the Ankuochün across the border into Shantung.

Meanwhile at Canton on 17 November, Chang Fa-k'uei seized control of the city on behalf of Wang Ching-wei and in opposition to Li Chi-shen, the local garrison commander, and Huang Shao-hsiung, the third principal member of the Kwangsi clique. While Chang tried to eliminate CCP influence among the long-established mass organizations, the communists staged their own coup on 11 December. The Canton Commune was suppressed within four days; the white terror that followed lasted longer. Wang Ching-wei, his political image now tarnished beyond repair by his dalliance with the communists in the summer of 1927, left for France on 17 December. Three days later Ho Ying-ch'in, elevated in prestige from the conquest of Hsuchow, publicly proposed that Chiang Kai-shek resume his duties as commander-in-chief.[48]

With the east–west railway line under control of the revolutionary coalition, Chiang was able to travel in person to Kaifeng to negotiate with Feng Yü-hsiang. The outcome was the February 1928 reorganization of all KMT-affiliated armies into four army groups, of which the old NRA under Chiang constituted the 1st, Feng's Kuominchün the 2nd, Yen Hsi-shan's Shansi-based forces the 3rd, and the Kwangsi clique under Li Tsung-jen the 4th. The Kwangsi generals dominated Hupei and Hunan since the fall of T'ang Sheng-chih, and shared control of Kwangtung with Li Chi-shen. The near equality of the four army groups reflected the realities of military power as the KMT edged toward the

48 Summarized from Jordan, *Northern Expedition*, pp. 143–50.

post-Northern Expedition phase. Chiang now transferred the Whampoa Academy to Nanking as the Central Military Academy, and revived the General Political Department, now purged of communists; these efforts at indoctrination had their greatest effect, as might be expected, on the units of the 1st Army Group (AG).[49]

Supported by the 2nd AG attacking from Honan, the 1st AG advanced north up the railway from Hsuchow into Shantung in early April 1928. The already much battered Sun Ch'uan-fang bore the brunt of the fighting. When his counter-offensive on 16–17 April failed, he had to evacuate Yenchou (Shantung) to escape encirclement; afterwards he attempted to hold the Shantung provincial capital at Tsinan and the railway line from there to the port city of Tsingtao. Ankuochün morale in general was weakening, and their forces were also hard-pressed along the Chihli borders with Honan and Shansi. When KMT troops cut the railway line to Tsingtao, Ankuochün units fled Tsinan to the north, across the Yellow River bridge.

The evacuation was the disorderly rout typical of retreating warlord armies, complete with robbery and violence. The Japanese Kwantung Army blamed the disorder on the KMT troops, and moved a brigade into Tsinan to protect Japanese civilians and interests. The left-inspired social violence of 1927 had left behind fears of the Nationalist movement among most foreigners in China, who thus relied on Japanese accounts of the Tsinan Incident. Since Major-General Tatekawa Yoshiji, afterwards central to both the murder of Chang Tso-lin (June 1928) and the Mukden Incident (1931), was also involved at Tsinan, it is difficult to doubt that Kwantung Army leaders were seeking a pretext for intervention. Large-scale fighting between the Japanese and the 1st AG broke out on 3 May. Chiang's response was politically astute. While maintaining his HQ in Tsinan, he ordered his men to transit the city quickly, to minimize occasion for provocation, and blamed Chang Tso-lin (falsely) for calling in the Japanese.[50]

On 9 May Chang Tso-lin ordered his armies to concentrate at Techou, Paoting and Kalgan, a defensive deployment intended to hold these railway line approaches to Peking.[51] Feng Yü-hsiang (2nd

49 Jordan, *Northern Expedition*, pp.151–5; Sheridan, *Chinese Warlord*, pp.233–9; Donald G. Gillin, *Warlord: Yen Hsi-shan in Shansi Province, 1911–1949* (Princeton, 1967), pp.106–10, alludes to the same events.

50 Jordan, *Northern Expedition*, pp.155–61; McCormack, *Chang Tso-lin*, pp.244–6, with analysis of the Japanese side.

51 McCormack, *Chang Tso-lin*, pp.214–15.

AG) and Yen Hsi-shan (3rd AG) both committed their forces enthusiastically at this stage, in order to be in at the kill. The Ankuochün still maintained a superiority in artillery, much of it railway mounted and highly useful in a withdrawal along the railway lines, but the morale of the Ankuochün units was collapsing. Chang Tso-lin was caught in a dilemma: he wanted continued Japanese support for his position in Manchuria, but was forced to denounce Japanese imperialism publicly in order to counter his long-standing reputation as a Japanese running dog. He had been heartened by Japanese intervention at Tsinan, but Japanese agencies were in conflict with one another and Japan's policy toward Chang was uncertain. Chang launched a massive counterattack on Feng Yü-hsiang during 17–25 May, committing some 200,000 troops, which broke up Feng's siege of Paoting and drove him back to Tinghsien. Reinforcements from Li Tsung-jen (4th AG) and a supporting attack from Yen Hsi-shan then turned the tide on the Paoting front, and meanwhile the 1st AG threatened Tientsin, southeast of Peking.

While Japanese Prime Minister General Baron Tanaka Giichi procrastinated, Chang Tso-lin determined to evacuate Peking and to try to hold out in Manchuria. The Japanese Kwantung Army leadership had decided to assassinate him, hoping that the disorders following his death would provide a pretext to take over Manchuria, a scenario finally enacted in 1931–2. Staff officer Colonel Komoto Daisaku made the necessary arrangements, and as Chang's train passed under a bridge of the Japanese-owned South Manchurian Railway Company south of Mukden at 05:30 on 4 June, explosive charges charges were detonated, and Chang died a few hours later. The Ankuochün position south of the Great Wall crumbled within days, and the KMT flag was raised over Peking.[52]

Chihli province (whose name meant 'directly attached' to the national capital, now at Nanking in accordance with Sun Yat-sen's wishes) was renamed Hopei ('north of the Yellow River'). Peking (Pei-ching) meaning Northern Capital was renamed Peiping (Pei-p'ing), often translated Northern Peace but actually referring to the fact that the region had been conquered ('pacified') from the south. When the Ming dynasty conquered the north in 1368, they had also imposed the name Peiping while maintaining their capital at Nanking (until 1421), an historical allusion not lost on educated Chinese.

52 Jordan, *Northern Expedition*, pp.162–8.

In Manchuria the result was not what the Japanese officers had expected. Chang Hsueh-liang, better educated than his father, and with experience and acceptance as his father's deputy, succeeded to control of the Fengtien clique, and held it together in control of Manchuria without any help from the Japanese, who had previously discounted him as a playboy and an opium addict. It soon became widely, and correctly, believed that Japan was responsible for Chang Tso-lin's death, which motivated his son to seek revenge. Accommodation with the KMT was the first step, and while the negotiations were time-consuming, the death of Chang Tso-lin had in fact made the total destruction of the Fengtien clique less necessary to the KMT. Chang Hsueh-liang hoisted the KMT national flag, and on 30 December 1928 was appointed by Nanking to command his own troops, now renamed the Northeast Border Defence Army.

The Northern Expedition had originally been launched with the objective of destroying the northern warlords; at its end the three major northern warlords had been coopted into the ruling military coalition, even though others had been eliminated. While warlordism remained a major force, Chiang Kai-shek was in a stronger hegemonial position, and the KMT government in 1928 had more widespread political legitimacy, than any Chinese government since 1912.

A US consular report in February 1929 credited Chiang Kai-shek's 1st AG with 240,000 men, Feng Yü-hsiang's 2nd AG with 220,000, and Yen Hsi-shan's 3rd AG with 200,000. The 4th AG of the Kwangsi clique and Li Chi-shen of Kwangtung had 230,000, while Chang Hsueh-liang and his father's surviving generals in the Manchurian provinces had 190,000 more. Lung Yun headed a much reduced Yunnan Army of 30,000, and some 540,000 other troops in Szechwan, Kweichow and other places rounded out the stated total of 1,620,000. While only a small percentage of China's population, it was many more troops than China could afford. In January 1929 a Disbandment Conference met at Nanking, divided the country into six disbandment regions (the territories of the five major warlords plus a sixth region composed of Szechwan, Yunnan and Kweichow), and announced that the army would be reduced to 65 divisions of 11,000 men each.[53]

53 Sheridan, *Chinese Warlord*, pp.242–3.

Also in February 1929 the politics of inter-warlord warfare resumed. Feng Yü-hsiang, faced with rebellion and famine in Kansu, was eager to expand into Shantung, while in Wuhan the Kwangsi generals, in control militarily since their defeat of T'ang Sheng-shih, resented the intrusion of Chiang Kai-shek's agent Lu Ti-p'ing as governor of Hunan. The issue was whether the revenues of the central Yangtze provinces would be used to support Chiang's troops or those of the Kwangsi clique. When the Kwangsi generals sent an army to attack Lu at Changsha, Chiang apparently bribed Feng to stay neutral by promising money and future rule over Shantung, and sent an army to take Wuhan. This move was planned by Colonel Dr Max Bauer, the de facto founder of the German military mission that exercised great influence over Chiang Kai-shek in the early 1930s. While Feng sent troops under Han Fu-chü, Nanking's men got to Wuhan first, and the Kwangsi leaders abandoned Hupei without a fight when it became clear that Feng would not fight on their side.

Even if Chiang had meant to honour such a promise, it would have been difficult for Feng to cash his claim to Shantung in 1929. While Feng was already in occupation of the small part of Shantung west of the Tientsin–Pukow railway line, the Japanese held the entire Tsingtao to Tsinan line tightly, and this isolated the northern peninsular area of Chefoo and its environs, where Liu Chen-nien, formerly commander of Dog Meat General Chang Tsung-ch'ang's bodyguards, had taken over. Liu was trying for recognition from the Nanking government, despite a comeback attempt by Chang Tsung-ch'ang in March–April, which the Japanese government denied bankrolling. It seemed that the Japanese would withdraw on schedule in early May, permitting Feng's subordinate Sun Liang-ch'eng to take control of the entire province. Instead, on 15 April Chiang ordered Sun not to send troops to Tsinan or the railway zone, and (as he did later to block the communists in 1945) asked the Japanese to delay their withdrawal until Nanking troops could replace them. Chiang was telling Feng he would have to fight if he wanted Shantung, and Feng had no allies. On 25 April Feng's supporters left their positions in the national government, and Feng concentrated his troops to defend Honan.

While the usual campaign of mutual denunciations in circular telegrams went on in public, negotiations behind the scenes led to the defection in May of Han Fu-chü and Shih Yu-san, key subordinates of Feng Yü-hsiang who together commanded some 100,000 Kuominchün troops of a total then estimated at 300,000.

Chiang at once appointed Han governor of Honan. These defections afterwards were widely regarded as the crucial factor in Feng's loss to Chiang. They did not halt the effort to build up an anti-Chiang coalition in the summer of 1929. While Feng negotiated with Yen Hsi-shan, and Chang Hsueh-liang's attitude toward intra-KMT politics remained carefully ambiguous, the KMT left under Wang Ching-wei escalated their calls for a 'reorganization' of the Nanking government that would eliminate Chiang Kai-shek.

On 17 September Chang Fa-k'uei, who had supported the campaign against the Kwangsi generals despite his continued allegiance to Wang Ching-wei, denounced Chiang Kai-shek and began military operations against him from his base in Yichang (Hupei). On 10 October Feng's generals signed a circular telegram calling on Feng and Yen to wage war on Chiang. Yen in fact accepted official appointments from both sides and remained neutral despite the encouragement he had earlier given to Feng. Even with the support of the Kwangsi generals, Chang Fa-k'uei failed to take Canton, which was strongly defended by Ch'en Chi-t'ang, Li Chi-shen's protégé and successor (Li had been under arrest since March because of his advocacy of negotiations with the Kwangsi generals). Chang Hsueh-liang, who would have been unlikely to support Feng Yü-hsiang in any case, was then tied up in an undeclared war with Soviet troops, who had succeeded to the prewar Russian special position in northern Manchuria. Feng's Kuominchün thus fought a battle of attrition without support against Nanking's forces. While the two sides were well matched, and at times the situation looked bad for Nanking, in late November the Kuominchün evacuated Honan.[54]

On 10 February 1930 Yen Hsi-shan publicly wired Chiang, urging him to resign and denouncing his policy of unification by military force. Yen in later years remained angry at Feng for having 'tricked' him into opposing Chiang at this juncture. In March the Kuominchün re-entered Honan, advancing on Kaifeng. Chiang assigned his best troops to the Honan front, ordering them to stand on the defensive in the expectation that the coalition against him would break up of its own accord. Covered by the action in Honan, Yen Hsi-shan's troops invaded Shantung, taking Tsinan and other key points against weak opposition. Yen's troops were considered qualitatively inferior to Feng's or Chiang's, but their presence in Shantung threatened the Hsuchow railway junction and, by

54 Summarized from Sheridan, *Chinese Warlord*, pp. 252–65.

extension, Chiang's entire army in Honan. At this high point of military success, Yen and his confederates brought together in Peiping a so-called Enlarged Conference of the Kuomintang that included all of the anti-Chiang elements, from Wang Ching-wei's Reorganizationists to Hu Han-min and the Western Hills group. The Enlarged Conference proclaimed a new government headed by Yen Hsi-shan on 9 September.

By then the military situation had turned dramatically in Nanking's favour. In July Chiang launched major offensives north into Shantung and west into Honan along the railway lines. By early September Shantung was secured and the Kuominchün forces at Chengchow (Honan) were under heavy attack. On 18 September Chang Hsueh-liang sent a public telegram urging resolution of national issues through proper channels by the 'Central Government'. He meant Nanking; four days later Manchurian troops entered Hopei, taking Peiping, Tientsin and other key locations. By early October Nanking's troops had mopped up Honan, and the war was over.[55]

Chang Hsueh-liang's tilt to Nanking had been decisive in 1930, but the outcome left Chiang Kai-shek strong enough to eliminate Feng Yü-hsiang as an independent warlord, to Chang Hsueh-liang's ultimate disadvantage. Feng went into exile, none of his comeback attempts amounting to much. His Kuominchün was not disbanded, but was broken up into smaller units that were incorporated into the Nanking army. His generals who joined Chiang Kai-shek faced Chiang's permanent distrust for all non-Whampoa officers. Yen Hsi-shan also had to go into exile, but was saved by the loyalty of his subordinates and by the fact that his regime in Shansi was too strongly entrenched for Shang Chen, Chiang's appointee as governor in Taiyuan, to uproot. As part of the general political crisis provoked by the Japanese takeover of Manchuria in late 1931, Chiang appointed Yen Pacification Commissioner of Taiyuan and Suiyuan, in effect re-establishing and confirming the autonomy in Shansi that Yen maintained until 1949, despite Japanese and communist invasions.[56]

Chiang's defeat of Feng and Yen left him more powerful than ever as 1931 opened, but he still had no actual control of the northeast, the extreme west, or the southern provinces. When Chiang arrested Hu Han-min in May 1931, the political leaders

55 Sheridan, *Chinese Warlord*, pp.265–7.

56 Gillin, *Warlord*, pp.110–24.

who had opposed him the previous year now came together at Canton and established a counter-government. These included long-time KMT leftists Wang Ching-wei, Sun Fo (Sun Yat-sen's son) and Eugene Ch'en as well as former Yuan Shih-k'ai Prime Minister T'ang Shao-yi, later joined by the Kwangsi generals. What made the new Canton regime possible in the first place, though, was the adherence of Canton garrison commander Ch'en Chi-t'ang, who had supported Nanking in 1930. The Canton–Nanking split was still unresolved when the Mukden Incident occurred in September. This forced Chiang to release those of his rivals whom he had arrested, and to appoint them to positions of at least nominal authority. From now on public opinion within the educated and articulate elements that supported the KMT urged Chiang to form and lead a coalition of all patriotic elements against the Japanese invaders. Chiang seems to have felt that public professions of patriotism were often merely a cloak for an anti-Chiang agenda. He believed that firm military unification of China was a necessary precondition to successful anti-Japanese operations.[57] After 1931 he was constrained against moving publicly against his remaining warlord and KMT rivals, but he increased his efforts against the CCP. The communists' rural insurrection had prospered alarmingly while Chiang's main attentions were devoted to the struggles with the Kwangsi generals and Feng and Yen.

THE BEGINNINGS OF CCP RURAL INSURRECTION

On 18 July 1927 at Kiukiang, Chu Te, Chou En-lai, Ho Lung, Yeh Chien-ying, Liu Po-ch'eng, Mao Tse-tung and others met to plan a response against the anti-communist measures inaugurated by Chiang Kai-shek in April.[58] This group included four of the ten marshals and the two most important political leaders of the future People's Republic of China. They planned a campaign beginning with the seizure of Nanchang, which Ho Lung accomplished on 1 August. KMT forces recaptured Nanchang a few days later, but the episode rightly marks the beginning of an independent Chinese communist military tradition.

57 A theme throughout Parks M. Coble's excellent, *Facing Japan: Chinese Politics and Japanese Imperialism, 1931–1937* (Cambridge, MA, 1991); see pp.27–38 for an account of the events of 1927–31.

58 William W. Whitson, *The Chinese High Command: A History of Communist Military Politics, 1927–1971* (New York, 1973), p.30.

Mao Tse-tung grew up in Hunan and, after a chequered educational career, was working as a library assistant in Peking at the time of the May Fourth Movement. Though one of the founding members of the Chinese Communist Party, he could not compete with such figures as Ch'en Tu-hsiu for intellectual leadership.[59] The CCP in its early years introduced the Marxist canon to the Chinese intellectual world, complete with the aversion to the peasantry characteristic of European Marxism. Urban, proletarian mass organizations and sincere acceptance of the KMT–CCP United Front and the need for a bourgeois revolution preceding the socialist revolution were logical corollaries. Chiang's massacres therefore took the CCP and their Russian advisers by surprise, and CCP response was hindered both by an historicist ideology that contradicted the reality of China in 1927 and by the felt need to refer major issues to a Soviet leadership that was both ruptured by the Stalin–Trotsky conflict and ignorant of conditions in China.[60]

Before and during the Northern Expedition, Mao had argued vainly for CCP efforts among the peasants. On entering Hunan, the Northern Expedition confronted a well-organized peasant movement whose articulate attacks on the existing system of land tenure frightened the NRA officer corps and contributed to the rightward turn of KMT politics. The CCP assigned Mao to investigate the Hunan peasant movement, and his March 1927 report, in which Mao argued eloquently that the peasants had the same degree of revolutionary consciousness, grasp of concrete issues, and ability to form mass organizations as Marxist theory had always assumed for the proletariat, established his credentials as a peasant expert on the eve of the destruction of the CCP's urban base.[61]

By October 1927 some of the survivors of the Autumn Harvest Rising and the brief communist seizure of Nanchang had congregated under Mao's leadership in the rugged Chingkangshan area on the Hunan–Kiangsi border. There they made a tense alliance with local bandits, raiding in the bandit manner, while Mao began to experiment with land redistribution. Lacking military training or experience himself, Mao came to view guerrilla warfare supported

59 In addition to the already cited Schwartz, *Chinese Communism*, Jerome Ch'en, *Mao and the Chinese Revolution* (New York, 1965), and Stuart Schram, *Mao Tse-tung* (Harmondsworth, 1966), offer accounts of Mao's Life from differing perspectives.

60 Isaac's vivid account in *Tragedy*, pp.238–71, remains valuable despite the author's Trokskyite orientation.

61 Mao, 'Report', in *Selected Works*, I, pp.23–59.

by a politically aroused peasantry as the correct CCP military strategy.[62] In later years he frequently cited the novel *Shui Hu Chuan*, a picaresque and enormously popular tale of rebels against the Sung dynasty (960–1276; the novel itself is set in the early twelfth century), as his inspiration – often to the annoyance of more professionally trained CCP soldiers.[63]

In May 1928 other remnant communist forces under Chu Te joined the Chingkangshan force, and Chu reorganized the operation along more conventional military lines. Chu was a graduate of the Yunnan Military Academy who had idolized Ts'ai O – the idealistic Yunnan general who began the resistance to Yuan Shih-k'ai's monarchical movement – in his earlier military career. Despite Mao's political and theoretical prominence, Chu was the principal communist military commander throughout the long revolutionary civil war, and the other leading commanders who later became marshals and generals shared an approach to military problems that had been shaped by training in local military academies and service in the warlord armies and the NRA. Thus, P'eng Te-huai had been a battalion commander under T'ang Sheng-chih, both the uneducated Ho Lung and Whampoa graduate Hsu Hsiang-ch'ien were officers under Chang Fa-k'uei, Liu Po-ch'eng had risen through the Szechwan military system, Lin Piao was also a Whampoa graduate, and Yeh Chien-ying was a classmate of Chu Te at the Yunnan Military Academy. Chu reorganized the 10,000 or so soldiers of the so-called 4th Red Army (only 2,000 of whom had rifles) into six regiments.[64]

Pressure of anti-communist forces on the Chingkangshan region led the CCP leaders to divide their forces in December 1928. P'eng Te-huai remained behind, while Mao, Chu Te and Lin Piao led the larger part in a fighting march across Kiangsi to the hills on the Fukien border. Around the same time, communist forces were surviving in the Oyuwan region, the hilly border between Hupei and Anhwei north of the Yangtze. These three sources produced different streams of communist military leadership.[65]

62 Mao's own account of this phase is 'The struggle in the Chingkang Mountains', in *Selected Works*, I, pp.73–104.

63 Whitson, *High Command*, pp.18–21, on the *Shui Hu Chuan* and other novels as part of the 'peasant model' of warmaking, and p.147, where (future PLA Marshal) Liu Po-ch'eng complains that citing such works is 'conceited erudition and empty pedantry'.

64 Whitson, *High Command*, pp.29–42 has biographical sketches of these and others.

65 Whitson, *High Command*, pp.42–3, 103–4, 125–8, 262–5.

- The later growth of the Mao Tse-tung cult of personality has tended to obscure the historiography of the period. Mao is credited with all the vision and victories; his opponents, primarily CCP Central Committee leader Li Li-san, are blamed for all the blunders and setbacks. The truth was more complicated. Li was trying to orchestrate for 1930 a combined attack of the scattered communist forces that would seize and hold a major urban centre as a base from which revolution could spread. While this seems shortsighted in view of the peasant-based, city-avoiding strategy that later brought the CCP to power, it should be remembered that there were no precedents for such a strategy in 1929. Emperors and warlords had come to power by seizing and holding the urban network; Li Li-san in this respect was merely following in the path of Sun Yat-sen. Mao was one of very few at this time who had any faith in a rural strategy. For most communists, going to the countryside was a last resort. It was simply the only way to survive the white terror in the cities.
- Mao's later interpretation[66] (December 1936) of pre-Long March CCP strategy emphasized the importance of land reform to win over the peasants and political indoctrination within the army; these and other elements would permit the Red Army to be the fish swimming in the sea formed by the people, and would permit an alternation between guerrilla and regular tactics that their opponents could not counter or imitate. Mao seems to have wanted to impose a Soviet-style commissar system on the Red Army in December 1929 and to have been opposed by military commanders who considered themselves as loyal to the party as Mao.[67] The rank-and-file certainly needed political indoctrination; many were prisoners of war who had no doubt joined to save their necks.[68]

Following Li Li-san's orders, P'eng Te-huai's force attacked Changsha in July 1930, held it for three days and then was forced out. Mao and Chu Te threatened Nanchang, but did not attack it. In September they collaborated with P'eng in a less successful attack on Changsha. Returning to southern Kiangsi, the Chu–Mao forces captured Chian on the Kan River (4 October), there discovering

66 'Problems of strategy in China's revolutionary war', in Mao, *Selected Works*, I, pp.179–254.

67 Whitson, *High Command*, pp.43–5.

68 Mao, 'On correcting mistaken ideas in the party', in *Selected Works*, I, pp.105–16, an important source for this period, notes (p.107) that 'many prisoners captured in past battles have joined the Red Army, and such elements bring with them a markedly mercenary outlook'.

documents revealing the KMT first encirclement and annihilation campaign scheduled for December.[69]

CAMPAIGNS OF ENCIRCLEMENT AND ANNIHILATION, 1930–1

More than the Long March or anything afterwards, the five KMT-launched campaigns of encirclement and annihilation during 1930–4 created a distinctively Maoist revolutionary strategy that depended on close connections between the Red Army and the peasant population in the area of operations. Mao's most definitive exposition of the theory of People's War is his December 1936 essay 'Problems of strategy in China's revolutionary war'.[70] Mao begins this by denying the existence of objective military science ('the laws of war in general, or, to put it more concretely, the military manuals published by the reactionary Chinese government') and rejecting the idea that either the Russian Revolution or the Northern Expedition can be a model for the communist revolution. After swipes at Ch'en Tu-hsiu and Li Li-san, Mao gives four characteristics that define the strategical situation: China's size, diversity and backwardness; the size and strength of the anti-communist forces; the weakness of the Red Army; and CCP leadership of the agrarian revolution. The final characteristic permits the survival of the Red Army, which the peasants will support with food and military intelligence, while denying the same to the enemy. The Red Army thus may disperse among the peasantry in times of adversity, and when the time comes to go over to the offensive may concentrate its entire force against one enemy column at a time, thus defeating the enemy in detail. Mao illustrates these principles by discussing the five encirclement campaigns, treating the first three (1930–1) – which he considered successful and for which he claimed the credit – in some detail, while using the fourth and the disastrous fifth chiefly as a means of attacking Li Li-san.

In the decades that followed, the doctrines of People's War introduced by Mao (the term, of course, came later) have enjoyed impressive successes, and not only in China. Nevertheless, such success depends on both the creation of real peasant support and the failure of the enemy to devise an appropriate counter-strategy. The degree to which CCP land policies were actually popular

69 Whitson, *High Command*, pp.46–9.
70 Mao, *Selected Works*, I, pp.179–254. The quotation is on p.180.

continues to be debated. Without denying the reality of exploitation in rural China, the social situation was complicated by inter-village and inter-group rivalries and by the fact that landlords and victims often were members of the same clan. 'Class struggle' as such often had to be invented anew in each county invaded by the Red Army, and sustained by the murder and humiliation of local leaders of some legitimacy. The traditional local leaders themselves had long experience devising control mechanisms for rural areas, and in the fifth campaign were able to cooperate effectively with national government forces, whose blockhouse strategy in turn was designed precisely to break the link between the Red Army and the people.[71]

As the first campaign opened, the Red Army held Chian on the Kan River in central Kiangsi, athwart the province's main line of communication. At Mao's urging, they abandoned this strategic but exposed position and retired eastward, concentrating their 40,000 combat troops in the hilly area of Ningtu county in the southeast of the province. Kiangsi provincial chairman (and Chiang Kai-shek appointee) Lu Ti-p'ing deployed about 100,000 men in twelve divisions surrounding the Kiangsi Soviet area. These were supplemented by special forces called the A-B (Anti-Bolshevik) Group intended to give the Nationalists warning of Red Army movements. Three divisions (8th, 24th and 50th), deployed north of Ningtu, had recently fought against Feng Yü-hsiang in Honan, but the rest were Hunan and Kiangsi provincial troops of lower quality. Chang Hui-tsan, a protégé of Lu, was the overall field commander; his 18th Division, backed up by the 5th and 77th, approached Ningtu from the northwest.

The Red Army employed a variety of ruses to lure the overconfident Chang Hui-tsan into a trap in the mountain defile of Lungkang. They sprang the trap in the predawn hours of 30 December, annihilating the 18th Division and beheading Chang. Putting on the captured Nationalist uniforms, the Red Army moved east and on 1 January 1931 surprised and routed T'an Tao-yuan's 50th Division as it tried to escape its entrenchments at Tungshao; about half of the division was wiped out. The 8th and 24th divisions then retired precipitately toward Toupi, and the other encircling divisions withdrew.[72]

71 William Wei, *Counterrevolution in China: The Nationalists in Jiangxi during the Soviet Period* (Ann Arbor, 1985), analyzes these issues brilliantly, with reference to earlier studies.

72 Whitson, *High Command*, pp.268–70.

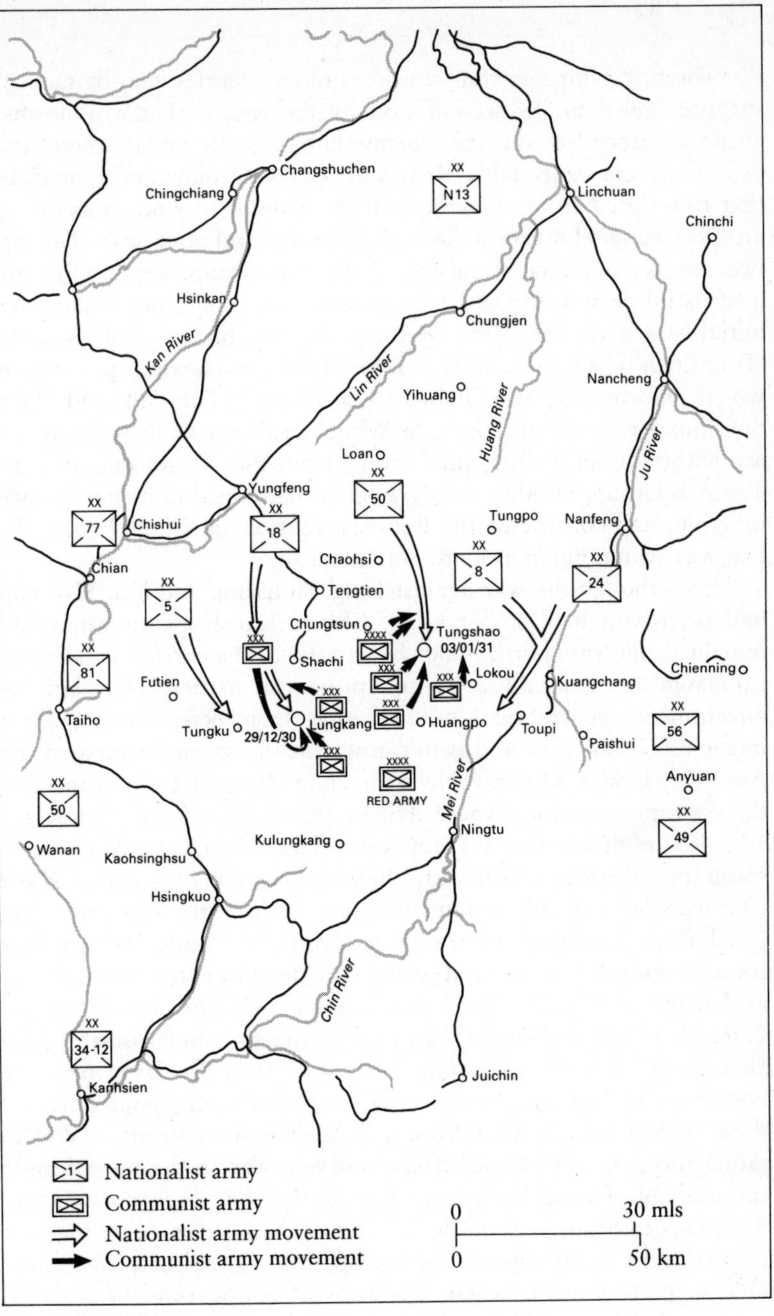

11. The first encirclement campaign, December 1930 to January 1931 (After: Whitson, *The Chinese High Command*)

The first campaign thus consisted of two battles won by tactical surprise, aided in the second case by the ruse with the uniforms. Surprise depended on the enemy entering the area where the peasantry was dependably Red, and Mao's account makes it clear that this varied from village to village. Thus it was not possible to attack Chang Hui-tsan's backup divisions at Futien and Tungku because 'the inhabitants, misled by the A-B Group, were for a time mistrustful of and opposed to' the Reds, who could not make their initial attack on the 50th Division, as they had wished, because 'Tungshao, where there were A-B Group elements, was a place from which information was liable to leak out.' The 8th and 24th divisions were safe at Toupi, 'a White area'. All of these locations are within about a thirty-mile radius from the Ningtu county seat. The A-B Group, in other words, while it had failed in its intelligence function, had constricted the Red Army's free operational zone; the fish was swimming in a pond, not an ocean.[73]

Even though the war against Feng Yü-hsiang and Yen Hsi-shan had been won by October 1930, Chiang Kai-shek's attention had remained on the north, and he regarded the first encirclement campaign as essentially a Kiangsi provincial matter. The Nanking government spent several months after their defeat organizing a larger (200,000 men) and better army for the second campaign. By April 1931 War Minister Ho Ying-ch'in directed from Nanchang the operations of four Route Armies (RAs): first, Ts'ai T'ing-k'ai's 19th RA (60th and 61st divisions) threatened the CCP area from the south by advancing from Kanhsien via Hsingkuo; second, Wang Chin-yu's 5th RA, whose four divisions (28th, 47th, 43rd and 54th, listed from southwest to northeast) were to advance by separate routes from the Kan River area and Yungfeng to enter the CCP area at Tungku and Shachi; third, Sun Lien-chung's 26th RA (25th and 27th divisions) advancing from the north; and fourth, Chu Shao-liang's 8th RA (5th, 8th, 24th, and 56th divisions) over the border in Fukien and invading by way of Kuangchang. None of these were Chiang's own troops. Ts'ai had been loyal to Wuhan rather too long after March 1927, and Sun was suspect as a former subordinate of Feng Yü-hsiang. The 5th RA had been put together for this campaign out of divisions that had never been together before, and the participation of the 8th RA was halfhearted at best. One suspects that, as usual, Chiang was considering the political aspects of the campaign: a victory might wipe out the communists,

73 Mao, *Selected Works*, I, pp.226–7.

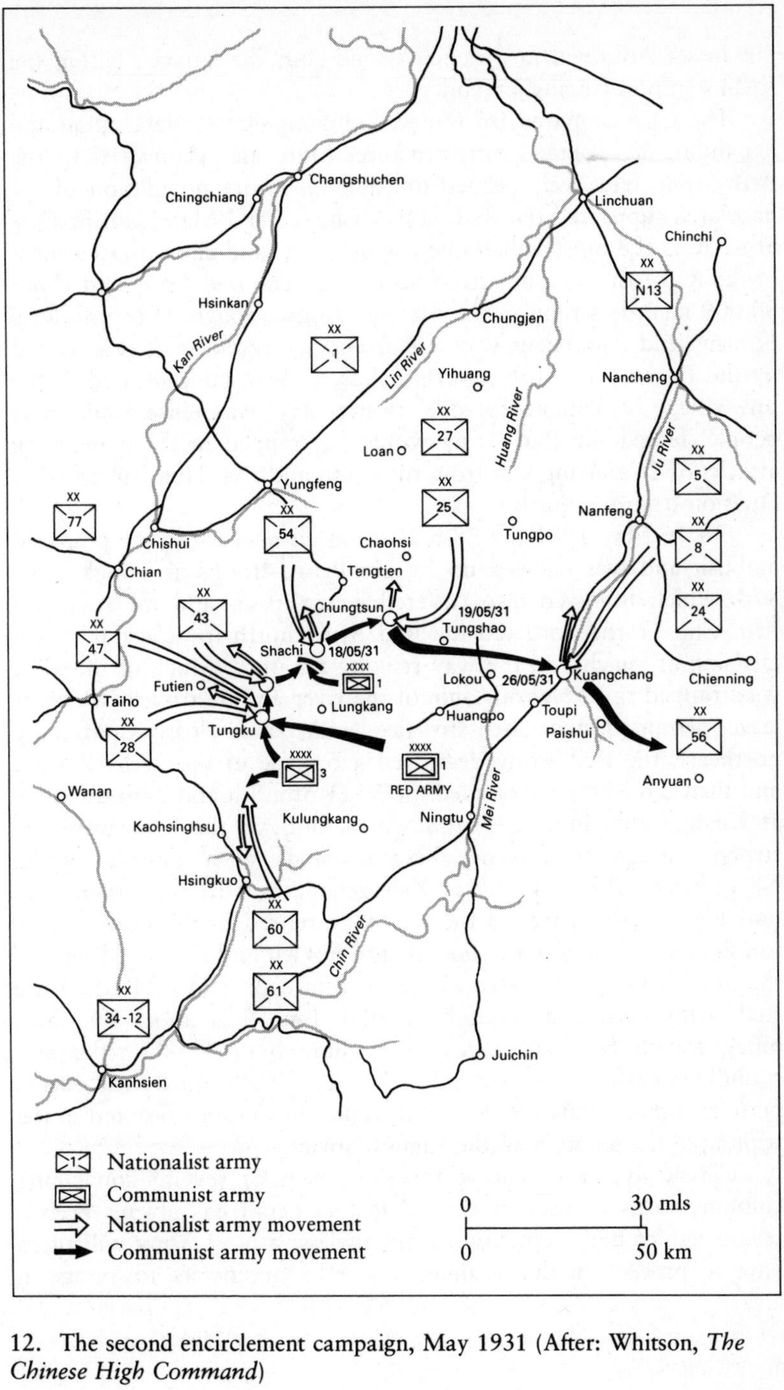

12. The second encirclement campaign, May 1931 (After: Whitson, *The Chinese High Command*)

but losses sustained in a defeat would shift the balance within the KMT camp in Chiang's favour.

The CCP prepared for the second campaign by developing and expanding its political infrastructure; Mao later claimed that 'the A-B Group had been cleaned up, and the entire population of the base area supported the Red Army'. Chu Te and Mao identified the 5th RA as the most vulnerable enemy force, and concentrated most of the Red Army at Tungku to wait for it. The Red Army had about 30,000 men, less than in the first campaign, though its overall level of arms and equipment was higher and its morale had been raised by the December victory. Nevertheless, to wait concentrated at the tiny village of Tungku for over twenty days was tense, and 'some people' feared the Red Army would be trapped in the converging attacks of Ts'ai T'ing-k'ai from the south and Kuo Hua-tsung's 43rd Division from the north.[74]

On 16 May 1931 the 28th Division advanced into the prepared ambush and was chewed up by Lin Piao's troops at Tungku; the 47th which followed also suffered heavy losses and the survivors fled. Chu Te then ordered the Red Army north to attack the 54th Division at Shachi, on the way striking the 43rd. Much of the 43rd was trapped on the wrong side of the river and destroyed, which at least permitted the 54th to flee with small loss. Continuing northeast, the Red Army destroyed a brigade of the 27th Division and then (26 May) surrounded the KMT 5th, 8th and 24th divisions at Kuangchang. In a sense this was a bluff, as the Reds were not strong enough to destroy these divisions in a pitched battle. Nevertheless, the divisions at Kuangchang had to fight their way out. P'eng Te-huai trailed them as they retired to the north, while Lin Piao struck across the border into Fukien and destroyed part of the 56th Division. As Mao noted, in fifteen days (16–31 May) the Red Army 'marched seven hundred li [one li is about one-third mile], fought five battles, captured more than 20,000 rifles and roundly smashed' the second campaign. The added armaments permitted more guns for the militia, and the victories resulted in the tripling of the territory of the Kiangsi Soviet.

Classically, coordinating the movement of several converging columns so as to prevent their defeat in detail has always been a severe test of high command. Nevertheless, a large army will often have to proceed in that manner if it is to employ its advantage in

74 For the Second campaign, Whitson, *High Command*, pp.270–2; Mao, *Selected Works*, I, pp.227–8.

numbers. Beginning with the US Civil War and Moltke's Königgrätz campaign (Austria–Hungary, 1866), military doctrine in the advanced countries had stressed the control of multiple columns through staff work and telegraphic communications. While the KMT armies did have some trained staff officers, there is little evidence either here or in the ambitious counter-offensives of the Sino-Japanese War that the Chinese command agencies had given serious thought to the command and staff problems of multiple-column campaigns. Neither telegraphic nor radio communications are mentioned. Mutually suspicious, depending on messengers for communications, and denied intelligence due to CCP control of the local population, the several KMT divisions were vulnerable to the defeat in detail inflicted on them by the fast-marching Red Army.

The third campaign of encirclement and annihilation got going within a month of the end of the second. Chiang Kai-shek took personal command at Nanchang, dividing his army into a centre under Ho Ying-ch'in (also at Nanchang), a right wing under Ch'en Ming-shu (Chian) and a left wing under Chu Shao-liang (Nanfeng). Mao's account credits Chiang with 300,000 troops and the Red Army with only 30,000. In fact the Red Army may have been as large as 55,000, since their victory in the second campaign permitted them to recruit and arm more men. In contrast the twenty Nationalist divisions were badly under-strength, aggregating some 130,000 men. But some of these divisions were from Chiang's personal troops, and Chiang's strategy, correctly reported by Mao, was to 'drive straight in', which was very different from the strategy of 'consolidating at every step' he used in the second campaign. The aim was to 'press the Red Army back against the Kan River and annihilate it there'.[75]

On the extreme left of the Nationalist deployment Ch'en Ch'eng's 18th Army (11th and 14th divisions, reinforced by the 6th and 10th) advanced from Nanfeng to Kuangchang and entered the Soviet area. To their right Chu Shao-liang's 8th Route Army (less the destroyed 56th Division) advanced on Tungshao and Shachi. Sun Lien-chung's 20,000-strong 26th Route Army remained near Loan. Further west the 47th and 54th divisions advanced south from Yungfeng toward Tungku, while the 23rd, 28th and 77th divisions remained west of the Kan River near Chian. Advancing from the south, Ts'ai T'ing-k'ai's 19th Route Army had been

75 For the Third campaign, Whitson, *High Command*, pp.272–5; Mao, *Selected Works*, I, pp.228–30.

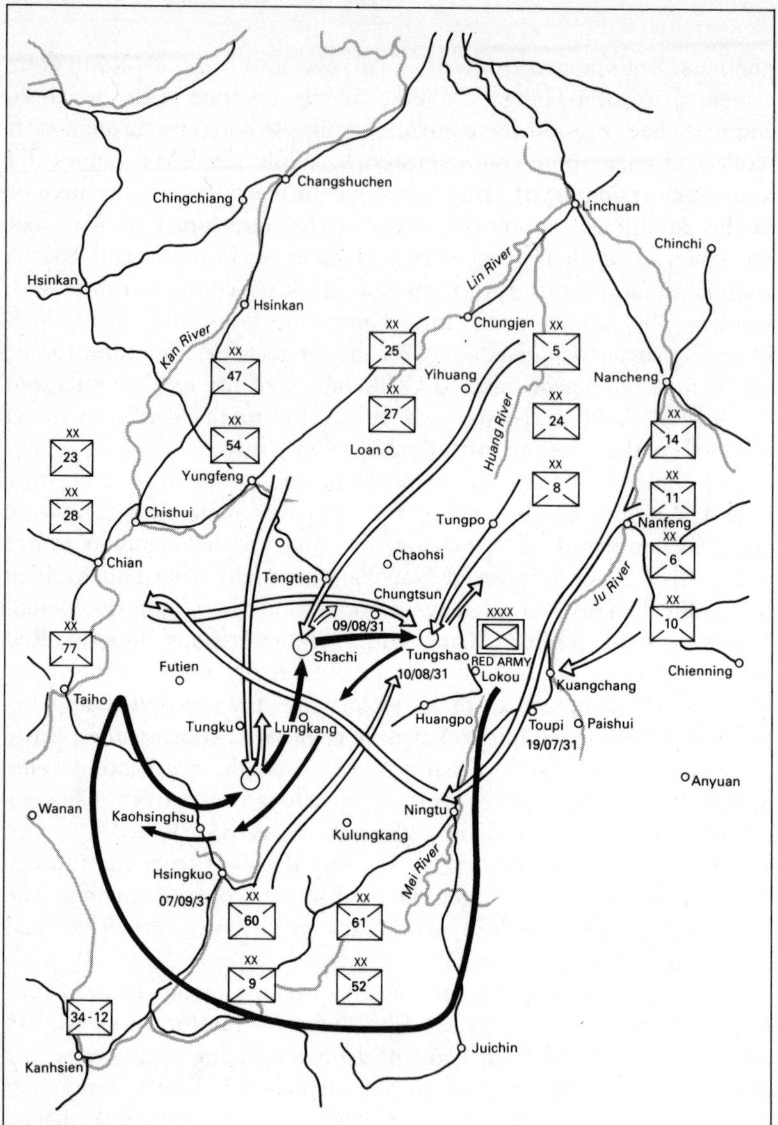

13. The third encirclement campaign, August–September 1931 (After: Whitson, *The Chinese High Command*)

reinforced to a strength of some 40,000 men by the addition of the 9th and 52nd divisions.

Mao and the Red Army leadership decided to fight in the Hsingkuo area, which was already menaced by the advance of Ts'ai T'ing-k'ai's forces in July. Leaving guerrilla forces behind to oppose Ch'en Ch'eng, the main Red Army made a 400-mile, two-week forced march from Ningtu to Juichin, then west around the rear (!) of Ts'ai T'ing-k'ai's forces, assembling at Hsingkuo in early August, undetected by the Nationalists. Meanwhile, Ch'en Ch'eng's powerful army 'made a deep but useless penetration' into the communist base area of southern Kiangsi. They ran out of provisions, and, frustrated by the passive resistance of the Red peasantry, began to harvest unripened rice, drink foul water, and suffer from dysentery.

Mao's plan was 'to move from Hsingkuo by way of Wanan, make a breakthrough at Futien, and then sweep from west to east across the enemy's rear communication lines'. But Ch'en Ch'eng and his subordinate Lo Cho-ying had completed their sweep across the northern part of the Soviet area and were waiting at Futien. Reversing course, the Red Army marched southeast, defeating the 47th Division at Kaohsinghsu on 6 August, then turned north to defeat the 54th Division at Liangtsun on 8 August and the 5th Division between Lungkang and Shachi the following day. In other words the Reds were deliberately avoiding the dangerous armies commanded by Ch'en Ch'eng and Ts'ai T'ing-k'ai while striking blows at exposed divisions already demoralized by defeat in the second campaign. On 10–11 August the Reds attacked Mao Ping-wen's 8th Division in the Huangpi-Tungshao area and defeated it, suffering heavy casualties themselves. 'At this point all the main enemy forces, which had been advancing westward and southward, turned eastward. Focusing on Huangpi, they converged at furious speed to seek battle and closed in on us in a major compact encirclement'. Nevertheless, on the night of 11–12 August the Red Army was able to slip away to the southwest through the seven-mile-wide corridor of mountainous terrain that still separated the closing jaws represented by the armies of Ch'en Ch'eng and Ts'ai T'ing-k'ai.

Reassembling at Hsingkuo, the Red Army was able to rest for a fortnight before the Nationalists found out where they were. Bad weather conditions and the fact that the Red Army was an all-infantry force had combined to make Nationalist air reconnaissance ineffective. After this string of successes, and no doubt feeling very cocky, the Red Army made a frontal attack on two of Ts'ai T'ing-k'ai's divisions entrenched at Kaohsinghsu. The two-day battle (7–9 September) resulted in the loss of one-fifth of the 20,000 Red Army troops committed; P'eng Te-huai was wounded.

This last battle of the third campaign was a setback for the communists, and enhanced the morale and prestige of Ts'ai T'ing-k'ai's forces, who later distinguished themselves opposing the Japanese in Shanghai in 1932. Mao tried to interpret this battle as a partial victory, and claimed that the third campaign ended because 'the enemy forces, hungry, exhausted and demoralized, were no good for fighting, and so decided to retreat'. In reality, the Red Army had failed to dislodge either the 18th Army or the 19th Route Army from the positions deep in the Kiangsi Soviet area that they had occupied. The third campaign ended because the Japanese takeover of Manchuria, commencing on 18 September, created some new political realities. While Chiang was relieved from the previously existing danger of intra-KMT military opposition coalescing around the Kwangsi clique, he also had to deploy his best troops to the Nanking–Shanghai area against the threat of full-scale war with Japan.

Mao was formally elected chairman of the Kiangsi Soviet in November 1931, and its area expanded from 5,000 to 14,000 square miles by late 1932. Ho Lung meanwhile led a ragtag communist force that barely survived in the Hunan–Kiangsi border area, while in the Oyuwan area of the Hupei–Anhwei border Chang Kuo-t'ao organized a Red Army force backed up by an indoctrinated peasantry. Using a strategy identical to that of the main Red Army, but independently evolved, the Oyuwan Soviet area had beaten off two encirclement campaigns, conducted by inferior Nationalist troops, by the end of 1931; a third was scheduled for January 1932.[76]

In the late summer of 1931, as the third campaign of encirclement and annihilation was progressing, Chiang Kai-shek seemed to have almost within his grasp the military reunification of China that was the first step in Sun Yat-sen's programme for national reconstruction. While demoralization with the corruption and ineffectiveness of the Nanking government was already widespread, Chiang was felt to be personally incorrupt, and he had symbolized his claim to be Sun's heir by reburying Sun in the elaborate mausoleum on the slopes of the Purple Mountain, east of

76 Whitson, *High Command*, pp.104–5, 129–37, 275.

Nanking. Chiang could also feel that, by defeating Feng Yü-hsiang and Yen Hsi-shan, he had concluded the Northern Expedition in a real, as opposed to a formal, sense. The adherence of Feng and Yen to the Northern Expedition had been strictly a ploy to preserve their status as warlords. Now Feng was out, and while Yen's subordinates were entrenched in Shansi, Chiang had been able to replace Yen himself by a governor of his own choosing. The so-called 'Southern Opposition' that had recently met at Canton had the army of the New Kwangsi clique as its strongest military support, which army Chiang had succeeded in ejecting from the Wuhan area in 1929. Chiang's military power rested on units descended from the 1st Army Group of the National Revolutionary Army as reorganized in February 1928, commanded by officers trained at or otherwise associated with the Whampoa Military Academy (and its successor, the Central Military Academy at Nanking) – collectively known as the Whampoa clique. These units controlled the central and lower Yangtze provinces and the major treaty ports. Feng Yü-hsiang's former army was broken up into smaller forces under their own generals, whom Chiang never trusted. Yen Hsi-shan's army narrowly averted the same fate, which the survivors of Chang Hsueh-liang's army suffered after the Manchurian Incident. Kwangtung and Kwangsi, along with other interior provinces such as Kweichow, Yunnan and Szechwan, remained under local militarist regimes that were individually and collectively so much weaker than Nanking's armies that their overthrow seemed only a matter of time. In Manchuria, Chang Hsueh-liang's army was much weaker than his father's Ankuochün had been, and the murder of Chang Tso-lin by the Japanese had disposed his son to adopt a nationalist agenda and to deal sincerely with Nanking. While the third campaign of encirclement and annihilation against the Kiangsi communists was not as strategically sophisticated as the later fifth campaign, it was on the verge of succeeding when it was derailed by the outbreak of the Manchurian or Mukden Incident.[77]

77 Lloyd E. Eastman, *The Abortive Revolution: China under Nationalist Rule, 1927–1937* (Cambridge, MA, 1974), pp.1–30, for demoralization within the Nationalist regime; Coble, *Facing Japan*, pp.26–32, for a summary of military factions.

THE MUKDEN INCIDENT

At 11:00 p.m. on 18 September 1931 a section of track of the Japanese-owned South Manchurian Railway at Mukden was destroyed by explosive charges, which the Japanese accused Chinese troops of setting (for a general map of the railways see map 2, p.30). In accordance with contingency plans previously worked out by Colonels Ishiwara Kanji and Itagaki Seishirō, troops of the Japanese Kwantung Army fanned out through the three northeastern provinces. On the instructions of Chiang Kai-shek, who wanted to fix the blame firmly on the Japanese, Chang Hsueh-liang ordered his troops not to resist, so most of them were disarmed. By February 1932 the Kwantung Army, originally not much more than one reinforced division in strength, had taken control of Manchuria and proclaimed its independence as Manchukuo (the country of the Manchus). Aisin Gioro (Henry) P'u-yi, formerly Ch'ing Emperor Hsuan-t'ung (1908–12), was brought out of his exile in Tientsin and installed as regent, and later (9 March 1934) as Emperor K'ang-te, of the new state, but control of all matters remained in Japanese hands. On 7 January 1932 Secretary of State Henry Stimson proclaimed that the United States would not recognize territorial changes in China that violated the Nine Power Treaty (1922) or the Kellogg–Briand Pact (1928). China's diplomats argued her case ably before the League of Nations, whose commission of inquiry led by the British diplomat Lord Lytton duly found that there was no Manchu nationalism or separatist sentiment in the northeast. Japan responded by leaving the League.[78]

The Kwantung Army's move had totally surprised the Japanese political establishment, foreign service, navy, and indeed much of the rest of the army, though the cooperation of sympathetic members of the General Staff contributed to its success. The Mukden Incident is usually and properly described in connection with the failure of collective security that led to the Second World War, the effect of the great depression in promoting political extremism in the advanced countries, and the Japanese military factions of the 1930s. Nevertheless, Chinese behaviour partly

78 The Mukden Incident, because of its importance in the origins of the Second World War, has generated much literature; see especially Sadako K. Ogata, *Defiance in Manchuria: The Making of Japanese Foreign Policy, 1931–32* (Berkeley, 1964); Takehiko Yoshihashi, *Conspiracy at Mukden: The Rise of the Japanese Military* (New Haven, 1963); James B. Crowley, *Japan's Quest for Autonomy: National Security and Foreign Policy, 1930–1938* (Princeton, 1966), pp.82–186; Coble, *Facing Japan*, pp.11–27.

explains the Japanese move, which in turn had a great impact on China.

Throughout the late 1920s Japanese Foreign Minister Baron Shidehara Kijūrō had advocated reasonable accommodation to Chinese nationalism as the best way of preserving Japan's investments and privileges in China. This was a difficult path to walk in view of the strikes, boycotts and acts of violence against foreigners that were part of the 1926–7 revolution, and the passive resistance, bad faith and non-compliance with treaties that had been standard Chinese responses to foreign pressures since the Opium War. Nevertheless, as of 1931 the various fires, of which the Tsinan Incident was the worst, had been put out diplomatically. The local Japanese consul-general (and future prime minister) Yoshida Shigeru hoped to do the same with the Mukden Incident, until his mind was changed by a Japanese major's drawn sword. On 23 November 1931 Chinese Foreign Minister Wellington Koo had proposed withdrawal of Chinese troops to Shanhaikuan while Chinese civil administration continued. Shidehara felt that this was an acceptable basis of negotiation, but the army leadership disagreed. Since the army had already rallied around the Manchukuo programme, Shidehara's position became impossible. The Wakatsuki Cabinet resigned on 12 December, and all the following Japanese Cabinets down to the end of the Second World War insisted, vainly, on international recognition of Manchukuo.

The Japanese invasion of Manchuria derailed the military unification of China that Chiang had been pursuing tenaciously since the start of the Northern Expedition. Chiang in fact never again attained the degree of hegemony over China that he had enjoyed in the summer of 1931. As noted previously, after September 1931 he was forced to permit Yen Hsi-shan to return to power in Shansi and had to make a deal with the Canton–Kwangsi coalition opposed to him, bringing their leaders into the Nanking government. He also had to end the third campaign of encirclement and annihilation against the Kiangsi communists, even though his best troops had not been defeated by the Red Army and still held much of the CCP base area. Chiang understood clearly that the communists' and the opposition warlords' talk of a coalition of all patriotic anti-Japanese elements was intended to get him off their backs. But at the same time the Japanese aggression mortally offended the Chinese nationalism that was strong and deep among China's educated classes and urban dwellers. Chiang knew that, were he to recognize Manchukuo in order to free his hands to deal with his domestic enemies, his own position would crumble. Nevertheless, for him the suppression of domestic resistance always seemed a necessary precondition for the war against Japan that he wanted to wage. As he expressed it, 'the Japanese are a disease of the skin; the Communists are a disease of the heart' – a statement that both explains and summarizes his policies from 1931 to 1937.[79]

79 Chiang expressed the same idea in various ways during 1931–7, 'first pacification, then resistance' being another common formulation; see Coble, *Facing Japan*, pp.56–89.

5 DISEASES OF SKIN AND HEART, 1931–7

Despite the Japanese takeover of Manchuria, Chiang Kai-shek until December 1936 pursued a policy of attempting to keep the Japanese at arm's length while concentrating his military and political energies on suppressing his domestic enemies, chiefly the Chinese communists. The anti-communist strategy was spectacularly successful. The blockhouse strategy used in the fifth campaign of encirclement and annihilation uprooted the communist base areas and forced the Red Army on to the Long March, during which most of the Red soldiers perished or deserted.

This success came at a price. Even after the Northern Expedition, warlord politics was a multi-player zero-sum game: anyone's gain was someone else's loss, and Chiang's effort to enhance his already hegemonial position continued to cause non-Whampoa elements – which otherwise had little in common – to combine against him. Informed opinion held that Chiang tried to keep his Whampoa-led units from damage, while allowing the casualties of the communist suppression campaigns to fall on less favoured units. Pursuing the Red Army on the Long March, Chiang's troops diminished or destroyed warlord autonomy in the provinces they traversed. In North China, the Japanese expansion that was intended to put pressure on China as a whole mainly affected local military commanders formerly affiliated with the Feng Yü-hsiang's Kuominchün or Chang Tso-lin's Ankuochün, whose reduction could be seen as benefiting Chiang. Successes against communists while the Japanese were not being effectively checked thus caused resentment among many military adherents of the Nationalist coalition who themselves were anti-communist. This resentment complemented the rising demoralization of the civilian supporters of the KMT as the regime sank into the corruption and favouritism that characterized the politics of the Nanking Decade, as the years 1927–37 have come to be called. Despite these perceptions, Chiang Kai-shek was sincere in his desire to turn in full force against the Japanese when the time was right, as he proved by throwing his best units into the Shanghai campaign in late 1937, where they were lost.

The creation of Manchukuo left successive Japanese governments with a diplomatic problem they could not solve. The Kwantung Army's unilateral action not only took Tokyo by surprise, but in fact wiped out Baron Shidehara's long-standing policy of coming to terms with the Chinese revolution. Confronted with international isolation but unable to withdraw from Manchukuo, the Japanese realized that Nanking's recognition of Manchukuo was needed to rescue Japan from her position of international isolation. Since Chiang understandably would not grant recognition, the military and political situation in North China was one of repeated crises papered over by settlements disguised as local military agreements, until the outbreak of full-scale war in 1937.[1]

By December 1936 Chiang imagined his pieces were in place, and was directing Shansi warlord Yen Hsi-shan and Chang Hsueh-liang, now headquartered in Sian (Shensi), to suppress the surviving communists assembled in the Yenan area. The kidnapping of Chiang and his forced agreement to an anti-Japanese United Front with the CCP preserved the Red Army and made war with Japan more likely.

MANCHUKUO AND JAPANESE AGGRESSION IN CHINA

Japanese aggression in Manchuria provoked anti-Japanese movements elsewhere. Chinese resigned from Japanese employment, boycotted Japanese goods and stores, demonstrated against Japanese installations, and subjected individual Japanese to verbal and physical abuse. Chiang Kai-shek resisted the pressure to declare war on Japan, placing his hopes instead on League of Nations mediation and on the US/UK support for the territorial integrity of China stated in the Nine Power Treaty of 1922. While US support came in

1 Parks M. Coble, *Facing Japan: Chinese Politics and Japanese Imperialism, 1931–1937* (Cambridge, MA, 1991), is an excellent recent study of this period which goes well beyond previous literature. From the Japanese view, James B. Crowley's classic *Japan's Quest for Autonomy: National Security and Foreign Policy, 1930–1938* (Princeton, 1966) can be supplemented by James W. Morley, ed., *Japan Erupts: The London Naval Conference and the Manchurian Incident, 1928–1932* (New York, 1984) and *The China Quagmire: Japan's Expansion on the Asian Continent, 1933–1941* (New York, 1983).

January in the form of Stimson's non-recognition doctrine, and US public opinion became and remained pro-Chinese, the USA was unwilling to go to war with Japan even as late as 1941, and without US participation League of Nations (meaning British and French) intervention was bound to be short of war and thus ineffective. Indeed, as of January 1932 the British and French were not yet ready for a public declaration of non-recognition.[2] Stimson's statement had been provoked by the Japanese seizure of Chinchou, southwest of Mukden on the railway line to Peiping, a move that seemed to portend the annexation of Jehol province and possibly a move on Peiping itself.

On 28 January 1932 the Shanghai Municipal Council, the governing body of the Shanghai International Settlement, proclaimed a state of emergency due to the boycott. Admiral Shiozawa, in command of all Japanese forces in Shanghai, then moved to secure the Japanese concession area by sending marines (technically Special Landing Forces, which were under the Japanese navy rather than the army) into the adjoining Chinese business district of Chapei. When fighting broke out with Chinese troops, Shiozawa ordered an air bombardment, which permitted foreign newsreel cameramen to film the numerous casualties among the congested civilian population. The Chinese troops of Ts'ai T'ing-k'ai's 19th Route Army, fresh from defeating the Red Army in Kiangsi, fought the Japanese for five weeks. When it was over, the Imperial Navy had been humiliated by asking the Imperial Army for assistance, and several divisions had been committed where the Japanese had thought a single regiment would suffice. Ts'ai and his soldiers became international celebrities, contributing to the overestimation of Chinese military power that distorted US strategy until late in the Second World War. Ts'ai in fact had been violating Chiang's orders by holding out in Chapei, and after he was expelled Nanking concluded (May 1932) a local settlement under which a twenty-kilometre-wide zone was created around Shanghai, from which Chinese troops were excluded.[3] By this time Chiang had neutralized the threat to his military authority (see Chapter 4) started by the Kwangsi–Canton faction of the KMT in May 1931, and so felt free to order the fourth encirclement campaign against the communists.

2 Crowley, *Japan's Quest*, p.155.
3 Coble, *Facing Japan*, pp.11–55.

Despite the emotions generated by the Shanghai Incident, the Japanese were exercising rights there that pertained to all foreign powers signatory to the various unequal treaties with China. Nevertheless, as the incident peaked, Stimson proposed that the USA increase her naval presence in East Asian waters, by implication threatening war with Japan. President Hoover and Secretary of War Patrick Hurley – later President Roosevelt's 'special representative' and US Ambassador to China – demurred, but the Japanese understood that the two Anglo-Saxon powers, who in their view had ganged up on Japan at both the Washington (1922) and London (1930) conferences, would not support Japanese rights even in an area like Shanghai where their own interests were also threatened. This reinforced the Japanese determination to settle the Mukden Incident only by direct negotiation with Chinese authorities, a position insisted upon by Baron Shidehara throughout his career. Involvement of the League of Nations appeared to the Japanese to be merely the old Chinese game of 'using barbarians to control barbarians'. In February 1932 the League Council condemned the Japanese takeover of Manchuria and appointed an investigating commission headed by the Earl of Lytton, a British diplomat. The response of the new Japanese government, headed by the allegedly moderate Admiral Saitō Makoto, a former governor-general of Korea and close associate of Emperor Hirohito, was to recognize Manchukuo in August.

By December 1932 the Japanese were aware that the Lytton report would condemn them, and the Saitō Cabinet approved the conquest of Jehol, which they had resisted until then despite the urging of the army leaders. Jehol and Shanhaikuan Pass were swiftly seized. In February 1933, when the League adopted the Lytton report (only Thailand supported the Japanese position), Japan left the League.[4] Since the USA and the League powers would not fight Japan over China, China was forced to sign the Tangku truce on 31 May. This agreement was signed by Huang Fu, a long-time close associate of Chiang who that month had been appointed chairman of the Peiping political affairs council, with jurisdiction over the affairs of the five northern provinces of Hopei, Chahar, Suiyuan, Shantung and Shansi. Since the Japanese were contemplating further separatist movements in North China, they were willing to deal through Huang, thereby laying the foundation for a claim that North China was somehow autonomous. For Chiang, this procedure

4 Summarized from Crowley, *Japan's Quest*, pp.159–86.

allowed him to delay Japanese expansion without formal recognition of Manchukuo by Nanking. Under the agreement Japan retained Jehol and Shanhaikuan, and a demilitarized zone was created between the Great Wall and the Peiping–Tientsin corridor, from which Chinese troops were barred, and in which order was to be maintained by Chinese 'police'.[5]

The Tangku truce ended the Manchurian crisis in the immediate sense, giving Chiang Kai-shek the breathing space he needed to launch the well-planned and successful fifth encirclement campaign. Despite the regrouping of Chinese politics that occurred after the 1936 Sian Incident, there is no doubt that much of the anti-Chiang KMT left in 1933–4 agreed with Chiang on the two basic points that China needed to suppress the communist rebellion and radically modernize its military forces before it could hope to wage war with Japan. Wang Ching-wei defended Chiang's policy of appeasement, and as Foreign Minister took much of the blame for it, before an attempt on his life on 1 November 1935 removed him for a time from active politics.[6]

For Japan the Tangku truce was a step on the path to the ultimate goal: Chinese recognition of Manchukuo and the conclusion of an anti-communist alliance among the three powers. The Japanese justified the hegemony they aspired to by the term 'Asiatic Monroe Doctrine', an explicit reference to the US Monroe Doctrine for the Western Hemisphere. In May 1934 a Japanese effort to secure a statement of sympathy for this idea was dismissed by Cordell Hull, the new US Secretary of State. In July the new Japanese Cabinet headed by Admiral Okada Keisuke decided to abrogate the Washington and London naval treaties; even greater naval strength was needed if Japan was to pursue, without allies, a policy opposed by the United States, Britain and the Soviet Union. In October Vice-Minister of Foreign Affairs Shigemitsu Mamoru proposed, in an internal policy memorandum, a radical attempt to gain China's support: Japan would call for the abrogation of the unequal treaties, the end of the treaty port/foreign concession system, and the removal of all foreign troops from China. The implied quid pro quo was Chinese recognition of Manchukuo. The leadership of the Imperial Army vetoed this seductive proposal, and on 7 December 1934 the government formally decided to detach the

5 Coble, *Facing Japan*, pp.106–19.

6 In addition to Coble, see John Hunter Boyle, *China and Japan at War: The Politics of Collaboration* (Stanford, 1972), pp.24–43.

provinces of North China from the influence of the Nanking government.[7]

On 29 May 1935 two Japanese colonels from the troop formations stationed in North China under the terms of the 1901 Boxer protocol called on the Peiping Military Council, and rather abruptly demanded the removal of all KMT political organs and Chinese Nationalist troops from the Peiping–Tientsin area. It seemed as if another Mukden crisis was being created, and within a few days the Japanese Naval Staff circulated an appreciation that argued against a North China crisis that might provoke Anglo-American intervention. When Lieutenant-General Umezu Yoshijirō, the commander of these Japanese forces, returned to his station, he found War Minister Ho Ying-ch'in, one of Chiang's most trusted subordinates, with instructions to meet the Japanese demands. The Ho–Umezu agreement signed on 10 June effectively eliminated the formal presence of the Nanking government in Hopei province, provoking panic in Peiping and angry demonstrations elsewhere. While the Japanese wanted to detach Hopei, they were not united among themselves as to how to accomplish this goal, and the Nanking government had in fact reacted weakly to a veiled threat that might have had little Japanese force behind it.

Meanwhile in Chahar, Major-General Doihara Kenji, already famous for his role in bringing Emperor Henry P'u-yi out of his Tientsin exile in 1932, was intriguing to set up an autonomous regime under the local military commander Sung Che-yuan, an old Feng Yü-hsiang subordinate who had no love for Chiang Kai-shek. On 18 June Chiang summoned Sung to Nanking, designating one of Sung's subordinates, Ch'in Te-ch'un, head of the Chahar Political Council. Doihara promptly escalated to threats, and on 23 June the hapless Ch'in signed the Ch'in–Doihara agreement, which provided for the withdrawal of Nationalist troops from half the province, elimination of KMT organs, restriction of Chinese immigration, and Japanese 'advisers' in the provincial government. Chahar was a less important loss than Hopei, and Doihara's threats more credible, but Doihara's ambitions extended beyond Chahar to Suiyuan and to the idea of arousing a pro-Japanese nationalism among the Mongols of Inner Mongolia.[8]

Japanese politics were thrown into more confusion than usual by the assassination of Major-General Nagata Tetsuzan – Chief of the Military Affairs Bureau of the War Ministry and a leading

7 Crowley, *Japan's Quest*, pp.196–201.

8 Crowley, *Japan's Quest*, pp.214–17; Coble, *Facing Japan*, pp.202–13.

proponent of technical modernization – on 14 August 1935, which led to the resignation of War Minister Hayashi Senjuro, the exposure of the deep rifts within the officer corps, and greater difficulty in controlling the field armies in China. On 24 November General Yin Ju-keng, who had been administering the demilitarized zone in eastern Hopei created by the T'angku truce, issued, with the backing of the Japanese Kwantung Army, a declaration of independence of the East Hopei Autonomous Anti-Communist Council (later government). Yin's declaration roasted the Nanking government for its failure to rid China of communism, and restored the old five-barred republican flag. It also set back General Doihara's plan to create a larger five-province autonomous state, to be called Huapeikuo ('North China') and to be composed of Hopei, Chahar, Suiyuan, Shantung and Shansi. Ho Ying-ch'in went north again, and after some involved negotiations the Nanking government on 12 December issued a mandate creating the Hopei–Chahar Political Council under 29th Route Army commander (and former Feng Yü-hsiang subordinate) Sung Che-yuan. Even though Sung was a slippery rascal, and was not really under anyone's control, the Hopei–Chahar Political Council was conceived as essentially the puppet of Doihara and the other expansionists associated with the Tientsin Garrison, afterwards the North China Area Army.[9]

In other words, as of late 1935, elements of the Japanese army, acting without much cooperation among themselves, much less reference to Tokyo, had created two north Chinese puppet regimes (the East Hopei Autonomous government and the Hopei–Chahar Political Council) outside of Manchukuo. Prince Te's Inner Mongolian movement may be considered a third. The proliferation of these entities permitted Chiang Kai-shek to disguise losses to the Japanese as concessions by autonomous local authorities, thereby avoiding the direct negotiations between Nanking and Tokyo leading to the recognition of Manchukuo that the Japanese government itself desired. The leading contemporary student of Japanese military politics notes that the 'political intrigues of the field armies in North China in the fall of 1935 fatally compromised the efforts of the foreign ministry to commit Chiang Kai-shek to some type of modus vivendi with the Japanese government.'[10]

9 Crowley, *Japan's Quest*, pp.224–30; Boyle, *Politics of Collaboration*, pp.39–42; Coble, *Facing Japan*, pp.267–77.

10 Crowley, *Japan's Quest*, p.237.

Japan in 1936 was convulsed by the February coup attempt of elements of the Tokyo-based 1st Division. The leaders of the coup had been inflamed by the rowdy public court martial of Lieutenant-Colonel Aizawa, the assassin of General Nagata, which had turned into a soapbox for extended denunciations of the existing regime and calls for direct imperial rule. The restoration of discipline following the revolt led to forced retirement or other penalties against many of the officers involved in the Mukden Incident and subsequent aggression in China, though most of these penalties were subsequently reversed. The new Cabinet (March 1936 to January 1937) headed by former Foreign Minister Hirota Koki concluded the Anti-Comintern pact with Germany and Italy in November, and emphasized naval construction and acquisition of modern weapons in its military policies. Expansion in China had a lower priority.[11]

Nevertheless the Kwantung Army continued to support the Mongolian autonomy movement led by Prince Te (Demchukdonggrub), who had been established in Pailingmiao in northern Suiyuan since April 1934. Chinese leaders since the 1911 revolution had refused to consider Mongol demands for a unified and autonomous Inner Mongolia; they preferred to continue the Ch'ing dynasty policy of divide and rule using the many Mongol princes. Shansi warlord and 'model governor' Yen Hsi-shan inherited this tradition. Fu Tso-yi, his governor of Suiyuan (1931–47), with the assistance of the Inner Mongolian communist leader Ulanfu (himself a prince), was able to break up Prince Te's operation in February 1936, driving him fully into the arms of the Japanese, with whom he had had prior dealings. The Japanese provided him with weapons and advisers, and after some other adventures including an attempt on his life in August, Prince Te returned in October 1936 leading a 15,000-man Manchurian–Mongolian army to retake Pailingmiao. Fu Tso-yi's men, reinforced with some Nanking units, put up an unexpectedly fierce resistance. On 24 November they took Pailingmiao back, capturing numerous documents that established Prince Te's Japanese connections and permitted him to be publicly declared a traitor.[12]

This victory of Chinese troops over Japanese surrogates

11 Crowley, *Japan's Quest*, pp.244–9, 262–76.

12 Crowley, *Japan's Quest*, pp.306–8; Coble, *Facing Japan*, pp.325–33; Donald G. Gillin, *Warlord: Yen Hsi-shan in Shansi Province, 1911–1949* (Princeton, 1967), pp.230–41.

provoked demonstrations of nationalism and created a feeling among many Chinese that China could challenge Japan successfully. This feeling contributed to the Sian Incident that began on 7 December 1936. Unfortunately China remained militarily very weak compared to Japan, despite the efforts at military modernization of the Nanking government.

KMT EFFORTS AT MILITARY MODERNIZATION

Chiang Kai-shek could fight the communists effectively with troops armed and trained at the levels of the early 1930s, and with political techniques drawn from the Chinese tradition; this was demonstrated by the partial success of the third encirclement campaign and the total success of the fifth. Fighting the Japanese, on the other hand, required the creation of a truly modern army with air support and technical services, and artillery, mortars and machine guns in adequate numbers and with appropriate supplies of ammunition. Such military modernization was beyond China's reach in the 1930s. Even if Chiang had finally been able to unify all the Chinese armies under his command, China's industrial infrastructure was no match for Japan's and was not likely to become one. Further, these industries were concentrated in the treaty ports and connected by sea and river transportation. China was thus extremely vulnerable to Japan's unchallengeable naval power, which, as the event showed, could reach up the Yangtze River past Wuhan. Despite the emotional satisfactions of calling for armed resistance to Japan, full-scale war was a losing proposition unless the Anglo-Saxon powers were willing to destroy the Japanese navy on China's behalf.

Such military modernization as could be achieved was a good thing in itself. As part of the KMT–CCP split of 1927, Chiang sent home the Soviet military advisers and hired Colonel Dr Max Bauer, retired from the German army of the First World War. Bauer had been Chief of Operations under General Erich Ludendorff and thus represented the elite of German General Staff training. In 1933 Colonel-General Hans von Seeckt came out to head the advisory mission, on the invitation of Lieutenant-General Georg Wetzell. Seeckt had been Field-Marshal August von Mackensen's Chief of Staff during the First World War and commanded the much reduced postwar army – the 100,000-man Reichswehr – from 1919 to 1926. He brought along General Alexander von Falkenhausen, who succeeded him in 1935. Chiang greatly respected the German officers, whose numbers peaked at about 100 in 1934,[13] and who were finally withdrawn at Hitler's order in May 1938. As late as 1944 the record of Major-General Albert C. Wedemeyer, USA, at the prewar Berlin Kriegsakademie smoothed his way as Stilwell's successor.[14]

Despite their deservedly high military reputations, the German advisers brought with them a set military doctrine that really could not be transferred to the China of the 1930s. German military theory, as it had evolved by the 1870s, depended on a mass army mobilized from a well-educated and highly nationalistic population, rapidly deployed using efficient railway and telegraphic systems, winning the campaign through a battle of annihilation (Vernichtungsschlacht) that in turn would permit an end to the war and a rapid demobilization of the soldiers to resume their civilian economic functions. Though new to China, the Germans quickly realized that the lack of an educated population and other infrastructure limited the transferability of the German model. Like their US successors during the Second World War, however, the Germans never came to terms with the way that military discipline and military professionalism were corrupted by Chinese social and political realities. Some Chinese generals in turn believed that German advice on 'operational matters was impractical because they did not understand the psychology of Chinese soldiers, or the historical backgrounds of particular units, or the intricacy of power relations between the commanders. What appeared to be rational, scientific ways of handling things were often politically untenable in China.'[15] One might add in passing that little has changed since then.

Given these constraints, it was difficult to achieve even much more limited goals. The Germans advised Chiang on troop demobilization, a matter in which political concerns had to be uppermost. They also gave advice on the strategy of the fourth and fifth encirclement campaigns. The decisive blockhouse strategy of the fifth campaign, however, owed more to Chinese historical precedents, in particular the experience of the nineteenth-century rebellion-quellers Tseng Kuo-fan and Tso Tsung-t'ang, than to the

13 Hsi-sheng Ch'i, *Nationalist China at War: Military Defeats and Political Collapse, 1937–1945* (Ann Arbor, 1982), pp.13–14.

14 F.F. Liu, *A Military History of Modern China, 1924–1949*, (Princeton, 1956), p.61; William C. Kirby, *Germany and Republican China* (Stanford, 1984), especially pp.190–232, for a general account of this period.

15 Ch'i, *Nationalist China*, p.14.

German assistance. Anticipating Stilwell in the Second World War, the Germans decided to create a cadre of sixty divisions within the Chinese army, organized, armed and equipped according to German prescriptions. This programme also offered markets for German arms industries, and the resulting products certainly looked German, some units retaining the distinctive German helmet throughout the Second World War. The Germans preferred to use trained units as cadres to train other units; this permitted the most rapid rate of expansion and was in fact the procedure they were using in Germany itself to transform the 100,000-man Reichswehr into the Wehrmacht of the Second World War. However, an army being trained and expanded in this manner was not available for operations, and Chiang slowed the training programme by using these divisions for the ongoing war against the communists.

According to a table published in February 1937,[16] the Chinese army contained 176 divisions affiliated factionally as follows:

31 Chiang Kai-shek (including 10 with German training)
18 ex-Chang Hsueh-liang Manchurian Army
12 ex-Feng Yü-hsiang
8 Yen Hsi-shan Shansi Army
6 Kwangsi clique (Li Tsung-jen, Pai Ch'ung-hsi)
15 Kwangtung
12 Hunan
9 Yunnan and Kweichow
27 Szechwan
38 miscellaneous northern (30) and southern (8) provincial

personal & regional, not a true national army.

Presenting the situation in this way understates Chiang's relative strength. The Szechwan troops were rabble even by warlord standards, and the same applied to most of the 'miscellaneous' divisions. Feng Yü-hsiang and Chang Hsueh-liang were in exile, with their divisions controlled by higher formations headed by Chiang supporters. The same might have happened to Yen Hsi-shan, but (as related on pp.154–5) his return to provincial power in Shansi was part of the fallout from the Manchurian Incident. Chang Hsueh-liang later (1934 and 1935) returned to operational command with Chiang Kai-shek's permission, an error that led up to the Sian Incident. In 1931, however, the Wang Ching-wei-led

16 Ch'i, *Nationalist China*, p.37.

southern opposition to Chiang was supported by the Kwangsi, Kwangtung, Hunan and Yunnan-Kweichow armies, all of which manifested elements of 'professionalism' and commitment to KMT goals. Each was individually weaker than Chiang's contingent, but united they potentially threatened Chiang's hegemonial status.

As part of the compromise with the southern opposition, Chiang gave up the chairmanship of the Executive Yuan to Wang Ching-wei from December 1931 to December 1935. He retained the chairmanship of the National Military Council (created March 1931), and the War Ministry, nominally subordinate to both bodies, remained (1930–44) under Ho Ying-ch'in, possibly Chiang's staunchest supporter. Chiang in other words retained his military power, but at the price of institutionalizing disunion within the KMT governmental structure. The transfer of Whampoa to Nanking illustrated another aspect of this disunion. Wang insisted on creating a Central Political Academy under his control, so Chiang's Central Military Academy was restricted to a more narrowly military role. Nevertheless, its work continued, it became a centre of German influence, and Chiang continued to regard even its youngest graduates as members of his own Whampoa clique.[17]

Despite the formal intra-KMT peace of these years, Chiang's policies were bitterly hated by those outside the Whampoa clique. The Fukien rebellion of 1933 illustrated this discontent. The 19th Route Army had been transferred to Fukien after its highly publicized battles, under the command of Ts'ai T'ing-k'ai, with the Japanese in Shanghai in 1932. Some observers, including former 19th Route Army commander Ch'en Ming-shu (vice-chairman of the Executive Yuan since December 1931), attributed the transfer to Chiang's jealousy that a non-Whampoa formation should gain such glory. Ch'en resigned his post in 1932 due to a corruption scandal, travelled to Europe, and returned determined to use the 19th Route Army against Chiang Kai-shek. In November 1933 Ch'en rebelled, creating a 'government' at Foochow nominally headed by Kwangtung elder statesman Li Chi-shen and nominally supported by anti-Japanese hero Ts'ai T'ing-k'ai. Nanking forces suppressed this rebellion in January 1934; the leaders fled to Hong Kong, formed a committee and issued calls for war with Japan, as had now become standard for all politicians opposed to Chiang Kai-shek.[18]

17 Liu, *Military History*, pp.78–83.
18 Coble, *Facing Japan*, pp.131–5.

Nanking's efforts at military modernization were only slightly successful, but even much greater success would not have permitted China to challenge Japan. F.F. Liu argues that 'had the war been delayed for two more years, China might have had 60 German-trained army divisions to throw against the invaders. In the air Messerschmitt and Stuka [*sic*] planes would have carried her markings and, under the sea, Chinese-manned U-boats would have harassed Japanese shipping in submarine wolf-packs.'[19] Apart from the overconfident anticipation of the Second World War developments, it is really not possible to imagine KMT China coping with the Japanese naval and air threats, no matter how long the war was delayed; the Japanese, after all, were not exactly standing still in these areas, and throughout the 1930s her navy and her air forces were comparable to (and threatening to) those of the United States and Britain. Hsi-cheng Ch'i argues the contrary: resistance like that of the 19th Route Army 'might have deterred further Japanese aggression' even at a high price, and Nanking 'lost a golden opportunity to exploit mass nationalistic fervour'. These are both good points, but Ch'i also states that 'exclusive concern with conventional military power . . . unnecessarily excluded unconventional forces and guerrilla warfare from the range of possible Chinese responses.'[20] Unfortunately, one can wage guerrilla warfare only in territories already lost by conventional means; urging the KMT to give up the coastal cities that were the economic basis of its strength and to rely on a guerrilla warfare that might not materialize (for example, there was no significant armed opposition to Japanese rule in 'Manchukuo') was simply not realistic. No amount of time would permit China to defeat Japan without foreign help. Defeating the communists was another matter.

THE FINAL ENCIRCLEMENT CAMPAIGNS AND THE LONG MARCH

Mao Tse-tung's elevation in November 1931 to the political leadership of the Kiangsi Soviet area had as one consequence his removal from direct command of troops. This elevation coincided with, and was part of, the general takeover of CCP affairs by the Returned Student or Twenty-Eight Bolshevik faction, which emphasized a more regular style of warfare and a return to urban

19 Liu, *Military History*, p.102.
20 Ch'i, *Nationalist China*, p.36.

revolution. 'Under the combined influence of Chou En-lai, Chu Te, P'eng Te-huai, Yeh Chien-ying and the Comintern adviser Li Te' Maoist military theory and practice 'faded from the scene'.[21] Most of these people repledged themselves to Mao after the débâcle of the fifth campaign, and Mao in his later writings blamed 'the Li Li-san line' for everything that went wrong, while attributing communist successes to the brilliance of his own leadership and – especially – to the novelty of the strategy later called People's War. In reality (as noted on pp.168–9) the Japanese seizure of Manchuria had forced Chiang to call off a still promising third campaign in 1931, even Mao's leadership would have been unlikely to produce victory in the fifth campaign, and similarly the Sian Incident saved the CCP at a critical moment. Without denying the importance of Maoist strategy, CCP victory was nevertheless greatly aided by circumstances beyond full CCP control.

In January 1932 the third encirclement campaign against Chang Kuo-t'ao's communist forces in the Oyuwan Soviet area began. Once again independently operating Nationalist columns penetrated a CCP area and were defeated in detail. In Anhwei the communist forces captured 15,000 rifles and some 20,000 prisoners, and then in March the German-trained and equipped division of T'ang En-po was defeated in southeastern Honan, adding its arms to the communist inventory. By the end of this campaign the Oyuwan communist forces totalled more than 70,000 men and 40,000 rifles, plus machine guns, mountain howitzers, mortars and wireless equipment.[22]

After the end of the Shanghai Incident in late April 1932, Chiang Kai-shek concentrated some 400,000 troops (33 divisions) against the Oyuwan Soviet. Lacking adequate room to manoeuvre against forces of this size, the CCP leaders waged a series of positional defence battles, which they lost. Forced westward, Chang Kuo-t'ao and his subordinates planned to break through the encirclement at its weakest zone along the Peking–Hankow railway in Hupei and march west into Szechwan, despite orders to the contrary from the Central Committee. Nationalist leadership was not perfect, and on one occasion two Nationalist divisions fought each other all night before the dawn's early light permitted mutual recognition. Nevertheless the Nationalists 'methodically constructed

21 William W. Whitson, *The Chinese High Command: A History of Communist Military Politics, 1927–1971* (New York, 1973), p.57.

22 Whitson, *High Command*, p.137.

fortifications in ever smaller concentric circles',[23] in other words anticipating the blockhouse strategy successfully employed in Kiangsi in 1934.

The Oyuwan forces broke out on 20 August 1932, beginning a four-year odyssey that eventually led them to Yenan and merger with the survivors of the more famous Long March from Kiangsi. They survived in large measure because their opponents were the squalid local warlords of Szechwan and Shensi, and because Chiang concentrated his efforts down to the end of 1936 first on the Kiangsi communists and then on the non-Whampoa Nationalist forces. After the communist forces merged, resentment of Mao Tse-tung's increasingly dictatorial stance led to Chang Kuo-t'ao's defection, but his subordinates remained important in CCP military affairs.

Also in August 1932, the main CCP leadership, meeting at Ningtu, Kiangsi, had stripped Mao Tse-tung of his remaining military authority and had shelved the idea of People's War. Chu Te led the senior CCP commanders, most with formal military education and experience in the warlord armies, who felt that the growth in power of the Kiangsi Soviet made possible an active defence 'beyond the borders' of the CCP controlled area. By this time the fourth campaign of encirclement and annihilation was already under way. Chiang Kai-shek had deployed 70,000 troops on the Kiangsi–Fukien border, 70,000 Kwangtung troops on the Kwangtung border, and 100,000 Central Army troops in rear area security and anti-communist operations in Kiangsi and Hunan areas beyond the Kiangsi Soviet area proper. This left a field force of only 154,000 (17 divisions) to confront 65,000 armed communists, but the Nationalists intended to build up the field force after the Oyuwan campaign. Lin Piao, armed with radio intercept warning of Nationalist plans, went south to attack Hsinfeng and then Namyung (Kwangtung), where the communists suffered heavy casualties in battle against Ch'en Chi-t'ang's Cantonese troops.[24]

Breaking off this battle, Lin and the main communist force returned via Hsinfeng to Kanhsien (July 1932) and continued north, marching rapidly through Hsingkuo, Loan and Yihuang, in the process driving weaker Nationalist forces away from the northern and western borders of the expanded Soviet area. Then they crossed the Ju River and regrouped at Chienning (Fukien) in December.

23 Whitson, *High Command*, p.138.

24 Whitson, *High Command*, pp.275–7.

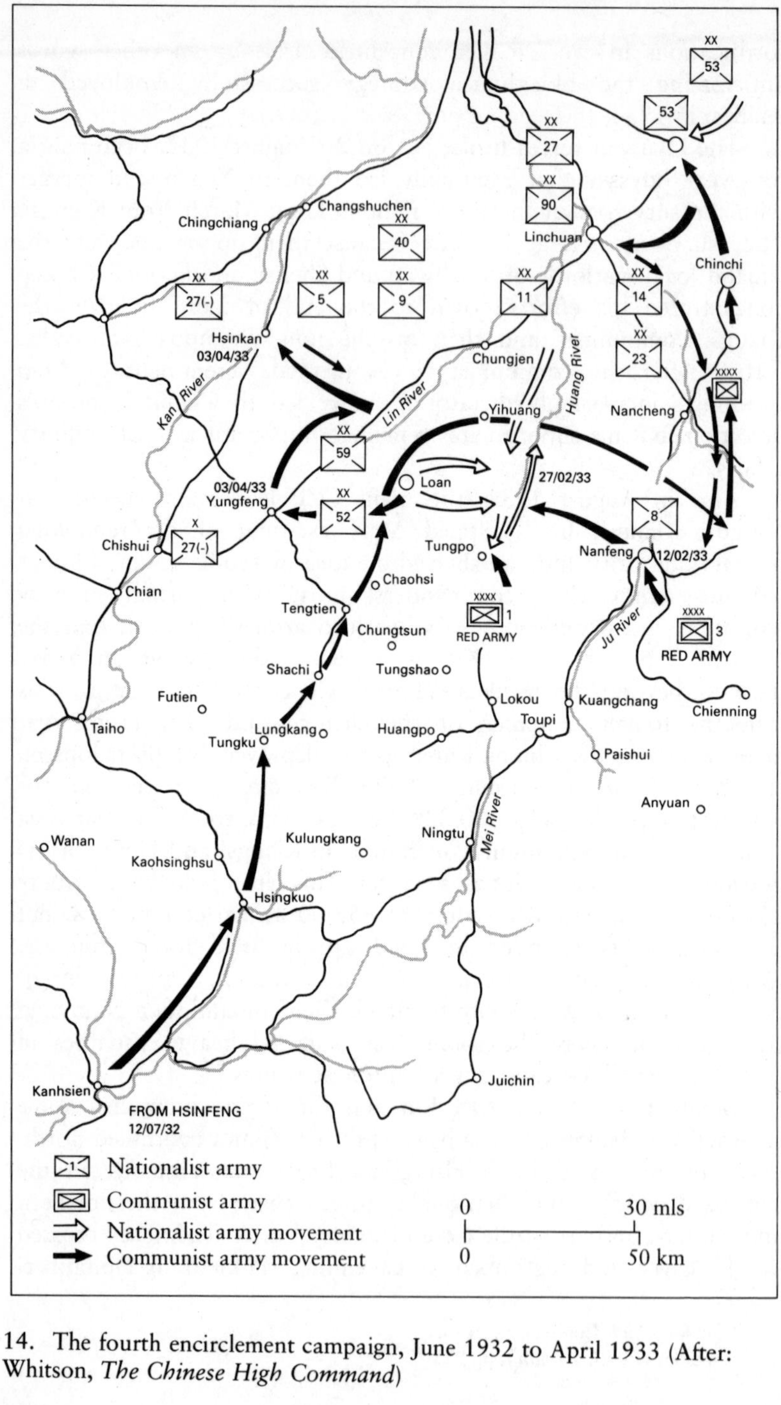

14. The fourth encirclement campaign, June 1932 to April 1933 (After: Whitson, *The Chinese High Command*)

Chiang Kai-shek then announced the official end of the campaign against the Oyuwan Soviet, which presaged more active operations in Kiangsi. Lin, the leading advocate of the theory of People's War in the 1960s, ironically argued in 1932–3 for a strategy of territorial defence that contradicted the basic concepts of People's War, declaring that 'not one inch of the Soviet would be trampled by Nationalist troops', and then striking pre-emptively to the north to raid Tunghsiang (January 1933) and then Ch'en Ch'eng's headquarters at Linchuan.

Returning, the communists laid siege to Nanfeng, whose Nationalist commander T'ao Chih-yueh conducted an exemplary resistance. Ch'en Ch'eng sent the 52nd and 59th divisions from Loan to relieve Nanfeng. Marching separately, they were separately ambushed on successive days (27–28 February) as they tried to traverse communist territory directly. One division was nearly wiped out, the other saved after heavy losses by the arrival of the 11th Division from Yihuang. While admitting that communist forces captured over 10,000 rifles, Mao's assessment that the Red Army 'in the main' had been victorious seems grudging.[25] In fact the strategy of pre-emptive attacks 'beyond the borders' of the Soviet area had been successful everywhere, even though it was also true that the principal battlefield success of the fourth campaign had been scored against Nationalist forces suffering the usual intelligence blindness after entering a territory inhabited by a hostile peasantry. In other words, victory in the fourth campaign, which ended on 29 April 1933, did not really tell the communists how to deal with the blockhouse strategy of the fifth. Even before the fifth campaign opened, the effects of a tightening Nationalist blockade on the agriculturally marginal lands of the Kiangsi Soviet area were being felt.

Communist victory in the first four encirclement campaigns in Kiangsi (sometimes partial, and with a boost from the Japanese in the third) had been won with the aid of a politically aroused peasantry that multiplied the operational effect of the Red Army. The Nationalist leadership was aware of the political dimension of the conflict, but their inability to provide a solution reflected the conflicts of purpose within the KMT coalition. Such political measures as were attempted (propaganda, police and administrative reform, cooperative societies, pao-chia and related militia-type

25 Mao Tse-tung, *Selected Works of Mao Tse-tung* (4 vols, Peking, 1961–5), I, p.231.

organizations) were half-heartedly and incompletely implemented. Land reform, as is well known, was not attempted by the KMT at all until its enforced exile on Taiwan after 1949, and only then under strong US pressure and supervision.[26] While the communist land law of 1 December 1931 had the ultimate effect of driving the rural elite into the arms of the KMT, it was popular among the poor peasants and the landless. William Wei concludes that down until the end of the fourth campaign in April 1933, KMT 'attempts to control the countryside were ineffectual. What control it did have continued to diminish because of provincial security forces, proclivities for milking the countryside of resources. Meanwhile the area under CCP control was growing.'[27]

Early in 1933 the communist government in the Kiangsi Soviet intensified the land reform, extending it to recently annexed areas. Meanwhile (as noted on pp.187–9), communist strategy during the fourth campaign took the Red Army 'beyond the borders' of the Soviet area. Faced with a communist movement that was both violently radical and evidently expanding, the Kiangsi rural elite became much more sympathetic to the KMT. Previously the landlords had benefited from an atmosphere of violence and lawlessness in which they were the strongest parties; now they looked to the state to convert the lands they held – often without clear title – into legally registered property and then to defend their property against attacks from below.[28]

For the fifth campaign the Nationalist leadership employed a radically different strategy. The Kiangsi Soviet area was surrounded by even larger numbers of troops, intensifying the economic blockade that was already noticeable during the fourth campaign. Nationalist columns overran the Soviet area, mainly from the north, but once each sector was cleared of regular Red Army forces it was sealed off by a line of multi-storey blockhouses, looking like small medieval castles, spaced close enough together to permit overlapping fields of fire. Communist doctrine metaphorically compared the Red Army to a fish swimming in the ocean of the people; the Nationalists now had designed a net to catch the fish. The

26 William Wei, *Counterrevolution in China: The Nationalists in Jiangxi during the Soviet Period* (Ann Arbor, 1985), pp.68–70. Wei's exposition of the effectiveness of KMT political measures during the fifth encirclement campaign period should be contrasted with Suzanne Pepper, *Civil War in China: The Political Struggle, 1945–1949* (Berkeley, 1978), on KMT political failures during 1945–9.

27 Wei, *Counterrevolution*, pp.99–100.

28 Wei, *Counterrevolution*, pp.101–2.

blockhouse strategy was labour intensive, and therefore needed the active cooperation of the rural elite and the labour resources they could coerce. The blockhouse strategy also required the rapid building of roads and bridges and stringing of telephone lines, so that the Nationalist columns could advance in a coordinated manner and be capable of mutual reinforcement.[29]

Mao Tse-tung blamed Chiang's German advisers for the blockhouse strategy. As noted previously (pp.182–3), the Prussian-German theory of war, articulated in Moltke's slogan 'march separately, fight together', was based on mutually supporting independent columns, and the Germans were impatient with the slow pace of the blockhouse strategy, which in their view permitted the escape of communist forces to the next sector while the blockhouses were being constructed. Far from being of German derivation, the blockhouse strategy was based on the strategy used by Tseng Kuo-fan, one of Chiang's heroes, to suppress the Nien rebellion in central China in the 1860s. Tseng's approach, itself based on some very ancient Chinese precedents, was followed by his disciple and collaborator Tso Tsung-t'ang to suppress Muslim rebellions in Shensi-Kansu and in Sinkiang in the 1870s and 1880s. In these rebellion-suppression campaigns, the rebellions had been suppressed sector by sector and the pacified areas secured by the planting of military colonies of soldiers demobilized from the armies that had done the suppressing. It will be remembered that Tseng and Tso were the founders of the 'militia army' concept, under which the Taiping rebellion had been suppressed by armies under civilian elite leadership, recruited from a relatively stable peasant population (rather than from the usual sources of Ch'ing soldiers) who could return effectively to farming.

Chiang made Tseng Kuo-fan one of the exemplary heroes of his New Life Movement,[30] and, while he did not imitate exactly the details of Tso's and Tseng's operations – historical circumstances having changed – the strategy of the fifth campaign resembled that of the nineteenth-century statesmen in two important respects. These were the slow and painstaking sector-by-sector suppression of the rebellion, and the creation of a system of rural control to prevent the rebellion from recurring. Both depended on the mobilization of the rural elite behind the KMT, which had the side-effect of driving

29 Wei, *Counterrevolution*, pp.104–19.

30 Wei, *Counterrevolution*, pp.76–81, on the New Life Movement and its limitations.

the KMT further to the right. In the shorter run, however, KMT alignment with the rural elite was a great success. At the time of the Northern Expedition, the radicalism of the KMT left and the alignment with the CCP made many landlords fearful of a KMT government, despite support of its nationalist goals. Now, threatened by the communist revolution clearly manifested in the land policies of the Kiangsi Soviet, the rural elite had good reason to support the KMT, which in turn needed them. Now peasants rounded up by the landlords built the blockhouses and the other infrastructure needed by the blockhouse strategy, while the landlord-led rural paramilitary groups provided both the information and the muscle needed to destroy the communist organizations in the areas from which the Red Army had been driven.

After months of preparation, the main operations of the fifth campaign got under way in April 1934. Advancing from the north were the Nationalist 8th Army (from Taiho on the Kan River), 7th Army (from Yungfeng), 3rd Army (from Yihuang) and 5th Army, which advanced up the Ju River from Nancheng and took Kuangchang on 28 April. These were supported on the east and south by the 10th Army (from Chienning, Fukien) and the 4th Army, which took Changting, Fukien, on 10 October. While the 800,000 KMT troops included some of Chiang's best formations, they varied widely in quality, but the same was true of the 150,000 troops the CCP classed as regulars, some of whom were recently promoted guerrilla units.[31]

As the campaign opened the communist leadership – Chu Te, Chou En-lai and the Comintern adviser Li Te – hoped to repeat the strategy of forward defence that had evidently succeeded in the fourth campaign. This time, contrary to the experience of the previous campaigns, successful cooperation between the Nationalist columns turned the opening stages of the campaign into a sequence of positional battles which the outnumbered communists lost. The Nationalists advanced slowly, three or four kilometres per day, refusing to be drawn into communist ambushes.[32] The lengthening lines of blockhouses prevented the Red Army from moving rapidly throughout the Soviet area, as it had in the first four campaigns. The fall of Kuangchang on 28 April was the occasion for meetings at Juichin in which the communist leadership began to consider the

31 Whitson, *High Command*, pp.278–80.
32 Whitson, *High Command*, p.278.

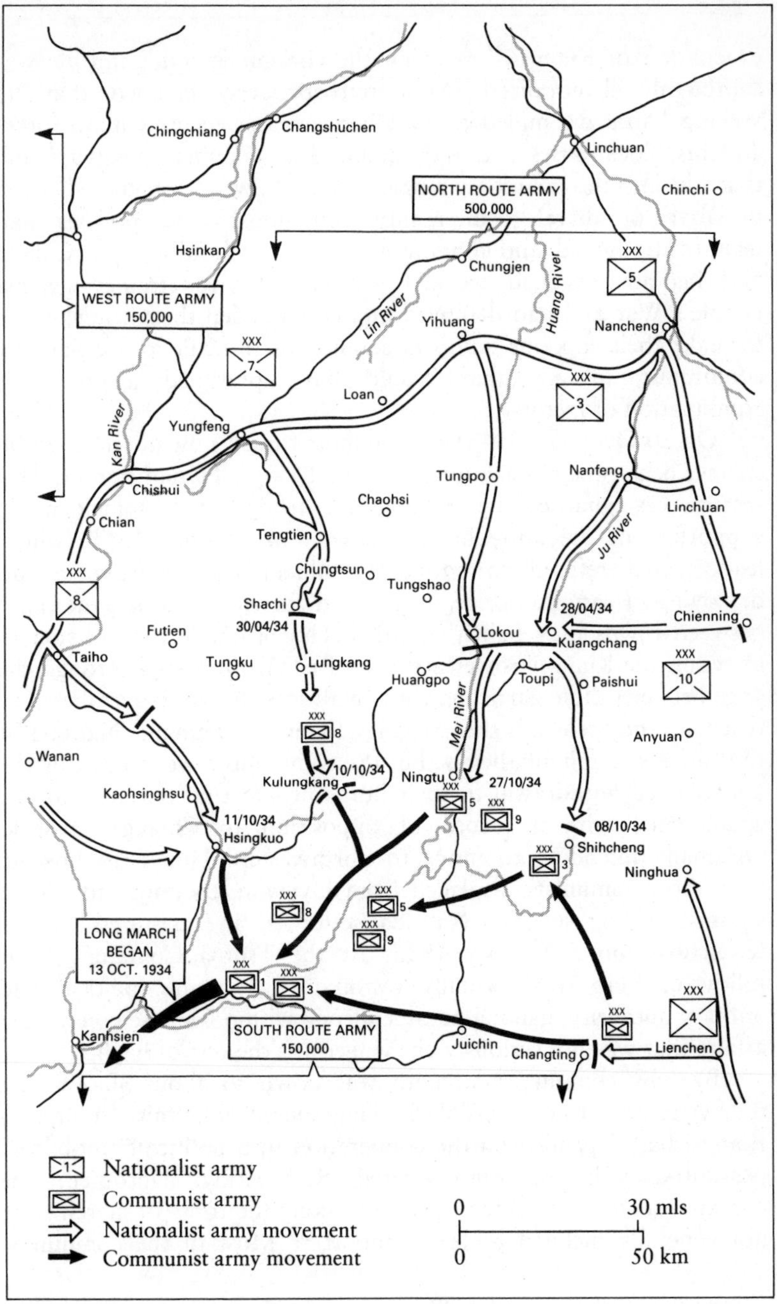

15. The fifth encirclement campaign, April–October 1934 (After: Whitson, *The Chinese High Command*)

evacuation of Kiangsi.[33] By then the communist rank-and-file was thoroughly demoralized. Mao retrospectively claimed that 'in seeking battle we milled around between the enemy's main forces and his blockhouses and were reduced to complete passivity' and that during the whole campaign 'we showed not the slightest initiative or drive'.[34] In reality communist land policies had prompted elite-led anti-communist rural mobilization, and Chiang and his advisers had worked out an effective strategy against People's War and had deployed and commanded their armies so as to make their superior numbers count. It is difficult to imagine any communist strategy that would have prevailed against this combination of factors.

On 20 October 1934 the communist forces, now about 102,000 strong, began their breakout along the Kiangsi–Hunan border. This sector was guarded by Kwangtung troops, not coincidentally supporters of the anti-Chiang tendency within the KMT, whose leaders had refused to adopt the blockhouse strategy, instead deploying in battalion or regiment-sized garrisons that left the space between towns only lightly guarded. Having made the decision to abandon the Kiangsi Soviet area, the Red Army passed through the gaps between these garrisons with small loss. In late November they reached and crossed the Hsiang River in Hunan; Nationalist resistance was initially heavy, but the communists were aided by the unexplained withdrawal to their home province of Kwangsi forces, again units with a record of opposition to Chiang Kai-shek. Originally intending to move to northwestern Hunan to link up with the communists displaced from Oyuwan, they instead turned south, avoiding superior Nationalist forces, and captured Tsunyi, Kweichow, on 5 January 1935. At the Tsunyi Conference that followed, Mao was formally restored to supreme political and military authority, gaining an ascendency within Chinese communist affairs that was not seriously challenged for the rest of his life.

By now communist strength was down to about 30,000 and they were in fact not particularly dangerous. Communist strength in Kiangsi had depended on the cooperation of a politically mobilized peasantry with the outnumbered Red Army. Uprooted, the communists discovered that 'peasants along the route of march were not generally inclined to lend support.'[35] Most of the communist

33 Whitson, *High Command*, p.281.
34 Mao, *Selected Works*, I, p.231.
35 Whitson, *High Command*, p.282.

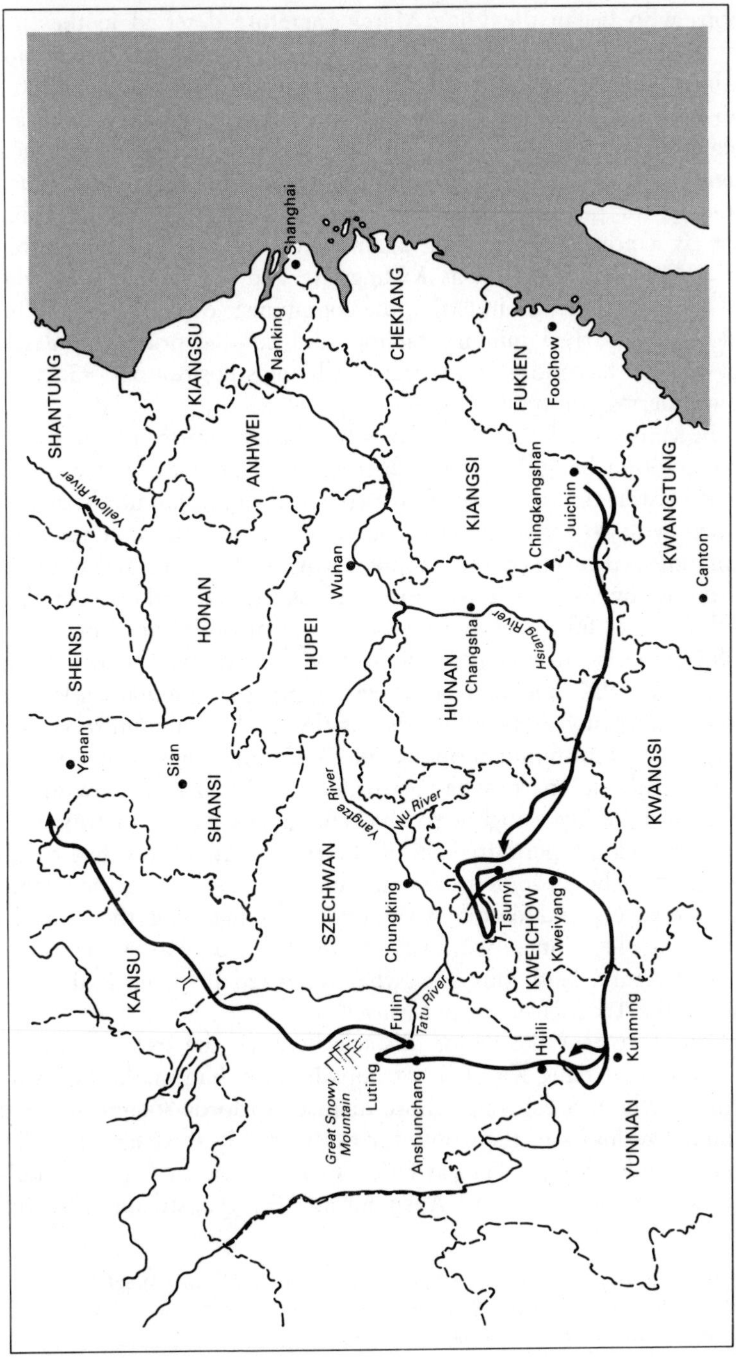

16. The Long March, October 1934 to October 1935

troops who began the Long March therefore deserted in the first few months. The remainder had, beyond survival, the two major goals of joining forces with the ex-Oyuwan forces under Chang Kuo-t'ao and founding a new base area. Even had they done so, Chiang Kai-shek had by now demonstrated that he understood their strategy and could root them out once again. Chiang has been much criticized for pursuing the communists halfheartedly and for using them as a pretext for moving against rival military factions within the KMT. As noted, it was Kwangtung and Kwangsi troops who had been instrumental in letting the communists escape in late 1934, and since the rival military factions did control provincial bases, they were in fact more of a threat to Chiang's position in 1935 than the wandering communist forces.

In March 1935 the communists first headed north in search of a linkup with Chang Kuo-t'ao, then reversed course, feinted south toward Kweiyang (the Kweichow provincial capital), and afterwards headed west toward Yunnan. Marching in multiple columns, the communists threatened the Yunnan provincial capital at Kunming, but in fact bypassed it, crossed the Chinsha River, and concentrated north of it at Huili in early May. Yunnan warlord Lung Yun, the Yi (Lolo) minority nationality militarist who had overthrown T'ang Chi-yao in 1927 and had later been appointed commander of the 13th Route Army by Nanking, essentially let the communists transit his province with minimal opposition. After some tense negotiations, during which all parties had to drink from a cup filled with the blood of a freshly slaughtered chicken, Lung's fellow Yi tribesmen in eastern Sikang permitted the Red Army to march north through their lands. The Yi looted the communists of everything they could take, however, and despite CCP efforts to highlight their shared hostility to the Chinese warlords of Szechwan, only a few Yi joined the Red Army. With this somewhat restricted help the Red Army reached the Tatu River by mid-May.[36]

The Tatu was the major obstacle between the two communist armies, since Chang Kuo-t'ao's troops by now had made their way across northern Szechwan, whose divided warlords sought as usual to minimize losses to their own forces. Normally travellers from the south would cross the Tatu at Fulin, strongly held by Liu Wen-hui's Szechwan troops, or at the Anshunchang Ferry upstream. The Red

36 Whitson, *High Command*, pp.283–6; Dick Wilson, *The Long March, 1935: The Epic of Chinese Communism's Survival* (New York, 1982), pp.137–43, on the treatment of the communists by the Yi.

Army in fact captured the ferry boat, but feared destruction if they relied on the single boat to ferry the whole army across, eighty men at a time. The communist leadership therefore decided to try for the iron chain suspension bridge at Luting, about 80 miles north and upstream from Anshunchang. This bridge had been built at Emperor K'ang-hsi's orders in 1701, and lay on the main road from Szechwan west to Tibet. The walled county town of Luting was on the east bank and was held by two Szechwan regiments. The defenders had removed the planking from the bridge as a defensive measure. On the night of 25 May Red Army troops crossed against machine gun fire, suspended on the bare chains above the turbulent and deadly waters (this episode has since become a stock theme of PRC calendar art). In the morning they were joined by the men who had crossed at Anshunchang and had marched up the east bank. The defenders fled.[37]

After Luting the communists marched east to Yaan, then north via Paohsing across the snow-covered and storm-ridden Chiachinshan mountains to Moukung. The Luting Bridge, the crossing of the Chiachinshan, and the later crossing of the grasslands of Sungpan provided the themes for much revolutionary art as the story of the Long March evolved into legend. At Moukung on 16 June 1935 the Chu–Mao column, technically the 1st Front Army, finally joined up with the Chang Kuo-t'ao column, officially the 4th Front Army. Chang in fact had some 45,000 men with 20,000 rifles, while the 1st Front Army was down to about 10,000 men.[38] Mao and the Central Committee were with the 1st, however, and they had numerous grudges against Chang: he had been too soft on the landlords during the Oyuwan period, he had abandoned Oyuwan precipitately, he had failed to make a serious effort to link up with the 1st Front Army, and his staff organization and general command style had too much of warlordism in it. It might be noted in fairness to Chang that a more accommodating policy toward the landlords aided the CCP in the 1937–49 period, and that the junction of the two communist columns required one of them to cross the Yangtze or the Tatu, which, as the Luting Bridge battle showed, was not an easy task.

As these tensions matured, the combined communist force marched north across the difficult and mountainous country of western Szechwan. Rallying at Maoerhkai, west of Sungpan, in early

37 Wilson, *Long March*, pp.151–61.

38 Whitson, *High Command*, pp.144–5, 287.

July, the leaders debated future strategy. Mao wished to move to northern Shensi, where local poverty would make People's War practicable, and where proximity to Japanese puppets (Prince Te's Inner Mongolian movement) would make the CCP's anti-Japanese posturings plausible even to non-communists. Chang wanted to create a new government in Szechwan, failing which he wanted to go to Sinkiang where direct contact with the Soviet Union would be possible. Mao's revolutionary romanticism and his constant citation of tactical ideas from the picaresque novels *Shui Hu Chuan* (*Outlaws of the Marsh*) and *Romance of the Three Kingdoms* had long grated on those communist leaders possessed of a more modern military education. These issues were not resolved, and Mao led those units whose commanders agreed with him on the difficult march around the fringes of the Sungpan grasslands into Kansu. After more difficult marches and battles with local forces, whose commanders once again failed to unite to destroy the communists, Mao's column reached northern Shensi in early October 1935. Mao and his followers dug in (literally as well as metaphorically; much of the rural population in this treeless area of thick loess topsoil deposits lived in caves, and the communist leadership enhanced its image by following their example) in the Yenan area and devoted themselves to creating Soviet organizations among the local peasantry.[39]

The column of the Long March led by Mao Tse-tung after his triumph at the Tsunyi Conference, and including Mao and the CCP Central Committee even before then, had traversed over 3,000 miles from southern Kiangsi to northern Shensi. From around 100,000 men at the time of the breakout from Kiangsi, the column had dwindled to about 10,000 who reached Yenan. Much of this loss, however, was the result of desertions shortly after the breakout, of Kiangsi natives suddenly confronted with awareness of the consequences of abandoning their home areas. The sheer hardships of the march accounted for much of the rest of the loss. Nationalist pursuit itself could have been more effective, but Chiang Kai-shek had some other concerns: there were two other marching communist columns – Ho Lung's from Hunan and Chang Kuo-t'ao's, the latter larger and better armed than Mao's, marching north of the Yangtze from the Oyuwan area on the Hupei–Anhwei border – and Chiang as usual was trying to use the situation to enhance the position of his own Whampoa group within the overall Nationalist coalition.

39 Whitson, *High Command*, pp.145–9.

The movement of the Mao column became known as the Long March, to the exclusion of the other columns, because the fall of Chang Kuo-t'ao left Mao's Yenan operation as the only significant communist activity in China.

Mao Tse-tung's flight to Shensi is often regarded as the end of the Long March, but Chang Kuo-t'ao retained the greater half of the Red Army including Chu Te, Liu Po-ch'eng, Hsu Hsiang-ch'ien and other famous leaders. Mao had radioed the other Red Army units to cross into Kansu and follow him. By now the passes used by Mao were blocked by Nationalist troops, some under Whampoa clique strongman Hu Tsung-nan, and the Cantonese General Hsueh Yueh was now commanding anti-communist efforts in Szechwan on behalf of Chiang Kai-shek. The split between the communist armies had been preceded by unpleasant political disputes in which Chang had been isolated and regularly outvoted by Mao's rubber-stamp majority on the CCP Central Committee. Chang now accused Mao of perfidy, formed a Provisional Central Committee under his own leadership, and planned a campaign to capture Chengtu, the capital of Szechwan province.

After failing to break through Hsueh Yueh's defensive positions in the Lushan–Tienchuan area in September 1935, Chang's troops retired to Moukung, whence they moved much further west to winter in Kantzu in northern Sikang from November 1935 to June 1936. During this period Chang learned that his plan to move his army west into Sinkiang had been personally approved by Joseph Stalin, who promised Soviet military assistance in that event. In June 1936 Ho Lung, who had conducted his own Long March from Hunan through Yunnan into Sikang, joined Chang at Kantzu with about 5,000 men. The combined force then left Kantzu and, aided by excellent early summer weather, retraced the route past Sungpan and crossed into the Minhsien region of Kansu against poorly coordinated Nationalist opposition.

So far Chang's troops had marched as if Chang intended to join up with Mao, but in fact Chang retained the support of most of the army for the Sinkiang venture. Seizing Chingyuan, Chang ferried about 1,000 troops a night across the Yellow River. By the time Nationalist pressure closed this off in mid-September 1936, some 22,000 men including Chang were on the west bank. The rest of Chang's 35,000-man army, including Chu Te, mostly made it to Yenan to join Mao. Chang's forces marched westward up the Kansu corridor, harried by the cavalry of Ma Pu-fang and the other Muslim warlords of his family, who despised the communists as atheists from another province. Near Chiuchuan in January 1937 most of them were wiped out. While the embittered survivors, including Hsu Hsiang-ch'ien, blamed Mao for not sending reinforcements, these events nonetheless destroyed Chang Kuo-t'ao's credibility as a military and political alternative to Mao Tse-tung within the CCP.[40] By then the Sian Incident had drastically altered Chinese politics.

THE SIAN INCIDENT AND THE DRIFT TO WAR

During 1935–36 Chiang Kai-shek was much criticized by his German advisers for pursuing the communists too slowly, and later historians have savaged him for allowing them to escape. In the circumstances of those years, Chiang was probably correct in viewing the fleeing communists less as a threat than as a means of consolidating his control of the KMT against the persisting opposition of the Kwangsi clique and the Hunan and Kwangtung forces allied to them. It will be remembered that these forces had allowed the communists to escape into the Long March in the first place. Pursuit of the Long Marchers brought central government troops, some under the formidable Hsueh Yueh, into Hunan, Kweichow and Szechwan, which Chiang honoured by his personal presence from March to October 1935.[41] Liu Hsiang, the principal Szechwan warlord, resented this, though he retained some of his eroding authority until his mysterious death in 1938. Liu Wen-hui, the second most important Szechwan warlord, made a deal with Chiang under which his troops were redesignated the 24th Army and he ruled Sikang from Yaan until the communist takeover.[42] Lung Yun in Yunnan also accepted Chiang's supremacy with a show of enthusiasm, and as a result retained his autonomous authority until the KMT coup of 1945.[43]

This left the old 'Southern Opposition' centring on Li Chi-shen and Ch'en Chi-t'ang of Kwangtung and the Kwangsi triumvirate of

40 Whitson, *High Command*, pp.150–4, citing Chang Kuo-t'ao's memoirs and Whitson's interviews with Chang; Wilson, *Long March*, pp.236–43.

41 Robert A. Kapp, *Szechwan and the Chinese Republic: Provincial Militarism and Central Power, 1911–1938* (New Haven, 1973), p.117.

42 Kapp, *Szechwan*, pp.124–41; A. Doak Barnett, *China on the Eve of Communist Takeover* (New York, 1966), pp. 215–29, evokes images of Liu Wen-hui's final days of power.

43 Lung Yun's biography in Howard L. Boorman, ed., *Biographical Dictionary of Republican China* (4 vols, New York, 1967–71), II, p.458.

Li Tsung-jen, Pai Ch'ung-hsi and Huang Shao-hsiung. This opposition derived legitimacy, from the KMT point of view, from the qualified support of Sun Yat-sen's old revolutionary associate Hu Han-min. When Hu died in May 1936, Ch'en and the others anticipated that Nanking would move against them. Ch'en, with Li Chi-shen's support, marched into Hunan in June, proclaiming loudly that he was going north to fight the Japanese since Chiang would not. Ch'en's position crumbled quickly. First the Canton air force and next (8 July) his chief subordinate Yü Han-mou defected to Nanking. Yü then accepted Nanking's appointment as governor of Kwangtung, while Ch'en left for Hong Kong on a British gunboat. He was soon joined by Li Chi-shen, who had gone to Kwangsi during this episode.[44] Kwangsi then fell into line and was forgiven, its troops receiving the designation 5th Route Army, and its leading generals (Li and Pai) serving very visibly in the long war to follow.

As Mao's communists congregated around Yenan, they became near neighbours of Shansi warlord Yen Hsi-shan. Yen, as befitted a Japanese Military Academy graduate (class of 1909), was personally well disposed toward the Japanese, and many Japanese soldiers returned the favour by fighting for him in the 1945–9 period. Nevertheless, Yen was threatened by the Japanese in 1935–6, and was no doubt correct in his belief that Chiang was willing to sacrifice Shansi, including Yen, as part of his general policy of appeasing Japan. Yen was also vulnerable to communist-led rural insurrection on the Kiangsi Soviet model. Despite Yen's heavily promoted schemes of economic development, Shansi remained poor and socially stratified. In February 1936 communist forces crossed the frozen Yellow River into southwestern Shansi, where they remained until April. They seem to have been foraging for food and recruits, rather than trying to establish a permanent base area, but nevertheless acted in their usual Robin Hood manner, killing the rich (including the richer peasants) who fell into their hands while being solicitous of the poor. The latter responded enthusiastically, while the resistance of Yen's army was apathetic. After the communists withdrew, Yen built a network of blockhouses along the Yellow River, and executed hundreds of people suspected of having collaborated with them.[45]

44 Boorman, *Biographical Dictionary*, I, pp.162–3 (Ch'en Chi-t'ang), and II, p.294 (Li Chi-shen).

45 Gillin, *Warlord*, pp.208–28.

Despite the foregoing, Yen Hsi-shan seems to have come to an understanding with the Chinese communists in the summer or autumn of 1936. In the end, Yen feared the Japanese army support of Prince Te in Suiyuan more than he feared the communists.[46] The latter were, of course, calling loudly for a United Front of all patriotic forces to resist Japan, and these calls were being echoed and amplified by KMT civilian supporters in China's major cities. Chiang Kai-shek resisted this pressure. He flew out to Sian in October to confer with his local commanders, who were Chang Hsueh-liang and Yang Hu-ch'eng. Chang, the former chief of the Fengtien military clique, had commanded various phases of the anti-communist campaigns since his return from Europe in February 1934 and had been at Sian since mid-1935, commanding Fengtien troops transferred away from North China as a result of the Ho–Umezu agreement.[47] As for Yang, though he had opposed the communist invasion of Shensi at the end of the Long March, he was nonetheless an old supporter of Feng Yü-hsiang, who was now hoping to ride to a comeback on the anti-Japanese wave.[48]

Chiang was unhappy with his October meeting with Chang and Yang. He ordered Whampoa clique general Hu Tsung-nan – a staunch Chiang loyalist and anti-communist – to attack the Shensi communists from his base in Kansu.[49] Chiang himself returned to Nanking, and then in November flew out to Taiyuan. There he praised Yen Hsi-shan's efforts in resisting Japan, promised him assistance, tried to persuade him to cooperate in destroying the communists, and in the end failed to overcome Yen's suspicions or win his support. Before the month was over, Yen's troops under Fu Tso-yi's command had defeated Prince Te's Japanese-equipped Inner Mongolian army at Pailingmiao, as noted previously.[50] Fu and Yen became national heroes, public opinion was reinforced in its conviction that resistance to Japan was militarily possible, and it was widely noted that the victory had been won by the Shansi troops on their own, without any assistance even from the Central Army units on the scene in Shansi.[51] Chiang, in the face of these

46 Gillin, *Warlord*, pp.228–33.

47 Boorman, *Biographical Dictionary*, I, pp.66–7, for Chang Hsueh-liang.

48 James E. Sheridan, *Chinese Warlord: The Career of Feng Yü-hsiang* (Stanford, 1966), pp.207, 273–6.

49 Lyman P. Van Slyke, *Enemies and Friends: The United Front in Chinese Communist History* (Stanford, 1967), pp.71–4.

50 Gillin, *Warlord*, pp.234–9.

51 Coble, *Facing Japan*, pp.325–33, especially for the impact of the Pailingmiao battle on Chinese opinion.

mounting pressures, still hoped to destroy the Chinese communists in one final campaign, and made arrangements to fly out to Sian again in early December and to place Chang Hsueh-liang and Yang Hu-ch'eng under the control of one of his most trusted subordinates, Chiang Ting-wen, a fellow Chekiang militarist who had been a star of the third and fifth Kiangsi campaigns.[52]

Before dawn on 12 December, troops of Chang Hsueh-liang's bodyguard surrounded Chiang Kai-shek's compound, shot his guards, and broke in. Chiang, awakened by the gunfire, fled in his nightshirt, only to be captured shortly afterwards. China held her breath for two weeks, until on Christmas Day Chiang Kai-shek and Chang Hsueh-liang flew back to Nanking on Chiang's private plane. Chang was promptly tried and convicted by a military court; still alive as of June 1994, he has spent most of his life since 1936 under house arrest, never giving a public account of his part in the Sian Incident. With the deaths of the other principals, it is unlikely that the many ambiguities of the event will ever be resolved.

Chiang Kai-shek had arrived at Sian on 4 December and had ordered the campaign against the communists to begin on the 12th. Evidently he also indicated that certain 'rebellious northeastern troops' (Chang's) were to be transferred south for 'reorganization'. Chang instead 'arrested' Chiang, confronting him with an eight-point demand (also released publicly) calling for all the usual good things: admission of all patriotic elements into the government, release of all political prisoners, end civil wars, etc. These demands not only closely paralleled CCP propaganda, but also resembled Feng Yü-hsiang's public stance after his betrayal of Wu P'ei-fu in 1924. Yang Hu-ch'eng, Feng's former subordinate, actually had more troops in Sian than Chang, and these celebrated Chiang's kidnapping with several hours of shooting and looting. Yang seems to have regarded himself as the proper warlord of the Sian area, and to have exploited this issue as an opportunity to keep central government influence out of the area.[53]

Chang Hsueh-liang telegraphed Yen Hsi-shan, who publicly condemned the kidnapping while endorsing the idea of a nationwide mobilization against Japan. Chiang Ting-wen was sent back to Nanking, where leading KMT luminaries such as T.V. Soong, Ho Ying-ch'in and Mme Chiang overruled proposals for an armed

52 For Chiang Ting-wen, see Boorman, *Biographical Dictionary*, I, pp.350–4.

53 Van Slyke, *Enemies and Friends*, pp.75–81, and the more recent detailed and critical account in Coble, *Facing Japan*, pp.342–61. There is also Wu Tien-wei, *The Sian Incident: A Pivotal Point in Modern Chinese History* (Ann Arbor, 1976).

expedition against Sian, preferring negotiations for the generalissimo's release. Stalin, and therefore the Soviet Union, promptly took the line that the kidnapping was the work of the Japanese or their Chinese sympathizers, and ordered the CCP to work toward his release. Despite Mao's reported anger at Stalin's highhandedness, a high-level CCP delegation including Chou En-lai and Yeh Chien-ying went to Sian and worked for the release of Chiang and the creation of a formal Second United Front (so called to distinguish it from the 1924–7 KMT–CCP United Front in effect during the Northern Expedition). As for Chang Hsueh-liang, whatever his motives were (and one may not doubt his hatred for the Japanese, who had murdered his father), they were at least in part altruistic. Chang may have felt that the popularity of his anti-Japanese stance would protect him and give him a further military role, but he must have known as he boarded the plane that he was also a hostage.[54]

In January 1937 the Nanking government's Bandit Suppression headquarters at Sian was formally abolished, but Chiang Kai-shek nevertheless inserted central government troops and removed Yang Hu-ch'eng from command. In February both the KMT and the CCP issued statements on the conditions for a United Front, under which the CCP agreed to stop trying to overthrow the national government and to stop confiscating landlords' land, and to designate the Soviet government a 'special region' of the Republic of China and the Red Army as a unit or units of the Chinese army as a whole. Formal agreement on these terms came only after the Marco Polo Bridge Incident.[55] The Red Army in Shensi was then given the designation, famous in later years, of 8th Route Army (under Chu Te, with P'eng Te-huai as his deputy) composed of the 115th (Lin Piao), 120th (Ho Lung) and 129th (Liu Po-ch'eng) divisions. The three divisions were the successors, respectively, of the Kiangsi Soviet (1st Front Army), Hunan communists (2nd Front Army) and Oyuwan forces (4th Front Army). The remaining organized communists in East China were redesignated the New 4th Army.[56]

Coming soon after the Pailingmiao victory, the apparent KMT–CCP reconciliation was wildly popular among students, city dwellers and others whose allegiance the KMT needed to keep.

54 Van Slyke, *Enemies and Friends*, pp.81–8.
55 Van Slyke, *Enemies and Friends*, pp.88–91.
56 Chalmers A. Johnson, *Peasant Nationalism and Communist Power: The Emergence of Revolutionary China, 1937–1945* (Stanford, 1962), pp.73–4.

Chiang Kai-shek was not able immediately to violate these sentiments by resuming war against the communists; this conflict really did not recommence until the New 4th Army incident of January 1941. Chiang seems to have concluded that he could not give in to the Japanese in the event of a new provocation, but he did not go out of his way to seek trouble with them. Yen Hsi-shan, whose troops had won the Pailingmiao victory, felt the same way, and spent the first half of 1937 trying to upgrade his army.[57] The communists and the lesser regional warlords similarly were preoccupied with local survival. The immediate effect of the Sian Incident and the Second United Front thus was not to increase the intensity of resistance to Japan but rather to freeze the political status quo in China. For the record, at least, Chiang had always claimed that once China was firmly unified under his leadership, he could wage war against Japan. This was less likely after December 1936.

The Japanese thought differently. A Foreign Ministry assessment in January 1937 concluded that 'although the terms of the compromise [at Sian] were not made known . . . we may not be too amiss is concluding that an agreement was reached at least on one point – namely, to resist Japan'.[58] For the next several months, however, domestic politics took precedence in Japan as the Imperial Army first brought down the Cabinet of Hirota Kōki (February), then blocked the formation of a Cabinet under General Ugaki Kazushige, who was considered too liberal by his fellow generals. General Hayashi Senjurō, the army's choice as prime minister, failed to create a majority in the Imperial Diet, and resigned in June. His successor, the Fujiwara aristocrat Prince Konoe Fumimaro, had been in office less than a month when the Marco Polo Bridge Incident confronted both Nanking and Tokyo with a crisis which contained the potential to escalate into all-out war, and from which neither government felt capable of walking away.

57 Gillin, *Warlord*, pp.243–50.
58 Crowley, *Japan's Quest*, p.310.

6 THE SINO-JAPANESE WAR, 1937–41

Full-scale hostilities between China and Japan resulted from the Marco Polo Bridge Incident of 7 July 1937. From 1937 to 1939 the Japanese army and navy overran the most important and heavily populated regions of China, suffering few setbacks in an essentially unbroken string of victories. Chinese leaders blamed their defeats on inferior armament and equipment, but Chiang Kai-shek's command practices, the factional splits in the Chinese military, and the continued distrust between the KMT and the CCP (despite the Second United Front) were also important factors. The Japanese army in this period, though attempting to modernize, remained largely an infantry force armed with rifles and machine guns, whose technical backwardness compared to contemporary European armies showed clearly in their defeat by the Red Army at Nomonhan in 1939.[1] While China could not cope with the Japanese naval power that blockaded her by sea and reached up her rivers, her small air force under Chennault achieved some surprising successes, and she might have done even better on the ground had her leadership actually been unified. Chinese were willing to die for their country in large numbers, but her leaders were still not willing to cooperate in her defence.

By mid-1939 the Japanese had conquered the densely populated, urbanized and (relatively) foreign-trade orientated parts of China that had previously been the main support of KMT rule. Peiping and Tientsin in Hopei had been conquered, along with lesser interior capitals such as Taiyuan and Kalgan. Japanese rule stretched down the railway lines past Shantung's capital at Tsinan to the great cities of Hangchow in Chekiang and Shanghai, Soochow and

1 Alvin D. Coox, *Nomonhan: Japan against Russia, 1939* (2 vols; Stanford, 1985), is the definitive account of this important undeclared war, in which the Japanese 23rd Division was decimated by forces commanded by future Marshal of the Soviet Union G.K. Zhukov. Stalin ended the conflict because of the outbreak of war in Europe in September 1939.

Nanking in Kiangsu. In 1938 the Japanese reached up the Yangtze River and took Wuhan in Hupei, whither Chiang had removed the national capital after the fall of Nanking. Meanwhile the Japanese, who were unchallengeable at sea, had captured all the major seaports: Tsingtao, Foochow, Amoy, Swatow and Canton itself, so that China was tightly blockaded by the sea routes over which her imports had traditionally come. Chiang Kai-shek had removed his government to Chungking in Szechwan province, and the Nationalists still held Kiangsi's capital at Nanchang and Hunan's capital at Changsha despite Japanese attacks. By breaking the Yellow River dikes the Nationalists had prevented the Japanese from taking the Honan railway junction of Chengchow and thereby completing the railway link from Peiping to Wuhan, and the Nationalists also held Sian and the rest of the Wei River valley in Shensi. The poor southwestern provinces of Szechwan, Kwangsi and Kweichow remained under Nationalist rule, as did Yunnan, from which the recently completed Burma Road into the British colony of Burma provided a low-capacity access to the outside world, as long as the British government could resist Japanese pressures to close it.

From 1939 to late 1941 the battle lines in China did not change very much. Indeed, the Japanese did not significantly expand the territory in China under their control until the ICHIGO offensive in 1944. But for Japan the China Incident was always conceived primarily as a means of pressuring the Chinese government to recognize the 'independence' of Manchukuo, and the threat and later emergence of Great Power conflict in Europe provided both dangers and opportunities for Japan. Policy debate in Japan considered and rejected a northern advance directed against the Soviet Union and opted for a southern advance against colonial Southeast Asia, whose metropolitan countries were either overrun by the Germans in 1940 (France, Netherlands) or fully preoccupied with fighting the Germans (Britain). Japan of course underestimated the United States, but correctly assumed that being on the winning side in a world war would permit her to settle the China Incident on her own terms.

The outbreak of the Second World War in Europe relieved Japan of the Russian threat at Nomonhan, but left her in control of more Chinese territory than she could effectively occupy, with no political solution in sight. Both Japan and China described the shooting war as an 'incident' in order to avoid triggering the US Neutrality Laws. Japan's preferred solution was US and Chinese recognition of Manchukuo in return for Japanese withdrawal from the rest of China. The USA consistently refused to discuss the

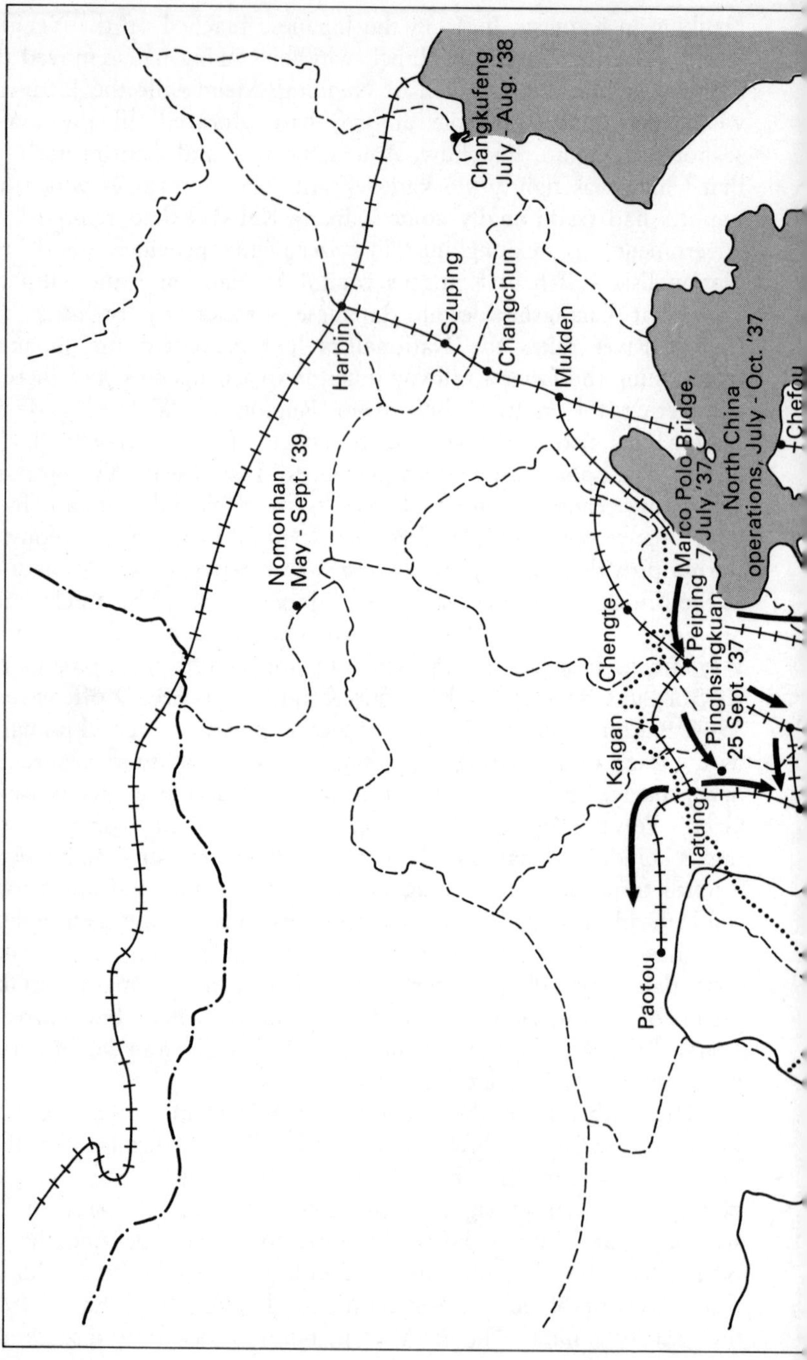
Changkufeng
July - Aug. '38
Szuping
Changchun
Harbin
Mukden
Marco Polo Bridge,
7 July '37
North China
operations, July - Oct. '37
Chefou
Nomonhan
May - Sept. '39
Chengte
Peiping
Pinghsingkuan
25 Sept. '37
Kalgan
Tatung
Paotou

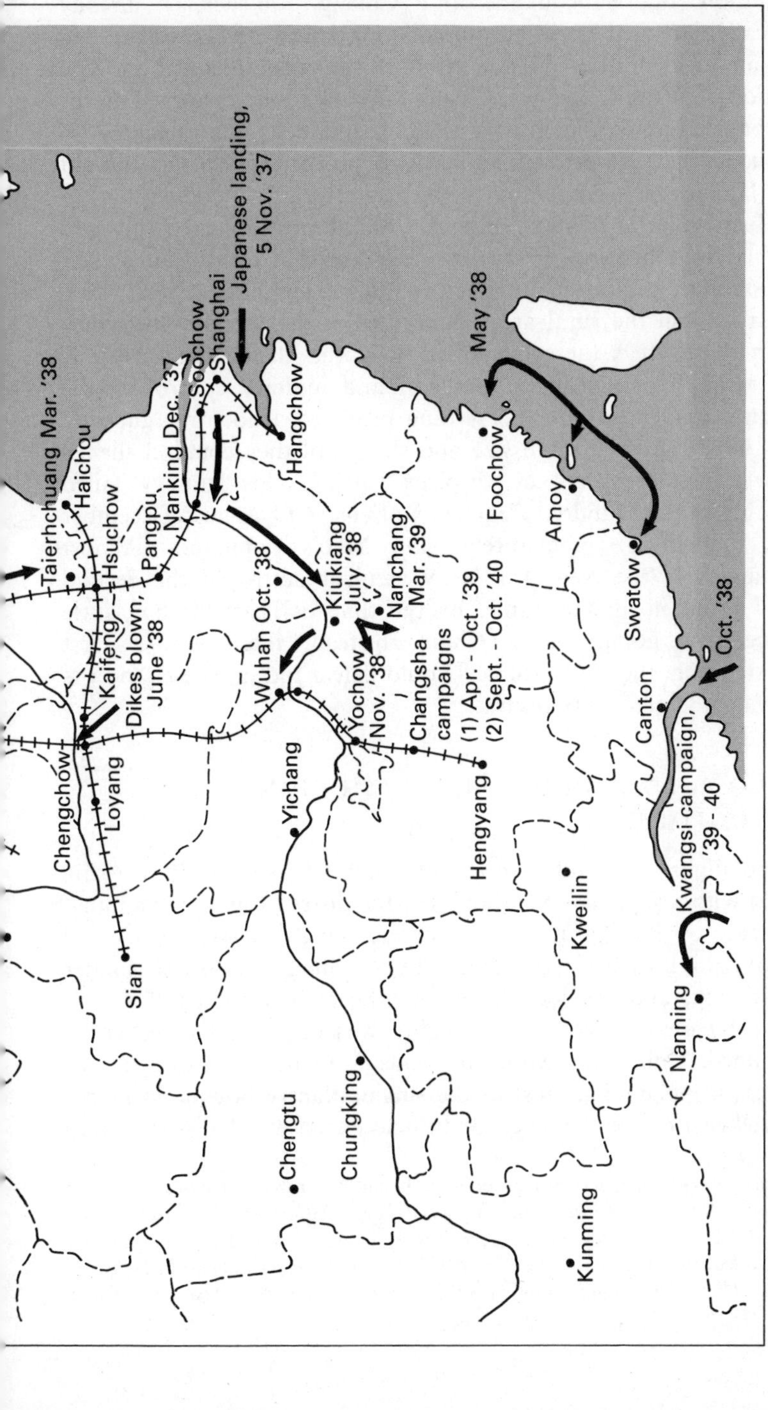

17. The Sino-Japanese War, 1937–1941

recognition of Manchukuo, and Chiang Kai-shek – already politically damaged by his accommodating attitude to Japan prior to the Sian Incident – could not afford to consider this option. The defection of Wang Ching-wei, Chiang Kai-shek's long-time rival on the left for the leadership of the KMT, permitted the Japanese to consolidate their puppet regimes in China proper in 1940, but did not make Japanese rule acceptable to the general Chinese population.

Meanwhile Japan's million-man China Expeditionary Army was stretched thin holding the major cities and the railway and river lines of communication connecting them. Japanese troops were seldom seen in the rural areas remote from the Japanese network, and in these areas the communists won the clandestine civil war against the Nationalists for political and military control of the resistance movements. Mao Tse-tung provided a doctrine: guerrilla forces would grow in both size and skill until they could challenge Japanese regular forces in set-piece battles. This strategy failed miserably in the Hundred Regiments offensive of August–December 1940, launched prematurely in Mao's opinion. Almost simultaneously the New 4th Army incident destroyed the Second United Front in all but name. By the time of Pearl Harbor, little fighting was going on in China. Instead, there was a tacit understanding: the United States would defeat the Japanese, and the civil war in China could resume.

MARCO POLO BRIDGE AND NORTH CHINA, JULY–OCTOBER 1937

On the night of 7 July troops of Sung Che-yuan's 29th Army clashed with a Japanese battalion near the district town of Wanping, southwest of Peiping near the famous Sung-dynasty constructed Marco Polo Bridge (Lukouchiao). By morning a Japanese soldier was missing, and the local Chinese officers had barred Wanping against Japanese search. Who exactly was at fault may never be determined. Unlike the Mukden Incident, there is no evidence of Japanese pre-planning: most of the single infantry brigade in Hopei was well east of Peiping, engaged in field exercises.[2] The US military

2 This follows the revisionist account in James B. Crowley, *Japan's Quest for Autonomy: National Security and Foreign Policy, 1930–1938* (Princeton, 1966), pp.322–42. Before Crowley, most students of the subject assumed that the Japanese had provoked the incident. See also the detailed study by Hata Ikuhiko in James W. Morley, *The China Quagmire: Japan's Expansion on the Asian Continent, 1933–1941* (New York, 1983), pp.243–86.

attaché, Joseph W. Stilwell, drove out from Peiping to investigate, but his party was forced back by gunfire before they reached Wanping.

For a few days it appeared that the Marco Polo Bridge Incident would be settled by a local truce between the opposed armies. Sung Che-yuan, who was also chairman of the autonomous Hopei–Chahar Political Council, was prepared to be flexible, as befitted a protégé of 'Betraying General' Feng Yü-hsiang. In Japan, the Konoe government, reflecting the views of the highest military and naval leadership, hoped to concentrate on the modernization of the armed forces. Settlement of relations with China was to rest on the three principles enunciated by Foreign Minister Hirota in 1935 (recognition of Manchukuo, an anti-Comintern pact, and suppression of anti-Japanese elements in China). Nanking rejected these terms then and on later occasions. Japan could achieve these objectives only through war, but in 1937 Japan's highest leaders hoped to defer war in China in favour of the modernization needed to survive a war against the Soviet Union or the Anglo-Saxon powers. Nevertheless, acting on the advice of the Kwantung Army staff, the Japanese Army General Staff recommended the mobilization and dispatch to China of five divisions, which the Konoe Cabinet approved on 11 July. On the same day the Chinese and Japanese commanders on the spot signed a local agreement that might have settled the issue.

Meanwhile Chiang Kai-shek was being goaded to action by the same elements that had been urging strong action against the Japanese since 1931. He ordered four divisions to Paoting, and instructed Sung Che-yuan, whom he did not trust, to take a stronger line. On 15 July the Japanese government gave Sung Che-yuan a 72-hour deadline for accepting the agreement signed on the 11th. Chiang Kai-shek, on the contrary, insisted that the incident be settled by negotiation between the central governments, and, in a much publicized speech at Kuling, declared that no more Chinese territory would be alienated to Japanese control. In the past, rhetorical defiance had preceded local accommodation, so the Japanese failed to take Chiang seriously this time. As bitter fighting developed around Wanping, Kwantung Army units moved into Hopei, and the Kwantung Army leadership, Prime Minister Konoe, Foreign Minister Hirota, and the Japanese press all began speculating about detaching Hopei–Chahar from China, Manchukuo-style. The Army General Staff continued to call for restraint, but despite the authority over operations that it theoretically had under the Japanese constitutional system, it did not prevail. The Japanese Cabinet endorsed 'autonomy' for North China on 7 August. Fighting also broke out at Shanghai, and full-scale warfare followed the bombardment of Japanese naval installations there by Chinese aircraft on 14 August.

In the war that followed the initial advantages were all with the Japanese. Japan was somewhat behind the European armies in the development of tanks, motorized transport and military aviation, but she was nevertheless well ahead of China in all these categories. Japanese divisions thus contained the machine guns, mortars, infantry guns, anti-tank guns, and field artillery called for in their tables of organization. They were served by trained crews, supplied with adequate amounts of ammunition, and commanded by officers trained in the proper cooperation of the various arms.[3] If the Japanese sometimes scorned firepower because of their contempt for the Chinese, they were nevertheless capable of returning after a setback and doing it by the book. In China, despite Chiang Kai-shek's efforts to develop elite units, weapons more powerful than rifles continued to be rare, and training in their proper use rarer still, partly because of uncertain ammunition supply. In China also, tables of organization – and indeed all military activities – continued to be affected by military politics, which led to endless organizational variety and unit inflation ('divisions' of only a few thousand men), so that uniform standards of training were not possible. In contrast to China, Japan's armed forces were well provided for by a strong domestic arms industry and a centralized system of military supply. Her German-derived military draft ensured a steady stream of trained replacements, all literate and indoctrinated to nationalism through her French-inspired education system. Against the USA in the Second World War, Japan's infrastructure proved inadequate, and US officers often marvelled at the slavish obedience to detailed and sometimes inappropriate written orders displayed by Japanese commanders. Against Chinese armies, the fact that Japanese commanders could expect to be

3 Both Roy M. Stanley, *Prelude to Pearl Harbor* (New York, 1982), and Frank Dorn, *The Sino-Japanese War, 1937–1941: From Marco Polo Bridge to Pearl Harbor* (New York, 1974), summarize Chinese and Japanese divisional organization. Basically, the Japanese were carrying out, and on paper the Chinese had already accomplished, the transition to the standard Second World War 'triangular' infantry divison: three infantry regiments of three battalions each, supported by several battalions of division artillery, engineers and other services. Most Chinese divisions contained only infantry.

obeyed gave them a great advantage. China's great size, and the fact that Japanese brutality and chauvinism stimulated Chinese nationalism and resistance, might have made the war unwinnable in the long run; the parallels with the USA's war in Vietnam are evident. But the Japanese continued to win most of their battles with Chinese units until the end of the Second World War, even though by then many of the Japanese divisions in China had little artillery and their advantage in firepower *vis-à-vis* the Chinese was correspondingly reduced.

Kwantung Army troops moved to Tientsin from Shanhaikuan while other Japanese columns moved on Peiping through Kupeikou. After some fights in which the elite Big Sword units of the 29th Army were duly slaughtered by Japanese machine guns, Sung Che-yuan's troops began to pull out of Peiping. At Tungchow, east of Peiping, false rumours of Chinese success led the local garrison to kill all the Japanese residents. The following day, 30 July, the Kwantung Army took the town, devastating it and massacring its Chinese population in retaliation. The 29th Army was already gone from Tientsin, whose Chinese city (the native quarter, as opposed to the area of international concessions that was still under Great Power protection) was bombarded from the air, and from Peiping, whose people could see the smoke from Tungchow and draw the obvious conclusions. But when the Japanese entered Peiping on 31 July their occupation was orderly.[4]

From the Peiping–Tientsin area, Japanese advances could be expected along the three major railway lines (Peiping–Suiyuan northwest to Inner Mongolia, and Peiping–Hankow and Tientsin–Pukow south to the Yangtze), control of which would facilitate the movement and supply of their armies. Having already defeated Sung Che-yuan's troops, advances along these axes would bring them into contact with Liu Ju-ming in Chahar and Han Fu-chü in Shantung, both also Feng Yü-hsiang protégés, and with Yen Hsi-shan in Shansi. In previous years allowing the Japanese to wipe out his competitors would have appealed to Chiang Kai-shek, but that game was too dangerous in the heightened nationalist atmosphere of 1937, and Chiang's personal troops were now at risk in the Shanghai area. As a gesture of national unity, Kwangsi clique leader Pai Ch'ung-hsi was named Chiang's Chief of Staff, which turned out to be an empty title since Chiang never trusted him.

4 Summarized from Dorn, *Sino-Japanese War*, pp.38–66.

Anticipating a Japanese invasion of Inner Mongolia, Chiang on 1 August appointed Yen Hsi-shan as Pacification Director of Taiyuan, and ordered a deployment of troops. 'As usual, the chain of command for the expected operations was one of those complicated puzzles of authority so dear . . . to the Chinese military mind – a . . . balance between doubtful generals, overlapping command, and provision for Chiang to bypass commanders when his intuitive sense of tactics inspired him to issue orders directly to subordinate units'.[5] Yen's authority over Liu Ju-ming's ex-Kuominchün troops, Lin Piao's 115th Division of the Communist 8th Route Army, or the Central Army contingents of Wei Li-huang and T'ang En-po in Shansi was never more than nominal. This did not really matter. Yen had been a provincial warlord long enough to have forgotten his early, and now obsolete, military education. His higher officers were 'with few exceptions, quite unfit to command', and his command style was identical to Chiang's, since from 'his headquarters in Taiyuan, a hundred miles away, Yen attempted to dictate tactics to the front, with often catastrophic results.'[6] As is evident from previous chapters, both Yen Hsi-shan and Chiang Kai-shek were extremely capable practitioners of the complex double dealing needed to survive in warlord politics, but the habits of command needed therein were extremely dysfunctional in a war against an enemy as powerful and as professionally organized as Japan.

Japanese forces, mainly the 5th Division and the 11th Independent Mixed Brigade, captured Nankow on 11 August and advanced into Chahar through Chüyungkuan Pass, abandoned by its defenders. They took Huailai after several days of fighting on 26 August. Liu Ju-ming's main force, the 143rd Division, then abandoned Kalgan and retired – all the way to southern Hopei. The Japanese occupied Kalgan on 3 September. They had been joined by numerous Mongol irregular cavalry, of slight military use, but politically valuable in support of the separatist regime of the Mongol Prince Te, which was duly proclaimed in November.[7]

A Japanese column from Kalgan advanced quickly into Shansi,

5 Dorn, *Sino-Japanese War*, p.57. Dorn was a Stilwell protégé and shared Stilwell's contempt for what US officers viewed as China's lack of military professionalism.

6 Donald G. Gillin, *Warlord: Yen Hsi-shan in Shansi Province, 1911–1949* (Princeton, 1967), pp.258–9.

7 Dorn, *Sino-Japanese War*, p.237.

making use of the railway, which the Chinese did not attempt to destroy. The Chinese abandoned Tatung on 13 September, falling back to a line from Yenmenkuan on the Great Wall east to the mountain pass of Pinghsingkuan. Yen Hsi-shan's troops became more demoralized, and detached parties were often mobbed by peasants, evidence of the general failure of Yen's political efforts. Japanese air supremacy created panic; villages, and even the provincial capital Taiyuan itself, emptied whenever the sound of propellers was heard. Eventually, during the Second World War, civilian populations in China and elsewhere would learn to maintain discipline under air attack, but in 1937 it was generally the case that they would panic. The assumption that civilians would panic under the threat of air attack in turn exerted a formative influence on air doctrine; intimidating the natives, for example, was defined in the 1920s and 1930s as a major mission of the British Royal Air Force. Events in China temporarily bore out these predictions.

The main body of the Japanese 5th Division went simultaneously by road from Huailai to Weihsien in Chahar to invade northeastern Shansi. It had a motorized transport column, but its rate of advance was determined by infantry marching over ox-cart roads. By the time they reached the Shansi border, Lin Piao's communist 115th Division, after a forced march from Shensi, was in place at Pinghsingkuan. This pass, west of Lingchiu on the road to Taihsien, was a narrow defile worn through the loess by centuries of ox-carts, with no exit for several miles except the road itself. Having pushed their way through many easily defensible positions, the Japanese were careless and contemptuous, and began their march through the pass without scouting or securing the heights on either side. At about 9,000 men, Lin's division was of respectable strength, and had enough rifles and machine guns to make an impression. In contrast to most Chinese armies, the communist soldiers had beliefs to fight for, and Lin was not obeying foolish orders from distant higher commands. At dawn on 25 September Lin attacked the head of the Japanese column, at noon the centre and rear. The battle consisted chiefly of Chinese troops shooting and throwing hand grenades into the packed mass of Japanese soldiers trapped in the defile about fifteen feet below their attackers. When it was over there were about 3,000 Japanese killed as against 400 Chinese casualties. Following the already well-established Japanese practice, the Chinese killed the enemy wounded and prisoners, as they often did in their own civil wars. The battlefield also yielded some 100 trucks loaded with supplies, and welcome quantities of weapons, ammunition and clothing.[8]

The KMT official history of the Sino-Japanese War deals with Pinghsingkuan in a sentence, without any credit to the communists.[9] CCP accounts, on the other hand, describe Pinghsingkuan as a typical example of Red guerrilla tactics, inspired by the wise counsel of Chairman Mao.[10] Unfortunately, like the equally atypical victory of Li Tsung-jen at Taierhchuang (see pp.225–7), Pinghsingkuan is to be explained by Japanese officers succumbing to what they came to call 'victory disease'. After a series of easy scores against inept opponents, they failed to take the most elementary precautions, despite knowing better. Japanese commanders seldom repeated the purely operational blunders that had led to Pinghsingkuan, but victory disease affected the whole Japanese army in other ways. Most importantly, it took the form of brutal contempt for the Chinese population, expressed in rape, robbery, torture and casual killing, either at the whim of individual soldiers or as the policy of senior commanders.[11] Such behaviour had the effect of stimulating patriotic feelings even among Chinese peasants for whom such abstractions had been remote. This added to the difficulty of finding a political solution to the China Incident.

On 14 October a Japanese column from Tatung took Kweisui, capital of Suiyuan province, and three days later took Paotou, then the end of the railway line, which the Japanese took intact as usual. Meanwhile the battle in the Shanghai area entered its critical phase.

SHANGHAI AND NANKING, JULY–DECEMBER 1937

The escalation of the fighting around Shanghai from 14 August surprised the Konoe cabinet and the top echelons of the Imperial Army and Imperial Navy.[12] The Japanese had until then insisted on a local settlement in North China of the Marco Polo Bridge Incident, and in consequence their behaviour in the Shanghai area

8 Dorn, *Sino-Japanese War*, pp.120–32.

9 Republic of China, Kuo-fang Pu, Shih-cheng chu, *History of the Sino-Japanese War, 1937–1945* (Taipei, 1971), p.197.

10 See the citations assembled in Chalmers A. Johnson, *Peasant Nationalism and Communist Power: The Emergence of Revolutionary China, 1937–1945* (Stanford, 1962), pp.218–19.

11 Meirion and Susie Harries, *Soldiers of the Sun: The Rise and Fall of the Imperial Japanese Army* (New York, 1991), pp. 475–84, offers a recent look at Japanese army atrocities.

12 Crowley, *Japan's Quest*, p.342.

had been, by Japanese standards, circumspect. Japanese authorities promptly repudiated the suicidal attempt of navy Lieutenant Oyama Isao to capture Hungchiao airfield singlehanded on 9 August. The Japanese maintained a substantial presence in Shanghai, including about 5,000 ground troops, barracks and other shore installations. Naval forces, including a Yangtze gunboat flotilla, were also based there. This was appropriate, as Shanghai was the major concession city under the unequal treaty system, and the other major treaty powers – France, Britain and the United States – also insisted on the right to maintain a military presence there. By early August Japanese residents of the smaller upriver and coastal treaty ports had been evacuated to, and women and children evacuated from, Shanghai.

On 13 August two Japanese divisions under General Matsui Iwane disembarked at Shanghai. They had been transported and escorted by ships of the Japanese 3rd Fleet, whose flagship, the pre-Dreadnought armoured cruiser *Izumo*, was moored at the Bund immediately opposite the central hotel and commercial district. The Japanese reinforcements were appropriate under long-standing treaty rights. However, the Chinese buildup in the suburbs of Shanghai violated the 1932 agreement to keep these areas demilitarized.[13] Chiang Kai-shek was thus opting for an all-out war with Japan in preference to a local settlement in the north, which would have involved humiliation and loss of territory. Fighting broke out in the Chapei area of Shanghai.

On 14 August the Chinese air force attempted to take out the *Izumo*. Instead they totalled a hotel and a department store, killing some 2,000 people, mostly Chinese civilians. Even before this, the Japanese navy had been urging the dispatch of additional troops to Shanghai. Now the army agreed, and the 3rd and 11th divisions were dispatched to Shanghai. By mid-September Matsui's force had grown to six divisions, well-provided with armour, artillery, air and other specialist units, totalling perhaps 200,000 men.[14] Japanese air supremacy was total, which had the unintended side-effect of protecting the population of Shanghai against repetitions of the Chinese air raid of 14 August. Matsui systematically drove the Chinese forces out to a twenty-mile radius of the city, and called for reinforcements and a drive on Nanking.

13 Hsi-sheng Ch'i, *Nationalist China at War: Military Defeats and Political Collapse, 1937–1945* (Ann Arbor, 1982), p.41.

14 Dorn, *Sino-Japanese War*, pp.67–74.

Meanwhile Chiang Kai-shek had built up the army besieging Shanghai to 71 divisions totalling around 500,000 men. These were the elite divisions of the Central Army, trained by German advisers and containing almost all the artillery and other specialist units in the Chinese army. Under Chiang himself as 3rd War Area commander, aided by Ku Chu-t'ung, were three Wing commands: Left (Ch'en Ch'eng, later vice-president), Centre (Chu Shao-liang) and Right (ex-Ironsides leader Chang Fa-k'uei), which in turn controlled army groups, armies and divisions. The army group commanders included the much admired Chang Chih-chung, Stilwell's later nemesis Lo Cho-ying, and Hsueh Yueh, scourge of the communists during the Long March. In fact the chain of command mattered little, as Chiang directed events from the rear, ordering unit commanders to attack without regard for casualties, and to defend positions to the last man. By 20 October the Chinese forces had sustained some 130,000 casualties in bitter infantry fighting, in the course of which they were generally forced back by the outnumbered – but better trained and better armed – Japanese.

On 5 November the Japanese 10th Army (three under-strength divisions with about 30,000 men) of Lieutenant-General Yanagawa Heisuke made an amphibious landing at Chinshanwei, on Hangchow Bay at the Kiangsu–Chekiang border. The north shore of Hangchow Bay is an old and famous seawall which may remind the student of amphibious operations of Dieppe. Undefended, however, the wall facilitated the disembarkation of the Japanese force, mostly infantry, from its carriers, mostly merchant-type ships only slightly modified. The landing thus gave a preview of the rapidly improvised Japanese amphibious operations of 1941–2. It also threatened the right flank and rear of the Chinese armies at Shanghai, whose collapse promptly followed. On 8 November the Japanese 10th Army took Sungkiang, northwest of Shanghai. Within a few days most of the Chinese divisions had disintegrated, and the survivors were trying to hold a line further north near Soochow. Chinese losses in the Shanghai campaign may have reached 300,000.[15]

No matter what the numbers were, the elite Central Army that Chiang had spent years and effort building was now destroyed, and this reduced both China's ability to fight Japan and Chiang Kai-shek's ability to control events in China. The Shanghai campaign demonstrated how limited China's ability to wage war with Japan actually was. Even the elite Central Army units, fighting

15 Ch'i, *Nationalist China*, p.43.

hard with good morale before 5 November, were pushed back on the ground by smaller Japanese forces. China's air and naval weakness meant that she was vulnerable to the amphibious stroke that decided the campaign, and that Japan could easily capture her coastal cities, which were both the political base of the KMT and the places through which any foreign assistance would have to come. While the Shanghai débâcle silenced critics who alleged that Chiang would never fight the Japanese, it also made it more difficult for Chiang to control his internal military opposition. Before the Sian Incident, Chiang's Central Army was methodically destroying its warlord and communist military opposition. Between the Shanghai débâcle and Stilwell's Burma campaign, the most significant Chinese successes against the Japanese were won by generals (Cantonese Hsueh Yueh and Li Tsung-jen of the Kwangsi clique) of non-Whampoa factions, whose victories thus were a threat to Chiang. It is against this background that Chiang's refusal to follow Stilwell's advice, insistence on militarily absurd but politically balanced chains of command, direction of operations from the rear, and monopolization of US aid may be understood, if not excused.

Events now moved rapidly. The Chinese abandoned Soochow without a fight on 19 November. The principal surviving headquarters, the 15th and 21st army groups, created a defensive line from Kiangyin to Wuhsi, which the Japanese broke through, and also outflanked with another amphibious operation across Lake Tai. Changchow fell on 29 November and Tanyang on 3 December. Most of the Japanese 10th Army marched around the south of Lake Tai, taking Wuhsing, Changhsing and Yihsing and approaching Nanking via Lishui. Chiang Kai-shek had already sent most of the government to Chungking, and had moved himself with his military agencies to Wuhan, whence he issued detailed and irrelevant orders for the defence of Nanking.[16]

On 13 December the Japanese broke into the city from the east and south, and began the well-publicized bloodbath known since as the Rape of Nanking. Estimates of civilian deaths range from 200,000 to 300,000. Large groups were made to dig trenches and then machine gunned to fall into them, or were lashed together, doused with kerosene, and set afire. Women were gang-raped and mutilated before being murdered. These atrocities went on for several weeks, much observed by European and American witnesses,

16 Dorn, *Sino-Japanese War*, pp.74–102.

who could not be murdered with impunity. Many of the Japanese wrote descriptions of their atrocities in their diaries, and took photographs which they sent home. General Matsui, who was later hanged as a war criminal, was in fact taken out of the command loop and had no part in the atrocities, which went on under the direction of Lieutenant-Generals Yanagawa, Prince Asaka (an uncle of Emperor Hirohito) and Nakajima Kesago and Major-General Suzuki Teiichi. These made no effort to control the troops, and in fact egged them on. The political purpose of these atrocities was to intimidate Chiang and the Nationalist regime into coming to terms. As the Japanese were aware, Nanking symbolized the progress that Sun Yat-sen and his heirs had hoped China would make under a republican regime. But the Japanese terror tactics failed, as such tactics usually do, and the popular revulsion at Japanese behaviour, including a world public opinion that had grown increasingly hostile to Japan since the Manchurian Incident and whose hostility was reinforced by the Nanking atrocities, made it more – rather than less – difficult for Chiang Kai-shek to come to terms with Japan, even as his ability to engage them in war diminished.[17]

On 12 December the US river gunboat *Panay*, evacuating Americans from Nanking, was attacked and sunk by Japanese naval aircraft. British gunboats were also attacked. The Japanese apologized for what they described as accidents (even postwar the aircrew who carried out the attacks have stuck to this explanation) and paid compensation promptly. Isolationism still remained strong in the United States, and Britain understandably was preoccupied by the worsening situation in Europe. Both Anglo-Saxon powers therefore accepted the Japanese apologies and did not threaten war. The combination of protracted Chinese resistance, Japanese atrocities, and the *Panay* Incident therefore failed to produce the foreign intervention for which Chiang had hoped.[18]

17 Harries, *Soldiers of the Sun*, pp.221–30, has a recent account of the Nanking massacre. David Bergamini, *Japan's Imperial Conspiracy: How Emperor Hirohito Led Japan into War Against the West* (New York, 1971), pp.22–48 needs to be read here: he was trashed by the professional Japanologists, and says too much that he cannot prove, yet it is hard to doubt that the Nanking massacre was deliberate policy, orchestrated at the highest levels in Japan.

18 Waldo H. Heinrichs, jr, *American Ambassador: Joseph C. Grew and the Development of the U.S. Diplomatic Tradition* (Boston, 1966), and Dorothy Borg, *The United States and the Far Eastern Crisis of 1933–1938* (Cambridge, MA, 1968), pp.486–518, both discuss the *Panay* Incident, with full bibliography.

HOPEI AND SHANSI, SEPTEMBER–NOVEMBER 1937

The fall of Nanking precipitated a mass flight of refugees away from the areas of Japanese operations. Within this flight was an organized dismantling of entire institutions, including factories, arsenals, hospitals and universities. Such of their equipment as was portable was transported by coolie labour and reassembled elsewhere, generally in southwestern China. Much of the latter effort was directed by the Harvard-educated General Yu Ta-wei, formerly Chiang's agent for foreign arms purchases, whose fiscal integrity had won Chiang's confidence. As a human epic, this migration of people and facilities deserves to be celebrated. In more mundane terms, however, most of the factories of the Shanghai region were neither moved nor destroyed, but simply fell into Japanese hands. Chiang's regime, which had been unable to stop the Japanese even when it controlled the resources of Shanghai and the other treaty ports, from now on survived confined to the least urban and least modern regions of China. At the same time Japanese behaviour had demonstrated to many millions of Chinese, not least those trapped behind the lines of Japanese occupation, that they had a personal stake in Chinese nationalism.

Temporarily safe at his new headquarters in Wuhan, Chiang Kai-shek in December 1937 reshuffled his army organization. Despite, or because of, the losses in the Shanghai–Nanking campaign, the new chain of command was based on the previous principles: non-Whampoa commanders were to be neutralized, Communists quarantined, and the best troops retained away from the front under Chiang's personal command. The arrangement of war areas (theatres of operations) instituted now lasted with minimal changes until 1945. Chiang loyalist Ch'eng Ch'ien's 1st War Area was to resist the Japanese move down the Peiping–Hankow railway, flanked by Kwangsi clique General Li Tsung-jen's 5th War Area on the Tientsin–Pukow line. Ho Ying-chin, Chiang's right-hand man, commanded the 4th War Area (Kwangtung and Kwangsi) and served concurrently as Chief of the General Staff, if that can be imagined, Kwangsi General Pai Ch'ung-hsi being demoted to Assistant Chief until Ho became Minister of War. Whampoa stalwart Ku Chu-t'ung's 3rd War Area commanded the Chinese remnants in southern Kiangsu and Chekiang, and Yen Hsi-shan's title as 2nd War Area Commander signified that he was on his own in Shansi. Chiang personally, if remotely, commanded the 8th War Area (Kansu, Ninghsia and

Chinghai) and the Sian Pacification Headquarters, both commands being devoted to blockading the communists, and controlled more closely the seventeen divisions directly under the National Military Council in the Wuhan area. These last were not to be confused with the equally large Wuhan garrison headquarters under Ch'en Ch'eng, another Chiang loyalist.[19]

By September 1937 the Japanese North China Area Army under General Count Terauchi Hisaichi had grown to a force of about 200,000 men organized in two subordinate armies, eight divisions (including the 14th under Doihara Kenji,[20] famous for his role in the creation of Manchukuo and the puppet regimes in North China) and various supporting units. As in the warlord wars, the railway lines were the natural axes of advance. The Japanese 1st Army broke out of Peiping on 17 September and captured Paoting on the 24th. Paoting since the turn of the century had been a centre not only of military but also of medical and agricultural education; it now received the loot, kill and burn treatment. Chinese forces, units as usual failing to maintain contact or otherwise cooperate, retired hastily southward in the direction of Chengting and Shihchiachuang. Chiang Kai-shek, masterminding the battle from Wuhan, now ordered the survivors to divide, some to hold Chengting and some to hold Niangtzukuan (Ladies' Pass) on the Shansi border west of Shihchiachuang, through which runs the railway to Taiyuan. The Japanese took Chengting on 8 October, and celebrated Double Ten, the Chinese national holiday, by capturing the important railway junction of Shihchiachuang. The Chinese had used all the available rolling stock to evacuate themselves south to the Anyang–Taming area, where Sung Che-yuan (ex-Kuominchün and more recently chairman of the Japanese-dominated Hopei–Chahar Political Council) and T'ang En-po (very Whampoa), the 1st War Area's principal field commanders, promised still more hard fighting. In fact, after a short lull in the fighting, Doihara captured both Anyang and Taming on 4–6 November. T'ang En-po withdrew his army into Shansi without orders, but as a Whampoa man of high status, he was not disciplined.

Sung Che-yuan had ended up in Honan after being thrown out of eastern Hopei by the advance of the Japanese 2nd Army, which took Tsangchow on 24 September. Theoretically the 5th War Area

19 Dorn, *Sino-Japanese War*, pp.75–102.

20 B. Winston Kahn, *Doihara Kenji and the North China Autonomy Movement* (Temple, 1973).

of the capable Kwangsi general Li Tsung-jen should have been facing the Japanese, but Han Fu-chü, military governor of Shantung (whose army was called the 3rd Route Army), was planning to defect to the Japanese, and had prevented troops from the south from entering Shantung. Chiang Kai-shek now appointed Han's old patron Feng Yü-hsiang to command a new 6th War Area composed of what was left of east Hopei north of Shantung. The opportunity for Feng to order Han to let Li pass through Shantung never arose, as the Japanese reached and surrounded Techou on the Hopei–Shantung border in a few days; it fell on 15 October, and on the same day the Japanese reached the north bank of the Yellow River near Tsinan. Operations then stalled for a while. Han Fu-chü destroyed the steel railway bridge spanning the Yellow River at Tsinan. One of his divisions counterattacked the Japanese and actually captured some prisoners, whom Han had publicly and gruesomely executed to demonstrate his loyalty to China. Meanwhile he mobilized most of his army on the southern border of Shantung against Li Tsung-jen.[21]

Meanwhile the Japanese resumed their invasion of Shansi, and this time they did it right. The main Japanese column, the Chahar Expeditionary Force, moved south from Tatung, basically along the line of the Tatung–Taiyuan railway, but not confined to it. By the end of the month they had breached the Great Wall (imposing here, but of little modern military significance) at both Yenmenkuan and Juyuehkou. General Itagaki Seishirō's 5th Division, seeking to avenge its humiliation on 25 September, advanced on Pinghsingkuan once again. By now the Chinese communists were gone, their place taken by the 34th Army, part of Yen Hsi-shan's forces, who on 30 September abandoned the pass and fell back for fear of the Japanese troops already to their rear at Fanchih. The 5th Division was therefore able to march rapidly to join the rest of the Japanese army to assault Taiyuan.

Chiang Kai-shek then ordered Whampoa General Wei Li-huang to move his 14th Army Group from the Shihchiachuang area to Taiyuan. At the same time, as already recounted, Chiang ordered other troops to evacuate Shihchiachuang to defend Niangtzukuan. After the fall of Shihchiachuang, the Japanese 20th and 109th divisions attacked Niangtzukuan. On 27 October a Japanese flank attack led the shaky Chinese defenders to panic and flee. The Japanese now were free to surround Taiyuan from the south.

21 Dorn, *Sino-Japanese War*, pp.114–20.

A regular siege of Taiyuan had now developed, both sides sustaining numerous casualties as the Japanese forced the Chinese back on the city. On 2 November Japanese engineers exploded a mine under Tungshan, a key position in the east of the city, and were then able to advance to the walled city itself. Most of the Chinese defenders abandoned the city 'in great disorder', leaving a depleted garrison under Fu Tso-yi. On 8–9 November the Japanese took Taiyuan by storm with great loss of life. Of course, even this disaster was overshadowed by the débâcle taking place in the Shanghai–Nanking region in the same time period.[22]

In November the Japanese government formally activated Imperial General Headquarters (Daihon'ei), wherein the emperor met regularly with the army and navy ministers and Chiefs of Staff, whom only the emperor could command under the Japanese constitution. This step indicated that the Japanese regarded the China Incident, still so-called due to US neutrality legislation, as a full-fledged war, requiring a coordinated policy. By now three Japanese field armies – the Kwantung Army in 'Manchukuo', the North China Area Army of about 280,000 men in Hopei and Shansi, and the China Expeditionary Army of about 260,000 men in the Yangtze area – were in China, and the Navy and other Japanese agencies had their own interests. Each of the Japanese armies was pursuing an independent political course. Japan was nowhere near the bottom of her manpower barrel, but otherwise her resources were very finite, and expansion of the war in China had to compete with a very expensive programme of naval construction and with military modernization in general.[23]

SHANTUNG AND HONAN, DECEMBER 1937 TO MAY 1938

Having failed to gain the political settlement they desired, the logical next step for the Japanese was to threaten Chiang's new headquarters at Wuhan by advancing southward along the railway

22 Dorn, *Sino-Japanese War*, pp.120–32; quotation on p.126.

23 Dorn, *Sino-Japanese War*, pp.133–6. Japan's strategic dilemma in 1937–41 has resulted in an enormous literature, which may be sampled in Herbert Feis, *The Road to Pearl Harbor* (Princeton, 1950), David J. Lu, *From Marco Polo Bridge to Pearl Harbor* (Washington, 1961), Robert J.C. Butow, *Tojo and the Coming of the War* (Princeton, 1961), and James W. Morley, ed., *Japan's Road to the Pacific War* (5 vols, New York, 1976–1984; cited by individual volume titles: I is *Japan Erupts*, II is *The China Quagmire*).

line from Shihchiachuang or westward up the Yangtze from Nanking. Han Fu-chü was still fence-sitting in Shantung, whose major port of Tsingtao was connected by rail with the provincial capital at Tsinan, on the other major north–south railway from Tientsin to Nanking. As in the warlord period, the scarcity of China's lines of communication added to their importance in military strategy.

Shortly after the fall of Nanking, General Hata Shunroku assumed command of the Japanese China Expeditionary Army and began occupying points north of the Yangtze. Theoretically Li Tsung-jen's 5th War Area had about 400,000 effectives in its 63 under-strength divisions, but in practice Han Fu-chü, whose 3rd Group Army had about 80,000 of them, had no desire to risk them in combat. When Japanese troops crossed the Yellow River on 24 December, Han concluded that Japan would not offer him a deal, and evacuated Tsinan in an armoured train carrying his silver coffin and the cash from the provincial treasury. Within a few days the mayor of Tsingtao and the chairman of the Tsingtao–Tsinan Railway Company exercised the same thoughtfulness in making their departures. The Japanese 5th Division, fresh from Shansi, marched unopposed from Tsinan toward Tsingtao, but the city actually surrendered on 10 January 1938 to Vice-Admiral Toyoda Soemu's 4th Fleet. By then Chinese mobs had smashed the breweries and the streets were awash in beer. Chefoo was taken from the sea soon afterwards, as was Lienyunkang near Haichou, the eastern terminus of the Lunghai Railway that linked the two north–south lines through junctions at Hsuchow and Chengchow. Han Fu-chü's last mistake was to abandon his army and flee to Kaifeng, where he was arrested, tried, and executed on 24 January.[24] Han's betrayal of his old master, Christian General Feng Yü-hsiang, had been crucial in enabling Chiang Kai-shek to destroy Feng in 1929. Now, as a non-Whampoa general with no army, he was disposable.

By then three Japanese columns were marching south, one from Tsining toward Kueite (west of Hsuchow), one from Tsouhsien directly toward Hsuchow, and the third from central Shantung toward Taierhchuang, a village of stone houses backing on to the Grand Canal northeast of Hsuchow, and served by a railway spur from Lincheng. Li Tsung-jen's headquarters at Hsuchow was thus threatened from the west, east and north, and on 9 February Japanese from the south crossed the Huai River at Pangpu and took

24 Dorn, *Sino-Japanese War*, pp.136–46.

Huaiyuan. The 5th War Area therefore faced the kind of annihilating envelopment called Kesselschlacht by the Germans. Chiang Kai-shek ordered reinforcements from Honan, including T'ang En-po's 20th Group Army whose mission was to hold Kueite on the railway line between Hsuchow and Chengchow. On 12 February a counterattack by the 3rd Group Army surprised the Japanese and recovered part of Tsining, and follow-up attacks kept the Japanese off balance. Similarly, attacks by the 51st Army failed to recapture Pangpu but did stabilize the Huai front for a while. Japanese forces were overextended, while – in the manner of soldiers everywhere – Chinese troops were encouraged even by transitory local successes.

In early March the Japanese concentrated their 10th Division at Tsouhsien. Chiang Kai-shek moved the 20th Group Army from Kueite to Hsuchow, brought in the 2nd Group Army by rail from Shansi, and ordered the 3rd Group Army to attack the Japanese rear from Tsining. On 14 March the Japanese 10th Division moved, and by 18 March had taken Tenghsien, Lincheng and Yihsien in succession. The Chinese resisted stubbornly in each place, and the Japanese had to employ their artillery, tanks and aviation to the fullest. East of Taierhchuang, the Japanese 5th Division approached Linyi from the north. Chinese troops fought them to a standstill during 14–18 March. The Japanese regrouped and resumed the attack on 23 March. Five days later they had forced the Chinese through Linyi, but the latter still held out south of the town.

The successful Chinese defence of Linyi created an opportunity to destroy the Japanese 10th Division. T'ang En-po's 20th Group Army took up positions between Yihsien and Linyi, while Sun Lien-chung's newly arrived 2nd Group Army moved into Taierhchuang, where the Chinese troops retiring from Yihsien were ordered to concentrate. Ch'ih Feng-ch'eng's 31st Division made a fighting withdrawal into Taierhchuang, whose stone buildings encouraged house-to-house fighting, while the Grand Canal to the rear discouraged retreat. A Stalingrad-like battle developed. Other divisions of the 2nd Group Army moved in to replace Chinese losses, while the Japanese became obsessed with Taierhchuang to the neglect of their flanks. On 26 March T'ang En-po struck at Tsaochuang and Yihsien, and drove the Japanese from both towns. T'ang also cut off and isolated a brigade sent by the 5th Division, by a wide flank march west of Linyi, to the aid of the 10th. To compound the 10th Division's isolation, a unit of the 3rd Group Army crossed the lake from the west and cut the railway north of

Lincheng. For the next week the surrounded Japanese fought against hunger and thirst and Chinese. As at Stalingrad, airdropped supplies fell mostly to the besiegers. On 7 April about 2,000 survivors fought their way out of Taierhchuang and fled, leaving some 16,000 corpses and most of the equipment of the 10th Division behind. The Chinese did not pursue effectively. They had suffered almost as many casualties.[25]

Taierhchuang was the most important of the few Nationalist victories against the Japanese in the eight-year Sino-Japanese War. As such it became the paradigmatic battle for the KMT view of the war, as Pinghsingkuan did for the CCP. Credit for the victory is usually assigned to Li Tsung-jen and his German advisers, but Chiang Kai-shek, who flew into Hsuchow at the critical point of the battle, claimed his share, and certainly deserves credit for sending both Sung Lien-chung's and T'ang En-po's armies into the battle. Chiang's remote and centralized system of command, reminiscent of the Western Front in the First World War, scored an unusual success here, but its applicability in general required the fronts to be stable long enough for his detailed paper appreciations to be relevant.

The aftermath was anticlimactic. When the Japanese 5th Division resumed the attack on 15 April, they forced the Chinese back to Peihsien but were held there by the same forces that had won the Taierhchuang battle. Meanwhile the Chinese were losing the campaign in the south. The Japanese sent reinforcements to both of their field armies in China, and made new crossings of the Yangtze at Chenchiang and Nantung. The Chinese forces along the Huai started to crumble, which permitted the Japanese to break out from Pangpu. By 12 May Japanese mechanized units were threatening Hsuchow from the southwest. On 15 May Chiang ordered the troops of the 5th War Area to break out. The forces resisting the advance of the 5th Division now fell apart, and on 18 May the Japanese took both Peihsien and Taierhchuang. On 20 May the Japanese entered Hsuchow.[26]

In Honan, the Japanese had reached the Anyang–Taming area by November 1937. In the following months the Chinese withdrew some of the best troops of the 1st War Area to meet the Japanese offensive in the east. In February 1938 General Terauchi deployed a force of about 45,000 men built around Lieutenant-General Doihara

25 Dorn, *Sino-Japanese War*, pp.146–58.
26 Dorn, *Sino-Japanese War*, pp.158–68.

Kenji's 14th Division to resume the offensive in northern Honan. The Japanese reached the Yellow River with little Chinese opposition, Chinese units either fleeing in panic or disintegrating to form guerrilla bands that, at this stage of the war, were not much more than bandit gangs preying on the peasantry. After the Japanese defeat at Taierhchuang, the 14th Division moved to the Puchow–Puhsien area and began preparations to cross the Yellow River. Doihara accomplished this on 14 May and two days later reached the east–west railway line near Lanfeng. Manoeuvring rapidly and confusingly, Doihara evaded the efforts of General Hsueh Yueh's Eastern Honan Army to trap him. The Chinese forced Doihara's men out of Lanfeng on 27 May, permitting them to evacuate men and save rolling stock from the Japanese columns now advancing rapidly westward from Tangshan.

'Fighting withdrawal' meant rout and 'guerrilla warfare' meant disintegration in the Chinese communiqués of this time. Chiang Kai-shek compounded the collapse by ordering (31 May) most of the troops of the 1st War Area to move west of the Peiping–Hankow railway. The forces assigned to defend Kaifeng thus were actually outnumbered by the Japanese attackers. Shang Chen's 32nd Army fought hard for six days, but Kaifeng fell on 6 June, and two days later Japanese cavalry reached Hsincheng, on the railway line south of Chengchow. Chiang then ordered the Yellow River dikes north of Chengchow to be blown open by explosive charges. Shang Chen stalled to evacuate his troops, but eventually carried out the order. The course of the Yellow River then shifted, to flow southeast into the Huai, accompanied by the flooding of much of Honan, Anhwei and Kiangsu provinces. Millions of people were either killed outright or died because the floods deprived them of their already marginal means of subsistence. Catastrophic shifts in the bed of the Yellow River had occurred many times, due to natural causes; Chiang was exceptional in using flooding as a deliberate strategy. In the long run, his evident disregard for peasant life contributed to the communist case against him, but in the short run, Chiang's strategy was successful: the flood caused the Japanese to retire to the east in a haste that bordered on panic.[27]

For Chiang Kai-shek and the KMT elite, and for the majority of the educated public as well, blowing the Yellow River dikes was an acceptable measure in the scorched earth campaign of total war that

27 Dorn, *Sino-Japanese War*, pp.171–9.

Chinese propaganda described without let-up until 1945. Afterwards, when Chiang ordered another sector of Yellow River dikes to be blown to stop the communist advance during the 1946–9 civil war, educated opinion interpreted this as showing Chiang's disregard for the suffering of the people. Accurate statistics on loss of life and destruction of infrastructure are difficult to come by, but the impressionistic accounts by eyewitnesses consistently tell the same story, and the generations of Chinese who lived through the period of 'military disorders' (ping-luan) – a term that incorporates the warlord period, the Sino-Japanese War and the civil war – are united in their fear of this state of affairs recurring. Nevertheless, as the 1953 census eventually revealed, decades of suffering and the loss of millions of lives in war-related causes in fact had little demographic significance. Furthermore, the blowing of the dikes was an extreme measure in a Chinese resistance that would eventually settle down to something like an accommodation with the Japanese invaders in many regions of China. In the immediate context of late 1938, the flood meant that the Japanese could not immediately seize control of the Peiping–Hankow railway line, and therefore that their attack on Wuhan would have to depend on an advance westward up the Yangtze River.

THE WUHAN CAMPAIGN, JUNE–NOVEMBER 1938

The Yellow River flood saved Chengchow for the time being, and thus prevented a Japanese move southward on the Peiping–Hankow railway line toward Wuhan. Since southern Anhwei was not flooded, the Japanese could still march up the Yangtze toward Wuhan, using the river as their line of communication. By early July General Hata's forces had expanded to some sixteen divisions with aviation and other supporting units, totalling 380,000 men. Most of these were organized into the 11th Army of General Okamura Yasuji of later 'three-all' fame and the 2nd Army of General Prince Naruhiko Higashikuni, in 1945 prime minister of Japan's 'Surrender Cabinet'.

Chiang Kai-shek and the National Military Council had anticipated Wuhan as the next Japanese objective, and had issued incredibly detailed orders deploying no fewer than 107 divisions with a theoretical aggregate strength of some 800,000 men to defend it. These were divided between the 9th War Area of Ch'en Ch'eng, formed from an expanded Wuhan garrison command and responsible for Wuhan itself and the adjoining region south of the

Yangtze, and the 5th War Area, now under Pai Ch'ung-hsi with fellow Kwangsi leader Li Tsung-jen as his deputy, responsible for the territories north of the river. Hsueh Yueh, Shang Chen, T'ang En-po, Sun Lien-chung, Chang Tse-chung and others who had distinguished themselves in the fighting so far continued to command formations, though these were much weakened by the circumstances of the 5th War Area's flight from Hsuchow. On the other hand, generals such as Liu Ju-ming, who had merely succeeded in escaping, also remained in responsible positions. The 1st War Area in northern Honan and the 3rd War Area, now confined to the hilly regions of Chekiang and Anhwei south of the Yangtze, were assigned 'supporting roles'. In reality, the Chinese on the south bank of the Yellow River made a local truce with the Japanese on the north bank, and food and other items were traded back and forth while the Wuhan campaign was fought.

The details of the Chinese deployment were soon made irrelevant by enemy action, but Dorn's summary deserves quotation. 'The whole tone of the directive was one of delay, step-by-step withdrawal, and defense in depth that presaged retreat and eventual acceptance of defeat. Like most antiquated Chinese military thinking, the operational guiding principles for the defense of Hankow were the product of a sort of dream world of correct words and resounding phrases. Not once in the long-winded document was a commander ordered to stand in place, face the enemy, and fight.'[28]

The Japanese offensive began on 10 June. A column from Pangpu had come south along the Hsuchow–Hofei branch railway line in Anhwei and had taken Hofei, from which the Japanese moved into southwest Anhwei. On 26 June the Japanese 6th Division ran into a coordinated Chinese counterattack of eight divisions in Taihu county (in Anhwei north of the Yangtze near the Hupei border), and had to retreat to avoid encirclement. Despite this success, the 'fortress' of Matang (Anhwei) on the Yangtze upstream from Anking, guarding against an upriver advance in the direction of Hupei and Kiangsi, fell to a joint Japanese army and navy attack on 27 June, despite stiff Chinese resistance. The Japanese then broke through the boom that the Chinese had stretched across the Yangtze and advanced upon Hukou, which the Japanese 101st Division conquered, after some hard fighting, by 8 July. This threatened Kiukiang, whose capture would seal off

28 Dorn, *Sino-Japanese War*, pp.180–5; the quotation is on p.185.

Kiangsi by both river and rail. Chiang ordered Hsueh Yueh to hold Kiukiang at all costs, but on 23 July the Japanese 101st Division crossed the river exiting the Poyang Lake and threatened Kiukiang from the rear. On 26 July some 45,000 Chinese troops fled Kiukiang, abandoning it to an attacking Japanese force of scarcely one-quarter their size, who celebrated by raping and murdering the civilian population.

A lull of several weeks followed. Much of the Japanese army was immobilized by dysentery brought on by drinking unboiled water. The Chinese did not use the opportunity to counterattack. They had run out of quinine, which aggravated their demoralization. Despite this, and despite Kiukiang and other fiascos, some Chinese units remained willing to put up a good fight to hold a definite position.

The Japanese 11th Army at Kiukiang attacked Juichang to the southwest on 22 August, and took it two days later. Afterwards their advance south and southwest was slowed by the stubborn resistance of Hsueh Yueh's troops. By 10 October the Japanese had taken 10,000 casualties and were less than halfway to Nanchang, both the 101st and the 106th divisions being unfit for further operations. The same fate befell the columns advancing northwest from Juichang along the south side of the Yangtze. After two weeks of assaults by land, air and water they captured the fortress of Matouchen on the south bank of the Yangtze in Kiangsi on 12 September. Repeatedly counterattacked, falling back, and resuming the advance, by 10 October they had barely crossed the Hupei border.

On the north bank of the Yangtze the Japanese had more success. The 6th Division beat off a Chinese attack on its base at Huangmei and advanced and took Kuangchi on 9 September. From Kuangchi it advanced to lay siege to Tienchiachen on the north bank of the Yangtze in Hupei, which fell on 29 September after resisting ten days. The Japanese executed the surviving Chinese defenders. Tienchiachen was the second and stronger of the two river fortresses that had been counted on to stop the Japanese. After it fell, the major Chinese formation on the north bank, the 11th Group Army of the 5th War Area, retreated – in good order but without fighting the Japanese – from Chichun to Hsishui. By this time the word that Chiang Kai-shek was evacuating Wuhan for Chungking, so that Wuhan would not be held, was spreading throughout the Chinese army, with the natural consequences for morale. The Kwangsi clique troops of the 5th War Area would be left behind to be decimated by the Japanese, while the Whampoa troops of the 9th War Area would be evacuated with Chiang – that at least was the interpretation that came naturally to soldiers with experience in the warlord wars. To compound the 5th War Area's problems, two more Japanese columns were making wide flank marches through Honan, south of the flooded area, to threaten Wuhan from the north.

On 27 August the Japanese 2nd Army moved west from Luan and Huoshan in Anhwei in two columns. The southern column captured Shangcheng (Honan) on 16 September and prepared to advance on Wuhan through the Tapieh Mountains. The northern column reached the outskirts of Hsinyang, on the Peiping–Hankow railway, by 30 September. When the Japanese cut the railway line to the south, the Chinese abandoned Hsinyang on 12 October. Once again, Chinese deployments for 'defence in depth' meant that engaged Chinese units were usually outnumbered by the Japanese, while unengaged units had too much opportunity to run away.

In October the Japanese 11th Army finally broke out of the box around Juichang (west of Kiukiang in Kiangsi) that had held it since August. Hsueh Yueh was forced to abandon Tean and retire south to the line of the Hsiu River, halfway to Nanchang. Chang Fa-k'uei's troops lost Yanghsin (Hupei) on 18 October, and on the following day the Japanese 106th Division had moved west and was attacking Huangshihkang on the south bank of the Yangtze; meeting minimal Chinese resistance after that, it reached the outskirts of Wuhan a week later. Meanwhile the 9th and 27th divisions marched overland from Yanghsin, and the 9th took Yochow on the Tungting Lake, the key to Hunan, on 12 November. Chang Fa-k'uei established defensive lines along the Hsinchiang River south of Yochow, and linked up with Hsueh Yueh's lines along the Hsiu River in Kiangsi.

North of the Yangtze in Hupei, Japanese 6th Division attacked the 5th War Area's now ineffective 11th Group Army at Hsishui. The usual formula of a frontal attack combined with a flank march, this time toward Huangkang, did wonders, and on 19 October the 11th Group Army collapsed. Japanese divisions now raced each other to Wuhan from various directions, the 13th and 16th from Tapiehshan, the 3rd and 10th from the Hsinyang area, the 6th from the east, and the 106th from the south. By this time the panicky evacuation from the city had mostly taken place, though some of the Wuhan garrison command of the contemptible Lo Cho-ying – who will be encountered later in Burma – did not flee fast enough, and were mauled by the Japanese, who entered the city on 25 October. Chiang had ordered the destruction of the city, but local property owners, looking to the future, removed most of the explosive charges. General Hata Shunroku entered the city in triumph and held his men to strict discipline, proving that it could be done if the Japanese high command so wished.

Perhaps a million Chinese soldiers were lost in the course of the Wuhan campaign. Accurate statistics are unlikely ever to be recovered. Compounding the numerical losses was the very strong sense that Chiang had abandoned the Kwangsi clique's 5th War Area in northern Hupei and the armies of Hsueh Yueh in Kiangsi and Chang Fa-k'uei in Hunan in order to secure the safety of what was left of his Whampoa-led Central Army. The nationalism reinforced by the Japanese invasion made overt manifestions of warlord-type behaviour politically incorrect, but beneath the surface the calculations typical of warlord politics dominated the minds of Chiang Kai-shek and his rivals in the Nationalist coalition, as American efforts to distribute aid in China were to show. Many of the Chinese troops not killed or wounded beyond recovery ended up as guerrillas. Despite KMT efforts to gain and hold control of the guerrilla movement behind Japanese lines, the CCP won out. As a result, these troops were doubly lost to the KMT regime.[29]

CANTON–NANCHANG–CHANGSHA, APRIL 1938 TO OCTOBER 1939

While the capture of Wuhan was not the last major operation of the Sino-Japanese War, afterwards military operations were affected by changes in the priorities of all the participants. For the Japanese the Changkufeng fighting (11 July to 10 August 1938) on the Korea–USSR border showed the Imperial Army to be inferior in weapons and technical services to the Soviet; this was emphatically confirmed in the May–September 1939 Nomonhan campaign on the desolate border between Japanese-ruled Manchukuo and the Soviet puppet state of Outer Mongolia.[30] Meanwhile the situation in Europe worsened, down to the outbreak of the Second World War. Japan therefore confronted the challenge of war with Russia and the opportunity of expansion to the south, but both required the

29 Summarized from Dorn, *Sino-Japanese War*, pp.185–224.

30 Alvin D. Coox, *The Anatomy of a Small War: The Soviet–Japanese Struggle for Changkufeng/Khasan, 1938* (Westport, 1977), and *Nomonhan* for these conflicts.

modernization of the Japanese armed forces and therefore the scaling down of the China Incident. While contemporary maps showed the Rising Sun spread over the most populous regions of China, in fact the Japanese had the men to hold only the major cities and the railway and river lines between them. In contrast to Manchukuo, where a viable collaborationist regime was functioning even in the rural areas, in China south of the Great Wall effective collaboration did not materialize. Japanese attempts to replace depreciated Nationalist money (fa-pi) with a currency of their own also failed miserably. Even the defection of Wang Ching-wei failed to change this general situation; Wang ended up losing his nationalist credentials earned from his early association with Sun Yat-sen and his leadership of the KMT left.[31]

Chiang Kai-shek and the Nationalist leadership never lost their hope of United States intervention, based on the Nine Power Treaty and the efforts of the missionary lobby. The USA remained unfriendly to Japan and maintained her non-recognition doctrine regarding any change in the territorial integrity of China. War on China's behalf, however, was out of the question. Public opinion was staunchly isolationist, and the Roosevelt administration, anticipating its Europe First strategy of the Second World War, regarded Nazi Germany as the primary potential threat to US security, and therefore tried to avoid escalating its confrontation with Japan. Japan actually benefited from the Cash and Carry amendments (November 1939) to the US neutrality laws: passed to permit Britain to continue trading with the USA despite the outbreak of the Second World War in Europe, they permitted Japan to continue trading with the USA on the same terms even if US courts held that the 'China Incident' was in fact a war, which would have been inevitable had Japan declared a formal blockade of any port on the China coast.

Meanwhile the Chinese communists expanded politically as well as militarily into the areas behind Japanese lines. While talking of defeating the Japanese, except briefly in 1940 they made few efforts to attack the Japanese directly. They did attack Chinese collaborators ('puppet troops') and effectively pre-empted the Nationalist agenda in the areas behind Japanese lines. The KMT recognized and resented the CCP success, and a covert civil war developed, breaking out into open fighting in the New 4th Army

31 This is the theme of John Hunter Boyle, *China and Japan at War: The Politics of Collaboration* (Stanford, 1972).

Incident of 1941.[32] By then a kind of political gridlock had set in in China: the communists could not defeat the Japanese, the Nationalists could not make peace with the Japanese without forfeiting their legitimacy to the communists, and the Japanese would not withdraw without Chinese recognition of Manchukuo.

Japanese amphibious expeditions took Amoy, Foochow and Swatow in May 1938.[33] This left Canton as the only important seaport still in Chinese hands. Canton's defenders (Yü Han-mou's 12th Group Army) hoped that the British presence at Hong Kong would keep the Japanese away. However, on 12 October, two weeks after the Munich Agreement demonstrated to the world the extent of British (and French) irresolution, the Japanese 21st Army (three divisions plus the usual support, about 70,000 men) appeared off the Bogue convoyed by the Imperial Navy. By 21 October they were parading through Canton, after an easy campaign with no military interest.[34] In February 1939 the same forces occupied Hainan Island.

Trickles of supply could still reach Yunnan through both French Indo-China and Burma until the evolution of tbe Second World War cut off these routes. Supplies from Russia could be imported into Sinkiang; where they went from there depended until 1943 on the ambiguous loyalties of Sinkiang's warlord Sheng Shih-ts'ai. And of course one could Fly the Hump from Assam across the Himalayas. China, in other words was tightly blockaded, which fact combined with the inflated order of battle of the Chinese armies to create the US delusion (much wondered at by both Churchill and Stalin) that hordes of eager warriors would spring from the Chinese earth if only arms could be supplied.

After the fall of Wuhan, Chiang Kai-shek held several conferences with his top generals, in which Chiang called for more emphasis on propaganda and guerrilla warfare, and for reorganization and better training of the regular troops. In fact internal politics prevented any significant consolidation of China's over 300 under-strength divisions, and the restructuring of the higher commands also amounted to little more than tinkering. The war area structure as reorganized in December 1937 (see pp.221–2) remained mostly in place, Chinese armies 'defending' the out-of-the-way parts of their original war areas that the Japanese

32 A general theme of Johnson, *Peasant Nationalism*.

33 Dorn, *Sino-Japanese War*, pp.168–70.

34 Dorn, *Sino-Japanese War*, pp.224–30.

did not intend to attack. Chang Fa-k'uei, who had moved his troops without authorization from Hunan to Kwangtung and Kwangsi, was rewarded by being made commander of the 4th War Area in those provinces.

In early 1939 General Okamura's Japanese 11th Army prepared to reopen the offensive against Hsueh Yueh's army, formally part of the 9th War Area, which had held the line of the Hsiu River between Tean and Nanchang throughout the Wuhan campaign. The thirty-five divisions of the 9th War Area in Kiangsi (there were twenty-four more in Hunan) outnumbered their attackers by 230,000 to 75,000 and by now had a considerable record of defensive success. Unfortunately Chiang attempted to direct the battle by detailed orders from Chungking, which meant, inevitably, that the initiative remained with the Japanese.[35]

On 18 March the Japanese 101st Division fought its way across the Hsiu at Tsaohsing, west of Tean. Chinese forces fell back quickly to within a few miles of Nanchang. Planned counterattacks were abandoned before being carried out, partly due to contradictory and irrelevant orders. The Japanese assaulted Nanchang from the north, west and south, taking it easily on 27 March. They then removed all of their troops except the 101st and 106th divisions to Hunan for the next stage of their planned offensive. They were surprised by the scale of the Chinese attack of 21 April, by the 49th and 74th armies, which persisted for two weeks and reached the outskirts of Nanchang. A combination of Japanese reserves and tactical air support broke up the Chinese effort on 8 May.[36] While this was going on, other elements of the 11th Army broke up a planned Chinese trap northwest of Anlu in northern Hupei, afterwards retiring to the railway line.[37]

From April to October 1939 the five divisions of General Okamura's 11th Army made a major effort to take Changsha, capital of Hunan. The plan was for three columns to advance simultaneously, one from Kaoan, the second from Johsi (both in Kiangsi) and the third and most powerful (built around the 3rd and 6th divisions) moved directly south from Yochow. The 9th War Area forces in Hunan were commanded by the courageous and capable Ch'en Ch'eng and numbered perhaps 365,000 men in formations of varying quality. The Japanese columns jumped off from 13 to 18 September. By 24 September the 3rd and 6th

35 Dorn, *Sino-Japanese War*, pp.244–51.
36 Dorn, *Sino-Japanese War*, pp.251–60.
37 Dorn, *Sino-Japanese War*, pp.260–4.

divisions had fought their way across the Hsinchiang River, and two days later, supported by an amphibious crossing of the Tungting Lake, had covered more than half the distance to Changsha. All very easy and typical, but Ch'en Ch'eng actually meant 'to lure the enemy into the vicinity of Changsha for a decisive battle'. On 27 September Chinese divisions pre-positioned on the flanks of the advancing Japanese counterattacked, and drove them back to Yochow with heavy losses by 8 October. Both of the columns attacking from Kiangsi suffered variants of this fate.[38]

THE CHINESE WINTER OFFENSIVES, 1939–40

Frustrated by their failure to settle the China Incident and angered by the defeat in Hunan, Imperial General Headquarters ordered the 21st Army, now under Lieutenant-General Imamura Kinichi, to conquer Kwangsi. On 15 November the Japanese 5th Division took Chinhsien, and soon afterwards Pakhoi and Hopu, the other small ports of western Kwangtung, in an amphibious operation. From Chinhsien the Japanese army advanced rapidly on Nanning, capturing the city on 23 November, and then sending columns to the north and to the west.

When the flamboyant but unreliable Chang Fa-k'uei had forced his appointment as commander of the 4th War Area, his predecessor Pai Ch'ung-hsi, head of the Kwangsi military clique, had been left in control of Kwangsi as 'director' of the generalissimo's Kweilin headquarters. The 190,000 men under his command outnumbered the Japanese by about three to one. Chinese counterattacks began on 18 December, and by the new year had killed several thousand men of the 5th Division and driven its advance columns back on Nanning.

The Japanese then appointed a new army commander and sent reinforcements, including the Imperial Guard Division, which took Pinyang north of Nanning on 2 February 1940. A week later it was forced to evacuate. The Japanese position in Kwangsi now consisted of Nanning, Chinhsien and the road between them. This situation remained in place most of the rest of 1940. After many battles in which Japanese efforts to expand from Nanning were successfully resisted by the Chinese, on 30 October the 21st Army evacuated Nanning and marched to Chinhsien, which the Japanese burned and

38 Dorn, *Sino-Japanese War*, pp.269–83; the quotation is on p.281.

abandoned on 17 November. By this time the evolution of the Second World War had led the Japanese (July) to occupy the northern part of French Indo-China, so they could argue that the objective of the Kwangsi campaign, to cut off imports through that colony, had already been achieved. In fact the loss of face was considerable. The Imperial Guard never quite recovered its elite status, and suffered much disparagement when it served under General Yamashita Tomoyuki's command in the Malayan campaign of 1941–2.[39]

Chiang Kai-shek had been heartened by the Chinese victory in the Changsha campaign and by the down-scaling of Japanese offensives since the Wuhan campaign. In his usual detailed manner he ordered all of his field commands to launch a concerted offensive in mid-November, believing that the reorganization of the Chinese armies coupled with the rotation of less combat-experienced Japanese troops into the China theatre offered a major opportunity. The results were disappointing. The 1st War Area briefly entered Kaifeng, and the 5th War Area made some poorly coordinated attacks. The 9th War Area tried unsuccessfully to interdict the railway line between Nanchang and Kiukiang, and the 4th War Area successfully resisted Japanese efforts to expand out of Canton. For the most part the field commands went halfheartedly over to the offensive and stopped quickly, justifying themselves by reporting exaggerated claims of enemy losses.[40]

TO THE SECOND BATTLE OF CHANGSHA, 1940–1

Chiang Kai-shek was encouraged by the reported successes in guerrilla operations coming from the war areas. Henceforth Nationalist propaganda would portray the war as a string of guerrilla operations in which the underarmed but heroic Chinese forces harassed the Japanese while avoiding standup battles with main force Japanese units. Communist propaganda and doctrine were in fact very similar, and both Nationalists and communists could claim a degree of success in such operations. Unfortunately, however, a declared strategy of guerrilla warfare may often be merely a rationalization for the desire to avoid battle. Preserving one's forces by not fighting, and 'harassing' the enemy by following at a safe distance without actually making contact, were consistent

39 Dorn, *Sino-Japanese War*, pp.284–303.
40 Dorn, *Sino-Japanese War*, pp.304–22.

with the warlord-derived vices of most Chinese military units, but were not really guerrilla warfare. And even very extensive guerrilla operations were unlikely to drive the Japanese from China, as long as they retained the political will to remain there.

By 1940–1 the war in China continued to absorb very extensive Japanese military forces, but meanwhile the outbreak of the Second World War actually reduced the effective pressure that the Soviet Union and the democratic powers could bring to bear on Japan to end the war. As noted previously (pp.207, 233), the Soviet Union ended the Nomonhan Incident, despite a clear victory in the fighting, when Germany invaded Poland in 1939. During the critical phase of the Battle of Britain (July–October 1940) the British government had no choice but to give in to Japanese demands to close the Burma Road, China's last supply line to the outside world. United States policy was Europe-orientated; as also noted previously (p.234), the 1939 Cash and Carry amendments to the US Neutrality Act actually benefited Japan. The USA was far from friendly to Japan, however; the move of the US Fleet from San Diego (California) to Pearl Harbor (Hawaii) in January 1940 was intended as a threat, and in July the USA ordered a partial embargo on trade with Japan in retaliation for the Japanese occupation of the northern part of French Indo-China. But it was only a year later, in July 1941, that the US total embargo started the war clock ticking, and US leaders were reluctant to accept the idea that Japan would fight the Anglo-Saxon powers under any circumstances.

Certain elements in the Japanese leadership had long entertained the idea of war with Britain and/or the United States. The two powers had been the theoretical enemies of the Imperial Navy in exercises for decades, and in the violent Japanese policy conflicts of the 1930s the Imperial Way generals who argued for a northern advance (war with the USSR) had been opposed by admirals calling – possibly with the tacit support of Emperor Hirohito – for a southern advance against western colonial possessions in Southeast Asia. The German triumph in Europe in May–June 1940 made these possessions extremely vulnerable to an opportunistic Japanese attack. Such a war would depend on the Imperial Navy (and its air force), which was no longer heavily engaged in the war in China after the conquest of the coastal ports. Victory would make the settlement of the China Incident more likely, by removing the possibility of intervention in China's favour by the defeated Anglo-Saxon powers. The bulk of the Imperial Army, meanwhile, would not be needed in the Pacific and could remain in occupation of those parts of China under Japanese control.[41]

The latter point depended on the ability of the Chinese economy of the occupied areas to sustain the Japanese forces, and on the Japanese ability to maintain themselves against Chinese guerrilla warfare. The Japanese army remained a predominantly infantry force, without the extensive fuel and spare parts logistical tail of contemporary British and US armies (this contrast was very noticeable in the Japanese conquest of Malaya and Burma from British Empire forces in 1942).[42] Logistical support therefore meant mainly food supplies. While the China Expeditionary Army was very large – eventually over a million men – it was interspersed in a Chinese economy of several hundred million people, which the Japanese exploited successfully, if wastefully and callously. Collaboration was a failure at the national, political level, but it was much more successful at the local, economic level. Regarding guerrilla warfare, many post-1949 analyses have depended too much on the exegesis of Mao Tse-tung's writings. In fact, serious guerrilla warfare resistance did not exist in Manchukuo throughout the Japanese occupation. In North China the Hundred Regiments offensive of August–December 1940 was the test of the theory that success in guerrilla warfare would permit the transition to the regular warfare needed to drive the Japanese from China. Mao Tse-tung had articulated this theory but opposed Chu Te's recommendation to go over to regular warfare at this time. Mao was correct. The Japanese defended their base – the major cities and the railway lines connecting them – killing millions of Chinese in the process.[43] Subsequent 'guerrilla warfare' was ironically analogous to the 'defence in depth' (i.e. remaining safely distant from the Japanese) practised by Nationalist forces. By 1945 the communists in North China were well positioned for the event of a Chinese civil war, but the Japanese did not regard them as much of a military threat.

41 These are my generalizations, but there is a large literature. See Butow, *Tojo*, Lu, *Marco Polo Bridge*, Feis, *Road*, the five-volume series edited by Morley, and Coox, *Nomonhan*.

42 A theme throughout the excellent volumes of S. Woodburn Kirby, *The War Against Japan* (5 vols, London, 1969), and also of Louis Allen, *Burma: The Longest War, 1941–1945* (New York, 1984).

43 William W. Whitson, *The Chinese High Command: A History of Communist Military Politics, 1927–1971* (New York, 1973), pp.69–71; Lincoln Li, *The Japanese Army in North China, 1937–1941: Problems of Political and Economic Control* (Tokyo, 1975).

These considerations help to explain the apparently indecisive winding-down of operations in the Sino-Japanese War. After the creation of the Wang Ching-wei government in March 1940, the Japanese hoped that it would win enough acceptance that they could sign with it a treaty to end the China Incident. By the time that hope evaporated, Japan was far down the road leading to war with the Anglo-Saxon powers. Both sets of circumstances inhibited plans to expand Japanese-occupied territory in China. Limited operations intended to destroy Chinese armies were seldom followed by occupation of new territory, so a pattern of advance-fight-withdraw developed in Japanese operations against both mostly communist guerrillas and mostly Nationalist 'regulars'. This remained the pattern of Japanese operations in the China theatre throughout the Second World War.

From April to June 1940 General Enbu Katsuichirō, now commanding the Japanese 11th Army at Wuhan, advanced into north-central Hupei. On 8 May the Japanese took Tsaoyang, and then had to fight their way out through encircling Chinese forces whose commanders included Taierhchuang veterans T'ang En-po and Chang Tse-chung, who was killed in these actions. Afterwards the Japanese concentrated another force at Shayang on the Han River, marched west and took Yichang, the largest river port between Hankow and Chungking, on 9–12 June. Hupei remained quiet except for sporadic guerrilla activity for five months. In November Enbu launched division-sized columns from Suihsien, Chunghsiang and Tangyang; they advanced, fought, devastated the countryside, and retreated on a prearranged schedule. In March 1941 the Japanese 13th Division carried out a similar raid from Yichang.[44]

Meanwhile General Enbu concentrated about five divisions at Hsinyang in southern Honan, and in late January and early February 1941 these marched through a wide area of central and southern Honan, aided by a Japanese column coming from Pohsien (Anhwei). Nimble Chinese forces avoided contact almost entirely with the Japanese soldiers, who therefore employed their time burning peasant villages and raping the women. The whole operation was not much more than a training exercise for the large number of raw replacement troops from Japan, but Chungking announced a great victory when the Japanese returned to Hsinyang.[45] Japanese violence against the rural Chinese population

44 Dorn, *Sino-Japanese War*, pp.323–38.
45 Dorn, *Sino-Japanese War*, pp.347–52.

was escalating, and peaked later in the year in the millions of deaths in the 'Three All' anti-communist campaigns in North China (see pp.253–4). This degree of violence was probably worse than the more sporadic violence of the warlord era, bad as the latter had been, and despite regional variations for both warlord and Japanese violence. However, the Japanese usually conducted 'punitive operations' in areas already written off as candidates for long-term Japanese rule and economic exploitation; in those areas they were even less concerned with the survival of the civilian population than previous warlord regimes, which needed to exploit the civilian economy, had been. And since the Japanese troops were all foreigners, their atrocities had the effect of stimulating Chinese nationalism in rural areas hitherto little concerned with such issues. The Chinese communists were the main beneficiary of this nationalism.[46]

In late March 1941 a Japanese force built around the 33rd and 34th divisions carried out punitive operations in northwestern Kiangsi. Despite the usual inept leadership of Whampoa clique General (and Chiang Kai-shek favourite) Lo Cho-ying, the Chinese 19th Group Army stood up to the Japanese at Shangkao, where hand-to-hand fighting on 22–25 March caused each side several thousand casualties.[47]

In May General Count Terauchi of the North China Area Army, angered by the rise in guerrilla operations in northern Honan, concentrated six divisions to destroy organized Chinese forces in that area and extend his occupied area all the way to the Yellow River. After the success of this operation, the Japanese in October made an unopposed crossing of the Yellow River and took the railway junction city of Chengchow, three years after their first attempt to do so had been frustrated by the blowing of the Yellow River dikes at Chiang Kai-shek's orders. But the Japanese did not bother to take over the railway line in Honan, leading from Chengchow to Hankow, until their ICHIGO offensive of 1944.[48]

From April to September of 1941 the Japanese did not launch any new offensives, and in consequence a lull amounting in most areas to a truce descended on the China theatre. Events elsewhere were breaking fast. On 22 June Hitler launched his invasion of the

46 The thesis of Johnson, *Peasant Nationalism*, which I believe to be correct. See Chalmers A. Johnson, 'Peasant nationalism revisited: the biography of a book', *China Quarterly* 72 (London, 1977), pp.766–85, for an entertaining survey of dissenting opinions, mostly from the 1960s.

47 Dorn, *Sino-Japanese War*, pp.352–7.

48 Dorn, *Sino-Japanese War*, pp.357–62.

Soviet Union, which had been heralded for some months by rising tensions and German troop movements. The world held its breath, but it soon seemed evident that the Wehrmacht was destroying the Red Army as easily as it had its previous opponents. Unknown to Hitler, and partly due to their defeat at Nomonhan, Japan's governing circles had by now rejected the idea of attacking the Soviet Union, and instead had embraced the goal of annexing the Western colonial empires in Southeast Asia. In July Japanese troops occupied the southern half of French Indo-China, thus coming within air-striking range of the British naval base at Singapore. For two decades British Far Eastern strategy had depended on holding Singapore and operating from it in the event of war with Japan.[49] The strong US reaction – freezing of all Japanese assets and a total embargo of trade with Japan – indicated a degree of cooperation between the British and US governments that took the Japanese by surprise. Since the Japanese armed forces were totally dependent on imported oil, most of which came from the United States, the embargo also started the clock running on the Pearl Harbor attack: with oil reserves calculated as good for about eleven months of normal operations, Japan had to resume oil deliveries by the end of the year in order to retain freedom of action. Assuming the United States would not lift its embargo, this meant the southward advance to seize the oil resources of the Dutch East Indies. This required troops who might otherwise have been used offensively in China. But despite these other priorities, the Japanese intended to avenge their defeat at Changsha.

The Japanese 11th Army, now under General Anan Tadaki, had been reinforced to a strength of about 125,000 men in four divisions and four independent brigades. In early September 1941 most of these were concentrated around Linhsiang, east of Yochow on the railway line. On 17 September, after several days of probing reconnaissance, they moved south and crossed the Hsinchiang River in four parallel columns, supported by an amphibious operation from Yochow. Three days later they had reached and crossed the Milo, against Chinese resistance that was more inept than it should have been, even granted the Chinese objective of luring the Japanese into a trap. The eastern Japanese column made a wide flank march, while the others crossed the Laotao River. By 26 September the bulk of the 11th Army was concentrated east of Changsha between the Laotao and Liuyang rivers.

49 James Neidpath, *The Singapore Naval Base and the Defence of Britain's Eastern Empire, 1919–1941* (Oxford, 1981), treats these issues with great intelligence.

The 9th War Area commander Hsueh Yueh had naturally hoped that his 300,000 or so regular troops would delay the Japanese longer and inflict more damage on them. Nonetheless, the Japanese were now where Hsueh wanted them to be, and their rapid advance made them careless of flank and rear security. Hsueh ordered his troops east of Changsha to hold their positions to the last man. The sudden stiffening of Chinese resistance threw the Japanese off balance, and they were surprised when Chinese reserves attacked from the east and northeast on 27 September. The encircled 11th Army fought to survive; three days later it broke out and fled to the north. The Chinese recovered their territory up to the Hsinchiang River. As usual, halfhearted pursuit robbed them of total victory, but this time the trail of dead Japanese and captured military equipment corroborated Chinese claims of success.[50]

An overview of the Japanese position in China in late 1941 provides material for contradictory interpretations. In Manchukuo a stable puppet regime served as the instrument for Japanese exploitation. This solution had failed in China proper (as described on pp.245–9) but nevertheless the Japanese continued to rule and exploit the coastal and riverine cities within reach of Japanese naval power, without challenge from any Chinese force. In North China the defeat of the Communist Hundred Regiments offensive in 1940 and the 'Three All' campaigns of 1941 (as described on pp.253–4), created the situation that lasted until 1945, wherein the Japanese controlled the major cities and the railway network that connected them, while communist-ruled 'liberated areas' controlled the rural areas between the railway lines. The 'guerrilla warfare' of the next several years meant sporadic attacks against Chinese 'puppet troops' of the Wang Ching-wei regime; the Japanese were able, despite this resistance, to draw both labour and agricultural produce from North China to support their occupying forces.

In South China, away from the coast, the situation was different. Twice now the Japanese had been defeated in attempting to conquer Changsha, the provincial capital of Hunan, by moving southward from Hupei. The Japanese campaign in Kwangsi also could only be seen as a defeat, which made a laughing-stock of the supposedly elite Imperial Guards Division. Southern Kiangsi remained under Chinese control, despite the fall of the provincial capital at Nanchang. In the hinterlands of Chekiang, Anhwei and Fukien irregular forces survived, mostly under Nationalist control

50 Dorn, *Sino-Japanese War*, pp.363–72.

despite the challenge of the communist New 4th Army. Chiang Kai-shek's Whampoa clique-led Central Army survived in Szechwan and Shensi, whose colourful local warlords were now mostly history. However, in Kansu the Chinese Muslim cavalry of the Ma clan ruled much of the province, and in Yunnan the Yi (Lolo) nationality warlord Lung Yun retained control for the time being.

What seemed important strategically about South China was the Chinese ability there to defend territory against Japanese attempts to conquer it. This argued, especially to the United States when that country entered the war actively in December 1941, that China was still fighting Japan effectively and that the China theatre could be important in the overall Allied war effort against Japan. Yet, as is so often the case with China, appearances were deceptive, and reality was the opposite of appearance. The Japanese defeats in the two Changsha campaigns had a lot to do with 'victory disease' – as the Japanese themselves called it – and the Kwangsi campaign had floundered partly due to lack of a clear objective. By this time the Japanese themselves were looking to a general Axis victory in the Second World War to settle the China Incident; this meant the southern advance and a consequent lower priority for military operations in China itself. From Chiang Kai-shek's point of view, the highly publicized Chinese victories against Japan had been won by the Kwangsi generals Li Tsung-jen and Pai Ch'ung-hsi, the Cantonese Hsueh Yueh, and perhaps Chang Fa-k'uei – all long associated with the non-Whampoa 'southern opposition' within the KMT. Chiang Kai-shek regularly discriminated against these armies in allocating US assistance, but Chennault's later air offensive against Japan (much desired by Chiang – see Chapter 7) depended on the ability of these out-of-favour armies to hold the airfields in these areas against Japanese ground attack. In the 1944 ICHIGO offensive, confronted with a clear operational objective, the Japanese easily overran these areas which had previously resisted them.[51]

COLLABORATION AND ITS FAILURE

As far back as the Twenty-One Demands of 1915 some Japanese policy-makers hoped to exercise Japanese rule within China through Chinese collaborators, and Japanese efforts to manipulate such

51 Graham Hutchings, 'A province at war: Guangxi during the Sino-Japanese conflict, 1937–1945', *China Quarterly*, 108 (London, 1986), pp.652–79, shows these processes at work in Kwangsi during the entire Sino-Japanese War period.

warlords as Anhwei clique patriarch Tuan Ch'i-jui and Manchurian militarist Chang Tso-lin continued this tradition. The 'Empire of Manchukuo' from 1932 on provided the model puppet state. Each Cabinet minister and each of the nine (ten after the incorporation of Jehol) provincial governors was flanked by a Japanese 'adviser' who in practice had all decision-making authority. Manchukuo did not win the loyalty of its Chinese subjects, but it remained free of guerrilla disturbances until the Chinese communists entered the area postwar. Its relative tranquillity was due to the fact that the 'empire' was rapidly established by the Japanese Kwantung Army without the extensive atrocities to the civilian population that characterized Japanese operations in China proper from 1937 on.[52]

On 24 November 1935, as part of the fallout from the Ho–Umezu agreement, the East Hopei Autonomous Anti-Communist Council came into existence, flying the old five-barred flag of the pre-Northern Expedition Chinese Republic. Its leadership represented the local landlord class, who at this point in time resented KMT interference in local affairs almost as much as they feared communist social programmes. From Doihara Kenji's point of view, the East Hopei government was a step toward the creation of a five-province North China modelled on Manchukuo, but it had less status: even Japan did not recognize East Hopei as an independent nation.[53] But even though East Hopei's leaders were despised as traitors by most Chinese, there was no significant guerrilla resistance in their area before 1937. The Hopei–Chahar Political Council at Peiping from 1935 to 1937 was under Sung Che-yuan, a Feng Yü-hsiang subordinate rightly distrusted by both Nanking and Tokyo, but who fought against the Japanese after 7 July 1937. Prince Te's Inner Mongolian movement, while wholly dependent upon the Japanese, nevertheless had a serious agenda in Mongolian nationalism. Neither of these was as much a Japanese puppet as Manchukuo and East Hopei.

On 4 September 1937 Major-General Kita Seiichi was placed in command of the Special Sections (tokumu-bu or -kikan) carrying out political activities in the sphere of the North China Area Army. Efforts to recruit Ts'ao K'un and Wu P'ei-fu – the leaders of the former Chihli military clique who could now be regarded as senior statesmen – to head a puppet government failed, so when the

52 F.C. Jones, *Japan's New Order in East Asia: Its Rise and Fall, 1937–1945* (London, 1954), includes discussions of Manchukuo institutions.

53 Boyle, *Politics of Collaboration* pp.39–40.

Provisional government of the Republic of China was inaugurated in Peiping on 14 December, its head was Wang K'o-min, a Shanghai banker and former Ch'ing official who had supported the losing side in the political struggles of the 1920s. While the Provisional government was thus a creature of the Japanese North China Area Army and was headed by a nonentity, its use of the KMT flag and constitution helped to discredit these symbols for many Chinese.[54]

During the active phase of the Sino-Japanese War, the Japanese Central China Area Army (later the China Expeditionary Army) reported to Tokyo independently of, and on a basis of equality with, the North China Area Army. It lacked a cadre of old China hands with blueprints for puppet regimes, so its Reformed government of the Republic of China, inaugurated at Nanking on 28 March 1938, was an even more perfunctory effort. Its chief Liang Hung-chih was a former associate of Tuan Ch'i-jui, and – like the now reluctantly dissolving East Hopei government – it flew the old five-barred flag.[55]

By mid-1938 the three Japanese army commands in China were thus supporting four different puppet regimes, including Manchukuo and Prince Te, both under the Kwantung Army. Japanese hopes for the settlement of the China Incident required either Chiang Kai-shek's recognition of Manchukuo, or, failing that, the amalgamation of the Peiping and Nanking regimes into a single government with enough legitimacy in China to make its recognition of Manchukuo meaningful. That meant attracting some major political figures, and the Japanese were already working on Wang Ching-wei.

Despite the prestige Wang retained among long-service revolutionaries who remembered his attempt to murder the Prince Regent in 1910, Wang was in fact washed up politically. The communists felt that he had betrayed them in 1927, Chiang resented his association with the repeated military conspiracies against his rule, and ironically the anti-Japanese voices in KMT China resented Wang's public support for Chiang's appeasement of Japan prior to 1937. As of the end of 1938 armed resistance to Japan had produced the predictable disaster, and – according to the admittedly suspect later testimony of Wang's supporters – Chiang and the leading elements of the KMT supported continued resistance only because they feared that otherwise 'the Communists, the Kwangsi Clique, Feng Yü-hsiang, and other anti-Kuomintang elements would

54 Boyle, *Politics of Collaboration* pp.84–92.
55 Boyle, *Politics of Collaboration*, pp.110–16.

use anti-Japanese slogans to build public support for their opposition to the Government, with a new eruption of civil war the inevitable result'.[56] Wang, who was already deeply involved in private negotiations with the Japanese, failed to convince Chiang in December that making peace with Japan and taking the consequences was the best policy.

On 18 December 1938 Wang flew to Kunming, where he failed to persuade the anti-Chiang warlord Lung Yun to support him, and then to Hanoi. Chiang was probably aware of Wang's intention to defect, but did nothing to hinder him or his numerous associates, who left Chungking the same day. Wang had been encouraged to defect by Japanese promises that were not kept at the highest level. Japanese prime minister Prince Konoe actually had no plan at this stage for creating an all-China government under Wang, and the Imperial Army adamantly refused to consider a definite date for troop withdrawal or to abandon its existing puppets and the policy of 'different regimes working together' (bunji gassaku) that they represented. Chungking stripped Wang of his party membership but for the time being was moderate in publicly denouncing him. After an attempted assassination in April 1939, Wang went to Shanghai under Japanese protection. In January 1940 two of Wang's key supporters defected back to Chiang, releasing documents that gave all the details of Wang's negotiations with the Japanese. The long delay in using Wang and the unwillingness of the Japanese to make any meaningful concessions to him meant that Wang was largely discredited by the start of his formal career as a Japanese puppet.[57]

Wang went through with it anyhow, being inaugurated in Nanking on 30 March 1940, with thousands of Japanese troops serving as honour guards. The following day a Japanese Foreign Ministry spokesman refuted some unkind allegations of puppet status by observing that Wang's regime was as independent as Manchukuo. Chungking now took the gloves off in denouncing Wang as a traitor to China (Han-chien) and putting a bounty on his head; it was a blessing for Wang that he did not survive the war.[58] Wang's use of the KMT flag and symbols, and his great political stature and the number of his supporters, however, fitted in nicely with the CCP propaganda line that the KMT did not have its heart in the war.[58] And both successes and defeats in guerrilla warfare

56 Boyle, *Politics of Collaboration*, p.208.

57 Summarized from Boyle, *Politics of Collaboration*, pp.210–76.

58 Boyle, *Politics of Collaboration*, pp.277–305.

meanwhile gave the CCP a handle on Chinese nationalism by the end of 1941.

THE CHINESE COMMUNISTS AND THE JAPANESE INVASION

The fallout from the Marco Polo Bridge Incident gave the advocates of war with Japan what they had been asking for, and most of the CCP leaders (Mao significantly excepted) were eager to fight the war in a conventional manner, placing their divisions side by side with other Chinese forces. The communist victory at P'inghsingkuan (previously discussed on pp.215–16), later used as a model for guerrilla units to emulate, was actually won by Lin Piao's regular division fighting as a component of a larger army. Fighting as regulars did not preclude the advancement of CCP political goals. The main immediate benefit of the Second United Front was the adherence of many patriotic urban intellectuals to the communist cause. Hastily trained at the Resist Japan Military Academy (K'ang-Ta), they afterwards served as cadres as CCP-led organizations expanded. But Mao's call for an emphasis on guerrilla warfare and organizational expansion was resisted.[59]

By May 1938 regular operations against the Japanese had led to catastrophic defeats, and more were on their way. Mao then stated that 'the enemy's design is to occupy Canton, Wuhan and Lanchow and link up these three points'.[60] Lanchow never fell, but the rest of the agenda was complete by the end of 1938. But as the Japanese presence in China expanded, they became thinner on the ground. The Japanese occupation came to resemble a net, whose strands were the railways, roads and river lines of communication and whose interstices were the provincial capitals and other major cities. Rural China, including most county (hsien) towns, did not see Japanese soldiers on a regular basis. The idea of nationalism had not spread widely among the peasantry as of 1937, and in Manchukuo and parts of north China the Japanese – whose military presence of course kept Chinese warlords out – exploited the country effectively through an administration of Chinese collaborators.[61]

59 Whitson, *High Command*, pp.67–8.

60 Mao Tse-tung, *Selected Works of Mao Tse-tung* (4 vols, Peking, 1961–5), II, p.137.

61 Johnson, *Peasant Nationalism*, p.31.

The 1937–8 fighting resulted in the disintegration of many Chinese formations, whose survivors fled into the rural areas, becoming indistinguishable (to Japanese eyes) from the regular inhabitants thereof. Some of these engaged in guerrilla warfare, and the Japanese sent punitive columns to the affected areas. The Japanese army meanwhile was inflamed by a combination of 'victory disease', racism and frustration, and committed brutal atrocities on the Chinese population as a matter of course. The Rape of Nanking was the example that gained the most worldwide attention, but Japanese columns in the countryside typically behaved in the same manner, and some of the best surviving evidence of this is in the diaries kept by Japanese soldiers (almost all of whom were literate), with their detailed descriptions of atrocities, especially rapes. Japanese reprisals and atrocities thus stimulated nationalism among the peasantry, which led to guerrilla warfare and more reprisals, continuing the process.

The communists were well positioned to take advantage of these developments. Japanese propaganda clearly identified the communists as their main enemy, and – reflecting ideas sincerely held within the Japanese leadership – castigated the KMT for failing to cooperate with Japan in the suppression of communism. Since after the inauguration of Wang Ching-wei's Nanking government in March 1940 the Japanese puppets used the KMT flag, and since the Chungking regime soon resumed anti-communist policies, Japanese propaganda had the perverse effect of raising the prestige of the CCP and lowering that of the KMT among the newly politicized rural population. Also, to make their adherence to the Second United Front more palatable to non-communists, the communists had muted their social policies. Radical land reform was indefinitely postponed, and 'patriotic' landlords and other elite members were welcomed and in principle given one-third of the positions in communist-dominated local government organs.[62] Just as the communists were able to maintain a stable currency in their base areas, they were also able to apply these broad policies at the local level. The increasingly demoralized, faction-ridden and urban KMT did not compete effectively in rural China.[63]

62 Johnson, *Peasant Nationalism*, pp.92–122, remains the classic English-language study of the growth of the base areas. Lyman P. Van Slyke, *Enemies and Friends: The United Front in Chinese Communist History* (Stanford, 1967), pp.142–53, on the 'three thirds' system.

63 Suzanne Pepper, *Civil War in China: The Political Struggle, 1945–1949* (Berkeley, 1978), may serve to introduce the reader to the considerable literature on

The incorporation of the Yenan communists as the 8th Route Army of three divisions was, among other things, a KMT effort to limit the size of the communist army to the approximately 45,000 required by the formal tables of organization. In contrast to the Nationalist army with its large number of under-strength divisions, the communists used the three-division restriction to mask the growth of their forces. Actual communist strength in the north may have been as high as 90,000 as of August 1937.[64] As the Japanese invasion developed, Lin Piao's 115th Division established itself in the Wutaishan area near Pinghsingkuan in northeastern Shansi, gaining control of adjoining portions of Hopei and Chahar to form the Chin-Ch'a-Chi (the term is an acronym formed by the names of the three provinces in Classical Chinese) Base Area. The 129th Division, with Teng Hsiao-p'ing serving as Liu Po-ch'eng's political commissar, moved into southeastern Shansi, south of the Taiyuan–Shihchiachuang railway line, and extended their influence to adjoining regions of Hopei and Shantung to form the Chin-Chi-Lu Base Area. Ho Lung's 120th Division remained in the Yenan area, expanding its influence from Shensi into parts of adjacent Kansu and Ninghsia to form the Shen-Kan-Ning Base Area. Each divisional leadership elite represented a different stream of CCP military history: the 115th the survivors of the Kiangsi Soviet and the Long March, the 129th the Oyuwan Soviet and the Chang Kuo-t'ao wing of the leadership, and the 120th the communist elements (a high proportion originally bandits) that had remained in Hunan when the main communist force invaded Kiangsi and established the Kiangsi Soviet. Other base areas grew in East Hopei and in Shantung. Even the remnant communists in the lower Yangtze, reluctantly recognized by Chiang Kai-shek as the New 4th Army in August 1937, were able to organize similar movements, both north and south of the Yangtze, and near the major urban centres of Shanghai and Nanking. By 1945 there were nineteen such base areas in communist-influenced regions of China.[65]

---

the demoralization and disintegration of KMT China. Though her emphasis is on the 1945–9 period, similar problems existed throughout the Sino-Japanese War of 1937–45 and, indeed, even in the Nanking Decade of 1927–37; cf. Lloyd E. Eastman, *Seeds of Destruction* and *The Abortive Revolution: China under Nationalist Rule, 1927–1937* (Cambridge, MA, 1974), passim.

64 Johnson, *Peasant Nationalism*, p.73.

65 Whitson, *High Command*, p.68.

In principle, each base area contained military forces at three levels of quality. Rural self-defence corps troops, poorly trained and poorly armed, were essentially villagers responsible for local security. Full-time guerrilla forces, the next higher level, often incorporated bandit gangs, whose members were also vulnerable to the nationalism generated by the Japanese invasion. The elite were the regular forces, officered by the veterans of the Long March. The Japanese North China Area Army estimated communist strength in December 1939 as about 88,000 regulars, 160,000 full-time guerrillas, and 500,000 to 600,000 in the rural self-defence corps.[66] Two years later the Japanese estimated the regulars at 140,000. In effect, each division of the 8th Route Army had grown into a theatre command, controlling several division-sized 'brigades' of – usually – three 2,000-man regiments. The guerrillas had a parallel chain of command, with the 'column' (tsung-tui) replacing the division and the 'detachment' (chih-tui) the brigade. Militarily, the strategy of the early Kiangsi Soviet period was the rule: the politically committed and organized peasantry would deny intelligence and supply to the Japanese while providing it to the communist regulars, thus enabling them to defeat invading enemy columns in detail. The Japanese initially lacked both the manpower and the ability to mobilize the rural elite that had enabled the KMT to use the blockhouse strategy to destroy the Kiangsi Soviet, even though they had studied this campaign and tried to imitate Chiang's techniques.[67] Their instinctive response was to escalate the brutality of their reprisals, which brought the communists more recruits.

The success of the 8th Route Army in surviving the Japanese onslaught and then expanding despite the occupation led Chu Te and the rest of the militarily-trained leadership cadre to hope that in due course they could engage the Japanese army and win. Mao argued against this idea in 'Problems of strategy in guerrilla war against Japan' and 'On protracted war', two major military essays released in May 1938. Mao argued that the war against Japan would be protracted, and that communist strategy should emphasize guerrilla warfare, political mobilization and the building up of base areas. He acknowledged that at some point a transition from guerrilla warfare to 'mobile warfare', meaning Chinese regular forces engaging and destroying Japanese regular forces, would be necessary. Premature transition to this phase would not only fail,

66 Johnson, *Peasant Nationalism*, p.76.
67 Johnson, *Peasant Nationalism*, p.209.

but also risk the destruction of the base areas vital to the CCP's survival. Also, 'China's strength alone will not be sufficient, and we shall also have to rely on the support of international forces'.[68] Mao was quite correct, even if the 'international forces' turned out to be the US Navy and its friends, rather than the workers' revolution Mao hoped for in Japan. But since China's strength was not sufficient, hanging on and hoping for the best really was the best strategy.

Nevertheless, by 1940 the growth in communist strength had been so impressive that Chu Te ordered a coordinated offensive by most of the communist regulars (46 regiments from the 115th Division, 47 from the 129th, and 22 from the 120th) against the Japanese-held cities and the railway lines linking them. From 20 August to 10 September communist forces attacked the railway lines that separated the communist base areas, chiefly those from Techou to Shihchiachuang in Hopei, Shihchiachuang to Taiyuan in central Shansi, and Taiyuan to Tatung in northern Shansi. They succeeded in blowing up bridges and tunnels and ripping up track, and went on for the rest of September to attack Japanese garrisons frontally, taking excessive casualties (22,000 regulars, compared to Japanese losses of 3,000 or 4,000).[69] From October to December the Japanese responded in force, reasserting control of the railway lines and conducting aggressive 'mopping up operations' in the rural areas near them.

This was the end of the Hundred Regiments offensive in the strict sense, and it seems to have persuaded the communist military professionals that they were no match, as yet, for the Imperial Army. The Japanese spent the spring of 1941 reconsidering their strategy in North China. When General Okamura Yasuji took command of the North China Area Army in the summer, the new approach was 'Three All' meaning kill all, burn all, and destroy all in those areas containing communist forces. The population of the communist base areas dropped from 44 million to 25 million[70] and the survivors were dragooned into blockhouse building and trench digging, with the objective of dividing the communist forces still further. Each railway line was protected by lines of blockhouses connected by trenches and barbed wire. The Japanese stimulated local collaboration by creating protected villages that received higher

68 Mao, *Selected Works*, II, p.140.
69 Whitson, *High Command*, pp.70–4.
70 Johnson, *Peasant Nationalism*, p.58.

food allocations and other favours, and by giving bounties for the identification of communist organizers. At harvest time Japanese columns roamed the countryside, defeating the communist 'regulars' and burning whatever part of the harvest the Japanese could not collect under their control. Villagers outside the system of protected villages therefore starved if they were not killed outright. Young men, all of whom could be seen as potential communist recruits, were pressganged for forced labour in Manchuria. Under these circumstances, a strategy of guerrilla warfare, and not much of that, was the only one possible for the 8th Route Army.[71] Mao used the subsequent rectification campaign (the Cheng-Feng movement) to reassert his personal authority over the party and over military strategy, and this meant the abandonment for the rest of the Second World War of any serious communist challenge to the Japanese position in North China.

The Three All campaign was launched at the high tide of Axis arrogance, in the months before Pearl Harbor when the Wehrmacht was chewing up Russia as it had previously done Poland and France. After Pearl Harbor, of course, all Chinese factions could see that Japan would be defeated by the United States. Since Japan now had other commitments, the war in China turned into somewhat of a backwater. While the Japanese army in China remained large, the best units were drawn off to the Pacific and lost or isolated there, while newly raised formations were sent to replace them. The communists during 1942–5 engaged in low-level guerrilla warfare against the troops of the Japanese puppet regimes, but were in fact no more seriously engaged in fighting the Japanese than the Nationalists were. Both sides were trying to win foreign sympathy and support for the civil war that both expected following the New 4th Army incident of January 1941, which effectively ended the Second United Front.

THE NEW 4TH ARMY INCIDENT AND THE KMT–CCP SPLIT

The expansion and consolidation of the CCP-led base areas in the rear of the Japanese occupation had a communist political component that transcended the approved United Front goal of resistance to Japan. While not destroying the landlords as a class, and accepting their participation in the government of the base

71 Whitson, *High Command* pp.164–5.

areas, the communists did redistribute some lands and reduced rents to three-eighths of the crop. Showing that the landlords could be contrained by an effective state power in turn made their organizing efforts welcome among the peasantry. The pure class struggle that had failed in South China before the Long March was much more effective in North China when mixed together with the anti-Japanese struggle.

This was understood by KMT and other non-communist leaders, and turf battles between communist and KMT-led guerrilla organizations broke out and escalated in 1939. Yen Hsi-shan, who had attempted to emulate CCP political techniques during his period of alliance with the communists, broke with them decisively in November–December 1939. His Sacrifice League and Dare to Die formations promptly defected to the communists.[72] Chang Kuo-t'ao, on the other hand, had defected to the Nationalists in April 1938, and was publicly denouncing the motives of the CCP leadership. The KMT gave wide circulation to a pamphlet (purportedly written by the principal of the Yenan Worker's School but generally considered a fabrication) that described CCP policy as 70 per cent expansion, 20 per cent coping with the KMT, and only 10 per cent resisting Japan.[73] One could argue in response that CCP expansion was a form of resistance to the Japanese. KMT-led guerrillas were usually politically undisciplined, plundered the peasantry in their operational areas, and therefore could not expand to a degree comparable to the more politically adroit communists.

Yeh T'ing's New 4th Army had been constituted in August 1937 from remnant communists in the lower Yangtze. After the fall of Shanghai and Nanking, its guerrilla activities spread throughout southern Kiangsu and southern Anhwei in cooperation (sometimes grudging) with (Whampoa clique leading figure and close Chiang Kai-shek ally) Ku Chu-t'ung's 3rd War Area. North of the Yangtze the rapid expansion of the New 4th Army resulted in clashes with Kwangsi clique leader and Taierhchuang victor Li Tsung-jen's 5th War Area. In 1939–40 communist guerrillas took over most of northern Kiangsu, confining KMT governor Han T'e-chin to the city of Paoying on the Grand Canal. The New 4th Army now consisted of six division-sized 'detachments' coordinated by a South Yangtze Command (Ch'en Yi) and a North Yangtze Command (Chang Yun-yi). Their principal competitor was the Loyal National

72 Van Slyke, *Enemies and Friends*, pp.130–42.
73 Van Slyke, *Enemies and Friends*, p.157.

Salvation Army controlled by Nationalist secret police chief Tai Li, whose guerrilla activities seemed more directed against the communists than the Japanese.[74]

The KMT leadership was both angered and frightened by the New 4th Army's expansion. During 1940 the two sides negotiated, apparently coming to an agreement under which the KMT would accept the loss of northern Kiangsu and in return the New 4th Army would evacuate the area south of the Yangtze. These negotiations were apparently carried out in good faith. However, on 4 January 1941, while the evacuation was continuing, Nationalist troops under Ku Chu-t'ung surrounded the New 4th Army HQ at Maolin, in Anhwei south of the Yangtze. A ten-day battle followed in which Yeh T'ing was captured and his deputy Hsiang Ying and many others on both sides were killed or wounded. On 17 January Chungking formally disbanded the New 4th Army. Actually Ch'en Yi took it over, and continued its operations both south and north of the Yangtze.[75]

The New 4th Army Incident was the end of the Second United Front and the revival of the KMT–CCP civil war in all but name. The KMT had been blockading the Shen-Kan-Ning border area since 1939; this blockade was now extended to all of the communist areas. As the KMT war effort stagnated, relations between Nationalist troops and nearby Japanese units often became commercial, if not actually friendly. But KMT hostility to the communists, and the blockade of their territories, remained intense. This frustrated the efforts of Stilwell and other US officials to distribute a portion of American supplies to the communists, and of course the isolation of the communist territories contributed to the impression that they were actively resisting the Japanese, once it became clear that the Nationalists were not.

THE WAR IN THE AIR AND THE AVG

Since Japan never produced a Trenchard or a Billy Mitchell, she was spared the inter-service conflicts attending the introduction of air power in both Britain and the United States. By 1937 both the Imperial Army and the Imperial Navy had air forces dedicated to supporting the surface activities of their parent service. As the war

74 Johnson, *Peasant Nationalism*, pp.123–36.

75 Johnson, *Peasant Nationalism*, pp.136–40; cf. also Whitson, *High Command*, pp.210–21.

developed, the air for the most part belonged to the Japanese. Army and navy aviation maintained battlefield superiority, bombed and strafed Chinese troops and other targets, and carried out reconnaissance. Air doctrine was still primitive in all of the major powers; Japanese efforts at the beginning were made with open-cockpit single-engine planes that often lacked radios, so their command of the air did not approach either the volume of ordnance or the degree of air–ground cooperation typical of Allied operations in the later stages of the Second World War. Nevertheless the Japanese were formidable by the standards of the day. It was remarkable that the Chinese kept anything in the air against them, and in the end the Chinese air effort had an important effect in shaping American public opinion of the war in China and on the US military presence in China during the Second World War.

Chiang Kai-shek had been an enthusiast for air power after its successes in the fifth encirclement campaign of 1934. Unfortunately he hired an Italian air advisory mission soon afterwards. Despite the great reputation of Italian ships and planes in the interwar period, Italy was militarily only a façade, and the Chinese air force in 1937 shared this characteristic. With a paper strength of 500 aircraft, only 150 were effective, and most of these were low-performance trainers.[76] Chiang ordered his wife and her brother T.V. Soong to use their American contacts to get pilots. They hired Claire L. Chennault, still (1937) only a captain after twenty years' service. They promised him a free hand in developing the Chinese air force. This promise was kept; the Chiangs trusted Chennault as much as they trusted the Whampoa clique, and he repaid them with a loyalty that was blind to the defects of their regime.[77]

Chennault believed that fighter planes were important. This contradicted the air orthodoxy of the day, which held that 'the bomber will always get through' and that nothing else really mattered. Chennault was also a master of improvised logistics. Arriving in China within weeks of the outbreak of full-scale fighting

76 Stanley, *Prelude*, p.137.

77 My account follows two recent scholarly studies: Daniel Ford, *Flying Tigers: Claire Chennault and the American Volunteer Group* (Washington, 1991), and Martha Byrd, *Chennault: Giving Wings to the Tiger* (Tuscaloosa, 1987). The popular impression of the AVG, based on the John Wayne movie, is not historically correct, and efforts of the USAF to appropriate Chennault into the air power pantheon make odd reading, in view of how Chennault was treated in his career. DeWitt S. Copp, *A Few Great Captains: The Men and Events that Shaped the Development of U.S. Air Power* (Garden City, NY, 1980), offers the undiluted USAF view.

in July 1937, he sorted out the mess and kept a few squadrons flying. In August 1937, despite the fiasco of the attack on the Japanese 3rd Fleet flagship *Izumo* at Shanghai, Chennault's fighters decimated unescorted Japanese daylight bombing raids, and he even gained some success using searchlights to control his fighters at night. These were some of the first examples anywhere of fighter interception of bombing raids. The Japanese suspended their air raids. When they resumed in September, they had concluded that bombers always required fighter escort (an insight resisted by the USAAF as late as 1943).

Despite these successes, the balance of attritional losses favoured the Japanese, and their conquest of Hangchow and Nanchang deprived the Chinese of their principal flying school and aircraft factory. After the fall of Shanghai, the Soviet Union provided some Polikarpov I-15 biplane fighters and air and ground crews. These were really not competitive against the Japanese Nakajima type 97s, and in any case Soviet help dried up in September 1939, due to the Ribbentrop–Molotov pact and the negotiated settlement of the Nomonhan conflict. In early 1940 the Japanese had over 1,000 first-line aircraft in China against a paltry 150 Chinese. In September 1940 the Japanese introduced the Mitsubishi type 00 (Zero) fighter, which instantly became the dogfight boss of the China skies. Chungking and other Nationalist cities were henceforth bombed regularly. Chennault created an effective early warning system using ground observers linked by telephone and short wave radio, but lacked an interceptor able to tackle the Zero in the air.[78]

In March 1939 the Burma Road opened to traffic. It was an engineering marvel of switchbacks and tunnels through the jungle-choked mountains between Kunming and Lashio, whose construction was prompted by the loss of the China coast to the Japanese. Foreign assistance to China increasingly depended on the Burma Road as the Japanese blockade tightened. Since the China war was officially only an incident, the British authorities in Burma ignored Japanese protests that they were behaving unneutrally by allowing Chinese arms purchased abroad to transit. This changed with the German conquest of France: too desperate to fight the Japanese as well, the British closed the Burma Road in July 1940. When they reopened it in October, Britain had survived the German air assault, and US policy had shifted from neutrality to support of

78 Byrd, *Chennault*, pp.65–103; Stanley, *Prelude*, pp.133–41; Ford, *Flying Tigers*, pp.28–48.

Britain by all measures short of war. While the Anglo-American emphasis remained European, Japan's association with Germany was clear. Her occupation of the Hanoi–Haiphong area in September threatened Britain at Singapore and the USA in the Philippines. When the USA passed Lend-Lease in March 1941, Chiang sent Chennault to Washington to lobby for a Chinese share.

T.V. Soong's purchasing agents found 100 P-40B Tomahawk fighters. While these were phasing out of the US active inventory in favour of the P-40C, they were nonetheless all-metal multigun monoplanes, and could withstand more damage than the faster and more manoeuvrable Zero. On 15 April President Roosevelt signed an executive order permitting reserve military personnel to join the American Volunteer Group (AVG) in the Chinese air force. Terms included higher pay than in the USA and a bonus for each confirmed kill.[79]

While the AVG was organizing, Germany attacked the Soviet Union in June 1941, and Japan occupied southern Vietnam in July. This led the United States to embargo all sales to Japan and freeze Japanese assets. As noted previously (pp.243–5), these steps led directly to the Japanese attack on Pearl Harbor, since the Japanese needed to conquer an alternative source of oil (Indonesia) within six months in order to maintain the operational capability of its armed forces. The AVG was still organizing when the Japanese attacked Pearl Harbor; it thus flew for only a few months (December 1941 to May 1942) and then was dissolved. During these months they captured the imagination of the American public. Half the planes were grounded to provide spare parts for the planes that flew. The latter had full sets of shark's teeth painted on their engine cowlings. Nicknamed the Flying Tigers, they were divided into three squadrons named the Adam and Eves, Panda Bears and Hell's Angels. Chennault's Chinese-manned ground organization gave effective warning (without radar) of Japanese raids, so the AVG often ambushed the raiders for a good score. Operating out of Kunming and Kweilin, the AVG continued to fight in the losing Burma campaign. Afterwards, Chennault and a few of his pilots rejoined the US Army Air Forces, so that the 23rd Pursuit Group in China could be described as the successors of the Flying Tigers, even though most of the actual AVG personnel fought the rest of the war elsewhere.[80]

79 Byrd, *Chennault*, pp.104–22.

80 Ford, *Flying Tigers*, passim, and Byrd, *Chennault*, pp.123–52.

Chennault had performed miracles with minimal resources. His successes created the impression that, given enough material assistance and technical advice, China could become a major factor in the war against Japan. Extensive upgrading of China's land forces, however, would inevitably change the power relationships between the Nationalists, the communists and the other Chinese military factions. This political rock ultimately sank the American dream of China as a great power, and led directly to Yalta. Chennault himself complicated the picture. As a late but eager convert to the theory of strategic air power, he claimed he could defeat Japan with a very small number of bombers, whose needs conflicted with the demands of ground force modernization.[81] American inter-service rivalries thus entered the China theatre in early 1942, and meanwhile the evolution of the Second World War guaranteed that the overall priority of China would remain low.

OVERALL ASSESSMENT OF THE SINO-JAPANESE WAR, 1937–41

The period of the (Second) Sino-Japanese War that ran from the Marco Polo Bridge Incident of July 1937 to the Japanese attack on Pearl Harbor in December 1941 subdivides naturally into two phases: first, the period of heavy fighting and Japanese conquest to early 1939, and second, the period of relative stagnation that followed. During the first period the Japanese captured the major cities and most of the railway network of North China, along with Shanghai, Nanking, Wuhan and the Yangtze River up to the Gorges, and Canton and the other major South China seaports. By the time Nanchang (Kiangsi) fell in early 1939, virtually all of the treaty port cities in which a partially modern economy existed were in Japanese hands. The Japanese had achieved this at the cost of only two important battlefield defeats – by the communists at Pinghsingkuan and by the Nationalists at Taierhchuang – that had more symbolic than strategic significance. In mid-1939 the character of the war changed. The Japanese were defeated twice in trying to take Changsha (Hunan), were frustrated in their Kwangsi campaign of 1939–40, and made no further effort to expand their area of control in China. Yet they easily maintained their position as of 1939, defeating both the Nationalist general offensive of 1939–40 and the communist Hundred Regiments campaign of August–

81 Byrd, *Chennault*, pp.172–220, is excellent.

November 1940. The Japanese obviously had been mistaken in believing that an intense war in China would force the Chinese quickly into a dictated political settlement, and Emperor Hirohito often criticized his generals for failing to keep their promise of a short war that would not divert resources from Japan's air and naval buildup. Yet the Imperial Army had in fact been overwhelmingly successful in battle against the Chinese. In September 1939 the outbreak of the Second World War in Europe and the evolution of the war afterwards created the possibility of settling the China Incident through action elsewhere, through the 'southern advance' favoured in naval circles and perhaps by the emperor himself. Fighting in China itself then became less important, and it is this – rather than 'guerrilla warfare' and 'trading space for time' – that explains the lower intensity of the fighting in 1939–41. The level of military activity in the China theatre declined even further during 1941–5, in which period fighting the Japanese was very low in priority for Chinese of all political persuasions, and fighting the Americans was the main problem for the Japanese.

The size of the Japanese army in China supports these conclusions. By late 1939 the Japanese had, in China, about 25 divisions and 20 independent mixed brigades, with 500 aircraft, totalling about 1,200,000 troops.[82] As of December 1941 the China Expeditionary Army controlled 22 divisions (of the 51 in the Imperial Army as a whole), 20 independent mixed brigades (out of 58) and only 16 air squadrons (out of 151). It remained at this relative level for the rest of the Second World War. The Kwantung Army, whose tasks included defending Manchuria against a Soviet attack, had 13 divisions, 24 independent mixed brigades and 56 squadrons, and eventually reached a strength of about 700,000 men. The Southern Army, tasked with conquering the Philippines, Malaya, the Dutch East Indies and Burma, controlled only 10 divisions and 3 independent mixed brigades – ground forces the Japanese correctly calculated would be adequate – but it had 70 air squadrons and was supported by the land-based 11th Air Fleet of the Imperial Navy.[83] Overwhelming air superiority was of course the key element in the rapid Japanese victories of early 1942, and the war in China did not prevent the Japanese from deploying almost all of their air assets elsewhere. While the number of ground troops

82 Ch'i, *Nationalist China*, p.56.

83 See the tables in Hattori Takushirō, *Dai Tōa Sensō Zenshi* (Tokyo, 1964), pp.183–206.

in China may appear large, in fact military manpower was never a problem for the Japanese in the Second World War. The empire's population of around 70 million was subject to an efficient German-style conscription system that produced plentiful numbers of trained reserves, and the regime could conscript Chinese and Korean labour to substitute for Japanese called up for military service. Despite the demands of the China war, the Japanese army expanded to 51 divisions by late 1941, supported by 1,500 aircraft, not counting the 3,000 first-line aircraft flown by the Japanese navy. According to certainly inflated Chinese sources, the Japanese suffered 2,419,000 casualties including 483,000 deaths in China during 1937–45, of which 1,111,000 casualties including 222,000 deaths were in 1937–9, and 523,000 casualties including 104,000 deaths in 1940–1.[84] Considering the experience of the European countries in the First World War, the intensity of Japanese nationalism and the pervasiveness of the Japanese belief in the moral value of dying in battle, the empire could probably have sustained these casualty rates indefinitely. Since the Japanese were exploiting Manchukuo without any armed Chinese resistance, and elsewhere were exploiting occupied China ruthlessly despite Chinese resistance, China was in fact paying the cost of the Japanese occupation. Under these circumstances it was naive to believe – as both Nationalists and communists at least claimed to believe – that Japan would eventually be worn down by her efforts in China.

Despite the Chinese defeat in the 1937–9 campaigns, the Chinese were still in some sense at war, and both Chinese and foreigners who cared about China have tried to extract something of significance from China's presence in the war. Lloyd Eastman's conclusion is typical. 'This dogged resistance contributed significantly to the total Allied war effort against the Axis powers. It tied up approximately a million Japanese troops on the continent of Asia – troops that might otherwise have been used to combat the island-hopping armies of the Western allies in the Pacific.'[85] Similar statements abound in the literature, usually with the intent of crediting this contribution to either the communists or the Nationalists. In fact the existence of the China theatre in 1941–5 may have hindered the overall war effort against the Axis, by diverting resources that might have been better used elsewhere. The Japanese troops in China were not tied up, or down, and many in

84 Eastman, *Seeds*, p.136.
85 Eastman, *Seeds*, pp.130–1.

fact were transferred to Pacific islands, to be either destroyed or left to 'wither on the vine'.[86] They were replaced by new formations for which China offered the prospect of training under slightly more realistic conditions than peacetime. But the defeat of Japan was due – and this point cannot be emphasized too strongly – to the Japanese inability to match US aircraft production, pilot training and shipbuilding, both of warships and merchant vessels. These problems would not have been affected even marginally had the one to two million Japanese troops 'tied up' in China and Manchukuo been available for other uses.

For the Chinese, their defeat by the Japanese meant that the military political balance existing in 1937 would be radically different when the civil war eventually resumed. The Chinese source cited above for Japanese casualties claims that the Chinese suffered 3,211,000 military casualties (including 1,320,000 deaths) of which 2,521,000 casualties (including 1,029,000 deaths) were in 1937–41. These statistics should not be taken literally: only 130,000 missing are reported for the entire war, and none prior to 1941, even though entire formations disintegrated in the 1937–8 débâcle especially. Nevertheless even bad statistics can be revealing: the high proportion of deaths to total casualties testifies to the low level of medical care commented upon by almost all foreign observers, and the Chinese figures also testify to how little fighting there was in China after the United States entered the war. While the Chinese figures for losses are certainly understated, even at face value they indicate a terrible problem: in contrast to Japan's, China's military forces were not served by a conscription system that automatically generated trained reserves. Soldiers lost from whatever cause had to be replaced by raw levies. While in theory China had the manpower to field enormous armies, in practice it was difficult to get men to serve even under compulsion, and the primitive nature of China's economy made it logistically difficult to operate troops far from their agricultural bases; much of the reported strength of communist 'guerrilla' or 'irregular' forces, for example, were really peasants

86 Hayashi/Coox, *Kōgun*, discusses the redeployment, usually to the Pacific, of Imperial Army formations during 1941–5. Hayashi's Japanese original (on which the English-language book is based) is neither the latest nor the best of the Japanese accounts of the Imperial Army during the Second World War, but it remains the only work in English that looks at the war from a Japanese Army General Staff viewpoint, which the popular histories such as John Toland, *The Rising Sun: The Decline and Fall of the Japanese Empire, 1936–1945* (New York, 1970) and Harries, *Soldiers of the Sun*, do not attempt.

who could only operate near their villages. But for China even more than for Japan, manpower was not in short supply. Weapons and equipment were, and shortages of these items continued to constrict the size of China's armies.

The Japanese invasion aggravated these problems. By early 1939 they controlled most of China's major cities including the traditional arsenal towns. The surviving Chinese armies were therefore at a lower technical and armament level than had been the case in 1937. The Chinese armies then had had a paper strength of about 2,000,000 including 100,000 in Chiang's elite German-trained Central Army and about 200,000 troops of lower quality under Chiang's firm control. The Shanghai–Nanking campaign devastated the Central Army, and in the subsequent Wuhan campaign Chiang tried to preserve what was left of the Central Army while letting the cost fall on the Kwangsi clique's forces. Chiang was no longer as powerful vis-à-vis the other warlords as he had been, and his hopes of postwar dominance had to rest on controlling the weapons and supplies that the USA would provide.

For the long-suffering Chinese people, the Japanese invasion meant death and deprivation on a scale that made the military anarchy of the warlord period look benign. The failure of the Japanese to establish a stable collaborationist regime in China proper, in contrast to Manchukuo, aggravated the suffering. Japanese policy was to repress resistance by harsh reprisals, regardless of civilian losses; Chinese leaders similarly talked about, and occasionally practised, equally ruthless measures. No statistics can be cited with assurance, but the two most dramatic cases of civilian loss (the breaking of the Yellow River dikes by the Chinese, and the Three All suppression by the Japanese following the Hundred Regiments campaign) each produced several million civilian deaths, and they were not the only examples.

Despite the Chinese propaganda that continues to cloud the analysis of this period, China had been soundly trounced by Japan, and only hope of external Great Power intervention kept her marginal belligerency alive as of late 1941. Japan, however, had made a great mistake by attacking the Anglo-Saxon powers just as the tide was starting to turn against Germany on the Russian front. In the end Japan would be defeated by US naval operations in the Pacific, compared to which the 1941–5 events in the China theatre were peripheral. This did not prevent the USA from dreaming of results from operations in China, or the various Chinese factions from exploiting these dreams for their own purposes.

7 CHINA AND THE SECOND WORLD WAR, 1941–5

The Japanese attack on Pearl Harbor on 7–8 December 1941 did not immediately alter the stalemate that had developed by then in the Sino-Japanese War. Initial Japanese operations elsewhere were unexpectedly successful. After conquering the Philippines and Malaya, Japan invaded and conquered Burma, thus cutting the Burma Road and ending for the time being Chinese hopes of effective assistance now that the English-speaking Great Powers had joined the war against Japan. While China could be supplied by air from India to a limited extent, the precondition for significant Chinese participation in the war against Japan was the reconquest of Burma and the reopening of the Burma Road. By the time this was achieved in 1945, Japan already faced imminent defeat, chiefly because of US naval victories in the Pacific.

Nevertheless, China remained an important object in US hopes and plans until the crisis of Stilwell's dismissal in 1944. Until the eve of Japan's surrender, US strategists assumed that, after the Japanese Empire had been dismembered by naval action, its separate parts would have to be conquered on the ground. Chinese troops should do their share of this unpleasant task, and China was also considered for the role (later won by Okinawa) of launching pad for the planned final invasion of the Japanese home islands. At bottom, American hopes rested on the sentimental view, propagated by merchants and missionaries for over a century, that the Chinese were basically fine people who deserved to be helped out of their low estate with material assistance and US know-how.

American hopes were firmly constrained by the realities of the Second World War. Roosevelt, Churchill and (obviously) Stalin all shared the Europe First view of strategy, within which China and the other anti-Japanese theatres had at best a secondary priority. The needs of the war against Japan were well advocated within the US leadership by Admirals King and Nimitz and General MacArthur, all of whom gave Pacific operations priority over China. Within the general China–Burma–India (CBI) region, the USA had to cooperate with British Empire authorities. The British had no illusions about Chinese military potential, and Britain had her own priorities for the war in Asia. Britain needed victories on the Burma front to safeguard her position in India, and regarded the reconquest of Burma as an end in itself, not as part of a larger game plan involving China. British proposals for amphibious landings in insular Southeast Asia were viewed by US leaders as thinly disguised schemes to restore European colonial rule, which the USA did not favour.

Low actual priorities, compounded by logistical difficulties of an extreme nature, embittered policy differences among the US personnel in China. The feud between Stilwell and Chennault and the acrimony over how to interpret the Chinese communists were among the consequences.

Both KMT and CCP essentially sat out the 1941–5 period, letting the USA beat Japan for them. Neither side has ever admitted this. Madame Chiang and other leading Nationalist figures regaled the American public with accounts of great victories won by Chinese troops, who would do even better if the USA helped them more. In fact the Nationalist command resisted US pressures for active military operations, no matter how much aid was provided. Chinese commanders made what amounted to informal local truces with the Japanese, and trade took place over what were supposed to be front lines. The Nationalist government used the war years to win important diplomatic concessions, including the ending of the unequal treaty regime (1943) and formal recognition as a Great Power (1944). Americans within China, on the other hand, saw not a great power but a corrupt and demoralized society, whose collapse could be charted by the progress of inflation. In the communist areas higher morale, a sense of purpose, and stable prices were evident, facts which led US observers to underrate their radicalism and overrate their military effectiveness against the Japanese. In fact, the CCP in this period made only limited military efforts, mostly against Chinese troops of the Japanese-sponsored puppet regimes, and concentrated their efforts on the political organization of the areas behind Japanese lines. The KMT meanwhile deployed many troops to blockade the CCP areas. When they faced the last Japanese offensive of the war in the summer of 1944, they crumbled quickly, abandoning territories they had defended staunchly as late as 1941.

STILWELL'S MISSION TO CHINA AND THE FIRST BURMA CAMPAIGN

Even before Pearl Harbor, China, like Russia, had secured a place on the distribution list for US Lend-Lease supplies. During the March 1941 negotiations that created the AVG, T.V. Soong had presented a shopping list calling for enough US equipment to arm thirty Chinese divisions. As part of the fallout from the Japanese occupation of southern Indo-China in July, Brigadier-General John Magruder, USA, was appointed head of a US military mission, which arrived in China in October.

From Magruder's reports on the Chinese army, 'the War Department received the impression of a heterogeneous force that had considerable potentialities but was not yet an effective, well-trained, well-disciplined army'. Its greatest liability was 'the failure of its war lord commanders to see their soldiers as anything more than counters in the unending game of Chinese politics'.[1] The historical roots of this attitude were of course very deep, but even if they could be overcome, the materiel situation was bleak. On paper the Chinese army contained 2,919,000 front line troops (246 divisions and 44 independent brigades) plus 900,00 more (70 divisions and 3 brigades) in rear areas. Each division had an establishment of 9,529 men and 324 machine guns, but all were under-strength and under-armed. There were perhaps 1,000,000 rifles and only 800 pieces of artillery in the whole country.[2] Chinese commanders had no idea how to employ artillery, and were careless in maintaining such vehicles and advanced equipment as they had.

Material assistance depended on the Burma Road, on which driving conditions were such that 14,000 tons of supplies had to leave Lashio (in Burma) for 5,000 tons to arrive in Chungking.[3] With honest management, the road might yield 30,000 tons per month, barely enough to sustain a single US or British army corps. Honest management would have to face the fact that most of the supplies carried over the Burma Road were disappearing into the Chinese black market. This was not a problem for Chinese officers, who 'believed China might be able to win this war without further fighting. They expected international diplomatic pressure to force Japan out of China.'[4]

1 Charles F. Romanus and Riley Sunderland, *Stilwell's Mission to China* (Washington, 1953), pp.32–3.

2 Romanus and Sunderland, *Mission*, pp.34–5.

3 Romanus and Sunderland, *Mission*, p.45.

4 Romanus and Sunderland, *Mission*, p.43.

Soon after the Japanese attack on Pearl Harbor, at Roosevelt's suggestion, an American–British–Dutch–Australian (ABDA) command was created under General Sir Archibald Wavell, then commander-in-chief of the Indian army, to coordinate the defence of Southeast Asia. ABDA was dead from birth. On 10 December the Japanese sank the British battleships *Prince of Wales* and *Repulse*, and the next day Lieutenant-General Iida Shōjirō began the advance of the Japanese 15th Army up the Kra isthmus toward the heartland of Burma. In both Malaya and Burma at this stage in the war, lightly armed Japanese armies consisting mostly of infantry were routinely able to march through swamp and jungle to surround and isolate numerically superior British Empire forces that, being much better equipped, were essentially road bound. Japan's total command of the air prevented the resupply by air of such isolated units (not that the British had adequate airlift at this time). Prospects in Burma were therefore bleak, but when Chiang Kai-shek offered both Chinese ground troops and the AVG to help with Burma's defence, Wavell's hesitation in accepting this Chinese assistance created considerable ill will in Chungking.[5]

In February 1942 Joseph W. Stilwell was ordered to China with the rank of lieutenant-general. Major Stilwell had served under Colonel George C. Marshall when the latter commanded the 27th US Infantry in Tientsin. General Marshall was now Chief of Staff of the US army, and earlier had selected Major-General Stilwell to command the first US offensive in Europe. Sending such an important officer signalled to the Chinese that they were being taken seriously, despite the reservations found in Magruder's reports. Stilwell spoke fluent Chinese and had great respect for ordinary Chinese people; he was familiar with the ins and outs of Chinese politics and despised Chiang Kai-shek and most other Chinese leaders. He also had a full share of the Anglophobia that was widespread, though far from universal, among senior US officers of that period. Stilwell deserved his nickname of Vinegar Joe, and his habit of articulating his prejudices forcefully did not help him to

5 H. P. Willmott, *The Great Crusade* (New York, 1989), pp.159–84, for a recent and brilliant overview of the initial phase of the Pacific War. Ronald H. Spector, *Eagle against the Sun* (New York, 1985), is a fine summary of the Pacific War; I share his view of MacArthur. Louis Allen, *Burma: The Longest War, 1941–1945* (New York, 1984), updates the account of the war in Burma given in S. Woodburn Kirby, *The War against Japan* (5 vols, London, 1969), the excellent British official history written when ULTRA was still secret.

carry out an assignment that was as much diplomatic as military. In his defence it may be noted that overcoming the political and historical obstacles to making the Chinese army militarily efficient was not something that could be done with tact. Stilwell's mission and authority were ambiguously defined; his highest card was the control of Lend-Lease allocations, but this could often be trumped by the ability of Chiang and others to go over his head.[6]

By the time Stilwell reached India on his journey to China, the situation in Burma had deteriorated still further. The 33rd and 55th divisions of the Japanese 15th Army had taken Moulmein at the end of January, had virtually destroyed the 17th Indian Division in the Sittang Bridge battle on 22–23 February, and had taken Rangoon on 7 March. During March and April the Japanese 18th and 56th divisions were landed at Rangoon as reinforcements. In April the aircraft carriers of the Japanese 1st Air Fleet made a sweep through the Indian Ocean, forcing the British Eastern Fleet (which had no aircraft carriers) to retreat to the African coast.[7] These developments deprived the Burma Road of most of its value as a supply route to China. Ships could no longer sail to Rangoon or even to Calcutta. Instead, supplies destined for China had to sail to Bombay, then go by rail to Calcutta (over an already badly overstrained railway system), then by narrow-gauge railway into Assam, whence they might motor to Burma over roads as difficult as the Burma Road itself.

Meanwhile, in January the Chinese 5th and 6th armies (each about division strength, and the former including the 200th Division, China's only mechanized formation) had moved into Burma to support the British. When Stilwell first met with Chiang and Mme Chiang on 6 March, he seemed to gain Chiang's consent

6 Theodore H. White, *The Stilwell Papers* (New York, 1948), published not too long after Stilwell's death in 1946, gives an often-cited introduction to his personality. Barbara W. Tuchman's popular *Stilwell and the American Experience in China, 1911–1945* (New York, 1970) is very dependent on Romanus and Sunderland. It should be noted that high rank was very rare in the US army in early 1942. As a lieutenant-general, Stilwell ranked with the commanders of the three major commands (ground forces, air forces, and service forces) into which Marshall had reorganized the army, and ahead of MacArthur, who had been recalled to active duty in his permanent rank of major-general. Arthur N. Young, *China and the Helping Hand, 1937–1945* (Cambridge, MA, 1963), is the principal study of US aid to China.

7 Arthur Marder, *Old Friends, New Enemies: The Royal Navy and the Imperial Japanese Navy* (2 vols, Oxford, 1981–90), is definitive on the British Eastern Fleet throughout the war, supplementing Kirby's excellent earlier account.

to his command of these armies. In fact, Chiang tied Stilwell down with detailed orders (his usual practice) and the Chinese generals routinely communicated with Chiang behind Stilwell's back. As of 21 March the 200th Division held Toungoo on the Sittang, while the 17th Indian Division held Prome on the Irrawaddy. Hopefully, central Burma could be defended on that line against the Japanese in the south. The 200th Division actually held Toungoo until 30 March, against repeated attacks by the Japanese 55th Division. Stilwell tried to force 5th Army commander Tu Yü-ming to move his other formations to support the 200th, but Tu (later to be a major player in the Nationalist débâcle in Manchuria) stalled and disobeyed. By then the Japanese had gained total air superiority in

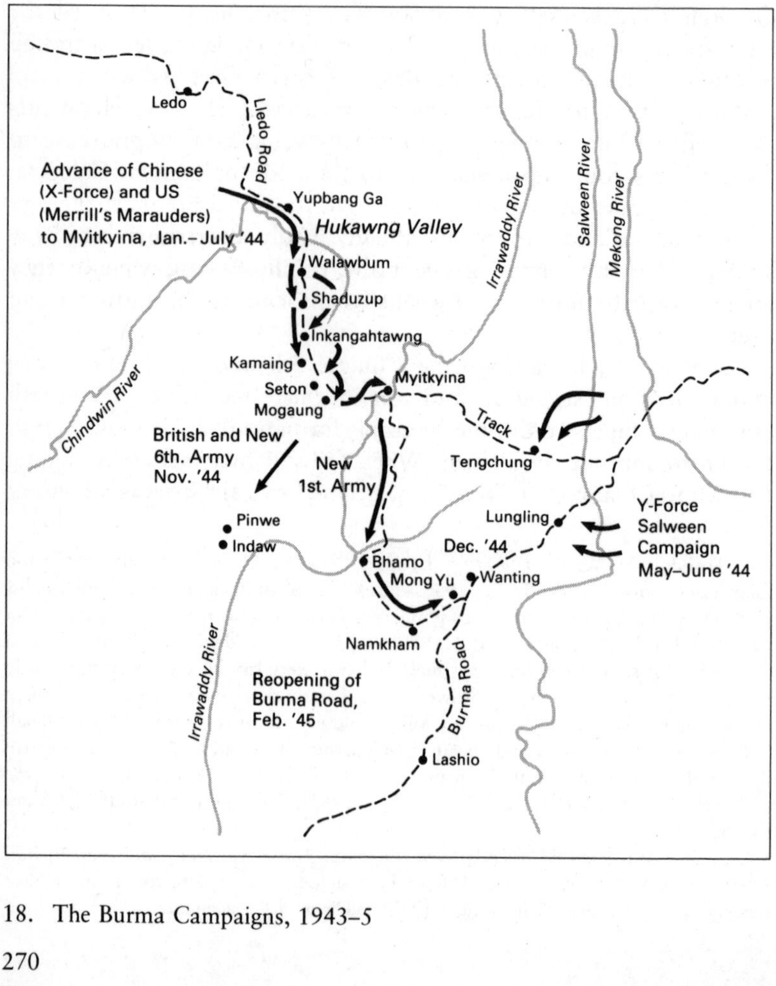

18. The Burma Campaigns, 1943–5

Burma, and the 15th Army afterwards was able to advance rapidly along three axes. In the east the 56th Division took Lashio on 29 April, while the Chinese 6th Army retreated through Kengtung and the barely engaged 66th Army went back to China via the Burma Road. In the centre the 18th and 55th divisions aimed for Mandalay, which fell on 1 May. In the west the 33rd Division advanced up the Irrawaddy from Prome. General Sir Harold Alexander, now the British commander-in-chief in Burma, felt that further withdrawals were inevitable. The British colonial government had largely collapsed. The Chinese obviously could not remain in Burma under these circumstances.[8]

In mid-April Stilwell proposed that some 100,000 Chinese troops be concentrated in India, where they could be armed with Lend-Lease equipment and trained by US instructors. Chiang concurred, and Stilwell determined to march to India with his Chinese troops. The 22nd and 38th Chinese divisions, with fragments of three others, reached India, while the rest of the Chinese troops withdrew into China on Chiang Kai-shek's orders. Lo Cho-ying had been appointed Stilwell's Chief of Staff, in theory to give Stilwell's orders more weight with the Chinese commanders. In practice Lo and the three Chinese army commanders (Tu, Kan Li-chu of the 6th and Chang Chen of the 66th) all communicated with Chiang, and carried out Stilwell's orders only after ascertaining that these had the generalissimo's approval. 'The Generalissimo had given Stilwell command of the Chinese Expeditionary Force in Burma and then treated Stilwell exactly as he did his other army commanders.'[9] Stilwell came to despise Lo Cho-ying, but could not get rid of him. On the other hand, he formed a lasting good opinion of 38th Division commander Sun Li-jen, like Marshall a graduate of the Virginia Military Institute. Stilwell's walkout attracted considerable press attention. When he arrived in India on 15 May he summed it all up: 'We got a hell of a beating. It was as humiliating as hell. We ought to find out why it happened and go back!'[10]

CHINA, CBI AND ALLIED STRATEGY

In late May 1942, from New Delhi and then Chungking, Stilwell made a number of proposals for the reconquest of Burma. He asked

8 Romanus and Sunderland, *Mission*, pp.93–148.
9 Romanus and Sunderland, *Mission*, p.118.
10 Romanus and Sunderland, *Mission*, p.143.

US Army Chief of Staff George C. Marshall for US troops who would join US-equipped and trained Chinese troops to invade Burma from India, in cooperation with other Chinese forces from Yunnan. To the generalissimo he proposed a sweeping reorganization of the Chinese army, merging under-strength divisions and purging commanders he considered corrupt or incompetent. The generalissimo ignored Stilwell's repeated suggestions, which were identical, Mme Chiang noted, to those made earlier by the German military advisers.[11]

Despite his personal regard for Stilwell, Marshall had to view requests from the CBI area in the context of the generally bleak Allied military situation in early 1942. Japan's threat to Australia meant that US troops whom Marshall would have preferred to send to Europe had to go to the South Pacific. Field-Marshal Erwin Rommel's drive to El Alamein meant that aircraft and supplies, already aboard slow convoys sailing around the Cape of Good Hope, that might have gone to India and China went instead to Egypt. To make such decisions, Marshall and the other members of the US Joint Chiefs of Staff (JCS) met with high-ranking British officers in the Combined Chiefs of Staff (CCS). Despite Roosevelt's insistence to a reluctant Churchill that China be considered a 'Great Power', CCS membership was denied to both China and the USSR, whose leaders naturally resented this. Marshall proposed transferring China's share of Lend-Lease supplies, now undeliverable due to the Japanese conquest of Burma, to British India; the British reconquest of Burma would then reopen the Burma Road, which was the necessary precondition of effective aid to China.

Chiang would have none of this. He absolutely rejected Stilwell's plans for army reorganization, for reasons which could not be stated for the record but which should have been clear to anyone (such as Stilwell) familiar with the politics of the warlord era. He regarded aircraft and modern weapons as ends in themselves, as tangible evidence of his power, regardless of whether they could be operated by men trained in their use. On 29 June, he threatened to drop out of the war unless three demands were met: three US divisions should be sent to India, an air force of 500 effective aircraft should operate in China, and air transportation over the Hump (from India to China) should be sustained at a monthly level of 5,000 tons.[12] The 5,000 ton figure came from an American

11 Romanus and Sunderland, *Mission*, pp.152–7.

12 Romanus and Sunderland, *Mission*, p.172.

estimate that that amount could be delivered by 75 twin-engine transports flying the Hump; actual deliveries to China were 80 tons in May, 106 in June and 73 in July.[13] China's Lend-Lease allocation, as opposed to delivery, had been dropped to 3,500 tons each for May and June, and then was to be eliminated. Stilwell was able to get the allocation restored. It might be noted that even 5,000 tons per month was a trickle compared to the (itself inadequate) 30,000 tons calculated maximum for the Burma Road. It was also quite inadequate to maintain a 500-plane air force; Chennault at this time was asking for 1,986 tons per month to support 100 fighters and 30 medium bombers.[14]

Chennault by now had returned to US service as a brigadier-general, subordinate to Stilwell through the 10th Air Force commander, now Stilwell's air deputy Brigadier-General Clayton L. Bissell. Stilwell trusted Bissell's advice on air matters, and Bissell was part of the USAAF bomber mafia, centred around H.H. Arnold (now commander-in-chief, US Army Air Forces), that had rejected Chennault prior to 1937. Bissell botched the job of inducting the AVG into the USAAF (only five pilots joined), and he resented Chennault's fame and the political clout that that conferred in the USA.[15] Chennault nevertheless was personally indispensable because of Chiang's confidence in him, and his promises of decisive results from an air-centred strategy evoked positive responses from the top echelons of US leadership, at a time when 'air minded' meant progressive.

Stilwell meanwhile secured a training base at Ramgarh, Bihar, for the training of the Chinese troops in India (afterwards X-Force, as CBI lingo evolved). Field-Marshal Wavell, now once again in command of the Indian army, objected to the presence of large numbers of Chinese troops in India, and Stilwell had to approach the CCS through Marshall on this point.[16] The US naval victory at Midway in June 1942 made the JCS favour limited anti-Japanese offensives to retain the initiative won in that battle. The Guadalcanal campaign followed, as did the commitment of US resources to CBI. The latter satisfied enough of Chiang's Three Demands to keep him placid, but the main hope was for a winter

13 Romanus and Sunderland, *Mission*, p.167.

14 Romanus and Sunderland, *Mission*, p.188.

15 Martha Byrd, *Chennault: Giving Wings to the Tiger* (Tuscaloosa, 1987), pp.142–9; Daniel Ford, *Flying Tigers: Claire Chennault and the American Volunteer Group* (Washington, 1991), pp.339–42.

16 Romanus and Sunderland, *Mission*, pp.211–20.

1942 offensive to reconquer Burma. Chiang promised to cooperate with a Chinese offensive from Yunnan.

By now the planned invasion of North Africa (TORCH) had priority for assault shipping, and even after Midway Japan was too strong at sea to make a 1943 Bay of Bengal amphibious operation feasible. An overland advance from India to Burma meant logistical dependence on exiguous dirt roads. Ground operations in the leech-infested jungle-clogged river valleys of Arakan and the upper Chindwin region of western Burma were barely possible during the (relatively) cool autumn and winter seasons, but in the summer the heat and monsoon rains stopped even the Japanese. Wavell's plan for the 1942–3 offensive had limited objectives, leaving Rangoon and the Irrawaddy Valley for the following year. The Chinese troops in India were assigned the Hukawng Valley in upper Burma as their area of operations. In other words, even if this offensive had succeeded in reopening the Burma Road, communication with China would still have been overland from upper Assam, and the logistical pipeline would have remained narrow.[17]

The British offensive in Arakan in 1942–3 was a failure. The Japanese counterattacked through the jungle in a replay of the tactics they had used to conquer Burma originally. Wavell replaced some subordinate generals, and planned a major offensive (ANAKIM) for the 1943–4 winter season, whose main operational innovation would be the air supply of forward units cut off by Japanese counterattacks. Meanwhile Brigadier Orde Wingate, unfortunately backed by Churchill, was convulsing the Indian army with his plan to convert much of it to lightly equipped Ranger-type units (LRPG: Long Range Penetration Groups, in Wingate's terminology; he also called them Chindits, after a fierce but mythological Burmese animal).[18] Churchill's support of Wingate paralleled Roosevelt's support of Chennault: both promised fast, dramatic results while orthodox military leadership seemed to be getting nowhere.

Chiang had put numerous obstacles in the way of creating a Chinese army to attack from Yunnan (Y-Force, the contingent training at Ramgarh being X-Force), including the appointment of the corrupt Tu Yü-ming, one of Stilwell's bêtes noires from the Burma campaign, as its prospective commander. Further

17 Summarized from Romanus and Sunderland, *Mission*, chs VII and VIII.

18 Summarized from Allen, *Longest War*, and Kirby, *War against Japan*. I share Kirby's sceptical view of Wingate.

negotiations resulted in Ch'en Ch'eng, whom Stilwell admired, gaining control of Y-Force preparations. What Stilwell could not stop, however, was the growing pressure from the Chinese to fight the war in the China theatre according to Chennault's prescriptions. At the TRIDENT Conference, Roosevelt decided in favour of Chennault; Marshall communicated this to Stilwell on 3 May 1943.[19] Chiang Kai-shek and his entourage trusted Chennault implicitly, and the latter had no political agenda within China. Stilwell's plans for comprehensive army reorganization, however, had unpleasant implications for the internal balance of power within China. Unlike the German military advisers of the 1930s, Stilwell spoke the Chinese language and was aware of Chinese realities, which his plans ignored. Chiang naturally returned Stilwell's dislike.

By this time the course of the war had changed dramatically in favour of the Allies. El Alamein, TORCH, and the German surrender in Tunisia had cleared the Mediterranean, while Stalingrad had ended any fears of a German victory on the Russian front. Final victory at Guadalcanal opened the prospect of a naval advance on Japan through the Central Pacific. These developments made China less important: as of mid-1943, even China's total collapse would not improve Japan's naval position, or add to the Japanese threat to India. Paradoxically, the improvement in the war situation added to the strains on shipping, with British plans for further Mediterranean operations conflicting with US plans for Pacific offensives and both competing with the cross-channel invasion (OVERLORD). All of these were more important than CBI in the CCS view. Giving Chennault a free hand, as the Chinese wanted, allowed the Anglo-Saxon leaders to postpone telling the Chinese how low they stood in overall priority. Chiang Kai-shek and the Nationalist leadership were not in on these decisions, but were aware that Roosevelt and Churchill were fighting the Axis elsewhere than in China, and that the European war came first. Nevertheless, the sincerely held American belief that the final defeat of Japan would require a ground war in China meant, for the Chinese leadership, that eventually a cornucopia of US supplies and equipment would descend on China, possibly along with a million-strong US army.[20] Chiang felt that he needed to be patient,

19 Romanus and Sunderland, *Mission*, pp.313–27.

20 See Tang Tsou, *America's Failure in China, 1941–1950* (Chicago, 1963), especially pp.57–87, for the importance of US ground force deployment in Chinese political calculations. Romanus and Sunderland, *Mission*, pp.327–41, 355–67 for TRIDENT and QUADRANT.

stall for time, insist on China's Great Power status and his own status as the sole legitimate government of China, and keep on reminding his allies of the potential importance of China. Chennault's air strategy was a way of keeping China in the eye of the US public and politicians.

CHENNAULT'S AIR STRATEGY

It was an insult to place Chennault under the officious Bissell, but USAAF chief H.H. Arnold wanted it that way. When both were promoted to brigadier-general, and later to major-general, Bissell's commission was dated one day before Chennault's, to preserve their relative seniority.[21] Chennault's China Air Task Force (CATF), as of now mainly the 23rd Pursuit Group, still depended on the human early warning network and other Chinese infrastructure and contacts that Chennault had built up. Chennault and Chiang were angered at not being given advance notice of the April 1942 Halsey–Doolittle raid on Tokyo, since the plans called for Doolittle's B25s to fly on to China in the hope that the Chinese would rescue their crews. They did, but the Japanese responded with brutal kill and burn operations in Chekiang and Kiangsi which lasted from May to September.[22]

Beginning in July 1942, Chennault proposed that, with an air force of 105 fighters, 30 medium bombers (B25s) and 12 heavy bombers (B24s), supported by 2,000 tons of supplies per month, he could win the war against Japan. He planned to 'destroy Japanese aircraft at the rate of ten to twenty to one' so that Japan would 'lose so many aircraft that the aerial defense of Japan will be negligible'. Then his heavy bombers would 'burn up' Japan's industrial areas while his medium bombers would cut Japan's sea communications. Japan could be defeated 'with comparatively slight cost'.[23] With the wisdom of hindsight, Chennault's plan deserves the ridicule it has usually received. Incendiary raids of upwards of a thousand bombers later in the war failed to force either Germany or Japan to surrender. In fairness to him, however, it should be noted that he had consistently achieved excellent kill-ratios and that his aircraft had been very effective in interdicting the wooden boat and

21 Byrd, *Chennault*, pp.149, 183.

22 Byrd, *Chennault*, pp.148–54; Saburo Hayashi, *Kogun: The Japanese Army in the Pacific War* (English translation, Westport, 1959), pp.49–50.

23 Romanus and Sunderland, *Mission*, p.253; Byrd, *Chennault*, pp.155–8, 172–82.

barge traffic that sustained the Japanese armies in south China. In stating that he could destroy Japanese industry with twelve heavy bombers, he merely reflected the official USAAF viewpoint that Japan's wood and paper cities would burn vigorously, given a little encouragement.

The mere ability to mount an air offensive, regardless of its prospects, depended on Chinese ability to defend the areas of the air bases against Japanese ground attack. As of mid-1942, the prospects for this looked good. The general scaling down of the Japanese effort in China created the impression elsewhere that the Chinese were tenaciously defending many positions that were in fact not being attacked. The most recent important action had been a Chinese victory. In the Third Battle of Changsha of December 1941 to January of 1942, 9th War Area commander Hsueh Yueh defeated Anami Yukio's 11th Army in a battle that was virtually a replay of the Second Battle of Changsha. The Japanese advanced to the outskirts of Changsha, were then attacked in the left flank and rear by three Chinese armies, and forced to retreat across the Hsinchiang River to the Yochow area, with considerable losses.[24]

In March 1943 Chennault was designated commander of the 14th Air Force.[25] Hump deliveries meanwhile averaged 3,000 tons per month until June.[26] Deliveries then went up, but enough uncertainties remained to make quarrels over the allocation of this tonnage very bitter. Chennault insisted, and gained Roosevelt's support, that his operations receive a fixed amount of Hump tonnage every month, regardless of the overall total delivered. The Chinese began constructing airfields in eastern China, while Chiang Kai-shek promised to hold them with Chinese troops 'in the event the enemy attempts to interrupt the air offensive by a ground advance on the air bases'.[27] Meanwhile Stilwell attempted to begin the training programme for Y-Force, the Chinese contingent that was to train in Yunnan and eventually to reconquer the Burma Road proper while X-Force invaded Burma from northern Assam. His problems were compounded by Chinese lack of interest, and by conflicts of face and jurisdiction between Ch'en Ch'eng, the senior Whampoa clique general designated as Y-Force commander, and Yunnan warlord Lung Yun.

24 Republic of China, Kuo-fang-pu, Shih-cheng-chu, *History of the Sino-Japanese War, 1937–1945* (Taipei, 1971), pp.362–75.

25 Byrd, *Chennault*, pp.183–8.

26 Romanus and Sunderland, *Mission*, p.284.

27 Romanus and Sunderland, *Mission*, p.320.

Roosevelt interviewed both Stilwell and Chennault before the Anglo-American TRIDENT conference in May 1943. Chennault's enthusiasm won the case; the president was particularly impressed by Chennault's promise to sink 500,000 tons of Japanese shipping if adequately supplied. Chennault's claim on the Hump tonnage thus was reconfirmed. The British delegates at the conference evinced doubts about ANAKIM, the planned winter offensive in Burma, proposing instead an assault on Sumatra, which would have struck at Japanese oil supplies while adding to the strain on Allied assault shipping and landing craft (and thus threatening the cross-channel invasion of Europe that was the centrepiece of Marshall's strategy). The US side killed this idea, and the outcome of the conference was a scaled-down ANAKIM, designed to open a land route to China in northern Burma, but with the capture of Rangoon and the Irrawaddy Valley deferred, for the second year in a row, to the following (1944–5) campaigning season.

During May and June the Japanese 11th Army made a five-division sweep into western Hupei to round up whatever river shipping they could find. In fact the Japanese were responding to the success of Chennault's raids against their river traffic, but Chiang Kai-shek worried that they were aiming for Chungking, and ordered Ch'en Ch'eng and 70,000 troops from Y-Force back to the 6th War Area to defend Chungking against the threat. When the Japanese completed their sweep and started falling back, the mood changed. The pro-Chiang lobby in the USA hailed this as a great victory; Chennault, writing to Roosevelt, claimed that the Japanese suffered 30,000 casualties out of a 100,000-man force. Actual Japanese casualties were 1,125 killed and 3,636 wounded. While Chennault's air offensive was now meeting stiff resistance in the air from the Japanese 3rd Air Division, leading the 23rd Fighter (formerly Pursuit) Group temporarily to abandon its advanced airfields at Hengyang and Lingling (both in Hunan) these bases now seemed even more secure against ground attack as a result of the reported Chinese victory.[28]

In August 1943 Churchill and Roosevelt and their staffs met again, this time in Quebec, for the QUADRANT conference. Dominating the agenda was the impending Italian surrender and the British wish for more extensive Mediterranean operations, which the Americans felt would further delay OVERLORD. British planners still felt the doubts about the feasibility of a Burma campaign, and

28 Romanus and Sunderland, *Mission*, pp.301–10, 335–7.

about the ultimate value of the Chinese contribution to the war, that they had often expressed. Churchill nonetheless made some changes in the British command arrangements, to maintain at least the appearance of interest. A new Southeast Asia Command (SEAC) was created, headed by Vice-Admiral Lord Louis Mountbatten, well known as a Churchill favourite, with Stilwell as his deputy. And Wingate was given carte blanche to turn more of the Indian army into LRPG. Stilwell originally welcomed Mountbatten's appointment, but predictably was soon turned off by Mountbatten's royal connections and British mannerisms.[29]

Taking seriously his position as Chief of Staff to the generalissimo, Stilwell had proposed offensive operations for China's essentially stationary field army, and had made the mistake of including communist formations in these plans. On 29 September he signed a document titled *Program for China*, in which he proposed eliminating half of China's divisions, weeding out incompetent officers regardless of seniority or connections, and concentrating training and equipping on sixty divisions to be trained in two echelons of thirty each. He felt politically stronger at this time, since Mme Chiang was supporting him as part of a feud with her brother T.V. Soong. He was therefore surprised when, during the visit of Lieutenant-General Brehon B. Somervell (head of Services of Supply in the US army, and a close confidant of Marshall), Chiang demanded his immediate removal. When Somervell, Marshall and Roosevelt stood up for Stilwell, Chiang backed down, blaming the 'misunderstanding' on Soong. He continued to dislike Stilwell, who did not heed Somervell's advice to treat Chiang ('Peanut' in Stilwell's letters and diary) more politely.[30]

THE CAIRO CONFERENCE AND THE CAMPAIGN IN NORTH BURMA

The immediate fallout from QUADRANT was a CCS directive ordering a north Burma campaign, whose objective was the capture of the Hukawng Valley and the Mogaung–Myitkyina area. This would permit a land link to China, through a road from northern Assam to link up with the old Burma Road, and it would also improve the air link by forcing Japanese fighters out of airfields in the Mogaung area, thus permitting transport aircraft to fly to China

29 Romanus and Sunderland, *Mission*, p.258.
30 Romanus and Sunderland, *Mission*, pp.367–81.

by a safer route skirting the highest mountains to the south. The Chinese troops being trained in India (X-Force) would bear the principal burden in this offensive.

The air war complicated the picture. Roosevelt was enthusiastic over a plan to base the new B29 bomber in China. In theory the B29s would fly in their own supplies over the Hump, without adding to the logistical congestion. Major-General George Stratemeyer, now commanding the USAAF in the India–Burma area, supported this plan in a scaled-down version, while pointing out the supply difficulties. Hump tonnage was increasing (August 5,674 tons, September 6,719, October 8,632).[32] Chennault expanded his operations, and on Thanksgiving Day attacked Taiwan in a brilliantly executed raid that destroyed 42 Japanese aircraft. Chennault was now asking for a force structure of 150 fighters (two groups), 48 B25s (one group) and 35 B24s (one group), which he hoped to expand to six fighter and two medium and three heavy bomber groups by the autumn of 1944. Chennault believed that, with air support, Chinese troops would be able to defend his air bases. He cited the alleged Japanese defeat in the western Hupei campaign (mentioned on p.278) as proof of this. Ironically, the raid on Taiwan stimulated the Japanese to begin planning a ground offensive against Chennault's bases.[32]

Stilwell did not agree with Chennault's analysis. He now ended Chennault's supply priorities, and began to build up a third group of Chinese divisions (Z-force, at Kweilin in Kwangsi) to defend East China. As with Y-force in Yunnan, the Chinese authorities made an initial show of enthusiasm, but they really wanted the US arms and supplies more than the training and reorganization (and weeding out of incompetents) that Stilwell considered necessary. He had been very successful with X-force, now about 30,000 strong in Assam with two divisions (Sun Li-jen's 38th and Liao Yao-hsiang's 22nd), supported by non-divisional army troops, all provided with US arms and equipment on a generous scale, which the Chinese troops had actually been trained to use properly. In October the 38th Division entered the Hukawng Valley, to begin the Chinese part of the winter offensive in Burma.[33]

By this time events elsewhere had made China even less important to the war against Japan. During 1943 the US navy

31 Charles F. Romanus and Riley Sunderland, *Stilwell's Command Problems* (Washington, 1956), p.18.

32 Romanus and Sunderland, *Command Problems*, pp.15–25.

33 Romanus and Sunderland, *Command Problems*, pp.26–48.

received delivery of several of the powerful *Essex* class aircraft carriers, and developed the strategy of a Central Pacific advance against Japan, involving the capture of selected islands which would serve as bases for further advance. The seizure of Tarawa atoll in the Gilbert Islands on 20 November inaugurated this approach. From the point of view of the USAAF, the Central Pacific advance would lead to the capture of the Marianas (actually accomplished in June–July 1944), from which a B29 offensive against Japan could be carried out without either the logistical difficulties or the need to deal with Chennault that would apply in China. The navy planned ultimately to seize Taiwan as the base for an amphibious attack on Japan, obviating both CBI and MacArthur's Southwest Pacific theatre, whose demands for landing craft conflicted with those of Mountbatten's SEAC (both theatres were peripheral from the Europe First viewpoint). Landing craft were now the naval bottleneck constraining the number of amphibious operations that could be carried out.

This applied in Europe as well, where British desires for additional operations in the Mediterranean and in Norway conflicted with the US and Russian insistence on a 1944 cross-channel invasion of Europe (OVERLORD). Churchill and Roosevelt met with Chiang Kai-shek at Cairo before their meeting with Stalin at Tehran in November. The Chinese proposals at Cairo represented a conflation of Stilwell's (support for the modernization of ninety Chinese divisions) and Chennault's (10,000 tons per month of Hump tonnage for the support of air operations in China) views. Chiang was critical of the limited scale of SEAC efforts for the 1943–4 campaigning season. On 25 November Chiang agreed to an expanded Chinese effort in Burma, even at the expense of Hump tonnage, provided that a major amphibious operation (BUCCANEER) were mounted in the Bay of Bengal.[34]

At Tehran a few days later, Roosevelt stayed at the Soviet embassy and got on warmly with Stalin, which left Churchill as the odd man out. When it became clear that he could not talk the other two out of the landing in the south of France (ANVIL) that they wanted to support OVERLORD, Churchill professed delighted surprise at Stalin's promise to enter the war against Japan after the

34 Romanus and Sunderland, *Command Problems*, pp.49–67. Tehran–Cairo was the major instance in the Second World War in which choices between major theatres were made at personal meetings involving all the Allied Great Power leaders, so these issues are discussed in virtually all general accounts of the war.

defeat of Germany, and proposed that BUCCANEER be cancelled to provide the landing craft for ANVIL. Stalin had first promised this at the October 1943 foreign ministers' meeting in Moscow, at which China had been declared a 'Great Power'. Since then Roosevelt had formed a very negative impression of China's potential at the Cairo conference. Russia could do – better – anything that China could do for the continental side of the war against Japan, and Roosevelt was now willing to sacrifice Chinese wishes in order to keep the three real Great Powers in alignment. He agreed to the cancellation of BUCCANEER, despite the protests of both CCS and JCS.[35]

THE 1943–4 BURMA CAMPAIGN

Stilwell, frustrated by Chiang's backing and filling and by his own failure to interest Roosevelt in his plans for reforming the Chinese army, went to Ledo determined to command in person the advance of the 22nd and 38th Chinese divisions toward Myitkyina. He also controlled Brigadier-General Frank D. Merrill's 5307th Composite Unit (provisional), alias Merrill's Marauders, a brigade-size US force organized on the same principles as Wingate's Chindits. These opposed the Japanese 18th Division, headquartered at Myitkyina. The Japanese 56th Division at Lung-ling faced, across the Salween River, eleven divisions of the Chinese Expeditionary Force (Y-Force), whose commitment to the campaign would depend on how angry Chiang decided to be about the cancellation of BUCCANEER. The latter also affected the offensive potential of SEAC troops. British IV Corps threatened the Chindwin Valley and XV Corps Akyab; they were expected to attack strongly enough to prevent the Japanese from reinforcing northern Burma.

The Japanese conducted their usual tenacious defence, holding up the 38th Division until the end of December at the village of Yupbang Ga. The Chinese fought methodically, by the book they had just learned, and Stilwell was often impatient with Sun Li-jen's excessive caution and delays. Nevertheless, artillery and other advanced equipment was employed correctly, and the Chinese units supported one another and did not run away when the Japanese attacked. Chinese morale improved greatly when they finally forced the Japanese out of Yupbang Ga by early January, but two months of only slightly more mobile operations were needed to get to

35 Romanus and Sunderland, *Command Problems*, pp.67–82.

Walawbum at the southern end of the Hukawng Valley in March 1944. Slow progress, but any progress was good against the Japanese, who were still the best jungle-fighting army in the world. CBI engineers built the Ledo Road behind the advancing Chinese troops, with the intention of ultimately linking up with the Burma Road proper.[36]

Limited as it was, the Chinese success in the Hukawng Valley led to the Japanese decision to launch a major offensive against the British. In February 1944 they attacked in Arakan, and in March launched the major Imphal–Kohima offensive, whose goal was to sever the Bengal–Assam railway in the Dimapur region, west of Kohima. Success here would have wiped out the potential of any north Burma campaign, by cutting the supply line between Calcutta and Ledo, over which supplies destined for the Burma Road to China would have to come as long as central and southern Burma remained under Japanese control. As in 1942, Japanese forces advanced through deep jungle and cut off large British formations. In 1944, however, the Allies had air superiority, and Sir William Slim, whose 14th Army controlled the British corps at Imphal and Kohima, ordered all isolated units to hold their ground and await resupply and reinforcement by air. After many weeks of very hard fighting, the British defeated the Imphal–Kohima attack. Their efforts drew off supplies that might have gone to Stilwell, and in London Churchill revived his arguments against the idea of a Burma campaign. Britain should instead attack Sumatra (Operation CULVERIN), break into the South China Sea, and approach Japan directly by sea, thus avoiding the China tangle. By now Churchill's strategic concepts had no credibility with Americans, and these arguments were ignored.[37]

At Walawbum a wide left-flank march to the Japanese rear by Merrill's 5307th had forced the Japanese withdrawal. The same tactic failed badly against Inkangahtawng later in March. The 5307th was forced back into the jungle and besieged, and its relief

36 Romanus and Sunderland, *Command Problems*, pp.119–59, is still the best account of this campaign. Leslie Anders, *The Ledo Road: General Joseph W. Stilwell's Highway to China* (Norman, 1965), on the road-building effort.

37 Allen, *Longest War*, and Kirby, *War against Japan*, have the best accounts of Imphal–Kohima; also William J. Slim's fine memoir *Defeat into Victory* (New York, 1961). Romanus and Sunderland, *Command Problems*, pp.160–72, on CULVERIN. Hayashi, *Kogun*, pp.92–101, and Meirion and Susie Harries, *Soldiers of the Sun: The Rise and Fall of the Imperial Japanese Army* (New York, 1991), pp.406–14, for Imphal–Kohima from the Japanese side.

had to wait on the advance of the Chinese units, which forced the Japanese out of Shaduzup on 29 March. The Japanese 18th Division now concentrated north of Kamaing and held out for two more months. Stilwell cursed and fretted at the dilatoriness of Sun Li-jen and Liao Yao-hsiang, his two division commanders, whom he suspected of communicating with Chiang Kai-shek behind his back. Time was getting short, if Myitkyina was to be reached before the onset of the rainy season. Eventually the 112th Regiment of the 38th Division made a left-flank march to Seton, several miles south of Kamaing, on 26 May. The Japanese then retired on Mogaung through the jungle, with great disorganization and loss of heavy equipment. They were unable to dislodge the 112th Regiment from Seton. Kamaing fell on 16 June and Mogaung ten days later.

Stilwell meanwhile had ordered a separate force, built around the Chinese 30th Division and the 5307th, to cross the Kumon range and take Myitkyina. They reached the outskirts of Myitkyina on 16 May, and seized and held the airstrip. Unfortunately the Japanese reinforced the town itself with troops from their 56th Division, and a regular siege developed. The Chinese 14th and 50th divisions joined the besiegers. The Japanese were probably never more than 3,500 strong, but they held out until early August, when the survivors evacuated the town. By then the 5307th had been pretty well wrecked as a combat unit.[38]

OPERATION ICHIGO AND STILWELL'S REMOVAL

The campaign leading to the fall of Myitkyina proved Stilwell's contention that properly armed and trained Chinese troops could defeat the Japanese in open battle, but it did not break the land blockade of China. The Japanese 56th Division blocked the Burma Road at Lung-ling. Dislodging it required action by the Chinese Y-Force divisions across the Salween, and that in turn meant motivating Chiang Kai-shek, whose interference had stalled the advance to Myitkyina, and who was angered by the cancellation of BUCCANEER and by the repossession of Lend-Lease supplies stored in India which could not be delivered to China. Chiang had demanded a billion dollar gold loan as his price for staying in the war;[39] in January 1944 Roosevelt threatened to cut off Lend-Lease

38 Romanus and Sunderland, *Command Problems*, pp.172–256.

39 Romanus and Sunderland, *Command Problems*, p.74; later discussion in Tsou, *America's Failure*, pp.109–16.

unless Y-Force attacked across the Salween. On 14 April War Minister Ho Ying-ch'in gave formal approval to such an attack.[40]

Chiang and Chennault were now warning of a major Japanese offensive planned for South China. In fact on 17 January Imperial General Headquarters had ordered an offensive (ICHIGO) to seize all of the Peking–Hankow, Canton–Hankow and Hunan–Kwangsi railway lines, objectives that included Chennault's airfields at Hengyang, Lingling, Kweilin and Liuchow. Chennault's success in interdicting Yangtze River traffic threatened the Japanese at Hankow, and his aviators had detected the Japanese reinforcement that preceded the launching of ICHIGO.[41] In April and May the Japanese occupied the Honan section of the Peking–Hankow railway against halfhearted Chinese resistance. As even the Chinese official history admits, the Japanese were able 'to operate at will'.[42] Chennault, who earlier had promised to stop the Japanese by air action alone, now argued that he had not received his promised supply allocations and that Stilwell had shortchanged Z-Force in favour of Y-Force. Stilwell's reaction was bitter: 'he tries to duck the consequences of having sold the wrong bill of goods, and put the blame on those who pointed out the danger long ago and tried to apply the remedy'.[43]

On the Salween front, the twelve divisions of Wei Li-huang's Y-Force were 40 per cent under-strength, aggregating 72,000 men. While qualitatively much inferior to X-Force, the arms, equipment and training they had received made them an elite component compared to the rest of the Chinese army. The plans called for the 53rd and 54th armies to attack Teng-chung, from which ran a mountain trail to Myitkyina that might be made into a leg of the Burma Road if Bhamo and Lashio were not recaptured. Meanwhile the 2nd and 71st armies concentrated on Lung-ling. Brigadier-General Frank Dorn represented Stilwell at Wei's headquarters. The Chinese forces crossed the Salween on the night of 11–12 May. On the right the Chinese spent the next month pushing on Teng-chung against Japanese resistance that was skilful and fanatical as usual. The Chinese troops fought bravely; their US advisers criticized them for poor equipment maintenance, poor coordination between arms,

40 Romanus and Sunderland, *Command Problems*, pp.297–314.

41 Romanus and Sunderland, *Command Problems*, pp.314–22; Hayashi, *Kōgun*, pp.86–91.

42 Kuo-fang-pu, *Sino-Japanese War*, p.421.

43 Romanus and Sunderland, *Command Problems*, pp.322–7. Byrd, *Chennault*, pp.207–57, is an excellent and balanced appraisal.

and excessive caution shown by their unwillingness to bypass isolated Japanese units. The two Chinese armies on the left fought their way to Lung-ling, from which they were thrown back by a Japanese counterattack. When the arrival of the rains suspended mobile operations, Y-Force was still cut off from the Chinese armies in Burma by the Japanese troops dug in on the Burma Road.[44]

The Japanese had concluded their Honan operations at a cost of 869 dead and 2,280 wounded,[45] bringing under their control the hitherto neglected stretch of the Peking–Hankow railway south of Chengchow. In June they moved in strength, five divisions with a second echelon of three more, against Hsueh Yueh's 9th War Area in Hunan. Hsueh's previous successes in defending Hunan have already been described (pp.243–4), and had won Hsueh Chennault's esteem. Nonetheless, Hsueh was not in Chiang's inner circle, and when CBI transferred some Z-Force supplies to Hsueh, Chiang's Kweilin representatives protested. Hsueh's army had not been improved by its relative inaction since 1942. In the new offensive, the Japanese 68th and 116th divisions approached Changsha by the railway line, the 3rd and 13th overland from Tung cheng (Hupei), while the 40th sailed across Tungting Lake, landing near Yuanchiang. The three Japanese columns converged on Changsha on 16 June, and occupied the city two days later. US observers reported Chinese troops fleeing, but 'knew nothing of any heavy fighting'. The 116th and 68th divisions pushed on to Hengyang, taking the airfield on 26 June. Major-General Fang Hsien-chueh's 10th Army held the walled city of Hengyang against repeated Japanese attacks, while 14th Air Force sorties hindered Japanese efforts to build up their strength there.[46]

As the East China crisis ripened, Stilwell recommended Chennault's removal, Chennault demanded that his Hump allocation be raised to 10,000 tons, and visiting US Vice-President Wallace recommended Stilwell's removal. This last was partly due to Chiang's statement that Stilwell did not understand 'political considerations' (he was already thinking of Wedemeyer),[47] and partly due to the recommendations of Lieutenant Joseph W. Alsop of Chennault's staff, a journalist in civilian life whose connections reached all the way to Roosevelt.[48] For Stilwell the fall of Changsha

44 Romanus and Sunderland, *Command Problems*, pp.329–60.
45 Romanus and Sunderland, *Command Problems*, p.371.
46 Romanus and Sunderland, *Command Problems*, pp.371–4.
47 Romanus and Sunderland, *Command Problems*, pp.374–9.
48 Byrd, *Chennault*, has a lot to say about Alsop; cf. p.179.

and siege of Hengyang proved that Chennault's air plan had failed. Political developments indicated why Chiang so favoured the air plan. On 21 July Brigadier-General Malcolm Lindsey at Z-Force radioed Stilwell to advise him of a plan to set up an autonomous government in Southeast China being worked out by Li Chi-shen, Chang Fa-k'uei, Yü Han-mou, Hsueh Yueh, Lung Yun and unnamed dissenters in Szechwan.[49] All of these non-Whampoa Nationalist generals had in the past supported various phases of the 'Southern opposition' to Chiang Kai-shek, yet most of them would have received US aid if Stilwell's plans for the Chinese army had come nearer to fruition. To add to Chiang's sense of beleaguerment, Wallace had pressured him to accept Stilwell's long-standing proposal for a US mission to the Chinese communist areas. This was the genesis of DIXIE Mission and it added to the strain in US–Chinese relations, as US diplomats in Chungking observed (rightly) that Chiang was preventing Lend-Lease aid from going to the CCP (or indeed to the non-Whampoa KMT), while arguing (wrongly) that the communists were actually fighting the Japanese.[50]

Hengyang finally fell on 8 August. Destroying the remnants of the 27th Group Army southwest of Hengyang, the Japanese advanced into Chang Fa-k'uei's 4th War Area in Kwangsi, taking Lingling on 8 September. Meanwhile the Japanese 23rd Army pushed north from Canton. Postwar, Field-Marshal Hata Shunroku, commander-in-chief of the China Expeditionary Army, opined that Pai Ch'ung-hsi and Li Tsung-jen of the Kwangsi clique had kept their troops out of action to conserve them 'for the future'. Arriving in Kweilin on 14 September, Stilwell noted that there was no military cooperation between Chang Fa-k'uei and Hsueh Yueh's 9th War Area. Chang was unhappy that Chiang Kai-shek had ordered him to defend Kweilin by putting his three best divisions within the city walls. In Stilwell's words, 'the place will then become another rat trap, like Changsha and Hengyang . . . We are getting out of Kweilin now, and will have to get out of Liuchow as soon as the Japs appear there.'[51] Stilwell was also upset by Chiang's attitude to the Salween front. Even though Teng-chung had finally fallen, Chiang was threatening to pull Y-Force back to defend Kunming unless the Chinese divisions at Myitkyina attacked toward Bhamo.

49 Romanus and Sunderland, *Command Problems*, pp.401–5.
50 Romanus and Sunderland, *Command Problems*, pp.374–9.
51 Romanus and Sunderland, *Command Problems*, pp.433–6.

The success of Operation ICHIGO had, in other words, precipitated a general crisis in the China theatre.

Stilwell had long believed, remarkably for someone with his experience of China, that if he were to receive full command authority over the Chinese army he could make something of it. Now ICHIGO had revealed the bankruptcy of the air strategy preferred by both Chiang and Roosevelt, swinging the latter behind Stilwell's ideas, to which Chiang also consented, at least for the record. Whenever Chiang had given Stilwell 'command' in the past, he had undercut him by continuing to deal directly with Chinese unit commanders. Stilwell expected this to continue. 'What the Peanut wants is an overall stooge, apparently foisted on him by the US.'[52] Roosevelt was now in Quebec negotiating with the British. The latter were buoyed by the success of their 14th Army in repelling the Imphal–Kohima offensive and resuming the attack in Burma. Roosevelt was correspondingly dismayed at Chiang's threat to pull back Y-Force. On 19 September CBI received a radiogram from Roosevelt telling Chiang bluntly 'to reinforce your Salween armies immediately and press their offensive, while at once placing General Stilwell in unrestricted command of all your forces'. Stilwell showed this to Patrick J. Hurley, now in Chungking as Roosevelt's personal emissary to Chiang, who recognized it as an ultimatum and asked to present it himself so as to soften its tone.[53] Stilwell demurred, feeling that too soft tones had led to misunderstandings in the past, and no doubt looking forward to humiliating Chiang. 'I've laid the Peanut low,' he exulted poetically to his diary afterwards.

Chiang, both humiliated and furious, dug in his heels and lobbied for Stilwell's removal. Hurley meanwhile had concluded that the USA had to work through Chiang, and that Stilwell had become an obstacle. In October Roosevelt agreed, recalled Stilwell, split CBI, and appointed Major-General Albert C. Wedemeyer to head the US military effort in China.[54] China no longer mattered in US strategy. The Central Pacific offensive had succeeded, the Japanese navy was largely sunk, and Japan could be bombed and invaded from island bases. Since Tehran, the USA had a promise of Russian assistance against the Japanese armies in China.

52 Romanus and Sunderland, *Command Problems*, pp.436–9.

53 Romanus and Sunderland, *Command Problems*, pp.443–6.

54 Charles F. Romanus and Riley Sunderland, *Command Problems*, pp.447–73; *Time Runs Out in CBI* (Washington, 1959), pp.3–45.

The latter kept on rolling. The Japanese army in Hunan pushed the Chinese slowly back into Kwangsi. Despite their promises to defend them, the Chinese evacuated both Liuchow and Kweilin, both sites of major air bases, on 10 November. The Japanese then advanced into western and southwestern Kwangsi, taking Nanning, the last of the important East China air bases, on 24 November, a step toward creating a land link with French Indo-China, which they opened on 10 December.[55] ICHIGO had in effect added Hunan and Kwangsi provinces, as well as central Honan, to the area under Japanese control by the end of 1941. The latter included Manchukuo (since 1931), the Yangtze Valley and the China coast, all areas in which Japanese control and exploitation was only weakly challenged by Chinese resistance. In North China the Japanese occupation of the major cities (Peiping, Tsinan, Taiyuan, and others) and the railway lines linking them was indeed challenged by the sporadic guerrilla warfare emanating from the communist-ruled areas between the railway lines. The population base of the communist areas had been so badly hurt by the Japanese punitive operations that peaked in late 1941, but continued thereafter, that the communist military was concentrating chiefly on mere survival, confining active operations to attacks on collaborators. The poor provinces overrun by ICHIGO were less valuable economically to the Japanese than the territories they had overrun earlier. They might have become centres of guerrilla warfare, but in fact previous communist organizations had been uprooted by the Nationalists, and the Japanese did not face significant partisan resistance to their conquest of these provinces. More ominously, the Japanese conquests suggested that the Chinese propaganda line of heroic Chinese resistance to the Japanese was false, and that even in late 1944, with Japan's navy and merchant marine largely sunk and its home economy collapsing from US air raids and lack of imports, the Japanese army in China could still march where it wished and take what it wanted. Including, perhaps, Chungking.

COMMUNIST EXPANSION DURING 1941–5

One of the factors in Stilwell's dismissal had been his insistence that Chinese communist forces receive a share of Lend-Lease supplies so

55 Romanus and Sunderland, *Time Runs Out*, pp.46–60; Hayashi, *Kōgun*, p.90.

that their troops, estimated at 475,000 'regulars' in October 1944,[56] could fight against the Japanese. DIXIE Mission was now functioning as a source of intelligence about the CCP, and the view from Yenan contrasted favourably with that from Chungking. The Chinese communists seemed idealistic and to be working together in pursuit of common goals. The corruption, demoralization, factionalism, black markets, and inflation that were so blatant in Nationalist China were not visible in the communist areas, where, ironically, currency and prices remained relatively stable. The communists seemed to be fighting the Japanese, and were at least talking about it. The Nationalists in contrast made local truces with the Japanese, had folded during ICHIGO, and routinely let slip in conversation that they expected the USA to do all the remaining work of defeating the Japanese, including sending a million-strong expeditionary force to China to root out the Japanese army.[57]

In reality, the parameters of KMT–CCP relations, and the degree of their resistance to Japan, were firmly fixed well before Pearl Harbor, and did not change significantly before the Japanese surrender in 1945. On the KMT side, the New 4th Army Incident of January 1941, in which Nationalist troops had attacked a communist formation in order to stop the expansion of communist-dominated guerrilla activities south of the Yangtze, meant a de facto repudiation of the Second United Front, and from that time some of the best KMT units were devoted to blockading the communist areas. The Nationalist leadership avoided, and indeed strenuously resisted, active operations against the Japanese, as Stilwell noted, and much of the 'front' became rather peaceful, since the Japanese from late 1941 were conducting their principal military operations outside of China. KMT policy was to let the USA defeat Japan, while Nationalist China stockpiled Lend-Lease supplies for the civil war to come. While this could scarcely be acknowledged for the record, it was still an open secret, with many friendly KMT officials confiding it to Americans who were expected to understand and sympathize.

56 US War Department, *The Chinese Communist Movement*, (2 vols, mimeographed, Washington, 1945), page v. I am indebted to Dr John A. Harrison for a copy of this report, which is often cited – e.g. Chalmers A. Johnson, *Peasant Nationalism and Communist Power: The Emergence of Revolutionary China, 1937–1945* (Stanford, 1962), p.214 – and which is the first extensive critical study of the Chinese communist movement in English.

57 War Department, *Communist Movement*, p.126.

The facts of life on the CCP side were more subtle. Students of Mao Tse-tung's thought could point to a corpus of articles, mostly from 1937–8, outlining a long-range strategy for the defeat of Japan.[58] Mao himself, however, was mostly concerned with avoiding a premature transition from guerrilla warfare to regular warfare aimed at breaking the Japanese hold on North China. After their defeat in the Hundred Regiments offensive, launched on Chu Te's initiative against Mao's wishes, the CCP leadership had tacitly abandoned the goal of eventually making the transition to regular warfare, henceforth concentrating instead on consolidating their base areas and surviving within them. Mao wrote no important military articles between 1941 and 1945, even though he did find time for 'Talks at the Yenan Forum on Literature and Art' (May 1942).[59] In effect, the CCP was stockpiling political capital for the civil war to come. While resembling the stance of the KMT, the differences were nevertheless important. Since CCP legitimacy and influence among the peasantry derived from anti-Japanese guerrilla activities, these had to be continued, even though in 1942–5 they were directed mostly against Chinese collaborators and posed little threat to Japanese control of the major cities and railway lines. And the political stance of welcoming all anti-Japanese elements into the coalitions that nominally governed the base areas tended to blur, for US observers, the serious communist convictions of the CCP's highest leaders and real rulers.

In July 1945 the US War Department prepared a classified study of the Chinese communist movement, whose remarkably objective assessments agree with subsequent research. Noting that many Nationalist (but usually not Central Army) troops had 'joined the puppet army to fight the Communists with Japanese support', the study referred to the 'virtual truce' between the Nationalists and the Japanese and puppet armies for 'several years' prior to ICHIGO. Prophetically 'many Chinese expect that the Japanese will withdraw without fighting' from their occupied areas, whose future allegiance therefore depended on whether the Nationalists or the communists 'will be the first to move in and take over control'. The puppet

58 Notably 'Policies, measures and perspectives for resisting the Japanese invasion' (July 1937), 'The situation and tasks in the anti-Japanese war after the fall of Shanghai and Taiyuan' (November 1937), 'Problems of strategy in the guerrilla war against Japan' (May 1938), 'On protracted war' (also May 1938), and 'Problems of war and strategy' (November 1938); Mao Tse-tung, *Selected Works of Mao Tse-Tung* (4 vols, Peking, 1961–5), II, pp.13–22, 61–74, 79–194, 219–36.

59 Mao, *Selected Works*, III, pp.69–98.

armies were important in these calculations. The communists accused the Nationalists of encouraging 'the desertion of troops to the Japanese in an effort to support the Japanese anti-Communist campaign'. This was unlikely due to the specific origins of the puppet troops, but nevertheless the latter figured in KMT plans to keep occupied China out of communist hands postwar. This attitude 'led to a form of indirect collaboration between the Chungking Government and Japan against the Communists'. While neither the Nationalists nor the communists would consider peace terms with Japan (especially this late in the war), unless the latter withdrew from China, the communists, also thinking postwar, from 1942 on began to moderate their stance toward the puppets. Meanwhile, throughout 1943 there was a 'serious threat of an all-out Kuomintang offensive against the Communists'. With KMT–CCP hatred so high, the communists also, like the Nationalists, were happy for a local arrangement with the Japanese, wherever they could get it. In Kiangsu there was 'a tacit arrangement between the New Fourth Army and the Japanese by which, and in return for the Communists not attacking the trains and railroads, the Japanese will not construct walls and dikes along the railroad as they have done elsewhere, and which would make crossing by the Communists next to impossible'. For the author of the study 'all evidence leads to the conclusion that while the Communists have been on the defensive against the Japanese, they have been on the offensive against the Chungking Government'.[60]

Even standing on the defensive involved fighting, in view of the anti-communist sentiments sincerely held by the Imperial Army leadership. But during the whole period of US involvement in the war, the communists refrained from large-scale anti-Japanese actions like the Hundred Regiments offensive, that could be guaranteed to provoke even larger-scale retaliation. During 1942–5 communist activities were not 'strong in terms of military power, but rather in terms of political-economic subversive activities against the Japanese'. The latter (as related in Chapter 6) began to employ the blockhouse strategy in 1940, leading to the Hundred Regiments offensive and the Japanese retaliation that followed. Afterwards the communists, like the Vietcong after Tet, emphasized smaller-scale operations employing land mines, other booby traps, and tunnelling. Communist operations meant that, in contrast to Manchukuo, the

60 War Department, *Communist Movement*, passim; quotations on pp.121, 127, 129, 131, 140, 142, 145.

Japanese 'never succeeded in consolidating their power' in North China and therefore could not exploit it as fully as they would have liked. In 1942 only 1 million Chinese migrant workers were sent to Manchukuo: the Japanese would have preferred 4 million; this was understandable since the Japanese actually controlled only about 27 million of the 70 million combined population of Hopei and Shantung, whence the migrants came.[61]

Nevertheless, and despite some of the reports coming out of DIXIE Mission, there was in fact little reason to believe that CCP operations were tying up a significant part of the Japanese war effort, or that Lend-Lease supplies given them would be used against the Japanese. The Japanese

> used China, and North China in particular . . . as a proving ground for their troops. The numerous 'annihilation campaigns' against both the Communists and Chungking Government forces were probably designed as much for the purpose of providing training for the Japanese troops as for defeating the Chinese. . . . The limited resistance offered by the Chinese provided an atmosphere of real war. The Japanese suffered casualties, but probably not so many as to render the annihilation campaigns truly costly to them. Because the Communist troops usually retreated before the Japanese few actual battles were fought during these campaigns. It was not the Communist armies that suffered so much as the people who were left a prey to Japanese vengeance.[62]

Postwar analyses confirmed both the low levels of Japanese losses and the degree to which the Japanese had stripped their armies in China, including the Kwantung Army, of their best formations by 1945.

The War Department analysis credited the communists as of October 1944 with 475,000 'regular' troops and 2,130,000 militia. The three divisions of the 8th Route Army (now renamed 18th Group Army) now controlled six military regions in North China, with eight weaker regions under the New 4th Army in Central China, and still weaker forces in the Canton area and Hainan Island. These are summarized in Table 7.1 (000s omitted). The

61 War Department, *Communist Movement*, pp.148–65; quotations on pp.148, 151.

62 War Department, *Communist Movement*, p.160.

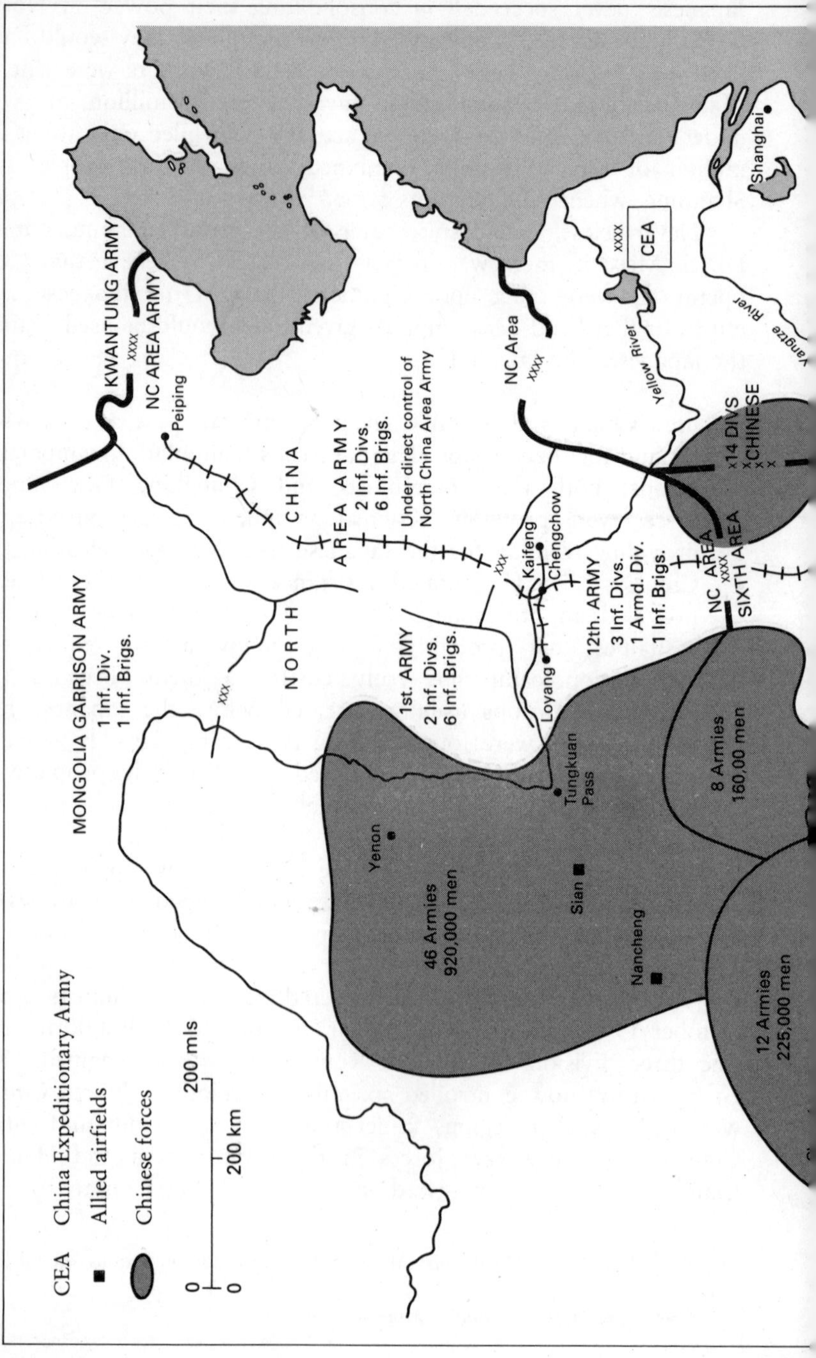
MONGOLIA GARRISON ARMY
1 Inf. Div.
1 Inf. Brigs.
KWANTUNG ARMY
NC AREA ARMY
Peiping
NORTH CHINA AREA ARMY
2 Inf. Divs.
6 Inf. Brigs.
Under direct control of North China Area Army
NC Area
CEA
Shanghai
Yellow River
Yangtze River
x14 DIVS CHINESE
SIXTH AREA
NC AREA
Kaifeng
Chengchow
12th. ARMY
3 Inf. Divs.
1 Armd. Div.
1 Inf. Brigs.
1st. ARMY
2 Inf. Divs.
6 Inf. Brigs.
Loyang
Tungkuan Pass
Yenon
Sian
Nancheng
46 Armies
920,000 men
8 Armies
160,00 men
12 Armies
225,000 men
CEA China Expeditionary Army
Allied airfields
Chinese forces
0 200 mls
0 200 km

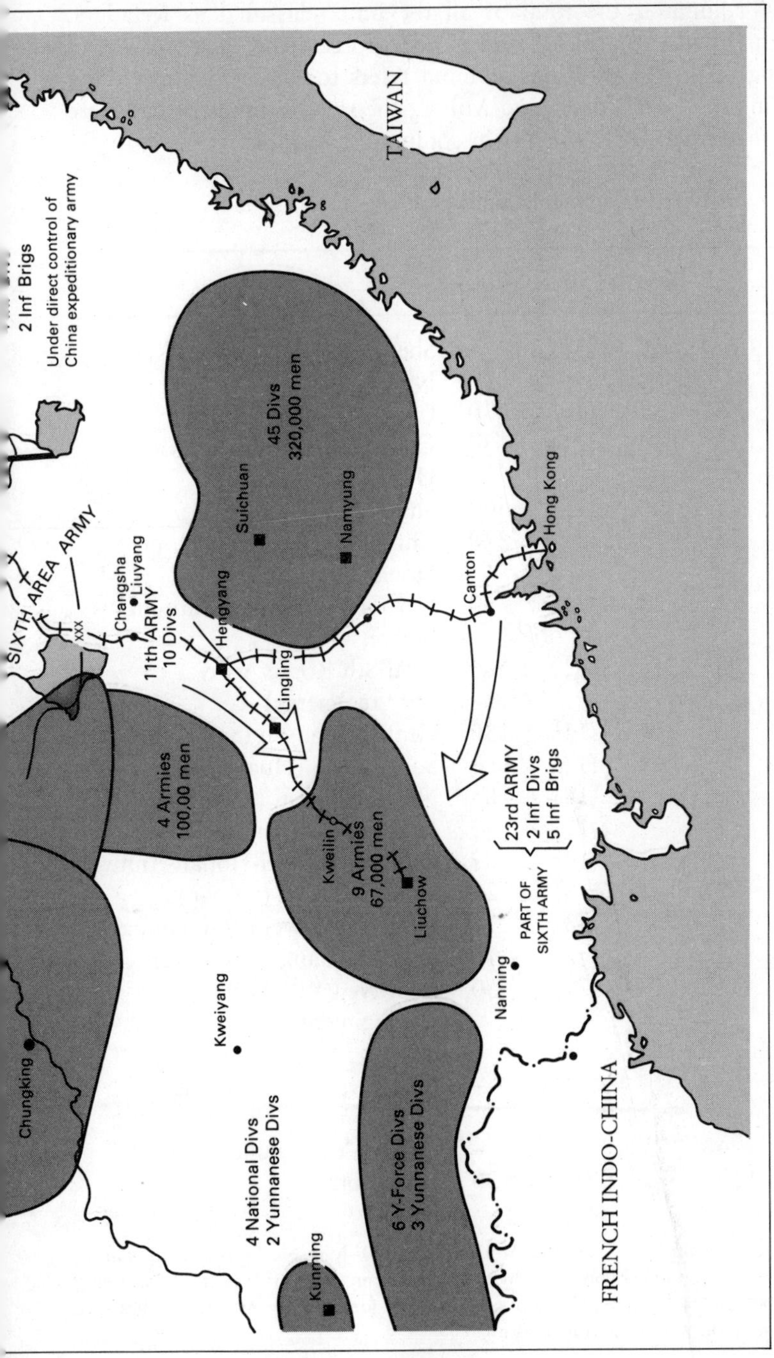

19. The military situation in China, October 1944 (After: Romanus et al., *Time Runs out in CBI*)

'Total' column is the total of all the units classified as Regulars, broken down into 'Field' and 'Local' forces, the latter of lower fighting quality. The 'Rifles' column refers to the Field forces only; counting the Local forces and Militia, the study estimated that there were altogether 282,000 rifles in communist hands.[63]

Table 7.1 Estimated communist military strength, July 1945

Field	Local	Total	Rifles	Militia	
50	–	50	(30)	–	Shen-Kan-Ning (Shensi-Kansu-Ninghsia)
26	5	31	(15)	50	Chin-Sui (Shansi-Suiyuan)
35	29	64	(21)	630	Chin-Ch'a-Chi (Shansi-Chahar-Hopei)
42	28	70	(25)	500	Shantung
50	25	75	(29)	320	Chin-Chi-Yü (Shansi-Hopei-Honan)
17	11	28	(11)	80	Chi-Lu-Yü (Hopei-Shantung-Honan)
220	98	318	(131)	1,580	total 8th Route Army (297 regiments)
19	?	?	(11)	130	Central Kiangsu (Su-chung)
21	?	?	(13)	?	South Huai (Huai-nan)
23	?	?	(14)	85	North Kiangsu (Su-pei)
18	?	?	(11)	?	North Huai (Huai-pei)
22	?	?	(14)	?	Oyuwan (Hupei-Honan-Anhwei)
6	?	?	(3)	25	South Kiangsu (Su-nan)
5	?	?	(3)	25	Central Anhwei (Wan-chung)
4	?	?	(2)	10	East Chekiang (Che-tung)
118	31	149	(71)	550	total New 4th Army (98 regiments)
3	–	3	(2)	–	East River (Tung-chiang, Canton area)
5	–	5	(3)	–	Chiung-Yai (Hainan Island)
346	129	475	(207)	2,130	grand total

63 War Department, *Communist Movement*, p.340. Johnson, *Peasant Nationalism*, pp.214–15, cites numbers provided by 8th Route Army Chief of Staff Yeh Chien-ying of 320,000 for the 8th Route Army and 153,676 for the New 4th Army; these are very close to the War Department estimate.

This summary documents the consolidation of communist power in the area of the Japanese North China Area Army. Politically, most of Hopei, Shantung, Honan north of the Yellow River, and the Chinese-settled portions of Inner Mongolia, along with most of Shansi (except the southwestern part of the province, where Yen Hsi-shan still held out) and the loess region north and west of Yenan, all were under the control of the six military regions of the 18th Group Army. In terms of their leadership, these were descended in pairs, respectively, from the 120th (parent of the Shen-Kan-Ning and Chin-Sui regions), the 115th (parent of the Chin-Ch'a-Chi and Shantung regions), and the 129th (parent of the Chin-Chi-Yü and Chi-Lu-Yü regions) divisions, each of which was now larger than a Nationalist Group Army. The Japanese still controlled the cities and railway lines but even they acknowledged that the communists controlled the people in the greater part of the region where Japanese troops could not be permanently stationed.

In Central China the situation was less favourable to the communists. The damage done by the New 4th Army Incident of 1941, in which Nationalist troops had attacked their communist 'allies' to prevent them from organizing communist guerrilla areas south of the Yangtze, and the stronger presence – compared to North China – of both pro-Nanking puppet troops and pro-Chungking guerrillas had inhibited communist growth, so that the eight military regions there were weak in all respects compared to those of North China. Overall, it is worth noting that the communist areas had already attained approximately this configuration by the time of the Hundred Regiments offensive in 1940, and that they did not expand significantly prior to the Japanese surrender. As of August 1945, they were still blocked from expanding in the northwest by the combination of Yen Hsi-shan and the strong Nationalist forces headquartered at Sian, were still facing KMT competition in the lower Yangtze, and had still failed to penetrate Manchukuo beyond the fringes of Jehol and Liaoning.[64]

In the wake of Stilwell's dismissal and ICHIGO, DIXIE Mission was recommending that the communists receive direct US support, since they seemed to be the only Chinese faction fighting the Japanese. Leaving aside the political implications of such a step – the argument over which became one of the most divisive issues in

64 See Romanus and Sunderland, *Time Runs Out*, p.382, for a breakdown of 'Chinese' forces as of August 1945. The 2,700,000 troops in 290 divisions summarized there include all the Chinese armies except the communists.

postwar US politics – it seems apparent that the communist army had little offensive potential in 1944–5. US support, coming through a fantastically long logistical pipeline, against the wishes of a KMT regime skilled in obstruction, would have been only a trickle. Stilwell's experiences at Ramgarh had shown how difficult it was to train Chinese peasants to be soldiers of a modern army, operating intricate machinery and coordinating advanced weapons on the battlefield. The communists' mobilization of the peasantry positioned them for a civil war against warlord-style Chinese forces, but offensive operations against the Japanese would have required army modernization that would have cut them off from their rural roots, and which they would have resisted, even had it been possible. Meanwhile only half of the Red Army's 'regulars' even had rifles, machine guns were even more scarce, and artillery almost nonexistent. Even the rifles lacked ammunition. 'All types of ammunition are exceedingly scarce, and the many different small arms calibers complicate the problem. . . . Ammunition is so scarce that practically none can be allotted for either rifle or MG training.'[65]

The limited military potential of the Chinese communists against the Japanese needs to be borne in mind when considering other US activities in China for the rest of the war. Hurley, who had advised Stilwell's removal on the grounds that he could never work with Chiang Kai-shek, became Roosevelt's 'special representative' and later US Ambassador to China, replacing Clarence Gauss. As a senior Republican politician and Cabinet member in the Hoover administration, Hurley was scarcely in Roosevelt's inner circle. He was also utterly ignorant of China (referring to Chiang Kai-shek as 'Mr Shek') and soon earned the contempt of his professional foreign service staff, whom he later repayed with accusations of communist sympathies. He viewed Chinese politics by analogy with US elections and party rivalries. Visiting Yenan in November, he greeted Mao Tse-tung and the other communist leaders with an Indian war whoop and tried to charm them into a coalition with the Nationalists. This got nowhere, but he did succeed in stopping the tentative efforts of the DIXIE Mission staff at US military cooperation with the Chinese communists, while reaffirming that US relations with China had to be through Chiang Kai-shek and the Chungking government.

65 War Department, *Communist Movement*, p.363.

These actions began a bitter polemical issue in US political and intellectual life, with the right blaming the 'loss' of China on a communist conspiracy abetted by US officials, while the left saw a wonderful chance for friendly relations with communist China aborted by Hurley's stupidity. The members of DIXIE Mission correctly reported the corruption and demoralization within the Nationalist regime and the depth of mass support for the communists in North China, and correctly predicted that 'power in China is on the verge of shifting from Chiang to the Communists'. Yet John P. Davies's description of the Chinese communists as 'backsliders' who 'have come to accept the inevitabilty of gradualness' or John S. Service's calling them 'a party seeking orderly democratic growth toward socialism' now seem strange. In fact the reasonableness of the CCP during 1936–49 was caused solely by their need to survive the Japanese invasion and then win the anticipated civil war. The CCP leadership in reality adhered strongly to radical revolutionary and communist views, as their post-1949 history demonstrates, and there is little evidence that a more positive US policy toward them would have influenced them to any great extent.[66]

WEDEMEYER AND THE END IN CBI

In the more immediate context of the final year of the Second World War, China did not matter much. Wedemeyer was much more tactful and diplomatic than Stilwell had been, but also had more limited objectives. Chiang never understood how much he had dropped in Roosevelt's estimation by his threats to pull back Y-Force, the billion dollar loan demand, and the failure of the Chinese armies to stop ICHIGO. By late 1944 the US Central Pacific offensive had obviously succeeded, the Japanese navy was finished, the Tōjō government had fallen, and Japan could be bombed and invaded from captured island bases without reference to China. Since Tehran, the USSR had replaced China as the uprooter-to-be of the Japanese armies in China, whose strength US intelligence continued to exaggerate. The failure to reopen the Burma Road in the 1944 campaigning season inevitably limited China's part in the rest of the war. In the belief that Stilwell's problems had been partly caused by wearing too many hats, Army

66 Tsou, *America's Failure*, pp.176–345; the quotations are on pp.201–3. Tsou's book was controversial when it appeared in 1963, but it is a good summary of the issues and cites earlier literature.

Chief of Staff George C. Marshall and his colleagues on the US Joint Chiefs of Staff split CBI into a China theatre and an India–Burma theatre. The latter, under Lieutenant-General Daniel I. Sultan, would control the advance from Myitkyina when active operations resumed in Burma. In the China theatre, Wedemeyer was given the task to 'advise and assist' the Chinese,[67] mainly through continued control of Lend-Lease. Air operations were declared to be the primary mission of US combat forces in China, and Stilwell's assignment of assisting in 'improving the combat efficiency of the Chinese Army' was shelved.

When Wedemeyer assumed his command in China on 31 October 1944, the Japanese 11th Army was moving on Kweilin from Lingling and the 23rd Army threatened Liuchow. Wedemeyer feared that the Japanese objective was the China terminus of the Burma Road at Kunming (Yunnan), whose capture would truly knock China out of the war. Trying to figure out why ICHIGO had been so successful, and whether Kweilin and Liuchow would hold, he quickly formed opinions similar to Stilwell's. He described the Chinese leadership as 'apathetic and unintelligent' and 'impotent and confounded' and unable to cope with the war situation because of 'political intrigue, false pride and mistrust of leaders' honesty and motives'. While the generalissimo assured him 'categorically' that Kweilin would be held, Wedemeyer noted that 'the disorganization and muddled planning of the Chinese is beyond comprehension'. Wedemeyer confined these assessments to his reports to Marshall, treating the Chinese with tact and courtesy; they responded by loving him as much as they had hated Stilwell. He also got on well with Chennault. By now it was clear that the latter's extreme air strategy had collapsed, yet ironically the Hump route was now delivering enough tonnage (34,914 tons in November 1944) to support both air and ground efforts. Meanwhile the Chinese evacuated both Kweilin and Liuchow on 10 November, and the Japanese 11th Army marched northwest, threatening Kweiyang (capital of Kweichow province) on the road to Kunming.[68]

Wedemeyer responded with the ALPHA plan, under which China's best troops would be concentrated at Kunming to back up the forces that, hopefully, would hold Kweiyang. Wedemeyer envisaged pulling the Chinese 57th Army from the anti-communist blockade at Sian and the 53rd Army from the Salween front, while

67 Romanus and Sunderland, *Time Runs Out*, p.15.

68 Romanus and Sunderland, *Time Runs Out*, pp.40–56.

the now-famous 22nd and 38th divisions would be flown to Kunming from north Burma. US efforts at Y-Force and Z-Force would be consolidated, and the whole affair run by a trained Sino-American staff under a senior Chinese general. Wedemeyer proposed Ch'en Ch'eng and got Ho Ying-ch'in, whose ability he rightly distrusted but whose appointment ('a decided blow') at least indicated Chiang's commitment.[69]

The movement by air of the 14th (in place of the 38th) and 22nd divisions was completed in early January 1945, despite SEAC commander-in-chief Admiral Lord Louis Mountbatten's initial opposition. Getting both the 53rd and the 57th armies actually to move required Wedemeyer's personal intervention with the generalissimo, after the orders had already been cut. The Japanese then saved the day by ordering their 11th Army to pull back from Kweichow province; on 10 December 1944 they instead completed the land link between their forces in Kwangtung and French Indo-China, which they had begun to forge by their capture of Nanning on 24 November. As Chiang remarked 'the advance on Kweiyang was not part of the enemy's plan'. The winding down of ICHIGO left airfields at Suichuan, Kanhsien and Namyung isolated behind Japanese lines in southern Kiangsi and northern Kwangtung, but still in control of Chinese troops under Hsueh Yueh. Even Chennault, whom the generalissimo continued to hold in high regard, had not been able to secure Chiang's consent to fly arms to Hsueh, who had been part of the 1944 separatist move. Chang Fa-k'uei in Kwangsi and Yü Han-mou in Kwangtung, both part of the same movement, had essentially opted out of the war by making local truces with the Japanese. Suichuan fell to the Japanese 27th Division on 29 January, but 14th Air Force planes were long gone.[70]

Operation ICHIGO thus ended, with the Japanese not taking Kunming more because they had not planned to than because of successful Chinese resistance. By then the 14th and 22nd Chinese divisions, which in India and Burma 'had become accustomed to being properly fed and to receiving their pay in full and on time', were in China. Chiang at once proposed that their pay be reduced to the level of troops in China, and that their US dollar subventions be paid to the Chinese government, rather than the troops directly. For Wedemeyer this matter symbolized Chiang's utter indifference to his army, of which the India-trained divisions were now the best

69 Romanus and Sunderland, *Time Runs Out*, pp.56–64.
70 Romanus and Sunderland, *Time Runs Out*, pp.142–79; quotation on p.165.

armed and militarily most effective units. During ICHIGO Wedemeyer had been besieged with demands that he sacrifice Kunming to save Chungking, and found it 'amusing and also tragic' to receive requests from senior Chinese officials to evacuate themselves and their families to America by air. 'Self-sacrifice and patriotism are unknown qualities among the educated and privileged classes.' He did not despair, however, and continued to push his plan to train an amalgamated Y- and Z-Force in China.[71]

Meanwhile the Burma campaign offered, for the third straight year, the prospect of reopening the land line to China. As of September 1944, while the British 14th Army attacked on the Chindwin and in Arakan, the Chinese armies in Yunnan and the Allied forces in northern Burma faced the Japanese 33rd Army (56th Division at Lung-ling, 18th at Bhamo, 2nd in reserve at Lashio). In October Sun Li-jen's New 1st Army (30th and 38th divisions) advanced due south from Myitkyina to attack Bhamo from the east, while the British 36th Division and Liao Yao-hsiang's New 6th Army (50th and 22nd divisions, until the evacuation of the latter as mentioned above) advanced southwest from Mogaung to the Indaw–Pinwe area. Combined USAAF and RAF efforts provided command of the skies, with air–ground liaison 'far ahead of that practiced in Europe' and numerous transports for the air supply of isolated units, so necessary in the jungles of Burma. As usual, the Japanese fought tenaciously, but Pinwe fell on 30 November to the British, who continued down the Irrawaddy. The two Chinese armies surrounded Bhamo by mid-November, and the Japanese there surrendered on 15 December. By this time, with considerable American prodding, Y-Force had attacked and forced the Japanese 56th Division out of China to the Wanting area. The Japanese knew through radio intercepts of the transfer of the 14th and 22nd divisions to China, and assumed that the Chinese advance in Burma would stop. They were thus surprised when the New 1st Army continued to advance in December 1944 and January 1945, taking Namyu, Namkham and Mong Yu in rapid succession, and Lashio in March. Since the Ledo Road in this section could be based on the prewar all-weather road from Bhamo to Mong Yu, truck convoys from Assam on the combined Ledo–Burma Road were already rolling, and the first reached Kunming on 4 February. The land blockade of China, imposed briefly in 1940 and permanently since 1942, was now broken, and British successes in the rest of Burma

71 Romanus and Sunderland, *Time Runs Out*, pp.165–8.

(Mandalay in March, Rangoon in May) offered the hope that the long detour through Assam and the Hukawng–Mogaung Valleys would not last much longer.[72]

By this time Roosevelt was dead, having, as his last major public act, gone to Yalta to plan the final stages of the war with Churchill and Stalin. Despite good reasons for doubt, Roosevelt continued until his death to hope that the USA and the Soviet Union would work together in the UN-centred postwar international order. He welcomed Russian participation in the final stages of the war against Japan, and was willing to have China pay a substantial price for it. The US military leadership believed that only a land campaign in Asia could force the surrender of the Japanese army there, and the reports of Stilwell and Wedemeyer did not encourage the belief that the Chinese army would be up to the task. In the final Yalta agreement, Stalin reaffirmed his promise to enter the war against Japan after the defeat of Germany, and in return was promised Port Arthur, the Manchurian railways and, in general, the whole Russian imperialist position in China as it had been prior to Japan's 'treacherous' attack in 1904. Roosevelt promised to obtain Chiang's concurrence to this, even though the agreement was to be kept secret from Chiang until the Russian deployment was completed. President Truman, who as vice-president had been excluded from Roosevelt's thoughts and councils, felt bound by the Yalta agreement, despite growing doubts of Soviet good faith.[73]

Since in the final outcome the Russian invasion of Manchuria was probably not necessary for Japan's surrender, while the Russians did give valuable assistance to the Chinese communists, it became easy to say afterwards that Yalta was clear evidence of a communist conspiracy in the upper reaches of the US government. Stilwell was one of the alleged plotters, and probably would have responded to these accusations with some vigour if not for his death in 1946. In reality Yalta amounted to the repayment, with interest, of Chiang's long-standing and often-demonstrated total unwillingness to take the land war against Japan seriously. Since the Chinese army would not be reformed, the Soviet army would do its job. Despite the long Chinese tradition of 'barbarian management', Chiang and his colleages had misread the signals from the American side, and failed to understand the revulsion of US military men at a massively corrupt KMT political establishment and an army that

72 Romanus and Sunderland, *Time Runs Out*, pp.77–141; quotation, p.92.

73 Tsou, *America's Failure*, pp.237–87, with references to the earlier literature.

refused to fight while demanding that the US commit a million of its own men. Luxuriating in the sense of victory over the dismissal of Stilwell, the end of the unequal treaty system and recognition of China's 'Great Power' status, the Chinese leadership failed to realize that since Tehran China had become strategically marginal to the USA.

Stalin has left no record of his innermost thoughts, and his often quoted characterization of the CCP as 'radish communists' (red only on the outside) may not have been entirely candid, but at the time of Yalta he may not have either predicted or wanted a total CCP victory in China. The extent of KMT disintegration was not evident to most people outside of China, and Stalin may have believed – as Chiang certainly did – that the Chinese communists would be uprooted and destroyed once the 'normal' conditions of pre-Sian Incident China were restored. Russian involvement with China in the 1920s had been largely the work of Trotskyite elements in the CPSU, whom Stalin had spent considerable effort in killing. The post-1927 CCP leadership had been thoroughly unresponsive to direction from Moscow, and the post-1949 Sino-Soviet friendship period was replaced by bitter polemics from 1960 on. At Yalta in 1945, Stalin probably felt that the specific terms he received were a good payment for the services of his troops.

Wedemeyer meanwhile continued the effort to upgrade the Chinese army. This was now centred at Kunming and involved the ALPHA force of thirty-six designated divisions (thirty-nine after the return of the New 1st Army) under Ho Ying-ch'in. Wedemeyer devised a parallel chain of command, with US advisers in each unit, whose advice the Chinese commmander rejected at his own risk. Supplying and equipping this force was now easier due to the reopening of the Burma Road, but training depended on first improving the appalling physical condition of these 'selected' troops. At one replacement depot 'one hundred percent were suffering from malnutrition, T.B. and other diseases'. The solution was the organization, under American auspices, of medical care and regular supplies of food to the Chinese units.[74]

From April to June 1945 the effectiveness of the training programme was tested when the Japanese 116th Division, reinforced, attacked westward from Paoching in three columns, threatening the airfield at Chihchiang, Hunan. The Chinese defenders were four 'armies' that aggregated barely 67,000 men while still outnumbering the Japanese attackers. Wedemeyer helped

74 Romanus and Sunderland, *Time Runs Out*, pp.231–47; quotation on p.242.

by blocking Chiang's attempt to control the battle directly and by airlifting the elite 22nd Division into Chihchiang, while the 14th Air Force continued to control the air. The Japanese finally called off the operation after taking some 6,500 casualties as against 20,000 Chinese. The Japanese noted a 'great advance' in Chinese tactics, and the Americans were gratified that the Chinese troops had fought, different arms and formations had cooperated, and that the supply and medical systems had functioned, even though there was room for improvement in all these areas.[75]

In concentrating on the ALPHA plan, Wedemeyer explicitly rejected the proposals for closer cooperation with the Chinese communists that continued to come from DIXIE Mission. The members of the latter naturally imagined that they were doing their job by discussing, on a hypothetical basis, ideas for US cooperation with the CCP, but both Hurley and Wedemeyer realized that such activities could be construed as treating the communists as an independent entity, with dismal consequences for relations with Chungking. Hurley's ill-advised efforts at KMT–CCP reconciliation were obviously getting nowhere, and he blamed DIXIE Mission for undermining him. The matter was complicated by the actions of other US agencies. The Office of Special Services (OSS) had conceived fantastic schemes of guerrilla warfare in cooperation with the communists, and the US navy was also dealing with them, since they wanted to station weather observers inside the communist areas. Wedemeyer's response was to forbid even hypothetical discussions with the CCP, and to lobby successfully to get the China operations of OSS and Naval Group China placed under his command. As the Second World War drew to a close Wedemeyer assumed, like everyone else, that Chiang would use his thirty-nine modernized divisions to crush the communists. US authorities were thus united in recognizing the KMT regime as the sole government of China, even though they were not blind to its defects.[76]

The end came suddenly. Following the atomic bombing of Hiroshima on 6 August, the Soviet army invaded Manchuria, destroying the once-powerful Japanese Kwantung Army and the 'empire' of Manchukuo in about a week.[77] Nagasaki was bombed

75 Romanus and Sunderland, *Time Runs Out*, pp.269–90.

76 Romanus and Sunderland, *Time Runs Out*, pp.249–59.

77 David F. Glantz, *August Storm: The Soviet 1945 Strategic Offensive in Manchuria* (Leavenworth, 1983), and *August Storm: Soviet Tactical and Operational Combat in Manchuria* (Leavenworth, 1983), for a recent and detailed analysis of this campaign.

on 9 August, and Emperor Hirohito made his surrender broadcast on the 15th.[78] By this time Japanese troops were already in withdrawal from the South China areas conquered during ICHIGO. According to the practice followed in the surrender of Germany, the Americans accorded Chiang Kai-shek the right, as commander-in-chief of the China theatre, to designate the officers to whom the commanders of Japanese formations should surrender. The sudden end of the war left the Russians in control of Manchuria, and the Chinese communists south and west of them in control of most of the hinterland of North China. For Chiang, the major problem was to get politically reliable troops in possession of the key cities in Manchuria and North China in order to forestall the communists. He therefore ordered the Japanese to hold their positions until they could surrender to officers designated by him, and he asked the USA for sealift and airlift to move his troops north.[79] These measures reopened the KMT–CCP civil war and placed the USA squarely on the KMT side, though US policy-makers were reluctant to acknowledge either of these facts.

THE SECOND WORLD WAR AND CHINA: AN OVERALL ASSESSMENT

Contrary to both the propaganda of the time and to many accounts since 1945, most Chinese leaders did their best to sit out the Second World War militarily, while using the war situation to position themselves for the resumption of civil war once the Japanese had departed. This generalization applied to the main Nationalist group (the Whampoa clique centred around Chiang Kai-shek), to the peripheral members of the Nationalist coalition (Yen Hsi-shan holding out in Shansi, the Kwangsi clique, and lesser generals such as Hsueh Yueh and Chang Fa-k'uei), and to the communists. While no major leader ever admitted this for the record, many Americans in Nationalist-controlled China heard variants of this theme: China had already exhausted herself fighting the Japanese in 1937–41, while the USA remained at peace, and it was now the USA's duty to finish the job, even if this meant sending a million-strong US army

78 William Craig, *The Fall of Japan* (New York, 1979), has the most complete account of Japan's surrender.

79 Romanus and Sunderland, *Time Runs Out*, pp.381–96; Suzanne Pepper, *Civil War: The Political Struggle, 1945–1949* (Berkeley, 1978), pp.7–41, on the KMT reoccupation of formerly Japanese-occupied China; Tsou, *America's Failure*, pp.300–16.

to China. Americans had much less contact with communist-controlled China, and tended to accept communist assessments of their war against Japan at face value. The communists claimed to be fighting the Japanese as vigorously as their means permitted; they would obviously do better if they got some of the American arms and equipment whose distribution was monopolized by the Whampoa clique. In fact postwar Japanese records and interrogations indicated that the Japanese were no more troubled by the communists than by the Nationalists. And for the Japanese as for the Chinese, the outbreak of the Pacific War in late 1941 created a new strategic situation in which China was peripheral. The Japanese had no reason to extend the territory under their control in China until the ICHIGO campaign of 1944, undertaken in reaction to Chennault's US-flown and US-backed air campaign.

At the end of Chapter 6 statistics were presented giving Chinese claims for their own and Japanese losses during the entire 1937–45 Sino-Japanese War. These indicated the great slowing down of active military operations after 1941, which confirms the impression given by the lack of major recorded operations or major changes in the territories controlled by either side. While the communists, and the Nationalists when talking to Americans, gave the impression of extensive guerrilla warfare behind Japanese lines, in fact the 1940 Hundred Regiments offensive represented the high point of Communist resistance to the Japanese (see pp.253–4). Afterwards, ruthless Japanese punitive operations and their adoption of the blockhouse strategy reduced communist guerrilla operations to a low-level threat. Despite their claims to DIXIE Mission, the communists concentrated on survival and political expansion during 1941–5, with such guerrilla warfare as existed being directed against Chinese puppet troops.[80]

80 In addition to material previously cited, see Lincoln Li, *The Japanese Army in North China, 1937–41: Problems of Political and Economic Control* (Tokyo, 1975), which is based in part on the extensive postwar Japanese official history. Exports from Japanese-occupied North China to Manchukuo and Japan more than doubled from 1941 to 1943 (pp.179–81), while imports remained stable. North China was in effect divided into zones of Japanese occupation and semi-occupation, guerrilla base areas, and neutral zones in between. Destructive raids into the base areas permitted the Japanese to continue drawing agricultural produce from the neutral zones (pp.197–204). Finally (p.233) Li anticipates the conclusion of the Civil War: 'Nationalist troops flown in by American planes replaced the Japanese as the ultimate victim of Communist power in North China. Every individual that the Nationalist Chinese flew in represented further military power lost.'

All of this did not imply that stability and peace reigned throughout the China theatre. While local accommodations between nearby Japanese and Chinese units could be long-lasting, they could also be disrupted without notice by Japanese action. While the Japanese did not try to expand their controlled territory prior to ICHIGO, they did use China as a training theatre for their army; this meant operations of the 'advance, burn, retire' variety, which were hard on the civilians in the operational area. Special circumstances, such as the rescue by Chinese of the downed US aircrew of the 1942 Halsey-Doolittle raid, were occasions for more extensive punitive measures. Punitive operations also frequently impacted upon the communist areas, which were both behind Japanese lines and nearer to Japanese forces than the areas under Nationalist rule. And for civilians in the cities, railway lines and contiguous areas of North China tightly controlled by the Japanese there was always the prospect of being conscripted, either to build blockhouses and trenches in the North China defensive system or for agricultural labour in Manchuria. For most of the people of North China, and for very many Chinese elsewhere, the Japanese invasion meant hardship, deprivation, danger and the risk of death on a scale much worse than during the wars and disorders of the warlord period, and the scaling down of the level of organized military operations after 1941 alleviated this only marginally if at all.

The Japanese in 1937 hoped for a short war followed by a political settlement including Chinese recognition. Despite the rapid sequence of military victories in 1937–8, and perhaps partly because of politically inspired atrocities like the heavily publicized Rape of Nanking, full-scale war stimulated Chinese nationalism and made a political settlement impossible. By late 1941, Chiang Kai-shek remained adamant in refusing to negotiate and the Japanese effort to create a legitimate puppet regime under Wang Ching-wei had failed miserably.[81] Nevertheless, any overall assessment of the Japanese political presence in China has to include the relative success of 'Manchukuo', whose Chinese population obeyed orders and worked for the Japanese until the end of the war. In China proper, the failure of collaboration at the national and symbolic level represented by Wang Ching-wei's Nanking government did not mean that the Japanese were unable to exploit occupied China

81 John Hunter Boyle, *China and Japan at War: The Politics of Collaboration* (Stanford, 1972), pp.306–35, for the final years of the Wang Ching-wei regime.

directly at the urban and local level. One can do a lot with bayonets. The Japanese-held cities remained under firm Japanese control, administered by traditional elites who collaborated with the Japanese as they had collaborated with changing warlord masters earlier. In the countryside the Japanese conscripted labour and requisitioned supplies either at will, or, if they had to fight, after fights which they usually won. In contrast to the starvation being experienced by cut-off Japanese garrisons in the Pacific in 1945, the China Expeditionary Army was reasonably well fed when it surrendered.

This leads to an effort to assess the extent to which the war in China in 1941–5 was a drain on Japan's overall war effort. This is an extremely difficult task. Much Japanese documentation was destroyed by the time of Japan's surrender, and even for the United States and Britain the economic historians of the Second World War have made few attempts to assess the relative costs of the war by theatre or by campaign. Nevertheless it may be stated with confidence that the continuing commitment to the China theatre did not provide the margin between victory and defeat for Japan in the Second World War. The China Expeditionary Army remained large (over a million strong) throughout the war, but during the war experienced divisions were rotated out for assignments in the Pacific, and were replaced by newly raised units, with a lower standard of artillery and heavy equipment. The Kwantung Army in Manchukuo was smaller but better armed; its tasks, however, included guarding against the threat from the USSR, something that would have been required even if not for the China war. During the 1937–8 active phase of the Sino-Japanese War, Emperor Hirohito repeatedly criticized his generals for failing to conclude the war quickly, as promised, and for the increased army expenditure that came at the expense of the naval and air buildup which he favoured. Despite this, Japanese naval and air power grew ominously down until Pearl Harbor. Afterwards, the military economics of the Japanese war effort were constrained by parameters within which the critical shortages were oil, merchant shipping, ship and aircraft production, and pilot training. Japan lost the initiative when she lost the Battle of Midway in June 1942. From then on, losses in merchant shipping weakened her industry by depriving it of oil from the Dutch East Indies, and inferior rates of ship and aircraft production and pilot training meant that her naval and air forces were increasingly outmatched when they met the Americans in battle. Nothing in the China theatre had much bearing on these processes. On land the Imperial Army remained formidable, as shown by the two 1944 offensives: ICHIGO in China and Imphal–Kohima in Burma. But nothing the Imperial Army did on the ground could offset the air and naval defeat of Japan in the Central Pacific, and the 'tying down' of the (largely self-sustaining) China Expeditionary Army by Chinese forces therefore neither contributed significantly to the Allied defeat of Japan nor imposed a great economic or human cost on Japan in prosecuting that war.

If all the above is understood, then the history of China during 1941–5 becomes a history of US efforts in the China theatre, of large hopes frustrated by intractable logistical realities, Chinese political intrigues, passive resistance and corruption. While the United States could not have operated in the China theatre without the support of British Empire authorities, the latter never shared the American belief that Chinese participation in the war was desirable or important. The British view, certainly correct in retrospect, was that resources diverted to China came at the expense of defending India on the Burma front, and that any offensive in that part of the world should target the sources of Japanese oil supply, beginning with Sumatra. Humouring the United States on China was part of the overall price that the British had to pay for American support.

The emotional and cultural roots of the American belief in the USA's 'special relationship' with China, the American suspicion of British imperialism and its hidden motives, and the refusal to entertain the same suspicions regarding the Soviet Union, have often been studied and go well beyond the topic of this work. What does require explanation, however, is the persistence until very late in the Second World War of the US military emphasis on China. As with so much else, the American experience in the Pacific War reinforced the view that a land war in China at some point would be needed to defeat Japan. While the US victory at Midway in June 1942 stopped Japanese expansion, it was followed by a long period – the Guadalcanal campaign and the 'island hopping' operations that followed until early 1944 – in which the Imperial Navy vigorously contested the US advance, creating the impression that a Central Pacific advance might take several years. Due basically to faulty torpedoes, the US submarine campaign against Japanese merchant shipping also got off to a slow start. The destruction of the Imperial Navy in the Philippine Sea (June 1944) and Leyte Gulf (October 1944) battles, the conquest of the Marianas as a B29 base, along with the success of the submarine campaign by then, meant that by late 1944 Japan could be attacked directly by air-naval means that bypassed her overseas armies. Even before Leyte Gulf, the US navy advocated this strategy, but MacArthur fought for and saved the Philippine operation.[82] In China at the same time, Chennault's airfields were falling to the Japanese in the ICHIGO operation, and US interest in CBI dropped dramatically. But it could not vanish entirely: Japanese resistance to the last man on every Pacific island that the USA did attack suggested that what the Japanese armies bypassed and left to 'wither on the vine' would all have to be uprooted and destroyed individually at some later time. At Yalta in 1945 the USA in effect paid the Soviet Union with concessions in China for undertaking this service in Manchuria, even though the surrender of the other Japanese armies indicated the price was too high. Ironically, the Chinese got the million-strong foreign army which they had been asking for, but in an unwelcome form.

82 Spector, *Eagle*, is the best recent summary of the Pacific War, with extensive bibliography.

8 THE CHINESE CIVIL WAR, 1945–9

In 1945 the Nationalist government took title to regions of China that had been under Japanese occupation, in some cases, since 1931. Their people, who had looked forward to the end of Japanese rule and the restoration of peace, were treated as traitors by the KMT regime. The latter, imperfect even before 1937, had become still more corrupt and demoralized during its years of isolation in Chungking, and its unwillingness to confront the most obvious political and military realities in and after 1945 defies explanation. The Northern Expedition of 1926–7 had been aided by the soundness of KMT currency, Chiang Kai-shek had devised and implemented an effective strategy against CCP rural insurrection, and he had undertaken a serious project of military reform before 1937. Now China's currency inflation was allowed to rage out of control, the best Nationalist troops were left isolated in northeastern cities where they were destroyed by weaker communist forces, and Chiang's military policy amounted to no more than favouritism to Whampoa clique hacks whom Chiang considered loyal. Nationalist hubris and hypocrisy perversely lent legitimacy to the CCP, and encouraged the belief, consistent with the concept of historical change widespread among the Chinese people, that the Mandate of Heaven was being transferred.

US involvement with China did not end in 1945. As the Cold War matured, a stable China aligned with the West seemed more important, and US guilt over Yalta increased. Nevertheless, the preferred American solution – a democratic China in which KMT, CCP and other parties could compete through electoral politics rather than war – was always a pipe dream. General George C. Marshall's mission to China was a sophisticated replay of Hurley's earlier bungling efforts to attain such a solution, and it too failed.

The civil war that followed was not a replay of the 1930s, as some China hands expected. The 'Southern Opposition' and the other once-strong warlords among Chiang's opponents had been weakened, as had Chiang himself, by the long Sino-Japanese War. The communists were the winners. They had gained in prestige by holding out in North China against the Japanese, their mass-mobilization techniques had been successful, and they were willing to coopt anyone, even capitalists and warlords, who was willing to join them. Government in the communist areas included stable currency, and seemed both more honest and more effective than the Nationalist alternative. Appearing more moderate than they in fact were, the communists seemed to provide a political ideology around which most Chinese could unite, something which had been missing since the disintegration of the Confucian system.

Militarily, the Nationalists played into the communists' hands by failing to revive the strategy of the fifth encirclement campaign. Once the best Nationalist troops were lost in North China, final communist victory was probably inevitable. Chiang continued his habit of 'command' via detailed written orders from Nanking, which helped to lose the decisive Huai-Hai campaign. Communist leadership in contrast was excellent, with the different army leaderships exercising initiative in their areas of operations while cooperating toward the common goal. When it was all over, Chiang fled to Taiwan, characteristically leaving his old rivals Li Tsung-jen and Yen Hsi-shan holding the bag on the mainland.

NATIONALIST CHINA, 1945–7, AND THE MARSHALL MISSION

Many policy-makers were caught by surprise when all of the Japanese armed forces, including Okamura's 1,050,000-strong China Expeditionary Army, obeyed their emperor's order to surrender.[1] By then Soviet forces under Marshal R. Ya. Malinovsky controlled Manchuria, adjoining the communist territories in North China. The Nationalists in contrast were confined to the south and west, and the Japanese surrender obviously cancelled Allied plans for a major amphibious expedition to open a port in South China. On the eve of the Japanese surrender, communist commander-in-chief Chu Te began to move troops into Manchuria, and Chiang on 12 August ordered them to remain in place.[2] Washington meanwhile, under the terms of the Japanese surrender, ordered

1 Charles F. Romanus and Riley Sunderland, *Time Runs Out in CBI* (Washington, 1959), p.351, for the strength of Okamura's army.

2 Tang Tsou, *America's Failure in China* (Chicago, 1963), p.305.

Japan to order that all Japanese troops in China (excluding Manchuria) surrender only to Chiang or officers designated by him.

Wedemeyer was angered by Chu Te's jumping the gun, and bent his orders to provide Chiang with airlift and sealift to move reliable Nationalist formations into North China. Peiping, Tientsin, Shanghai and the other major cities were reoccupied, and up to 500,000 Chinese troops moved in the process. US Marines landed at Tientsin, even though MacArthur rejected Wedemeyer's request for two US army divisions. Japanese units remained in being and defended these locations against communist occupation until the Nationalists arrived. Many continued to fight for the Nationalists afterward; Yen Hsi-shan's post-1945 position in Shansi depended on 'Japanese soldiers, dressed in Yen's uniforms, but fighting under their old commanders'.[3] Some 240,000 of the 350,000 puppet troops also joined the Nationalists. The combination of these measures in effect made the Nationalists the heirs of the Japanese position in North China, in control of the cities in alliance with puppet and some Japanese troops, while the communists still held the countryside.

Within the cities newly liberated from Japanese occupation, the Nationalist officials soon wore out their welcome. While inflation was raging in Nationalist China, the exchange rate between puppet and Nationalist money was set at 200 to 1, wiping out all savings in the newly annexed areas.[4] Less ingenious forms of rapacity and violence soon convinced the people of urban China that the Nationalists regarded them as collaborators with the Japanese and as fair game. Yet the lower Yangtze region had been the political and economic heartland of the KMT before 1937, so Chiang's indifference to establishing political support there is surprising. On Taiwan, whose people had come to expect predictable authoritarianism in fifty years of Japanese rule, KMT maladministration led to rebellion and brutal suppression.[5]

Most of the Nationalist troops sent to the north in 1945 came from the ALPHA forces, not so much because of their higher military quality as because these units had been selected in the first

3 Donald G. Gillin, *Warlord: Yen Hsi-shan in Shansi Province, 1911–1949* (Princeton, 1967), p.285.

4 Tsou, *America's Failure*, p.312; Suzanne Pepper, *Civil War in China: The Political Struggle 1945–1949* (Berkeley, 1978), pp.7–41, for an extensive treatment of these themes.

5 George H. Kerr, *Formosa Betrayed* (Boston, 1965), remains the classic account of the reversion of Taiwan to Chinese rule.

place because of their presumed reliability and loyalty to Chiang. In South China, due to his continued control of US supplies, Chiang felt strong enough to move against his warlord rivals. The Kwangsi–Kwangtung generals who had floated the coup attempt at the high point of ICHIGO were ignored politically and discriminated against in supply allocations. When most of the Yunnan Army under Lu Han, brother of Yunnan's Yi (Lolo) warlord Lung Yun, went to occupy North Vietnam after the Japanese surrender, Chiang sent his trusted Whampoa clique follower Tu Yü-ming to Kunming to depose Lung Yun in October 1945.[6] The army reorganization plan adopted in 1946 imposed asymmetric reductions on the non-Whampoa components of the Nationalist Army, which both undercut the power of their leaders and disposed them to make deals with the communists.

Meanwhile US Ambassador to China Patrick J. Hurley was still trying to get CCP and KMT to accept a US-style political solution to their differences, and got Mao to come to Chungking (28 August to 11 October 1945) for negotiations. Even though the Russians had obstructed Nationalist efforts to occupy Manchuria and had turned over captured Japanese equipment to communist forces there, Mao could not be certain of the extent of Stalin's support. The USSR gains at Yalta depended on KMT rule enduring, Stalin had voiced disdain for CCP prospects, and US military power had only begun its postwar erosion. Mao tried to secure specific concessions, chiefly KMT recognition of CCP rule in some, but not all, of their 'liberated areas' and control of 20 (out of 120) divisions of the reorganized army.[7] For Hurley these were irritating 'details' to be solved after a political settlement had been reached, and the negotiations failed. When Hurley resigned (27 November 1945) the Nationalists were still in the process of pushing their way into Manchuria. The Russians stalled on their own evacuation until 1946, and looted everything portable while they remained. But in the end they did go, and the KMT, for all its internal corruption, seemed to be consolidating its grip on China.

President Truman named General of the Army George C. Marshall as his 'personal representative' to China in December 1945. Marshall was an 'old China hand' who had commanded the

6 See the biographies of Lu Han and Lung Yun in Howard L. Boorman, *Biographical Dictionary of Republican China* (4 vols, New York, 1967–71), II, pp.445–7, 457–9.

7 Tsou, *America's Failure*, pp.321–3.

US 27th Infantry Regiment in Tientsin in the 1930s; he was more famous, however, as architect of the Europe First strategy while US Army Chief of Staff during the Second World War, and was familiar with the underside of the Nationalist regime through the reports of his protégé, Joseph W. Stilwell.[8] US policy was to create a 'strong, united and democratic China' under Nationalist rule. American military and other assistance would provide enough leverage to force the KMT into a coalition government with the CCP – 'so-called Communists' according to Secretary of State Byrnes – thus eliminating the one-party nature of KMT rule and the danger of civil war at one stroke. Continuing the tradition of medical metaphors begun by Chiang's 'diseases of skin and heart' comparison, Ch'en Li-fu of the CC clique described the communists as a 'bad appendix that has to be removed'.[9] The CC clique represented the pro-Chiang right wing of the KMT, and, while Marshall was pushing the coalition government idea, Chiang, through the agency of the CC clique and Tai Li's secret police, was trying to eliminate those elements of the KMT and the minor parties (the so-called Third Force) that were willing to accept a political solution including the communists. Chiang, in other words, actively wanted civil war, and went along with Marshall only to keep the US aid flowing.

Marshall's mission seemed successful at the beginning. He secured a cease-fire in Manchuria (10 January 1946) and CCP agreement to participate in the Political Consultative Conference, an all-party assembly preliminary to the formal drafting of a constitution.[10] In February 1946 he secured KMT and CCP assent to the reduction of the Chinese army to sixty divisions, of which ten were to be communist and fifty Nationalist. Marshall then went back to the USA and secured a substantial aid package. By the time he returned to China, the Manchurian cease-fire had broken down, and the communist capture of Ch'angch'un had provoked a successful Nationalist counter-offensive. Meanwhile the public release, also in February 1946, of the terms of the Yalta agreement had given the Nationalist regime a powerful propaganda weapon.

While pushing toward a military solution of the communist problem, which was in itself both understandable and consistent

8 Forrest C. Pogue, *George C. Marshall* (4 vols, New York, 1963–87), is the standard life.

9 Tsou, *America's Failure*, pp.351–4.

10 Tsou, *America's Failure*, p.418.

with Chiang Kai-shek's long-standing policy preference, Chiang did not pay sufficient attention to the military forces required to win such a confrontation. Chiang's hostility to Stilwell's proposals to upgrade his ground forces during the Second World War has been frequently alluded to, and it continued after the war. Nationalist troop strength fell from about 3.0 million at VJ day to 2.6 million in mid-1946, rising to a civil war peak of 2.7 million in 1947.[11] These continued to be organized in over 300 divisions, few of which had more than half of their authorized strenth of 10,977. Despite US supply, which reached its highest levels in the months before the Japanese surrender, establishment tables continued to be 'utopian', especially as regards crew-served weapons and vehicular equipment. The 1946 reorganization, aimed in part at weakening the non-Central Army part of the Nationalist forces, reduced many of the more under-strength armies and divisions to reorganized divisions and reorganized brigades respectively, but as the Nationalist position deteriorated, military-political considerations led to the restoration of the original designations, without any corresponding increase in strength. (The term 'formation' often encountered in reports of this period refers to units of a few thousand troops functioning as division-equivalents, but sometimes designated as brigades or even armies.) At the beginning of the civil war the Nationalists had a great superiority over the communists in numbers of vehicles and heavy weapons, but the advantage this might have conferred failed to materialize due to Nationalist inability to create a dependable supply and maintenance system. Similar weaknesses vitiated the Nationalist monopoly on air power. With an inventory of over 1,000 aircraft at VJ Day, the Chinese air force was down to 277 effectives by mid-1947.[12] While isolated Nationalist city garrisons grew overly dependent on supply by air, the combat aircraft did not fly often enough to provide adequate air reconnaissance, and were not a great threat to communist ground forces.

The communists in contrast expanded their military forces as rapidly as means permitted, going from 475,000 regulars in mid-1945 to 1,278,000 in mid-1946 and 1,950,000 a year later. Despite the windfall in Manchuria, these troops were not well armed. However, communist political control in their North China

11 E.R. Hooton, *The Greatest Tumult: The Chinese Civil War, 1936–1949* (London, 1991), pp.65–8.

12 Hooton, *Greatest Tumult*, p.75.

base areas was a reality, and this permitted them to mobilize both replacements and labourers (for a logistical system that depended on human bearers) from the rural areas. After a false start, they were able to achieve the same results in Manchuria. Nationalist efforts to create paramilitary and police forces in areas of communist influence therefore generally meant that the arms of such units were quickly captured by the communists. Once the communists began winning victories, their numbers expanded (2.8 million troops by June 1948, 4.0 million by February 1949) and their level of armament improved as a result of extensive captures from the other side (such as 12,667 mortars, 199,692 machine guns, and 2,992,258 rifles, along with several thousand artillery pieces of various calibres, meticulously accounted for by the communists).[13] As the communist forces expanded, they were reorganized according to a triangular pattern similar to that used by the Nationalists. By late 1949 the People's Liberation Army had grown to 219 divisions, each with an establishment of about 10,000 men, subordinated to 73 armies, which were in turn subordinated to 23 group armies that reported to the five field armies.[14] While each field army leadership represented a distinct strand within the military history of the communist movement, a respect in which both the communist and the Nationalist armies showed their warlord origins, the greatest single strength of the communist forces during the civil war period was the ability of the diverse field army leaderships to cooperate with one another despite the absence, often, of detailed directions from the central leadership.

During May 1946 the Nationalist armies occupied the central region of Manchuria. Fortified by military success, Chiang Kai-shek took a much tougher line in his negotiations with the communists, and became explicit in his determination to crush the Chinese communists by force, regardless of the opinions of Marshall or other Americans. The communists, militarily the losers in this period, called publicly for the restoration of the cease-fire, and accused the US government, with some justice, of not being even-handed in the KMT–CCP conflict. Marshall was caught in the middle of an inherently unworkable US policy. Recognizing the Nationalists as the sole legitimate government of China implied, for Americans of the time, broadening the regime by including its

13 Hooton, *Greatest Tumult*, p.190.

14 See charts in William W. Whitson, *The Chinese High Command: A History of Communist Military Politics, 1927–1971* (New York, 1973), pp.102, 114, 124, 186, 202, 244, 288, 332, 338, 352.

implacable opponents. US logistical support had made possible the Nationalist occupation of Manchuria and the cities of North China, but Marshall now tilted against the Nationalists. Allowing the CCP to veto Wedemeyer, he arranged the appointment of John Leighton Stuart, president of Yenching University in Peking, who had previously called for Chiang's resignation, as ambassador to China, and imposed an embargo, effective in August, on arms shipments to the Nationalists.[15]

The latter were still riding high on shipments made during the war, supposedly for use against the Japanese, and continued their advance. In October, after the Nationalists took Kalgan (occupied by the communists since 20 August 1945), Marshall recommended to Washington that he be recalled. This got KMT–CCP negotiations going again for a while, though by now it was obvious to all parties that these were merely a cover for a military solution. In November the National Assembly met at Nanking, and over the next few months proceeded to enact Sun Yat-sen's Five Yuan Constitution and to elect Chiang formally as president. The Nationalist high tide continued with the capture of Yenan in March 1947.

Meanwhile, Marshall had returned to the United States, convinced that his mission had failed, and blaming 'irreconcilable groups within the Kuomintang, interested in the preservation of their feudal control of China' for the breakdown of negotiations.[16] Marshall's experience with China went back to the 1920s, and he had been on the receiving end of Stilwell's reports during the Second World War; his negative assessment of the KMT deserves respect. Truman, who came to the White House ignorant of Chinese affairs, relied on Marshall, and in December 1946 reaffirmed his previous commitment that the United States would not become involved in any Chinese civil war. Prior to 1947 this position had the support of virtually all of the US political establishment, even those who later made Marshall a principal villain in the 'loss' of China. The communist insurgency in Greece and the general evolution of the Cold War in Europe, coupled with the election in 1946 of a Republican majority in Congress looking for a political issue, made it difficult for the US government to ignore completely the communist takeover of China. Nevertheless, the Truman administration adhered generally if imperfectly to the policy of non-intervention, and was certainly correct in feeling that even

15 Tsou, *America's Failure*, pp.424–8.

16 Cited in Tsou, *America's Failure*, p.438.

massive American support could not win the war for the Nationalists. Despite the tragedy that communist rule came to mean for China, during the civil war a CCP with outstanding political and military skills confronted a KMT bankrupt in both categories.

The oft-reiterated American position, that Chiang Kai-shek was the sole recognized government of China, had made him the sole beneficiary of US assistance. The helping hand not only meant that Nationalist troops were lavishly armed and equipped compared to their communist adversaries, but also helped the Nanking government to continue in operation despite the runaway inflation that was destroying the modern sector of the economy.

Yet in the end, when the Marshall Mission failed, President Truman and Secretary of State Dean Acheson decided to let the dust settle in China. The civil war had in fact gone on with little interruption since the Japanese surrender, despite the cease-fires, political negotiations and talk of a 'Third Force'.[17] It became more overt and intense following the Nationalist capture of Yenan, and its course opened the fault lines in the outwardly imposing edifice of Nationalist rule. Chiang is usually blamed for failing to institute land reform or curb inflation. In fact land reform probably would have meant a net loss of rural support for the KMT, whose in group – the looting classes, as it were – also benefited in certain respects from the inflation. Chiang's most serious failure during 1945–7 was his inability to reconstitute his own military forces in a manner that would have made the best use of his American assistance. This would have required his personal concern with the health, welfare and training of the troops, and with regular pay, supply and maintenance schedules, without which modern weapons and equipment become mere totem objects. His second greatest failure was his total refusal even to attempt to coopt the non-Whampoa generals. He might have failed in such an attempt. Li Tsung-jen, Pai Ch'ung-hsi, Hsueh Yueh, Yen Hsi-shan and the rest had disagreed with him often and had let him down at crucial junctures, some as recently as the 1944 ICHIGO crisis. But they, and the now patronless generals of Feng Yü-hsiang's and Chang Hsueh-liang's former armies, certainly shared with Chiang a desire for a China whose future development did not attempt to destroy traditional social relationships and private property.

17 The term used by liberal intellectuals looking for an alternative to both the KMT and the CCP. See Carson Chang, *Third Force in China* (New York, 1952), and especially Pepper, *Civil War*, pp.132–94.

In the period of the Northern Expedition, Chiang had been willing to coopt non-Whampoa elements in the struggle against the northern warlords, but in the 1930s he had shifted to a strategy of manipulation, in which conflict with the Japanese or the communists ideally would weaken non-Whampoa elements while preserving the elite forces he considered loyal. He had lost these in the 1937 Shanghai–Nanking campaigns, but had now reconstituted them – though perhaps not as well as he had imagined – with American help, which he had no intention of sharing with non-Whampoa warlords. The latter naturally became vulnerable to communist inducements, and many ended up as 'democratic personages' in post-1949 China. Chiang also continued into the civil war period the damaging leadership style – specifically the unwillingness to delegate authority and the attempt to control operations through written orders that were usually out of date when delivered – that was evident throughout the Sino-Japanese War.

GROWTH OF COMMUNIST POWER, 1945–7

Communist success in establishing themselves in Manchuria in 1945 extended the total territory under their control during the years 1945–7, but in fact the communists were hard pressed to hold all of the specific territories they had organized during the Sino-Japanese War. Communist resistance was conventional, in a military sense, and when they abandoned cities and the railways between them it was because they could not hold them, rather than as part of a strategy of 'People's War'. Just as the communists had called for a united front against Japan in the 1930s, to relieve them from the pressure of Chiang Kai-shek's offensives, so during 1945–7 they feigned cooperation with the various American efforts at cease-fires and political settlements for the same reason.

Communist military commander-in-chief Chu Te had vigorously protested the August 1945 order that Japanese troops surrender only to officers designated by Chiang Kai-shek, but the Japanese nevertheless obeyed. Similarly, despite a CCP party line mandating favourable treatment for surrendered puppet troops, most of the latter had joined the KMT. Despite these setbacks, the communists attempted to expand their territories as soon as the Japanese surrendered. The major prize was Manchuria. There the acceptance of any Chinese authority depended somewhat on the attitude of the occupying Russian forces.

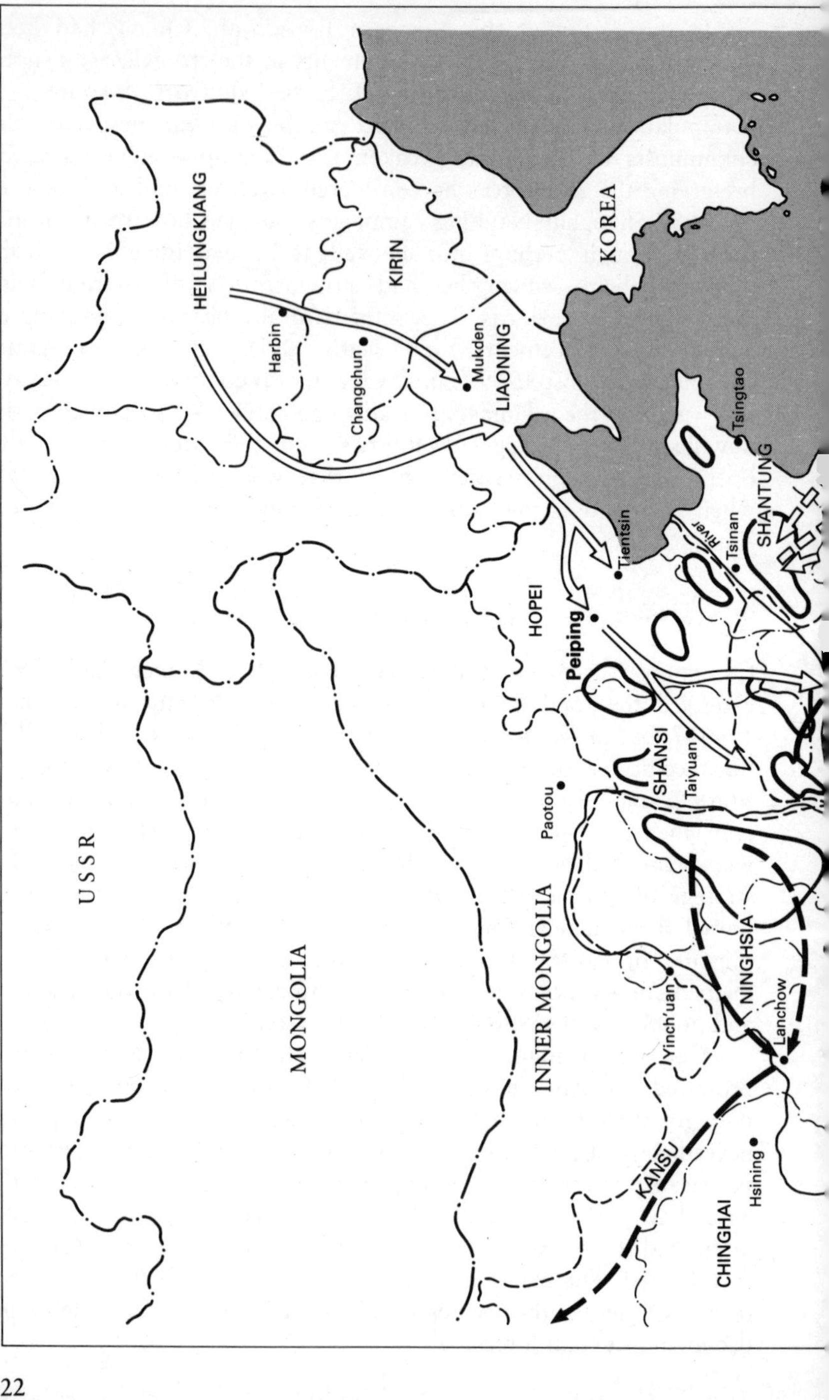

USSR
MONGOLIA
HEILUNGKIANG
KIRIN
KOREA
Harbin
Changchun
Mukden
LIAONING
Tsingtao
SHANTUNG
Tientsin
Tsinan
River
HOPEI
Peiping
SHANSI
Taiyuan
Paotou
INNER MONGOLIA
NINGHSIA
Yinch'uan
Lanchow
KANSU
Hsining
CHINGHAI

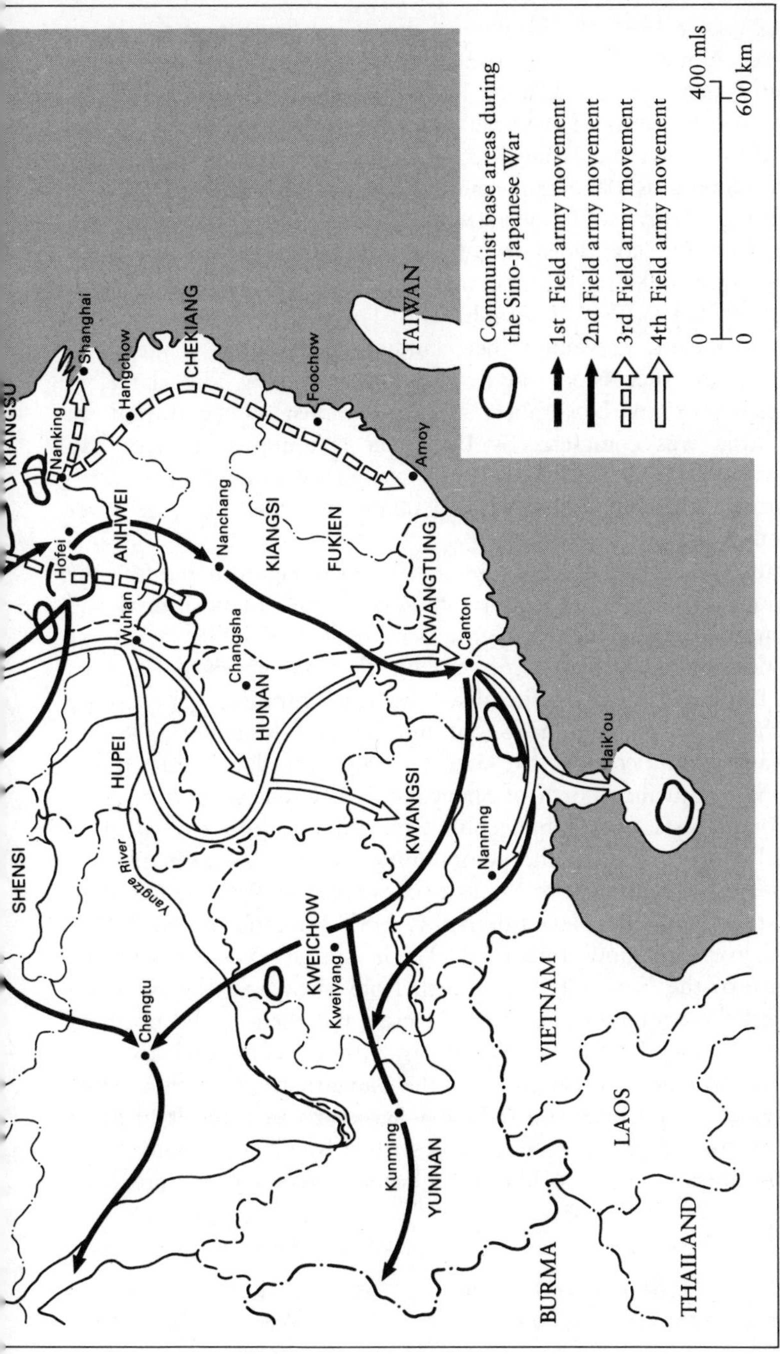

20. The communist conquest of China (After Whitson, *The Chinese High Command*)

In August 1945 60,000 men of the 343rd Brigade of the 115th Division, along with about 40,000 other communist troops, some formerly members of Chang Hsueh-liang's Northeastern Army, began to move into Manchuria under the overall command of Lin Piao, P'eng Chen and Hsiao K'o. The obliging Russians turned over to the communists the tanks and other weapons of the Japanese Kwantung Army, 600,000 strong at the time it surrendered. Meanwhile the six divisions of the Nationalist 13th and 52nd armies were sailing to Manchuria on the ships of Vice-Admiral Daniel Barbey's US VII Amphibious Force. The Russians, with various excuses, prevented their landing at Hulutao, Talien and Yingkou in succession, and when they finally did land at Chinhuangtao in November, the communist concentration in Manchuria was complete. By December communist strength had grown to 200,000, and due to the captured weapons these forces – the future 4th Field Army – had a qualitative edge over the other communist forces.[18]

This was fortunate, because for the next eighteen months the communist troops in Manchuria fought a series of positional and conventional engagements against Nationalist units that, whatever their deficiences, were part of the elite that had received US arms and training. The Nationalists swiftly captured the other Manchurian ports and advanced into central Manchuria, taking Shenyang (Mukden) on 15 January 1946. Lin Piao resisted the Nationalist advance north of Shenyang at heavy cost, and in April the communists took Changchun from Manchukuo troops. This yielded more arms for the communists, but it also escalated the Nationalist commitment to Manchuria, where the New 1st Army (of Sun Li-jen) and the New 6th Army, both veterans of the Burma campaign, were now operating. While spring rains slowed the advance of the New 1st Army north from Shenyang, the New 6th defeated the communists east of the city, and then turned north to join the New 1st. Both Nationalist armies combined to take Szup'ing and push north to cross the Sungari in June 1946. Only another cease-fire order on 6 June – agreed to as a result of great pressure from Marshall and later described by Chiang as his 'most grievous mistake' – saved Lin Piao's headquarters and permitted the

18 Whitson, *High Command*, pp.299–302. Daniel E. Barbey, *MacArthur's Amphibious Navy* (Annapolis, 1969), offers a sceptical American view of these supposedly elite Chinese troops.

central Manchurian front to stabilize along the Sungari for the remainder of 1946.[19]

In southwestern Manchuria in August 1946 the Nationalist 13th and 53rd armies, with the 93rd in reserve, attacked and captured Chengte (Jehol), Lunghua and Weichang, thereby securing the Peiping–Shenyang railway line. In southeastern Manchuria the Nationalist New 6th Army, withdrawn from the Sungari front, and the 52nd Army spent the last half of 1946 driving the communists back to the Yalu River.

By the end of 1946 the Nationalists had evidently overcome the early communist lead to establish their authority in the most important urban-industrial regions of south-central Manchuria. In fact the military operations were only part of the picture. Chiang had originally appointed Hsiung Shih-hui to command the Northeast Provisional Headquarters in control of both military operations and the restoration of Chinese civil authority. When Hsiung came under criticism from the KMT right wing (for trying to enforce the terms of the Yalta agreement, at Chiang's orders), Chiang replaced him with another leading Whampoa figure, Tu Yü-ming, fresh from his success in overthrowing the Lung Yun regime in Yunnan. Tu was considered unusually corrupt even by the standards of the time, and under his rule urban, Nationalist Manchuria became a kleptocracy whose citizens had little reason to fight the communists. The latter carried out land reform and established their well-tried system of political organizations in the rural areas, including the areas between Nationalist-held cities. The military operations commencing in 1947 made it apparent that the Nationalists in Manchuria were really over-extended and vulnerable.[20]

In the communist Chin-Chi-Lu-Yu region the Central Plains (later 2nd) Field Army led by Liu Po-ch'eng, Teng Hsiao-p'ing and Hsu Hsiang-ch'ien had grown to a strength of about 120,000 regulars by September 1945. Successful operations against low-quality Nationalist troops, some of them ex-Kuominchun with pro-CCP sympathies, swelled the ranks and provided additional stores of weapons. These communist forces also used the January 1946 truce for training purposes, and, like Lin Piao's troops in Manchuria, emerged a more 'professional' force, perhaps 200,000

19 Whitson, *High Command*, pp.302–4; Tsou, *America's Failure*, pp.420–1.

20 Whitson, *High Command*, pp.304–6; Pepper, *Civil War*, pp.278–80; Hooton, *Greatest Tumult*, pp.81–6.

strong by March 1947. Liu Po-ch'eng's forces failed in their attempts to cross the Yellow River and to deny the Peking–Hankow railway to the Nationalists, but in the process they inflicted heavy casualties and drew off forces that otherwise might have destroyed the communist forces to the east.[21]

These – the Shantung Military Region, later Ch'en Yi's East China (afterwards 3rd) Field Army – unsuccessfully resisted efforts commanded by Whampoa clique luminary T'ang En-po to secure the Tientsin–Pukow railway line to North China. After sustaining heavy losses against better-armed Nationalist troops, some with US training, the surviving communist forces withdrew to the mountainous areas of Shantung east of the railway and the Grand Canal by late 1946. While guerrilla units supported the communist regulars, the latter fought an essentially conventional war in defence of positions that actually did have strategic importance.

In early 1947 the Shantung troops faced 'a major Nationalist offensive, which sought to eradicate Communist military power in southwestern Shantung'. Communist forces under the overall command of Su Yü struck pre-emptively at the Nationalist garrisons of Linyi, Hsiangcheng, Yihsien and Tsaochuang in early January. They surrounded and destroyed the Nationalist 26th Division near Hsiangcheng, and mauled the US trained 77th Division as it marched to the relief of the 26th. The communists advanced west to take both Yihsien and Tsaochuang in hard-fought sieges, wiping out the Nationalist 51st Division in the latter place. Overall Nationalist casualties were about 40,000 in this sharply fought campaign, and the communists also captured weapons including tanks and artillery. However, the most interesting feature of this campaign was the way in which it portended the future Nationalist débâcle in Manchuria. Instead of following the successful blockhouse strategy of the fifth encirclement campaign, the Whampoa-led Nationalist forces now followed the vices of the southern armies in 1934: by remaining concentrated in comfortable (by Chinese standards) garrison towns, they failed to contain the communist columns, and were themselves vulnerable to being isolated and destroyed.[22]

The Nationalists responded with a counter-offensive aimed at Ch'en Yi's headquarters at Linyi. Once again Su Yü commanded the communist field forces. Leaving Linyi to the Nationalists, Su trapped the Nationalist 73rd Army and 46th Division northwest of

21 Whitson, *High Command*, pp.170–4.

22 Whitson, *High Command*, pp.231–5.

the city. The Nationalists lost 37,000 out of 40,000 men and all of their equipment, and the Tsingtao–Tsinan railway was closed. While the Nationalists went on to yet another offensive against the Shantung communists, the latter were now swollen to 250,000 regulars, and their response merged with the general communist seizure of the initiative that marked the civil war as a whole in 1947.[23]

For the communist forces left behind in Chin–Ch'a–Chi (Shansi, Chahar and Hopei; afterwards the North China or '5th' Field Army) while Lin Piao's troops moved to Manchuria, the years 1945–7, and indeed the civil war until 1949, were devoted essentially to harassing Nationalist forces holding Peiping, Tientsin and the railway lines. In late 1945 Nieh Jung-chen sent Hsiao K'o's troops to interdict the Paotou–Chining railway line in Inner Mongolia. From Kalgan the communists moved westward, capturing Chining in October 1945 and then surrounding Paotou, a siege they later had to abandon. In early 1946 the Nationalists made great efforts to seize the railway line northwest of Peiping, and in mid-1946 (as previously related on pp.324–5) the Nationalists won the struggle to control the railway between Peiping and Manchuria. Guerrilla warfare and the communist 'surround the cities' strategy are not features of these campaigns, which indeed were fought within the familiar parameters of inter-warlord warfare, with the railways as the major strategic prizes.

In August 1946 the communists, still holding Kalgan and Chining, laid siege to Tat'ung. While the communists allowed themselves to be drawn in more deeply there, the Nationalists Sun Lien-chung and Fu Tso-yi reached for their rear, attacking both Chining, which they captured on 14 September, and Kalgan. Fu and Sun continued to cooperate effectively and, committing all their forces, defeated the communists in a pitched battle at Huailai, took Kalgan on 10 October, and cleared the entire railway line from Peiping to Paotou. Communist withdrawal away from the railway was more a consequence of defeat than of strategy. Fu Tso-yi gained the most credit for the Nationalist victory, and eventually (December 1947) was rewarded with the Nationalist supreme command in North China; but as Yen Hsi-shan's principal field commander, he was never trusted by Chiang Kai-shek. In the first half of 1947 Nieh Jung-chen's forces repeatedly attacked the railway lines in Hopei and Inner Mongolia, occasionally interrupting traffic

23 Whitson, *High Command*, p.236.

but not attempting permanent interdiction until the general communist offensives later in the year.[24]

The end of the war with Japan found the Shen–Kan–Ning (Shensi–Kansu–Ninghsia) area including the communist capital at Yenan somewhat isolated from the main block of communist territory in the northeast. Communist forces there were constituted as the Northwest (later 1st) Field Army in November 1945 under the command of P'eng Te-huai aided by Ho Lung. This was a demotion for Ho, who, despite his poor education and bandit past, had led these communist cadres since Chingkangshan days. With fewer and poorer weapons than the other communist armies, their task was to defend Yenan while the other communist armies overran Manchuria. Their opponents were the Muslim cavalry of Ma Hung-k'uei and his clan and the troops of Whampoa clique General Hu Tsung-nan, who had resisted the communist entry to Shensi in 1935. Both generals had strong local roots and firm anti-communist convictions, and were largely successful through mid-1947. Indeed, Hu Tsung-nan's capture of Yenan in March of that year in a sense marks the Nationalist high water mark in post-Second World War China.[25]

While the KMT–CCP civil war begun in 1927 had never really ended, during 1945–7 there was at least much discussion of political solutions to the conflict. Meanwhile both sides were creating facts on the ground. Superficially the Nationalists had been more successful. In Manchuria they had driven the communists north of the Sungari River and into the rural hinterland. In North China they held Peiping, Tientsin and the railway lines, and had held Tatung and cleared the communists from Kalgan and the other major points on the line to Suiyuan province. In Central China the Nationalists had frustrated communist efforts to cross the Yellow River and cut the railway between Chengchow and Hsuchow. In Shantung, despite some bad setbacks and continuing communist presence on the Tsinan–Tsingtao line, the Nationalist counter-offensive reopened the north–south railway line through the province. And in the northwest the capture of the communist capital at Yenan in March 1947 followed a long period in which the Nationalists had kept their opponents on the defensive.

24 Whitson, *High Command*, pp.346–8.

25 Whitson, *High Command*, pp.111–12; Hooton, *Greatest Tumult*, pp.117–19; Hu Tsung-nan and Ma Hung-k'uei in Boorman, *Biographical Dictionary*, II, pp.175–7, 468–9.

However, Nationalist territorial expansion masked serious weaknesses. Nationalist troop strength, estimated at 2,700,000 in mid-1947, had actually declined since the end of the Second World War. Communist strength had increased from an estimated 475,000 to 1,950,000, and, while the communists continued to be less well armed than the best Nationalist units, Japanese and captured arms had greatly improved the fighting power of the communist forces.[26] With the threat of Japanese punitive measures removed, the communists could be more aggressive in expanding the rural areas under their control, thus assuring a steady supply of bearers and replacements. The Nationalist inflation and their predatory administration in the areas of China 'liberated' from the Japanese meant that there was no rally of the elite against the communists, as had been the case in the fifth encirclement campaign of 1934 in Kiangsi, and this in turn meant that the communists could use land reform and other radical social policies to rally the peasants, without fear of negative consequences.

Militarily, by mid-1947 the Nationalists had put themselves in an extremely vulnerable situation. Most of their best troops were now deployed in North China or Manchuria in cities strung out along railway lines, where they could be maintained only if rail communication were kept open. During the warlord period, when the peasants had been passive spectators or victims, such a strategy had been correct. During 1937–45 the Japanese had been willing to kill as many peasants as they had to in order to keep the railway lines open. During 1945–7 the communists tore up 16,515 kilometres of track of which the Nationalists restored only 6,398.[27] The Nationalists lost the war when they deployed their army to make it dependent on a communications network whose disintegration they could not prevent.

CIVIL WAR: THE MANCHURIA PHASE, 1947–8

In 1947 the communists went over to a general offensive, employing a battle-intensive strategy based on destroying main force Nationalist units, rather than capturing and holding cities as such. As in the Kiangsi Soviet period, rural mobilization would multiply the effect of communist regular forces. This strategy was carefully

26 Hooton, *Greatest Tumult*, pp.65–6.

27 Hooton, *Greatest Tumult*, pp.74–5, who also notes that air transport could not make up the difference.

articulated to subordinate units and diligently followed. The destruction of the powerful Nationalist Army in Manchuria set the pattern of the communist military victory.

As 1947 opened, Lin Piao launched a series of small-scale offensives across the Sungari River in Manchuria, then in the grip of winter. The first of these (6–17 January) lured the Nationalist 50th Division from garrison at Tehui and destroyed two of its regiments. In February, when several communist columns crossed the Sungari, the Nationalists concentrated their troops at Changchun rather than risk another ambush. In March another drive south of the river destroyed much of the Nationalist 88th Division and led to the capture of large quantitites of weapons and ammunition. The 50th had fought in Burma as part of Sun Li-jen's New 1st Army and the 88th had been part of Y-Force on the Salween front. If the communist forces could inflict even partial defeats on such elite Nationalist forces, then perhaps it was time to go over to the offensive and seize the initiative.

This was not evident to all observers. As May 1947 opened

> the Communists' strategic position was not impressive. Yenan had fallen, and Mao was a refugee in northern Shensi. Liu Po-ch'eng was about to strike desperately into Nationalist-held territory in the Tapiehshan, in the hope of diverting some of the massive Nationalist pressure then being exerted against Ch'en Yi. Ch'en's forces had been driven north from Kiangsu and Anhwei into southwestern Shantung, where the battle of Nanma had forced a further Communist withdrawal into northern and eastern Shantung. Nieh Jung-chen was barely holding his own in western Hopei.

Lin Piao's offensive began to reverse the sequence of communist defeats.

Lin mobilized some 400,000 troops and 200 guns against Tu Yü-ming's smaller (250,000 men) but better armed army, which was supported by an air force with 130 P51 fighter planes. Lin's troops swiftly surrounded and isolated the Nationalist garrisons at Changchun and Kirin city, while a strong column moved past Szuping south towards Shenyang. Tu Yü-ming withdrew forces from Antung and Tunghua near the Korean border and concentrated them to defend Shenyang. Meanwhile the communists surrounded Szuping, isolating Ch'en Ming-jen's 29,000-strong 71st Army within the city. In June the communists began a series of frontal assaults on

Szuping, which eventually cost them 40,000 casualties. Meanwhile Tu concentrated the New 6th, 52nd and 53rd armies around Shenyang. On 24 June the Nationalists, supported by their P51s and B25s, advanced on Szuping up the railway, while the three-division garrison of Changchun broke out and marched on Szuping from the north. On 28 June Lin Piao ordered a withdrawal, and the communist columns retired north of the Sungari, helped by Tu Yü-ming's unwillingness to pursue.

The May–June offensive was a defeat for Lin Piao, who faced criticism for the Szuping losses. The communists followed it up with an extensive land reform and the forced recruiting of many more troops. On the Nationalist side, Chiang replaced Tu Yü-ming with Ch'en Ch'eng, a much admired general whom Wedemeyer had wanted as ALPHA Force commander in 1944. He was also by now the most important Whampoa clique leader after Chiang himself, having won out over his long-time rival Ho Ying-ch'in in the struggle for influence. Ch'en, a 'bold, impetuous, intolerant and impatient leader', persuaded Chiang to put more troops into Manchuria, to a total of 500,000 by October.

From September to November Lin Piao masterminded another major offensive, this time avoiding frontal assaults on strongly held cities while concentrating on hitting the railway lines between them. The Nationalists held on to Chinchou – the seaport most convenient to the Manchurian railways – as well as Shenyang, Szuping, Changchun and Kirin, but rail traffic between these strong points became unreliable due to communist operations. Attacks against detached Nationalist forces eroded both Nationalist troop strength and morale, and the communists received defections from ex-Manchukuo soldiers whom Ch'en Ch'eng publicly disparaged. Chiang then sent the 73rd and 92nd armies into Manchuria. Reinforcements did not quite balance losses: the eight Nationalist armies in Manchuria in January 1948 now had an aggregate strength of only 300,000. No fewer than five (New 1st, New 6th, 53rd, 71st and 73rd) of these, however, were drawn from the thirteen US-trained armies of ALPHA Force.

Lin Piao began another offensive in January 1948, feinting against Changchun and Szuping while making the main thrust against the railway line southwest of Shenyang. Communist troops under Li Tso-p'eng destroyed the Nationalist New 5th Army (a unit of mostly ex-Manchukuo troops) and then attacked the Nationalist 60th Army at Kirin. In the east, communist columns took Liaoyang, Anshan, and then the seaport of Yingkou in late February. Lin Piao himself directed the communist capture of Szuping on 13 March, which wiped out the Nationalist 88th Division.

As a result of these operations, communist strength grew to some 700,000 men, and, once again, the fighting strength of the communist forces grew even more, due to the capture of arms and ammunition. The Nationalists were now totally excluded from the rural hinterland of Manchuria. Ch'en Ch'eng was soon replaced by Wei Li-huang, who was not an improvement; he 'faced rampant corruption among his logistical commanders', and his forces, though larger than in January, were mostly isolated in Shenyang (230,000 men) and Changchun (80,000 men), both of which could communicate only by air with each other or the Nationalists at Chinchou (120,000 men).

In the next phase of their offensive, the communists feinted at Changchun to conceal their main thrust at Chinchou. Despite Nationalist air superiority, Lin Piao was able to move his forces with relative freedom over the Manchurian railway system at night. When the main communist attack fell on Chinchou in September, Wei Li-huang, still concerned about Changchun, was slow to respond. Fan Han-chieh, commander of the Nationalist 6th Army in Chinchou, was pleading for help; Chiang Kai-shek sent Ku Chu-t'ung, now Chief of the General Staff, to Shenyang, and came there himself on 1 October. As a result, a force composed of the 39th, 54th, 62nd and 92nd Nationalist armies advanced up the coast from Shanhaikuan toward Chinchou, with naval support, while Liao Yao-hsiang (who had commanded the 22nd Division under Stilwell in Burma) broke out westward from Shenyang and captured Changwu, thereby cutting the railway from Manchuria that supported the communists at Chinchou. To no avail. Chinchou surrendered on 15 October.

Two days later Tseng Tse-sheng, commanding the Yunnanese troops of the 60th Army isolated at Changchun, surrendered and joined the communists. Other isolated forces surrendered around this time. More importantly, the fall of Chinchou made it possible to destroy Liao Yao-hsiang's powerful elite force (New 1st, New 3rd, New 6th, 49th and 71st armies). Liao allowed himself to be drawn into a frontal battle at Heishan south of Hsinlitun. By the time he tried to break out it was too late, and the remnants of his forces surrendered on 28 October. Chiang Kai-shek, Ku Chu-t'ung and Wei Li-huang had already flown out of Shenyang, and the best elements of the Shenyang garrison had gone into Liao Yao-hsiang's now destroyed column. Chou Fu-ch'eng was left with a demoralized remnant of 100,000 men including the 53rd Army. He surrendered promptly when the communists launched a general assault on 1 November. On 9 November Tu Yü-ming, in command once again, hastily evacuated the 140,000 Nationalist troops at Hulutao, who had come from Shanhaikuan. This left Manchuria entirely in communist hands.

Chiang had committed elite forces to Manchuria despite the advice of Wedemeyer, who had urged him to consolidate south of the Great Wall (itself a tall order) first. Ch'en Ch'eng, one of the few Chinese generals whose military ability was praised by the US advisers, had compounded the débâcle by calling in reinforcements that also were lost at the end. Communist attention to rural mobilization had contributed greatly to their victory, but it was a near thing: the communists had had little presence in pre-1945 Manchukuo, their methods were more coercive than usual, and they were aided by KMT indifference to the displaced landlords, which spread the impression that the communists were going to be the winners. While the communists certainly did 'surround the cities from the countryside', what mattered in the end was the ability of the communist main forces to engage and defeat, using their mostly captured armaments correctly and effectively, the elite Nationalist armies opposing them. Nationalist air superiority did not help them much. They had enough transports to become overly dependent on resupply by air, and thus less careful than they should have been to maintain the rail links between their garrison cities. At the same time their fighters and bombers, too few in numbers to have a decisive impact in any case, flew seldom in the daytime and never at night. The communists were therefore able to deploy and supply their armies by rail, running the trains all night long.[28]

CIVIL WAR: EAST AND CENTRAL CHINA, 1947–8

As the conflict in Manchuria ripened, the communist armies in East and Central China also seized the initiative. They crossed the Yellow River, advanced to the south to establish new base areas, and cut the major railway lines, thereby converting the once-aggressive Nationalist army into an aggregation of trapped city garrisons, as in Manchuria.

28 This section from Whitson, *High Command*, pp.306–19 (quotations pp.307, 310, 312); cf. Hooton, *Greatest Tumult*, pp.87–102.

On 30 June 1947 Liu Po-ch'eng's communist forces in Central China crossed the Yellow River near Puyang (then in Hopei), and headed south for the Tapiehshan range in western Anhwei and eastern Hupei, formerly the location of the Oyuwan Soviet area. The river crossing followed several days of well-coordinated diversionary attacks. During July Nationalist troops contested the communist advance along the line of the Lunghai railway, suffering some 50,000 casualties by Liu's estimate, and as usual yielding arms and supplies to the communists. In August the communists fought their way across Honan and Anhwei, a region devastated even more than the rest of China by the Sino-Japanese War and the Yellow River flood, to the Tapiehshan. By the spring of 1948 they had in effect recreated the Oyuwan base area and were once again besieged by the Nationalists. Liu Po-ch'eng sent the majority of his troops elsewhere, some to western Honan, others eastward to cooperate with Ch'en Yi's efforts. Hsu Hsiang-ch'ien meanwhile recruited more troops in the Taihang district of the old Chin-Chi-Yü-Lu base area; these later joined the final offensive against Yen Hsi-shan in 1949.[29]

Ch'en Yi's East China troops, who were heartened by their victory in Shantung in early 1947, faced a major Nationalist effort to eradicate them in April. Ku Chu-t'ung commanded the 400,000 troops (60 divisions) of the Hsuchow Pacification Headquarters, whose elite were the six divisions under T'ang En-po. Communist forces numbered about 250,000, and had retired into the pro-communist mountainous region of central Shantung. This set the stage for a replay of the earlier encirclement campaigns against the Kiangsi Soviet, whose outcome suggested that the Nationalists had forgotten their historical experiences there. While the 25th and 74th divisions entered the mountains from the northeast and the 48th and 83rd from the southeast, the 20th and 64th tried to protect the railway line against communist raiders in the southwest. In the northwest, one communist column surrounded and destroyed the Nationalist 72nd Division at Taian in late April; this drew the 5th, 11th and 75th divisions in what amounted to a wild goose chase. The separate Nationalist columns, in other words, failed to support one another and instead blundered about in the midst of a hostile population, inviting defeat in detail.

On 14 May the 25th and 74th divisions, attempting retreat, were surrounded at Mengliangku and wiped out. Chang Ling-fu's

29 Whitson, *High Command*, pp.174–7.

74th Division was referred to by the communists as one of the 'five main forces' of the Nationalists, the others being the US-trained New 1st and New 6th armies in Manchuria, the 5th Army at Hsuchow and the 18th Army near Wuhan.

Six weeks after the Mengliangku defeat, the Nationalists returned to the offensive, and this time they did it better. Deploying some twenty divisions on a line between Taian and Linyi, they advanced slowly but steadily in a general northeasterly direction, maintaining contact for mutual support, and in effect driving the communists before them and temporarily regaining control of the Tsingtao–Tsinan railway line. When the latter finally attacked the 8th and 11th divisions at Nanma, they left 5,000 dead to superior Nationalist firepower. While Ch'en Yi withdrew into northern and eastern Shantung, Liu Po-ch'eng's troops crossed the Yellow River, as related on pp.333–4. Nationalist units were drawn off to this new campaign, which 'may have saved Ch'en's columns from complete annihilation'. For the next several months, until early 1948, Ch'en's troops dodged a reduced Nationalist force in what the Nationalists called a 'mopping-up operation'. In reality the communists maintained their political hold on the Shantung population, which had been consolidated during the Sino-Japanese War, and this both provided them with recruits to expand their armies and hindered Nationalist operations.[30]

By early 1948 Ch'en Yi's numbers had grown to about 400,000. They were now reasonably well supplied with artillery and other specialist equipment, and had been able to train over the winter despite the Nationalist attacks. The Nationalists were increasingly demoralized, and in Shantung as in Manchuria they deployed their troops in concentrated garrisons in the towns along the railway lines, a policy that failed either to secure the railways or to cordon off the communists. On 9 March 1948 the latter attacked several railway town garrisons simultaneously. When the main Nationalist forces at Tsinan failed to react strongly, the communists surrounded Weihsien, whose fall cut the Tsingtao–Tsinan line once again, this time for the rest of the war.

Meanwhile communist forces of the East China Field Army, coming south from Hopei and western Shantung, and those of the Central Plains Field Army, moving north from eastern Honan, threatened the east–west Lunghai railway, which Liu Po-ch'eng's army had crossed but not permanently cut in their march to

30 Whitson, *High Command*, pp.236–9.

Tapiehshan the previous year. Loyang fell in April and Kaifeng in June, though the communists were later ejected from the latter. One Nationalist column that attempted to reopen the railway between Hsuchow and Chengchow was blocked and forced back. Another effort led to a bitter battle at Suihsien (28 June to 2 July) in which three Nationalist divisions were brought to the brink of destruction before a relief column from Hsuchow arrived.

Simultaneously, communist forces from eastern Shantung surrounded Yenchou on 10 June. Yenchou fell on 13 July, with a relief column from Tsinan only fifteen miles to the north. This of course cut the railway connection between Tsinan and Hsuchow and left Tsinan vulnerable. Ch'en Yi spent about six weeks redeploying his columns to tighten the noose around Tsinan, which came under attack on 14 September and surrendered ten days later after heavy fighting (22,000 Nationalist casualties out of a garrison of 86,000). The fall of Tsinan left Linyi and the seaport city of Tsingtao as the only Nationalist garrisons left in Shantung. The Nationalist position in Manchuria was also collapsing, (as already related on pp.331–3), and Nationalist forces in Peiping were threatened with isolation by the communist seizure of the Shantung part of the Tientsin–Pukow railway. While Tsinan was under siege, the staffs of the communist East China (Ch'en Yi) and Central Plains (Liu Po-ch'eng) field armies cooperated in the planning of an encirclement campaign whose objective was the railway junction at Hsuchow, the key to the North China Plain since the beginning of the warlord era.[31]

THE HUAI-HAI CAMPAIGN, 1948–9

Given the fall of Tsinan and the strong communist presence in western Anhwei and Honan down to the Tapiehshan range, the Nationalist forces in and around Hsuchow were in danger of being surrounded, as those in Manchuria and Peiping already had been. For Chiang, however, holding Hsuchow was necessary as part of his 'strategy' of reconquering the north, and so he magnified his subsequent defeat by pouring what were left of his reserves into the Hsuchow area. In November 1948 there were about 250,000 Nationalist troops at Hsuchow itself, supported by the 7th Group Army of 70,000 under Huang Po-t'ao at Nienchuang (east of Hsuchow on the Lunghai railway about halfway to the Grand

31 Whitson, *High Command*, pp.240–2.

Canal), the 12th Group Army of 80,000 (including the US-trained 18th Army) under Huang Wei (eventually trapped at Shuangtuichi, southwest of Suhsien, or about halfway to Pangpu on the north–south railway line), and 120,000 more at Pangpu. On a map these might look like mutually supporting dispositions, all linked by rail, but as in Manchuria the separate Nationalist forces were vulnerable to communist political strength among the rural population, which helped the communists to interdict the already damaged rail system.

Nationalist problems were compounded by their usual factionalism, which now included fissures in the Whampoa clique. Minister of War Ho Ying-ch'in and Chief of the General Staff Ku Chu-t'ung had installed Liu Chih as commander-in-chief at Hsuchow. Chiang Kai-shek no longer trusted these Whampoa leaders as implicitly as he once had, and imposed Tu Yü-ming – whose most recent credits were defeat and massive corruption in Manchuria – as Liu's deputy. Ch'iu Ch'ing-chüan, another general whose sole qualification was Chiang's personal confidence, commanded the 2nd Group Army, whose 80,000 men were the largest single formation at Hsuchow. Ch'en Ch'eng, leader of a faction of younger Whampoa generals, had also been defeated in Manchuria, but unlike Tu was in disgrace for it; this added to the isolation of his clients Huang Wei and Hu Lien, both of the 12th Group Army. Huang Po-t'ao's troops at Nienchuang were mostly his own Cantonese, but included the 59th and 77th armies of former Feng Yü-hsiang troops who defected to the communists at the first opportunity. Chiang seems not to have had any confidence in Liu Chih, and proposed putting Kwangsi clique leader Pai Ch'ung-hsi in overall command at Hsuchow. This may have been no more than a poisoned apple, but Ho and Ku killed the idea anyway, and Chiang reverted to his preferred command style of issuing orders to all major formations from the Ministry of National Defence in central Nanking.

The communist command situation was different and altogether better. Even though Liu Po-ch'eng's and Ch'en Yi's troops grew into the 2nd and 3rd field armies, respectively, and had different histories reaching back to the 1930s, they nevertheless planned the campaign together, establishing a special headquarters under Teng Hsiao-p'ing. They maintained liaison, acted independently in pursuit of common goals, and mobilized the peasantry both to provide coolie logistics for the communists and, as usual, to deny intelligence to the Nationalists.

During 7–22 November the East China Field Army, about 420,000 strong and commanded in action by Su Yü, surrounded Huang Po-t'ao's Nienchuang garrison. The defection of the former Feng Yü-hsiang troops (noted on p.337), permitted the communists to cross the Lunghai railway line and completed the encirclement of Nienchuang. The Hsuchow Nationalists attempted to relieve Nienchuang, spearheaded by the US-trained 5th Army, which included their only armoured division (the 200th) and which was commanded by Chiang Kai-shek's son Chiang Wei-kuo. These efforts were beaten off, and on 19–20 November the surrounded Nienchuang garrison was overrun and destroyed.

Meanwhile some 130,000 communists from the Central China Field Army advanced from the southwest and took Suhsien on 15 November, severing the rail connection between Hsuchow and Pangpu, and resisting relief efforts from both directions. Chiang had earlier ordered the 12th Group Army, previously based at Wuhan and operating against the Tapiehshan base, into the Hsuchow battle. When the communists surrounded it at Shuangtuichi (23–25 November), Chiang ordered it to break out. Huang Wei tried twice, the second time on 28 November, employing as his forlorn hope a former Yang Hu-ch'eng division that promptly defected to the communists and informed them of Huang Wei's dispositions and plans. Chiang now ordered Huang Wei to stay in place and wait for relief from the entire garrison of Hsuchow, now swollen to some 300,000 from the wreckage of other Nationalist armies.

Nationalist commander-in-chief Liu Chih, 13th Group Army Commander Li Mi, and Chiang Wei-kuo evacuated themselves to Pangfou on 28 November, and – encouraged by their betters – the Nationalist troops in Hsuchow began to pull out in disorder on the 30th. The following day Tu Yü-ming – who was experienced in disaster, if unsuccessful in overcoming it – led the main army out of Hsuchow, with the goal of rescuing Huang Wei. Forced west rather than south by communist pressure, this army was surrounded and immobilized at Chenkuanchuang (near Yungcheng) on 4 December. The success of Ch'en Yi and Su Yü against Tu Yü-ming added to Liu Po-ch'eng's pressure against Huang Wei. Both surrounded Nationalist forces endured bombardment by communist artillery, US made and recently captured from the Nationalists. The 23rd Division at Shangtuichi defected to the communists on 8 December, and the 14th Army soon afterwards followed their example. The 18th and 85th armies fought until their ammunition was exhausted, but were overrun on 15 December.

The three group armies (2nd, 13th, 16th) surrounded at Chenkuanchuang received some supplies by air until the weather turned bad around 20 December, but despite air supply, food, fuel and ammunition soon became critically short. Communist attacks temporarily broke apart the pocket, and the Nationalists were demoralized to hear of the destruction of Huang Wei's army. Until then Chiang Kai-shek had responded to Tu Yü-ming's radioed pleas for help by ordering Tu to march to Huang's assistance. From 22 December the communists ceased their attacks, resorting to leaflets and other propaganda. On 1 January 1949 Chiang Kai-shek publicly offered to negotiate with the communists, who rightly interpreted this as a sign of weakness and renewed their demands for unconditional surrender. On 6 January the final communist offensives against the Chenkuanchuang pocket commenced. The Nationalists did not surrender, but fought on until they were out of ammunition and their unit cohesion destroyed. They ceased to exist as a military force by about 12 January. Three days later the Nationalists ordered all of their mobile formations to withdraw south of the Yangtze, thereby effectively ceding North China to the communists and setting other political developments in motion.[32]

The Huai–Hai campaign was the most dramatic battle of the entire civil war. The Nationalists lost essentially all of the over half a million troops they had committed, and these included many formations, such as the armoured 200th Division, that were 'elite' in the sense of being lavishly armed and equipped. Foreign commentators generally have noted the importance of the Huai–Hai campaign and lavished praise on the leadership of the communist commanders Ch'en Yi and Liu Po-ch'eng. Yet, as in Manchuria and as in the civil war as a whole, the Nationalists' wounds were to a large extent self-inflicted. By spreading out their forces beyond the possibility of mutual support, but still concentrated in a few large masses while the intervening territory was tacitly conceded to the communists, the Nationalists invited the defeat in detail that they received. Communist professionalism in inflicting this defeat was admirable, but routine; fighting the way they chose to fight, the Nationalists would have been defeated by any reasonably professional force. Chiang Kai-shek compounded the problem by failing to solve the command issue and by trying to direct the battle from Nanking. Lacking a command system in which they had

32 Whitson, *High Command*, pp.174–86, 240–2; Hooton, *Greatest Tumult*, pp.143–9.

confidence, and by now feeling that time was running out for the Nationalists, the troop formations and individual soldiers trapped in the several pockets of the Huai–Hai campaign reacted in diverse ways. Some Central Army formations fought on as long as they could, while at the other extreme, formations originally raised by non-Whampoa warlords and dragooned reluctantly into the Nationalist coalition defected en masse to the communists, whose political line actively tried to recruit such elements. But many troop formations simply disintegrated as their officers and men fled or surrendered individually.

NORTH CHINA OPERATIONS, 1947–9

Fu Tso-yi's 1946 victories had given the Nationalists control of Tatung, Chining and Kalgan, temporarily securing the Inner Mongolian railway connection with Peiping. Nieh Jung-chen withdrew his defeated communist forces into the familiar Wutaishan base area southwest of Peiping on the Hopei–Shansi border, where they continued to oppose the Nationalists as they had previously opposed the Japanese. The Nationalists at this time were of course on the offensive in both Manchuria and Shantung. During the spring and summer of 1947 Nieh launched a series of offensives aimed mainly at the Peiping–Hankow railway line, with little result except for the occasional interruption of traffic. The Hopei and Shansi peasantry had been organized by the communists in the early years of the Sino-Japanese War; given these circumstances, the ability of the Nationalists to maintain rail communication to Peiping – admittedly over a somewhat rickety rail line – shows the limitations of a purely guerrilla mode of operations.

In October 1947 Nieh Jung-chen's troops, now expanded by recruiting and improved by training, cut the railway between Paoting and Shihchiachuang. The Nationalists naturally sent columns from both places. Nieh's troops held off the Paoting force, defeated the 3rd Army from Shihchiachuang, and went on to besiege and capture Shihchiachuang itself (19 October). Shihchiachuang was a major railway hub, since railways from Shansi and Shantung join the north–south line there; this made it a major depot for US arms and equipment, which the Communists captured. Nieh did not attempt to hold Shihchiachuang, as he was still not strong enough. During the rest of 1947 and the first part of 1948 Nieh remained based in the Wutaishan region, conducting raids of increasing magnitude on the railway lines radiating from Peiping. Hsu

Hsiang-ch'ien did the same from his base area in the T'aihangshan in southeastern Shansi. In April 1948 Nieh's and Hsu's troops were merged into the North China Field Army under Nieh's command.

While the Nationalists were going down to their final defeats in the Manchurian and Huai–Hai campaigns, the North China Field Army continued to threaten the rail lines from Peiping, provoking a massive counter-offensive by Fu Tso-yi in October 1948 that succeeded in recovering the lines to the south and west. Peiping was no longer needed to support Nationalist operations in Manchuria, and Fu was increasingly worried about being cut off there, but unfortunately for him the city was too important symbolically to be simply abandoned. In November Fu sent his 35th Army westward to reopen communications with Kalgan. It was surrounded and besieged at Hsinpaoan, southeast of Kalgan, and this permitted the communists to surround the 104th Army at Kalgan as well. Both armies were overrun and destroyed during 22–24 December.[33]

While Nieh Jung-chen's North China Field Army cut the rail lines west of Peiping, Lin Piao's Northeast Field Army, now grown to some 760,000 well-equipped regulars, attacked Fu Tso-yi's main bases at Peiping and Tientsin. Lin deployed his forces in three route armies, of which the right cooperated with Nieh's troops in the Kalgan campaign while the centre took Chengte (Jehol) and drove the Nationalist 13th Army back to Kupeikou on the Great Wall north of Peiping. The left route army meanwhile drove the Nationalist 86th Army out of Chinhuangtao on the coast of the Gulf of Chihli on to the 62nd and 87th armies in the Tientsin–Taku area, which the communist forces reached on 5 December. Fu Tso-yi's well-armed but politically heterogeneous army had about 500,000 troops at the start of these campaigns. The communist move on Tientsin–Taku threatened their possible evacuation by sea, movement to the north or south was precluded by the communist victories already recounted, and Fu's effort to maintain rail communication with his old patron Yen Hsi-shan in Shansi had led directly to the above-mentioned Kalgan and Hsinpaoan defeats. While these battles were going on, Lin Piao scaled down the action on his centre and left until more communist troops came in from Manchuria.

Communist regular forces now entered central Hopei in force,

33 Whitson, *High Command*, pp.348–52; Hooton, *Greatest Tumult*, pp.109–15.

once again moving freely among a rural population already accustomed to communist organization, while the Nationalist position once again degenerated to several isolated city garrisons. On 14 December communist troops occupied Nanyuan airport south of Peiping, thereby effectively trapping Fu Tso-yi and 250,000 troops within the city walls. The communists concentrated first on Tientsin, however, whose 130,000-strong Nationalist garrison tried to hold the communists off by flooding the surrounding terrain. On 14–15 January 1949 the communists took Tientsin by storm, and Taku fell two days later.[34]

After the fall of Nanyuan airport, Fu Tso-yi's troops had rapidly withdrawn within the walls of Peiping. There they could not hold out against a communist assault, as the entire built-up area was vulnerable to communist artillery fire; their main remaining weapon was the communist desire to capture Peiping intact so as to make it their capital. Fu was already considering a deal with the communists. Only about a quarter of the troops trapped in Peiping were Fu Tso-yi's own, and even these were demoralized and yearning for peace. The blockade of the city, while never perfect, nevertheless added to the general misery. A. Doak Barnett, an articulate witness of these events, summarized the mood of January 1949 as

> slow, but definite, social disintegration. No effort was made by the authorities to explain, to either soldiers or civilians, what was being done and why. On top of the past accumulation of dissatisfaction with the ineffective Nationalist regime, the deterioration caused by the siege resulted in the complete undermining of whatever popular support the Nationalist regime had previously enjoyed. No will to resist existed among the rank and file of soldiers or civilians. With few exceptions, people wanted one thing: peace at any price. They hoped the Communists would take the city soon and finish the siege. Only a small minority looked forward to Communist rule with enthusiasm, but the majority, although skeptical of what Communist rule might mean, no longer had any reservations about accepting it as an alternative superior to existing conditions.[35]

On 21 January Chiang Kai-shek announced his retirement from

34 Whitson, *High Command*, pp.319–21.

35 A. Doak Barnett, *China on the Eve of Communist Takeover* (New York, 1966), p.342.

office. This was more the result of the Huai–Hai campaign than of the situation at Peiping, but it had implications for the latter. Chiang's 'resignation' was the prelude to his successful attempt to concentrate all the portable assets of the Nationalist regime on Taiwan for the benefit of his immediate family and his Whampoa-clique loyalists. The decades of continuous progress on Taiwan since then have vindicated this decision, but its immediate effect was to leave the new president, Kwangsi clique leader vice-president Li Tsung-jen, and all the other non-Whampoa military factions within the Nationalist regime, holding the bag and taking the blame for the loss of the mainland. Fu Tso-yi – whose origins in Yen Hsi-shan's Shansi clique Chiang had never forgotten and whose Pailingmiao victory over Japanese-backed Mongol puppet troops had done so much to bring on the Sino-Japanese War that Chiang had wanted to postpone – in fact had agreed the day before to surrender Peiping and incorporate his army into the Chinese Communist People's Liberation Army (PLA).

SHANSI AND NORTHWESTERN CHINA, 1947–9

While the Nationalist capture of Yenan on 19 March 1947 was reported as a major victory in the opening campaigns of the unrestricted civil war, in reality Yenan and the Shen–Kan–Ning liberated area had only peripheral significance. Since the early years of the Sino-Japanese War the Nationalist regime had deployed vast numbers of troops (920,000 at the height of the ICHIGO crisis)[36] to the blockade of Shen–Kan–Ning. The presence of both the Japanese and Yen Hsi-shan in Shansi inhibited communication between Shen–Kan–Ning and the communist areas in East China, and the latter had grown into the main source of communist strength by 1945. Northern Shensi was arid, underpopulated (Shensi as a whole had only 16 million people in the census of 1953) and poor, and this was even more the case in the semi-desert areas of Kansu and Ninghsia (together 13 million, overwhelmingly in Nationalist areas) also included in Shen–Kan–Ning. In East China the communists had access to the provinces of Hopei (36 million people in the census of 1953), Shantung (49), Honan (44) and Kiangsu (41), whose populations remained very large despite the loss of life in the

36 Romanus and Sunderland, *Time Runs Out*, p.48.

Japanese reprisal campaigns.[37]

Many of the Nationalist troops in the northwest were local, either recruited in Shensi by Hu Tsung-nan – the Whampoa clique leader who was Chiang Kai-shek's strongman in the province – or Chinese Muslims loyal to the extended Ma family. Hu and the Mas were relentless anti-communists. Following their conquest of Yenan, they drove the communist Northwest Field Army, then about 70,000 strong and under the overall command of P'eng Te-huai rather than Ho Lung, to the arid region of Shensi north of the Wuting river. P'eng recovered, recruited replacements from the pro-communist peasantry of the region, recaptured Yenan (April 1948), and then defeated a Nationalist force west of Yichuan. P'eng then swung south and west, failed to take Paochi on the upper reaches of the Wei River, and then was badly defeated at Chingchuan. The Nationalists recaptured Yenan, and the communists took it back. In October 1948 P'eng began an offensive whose target was Tali on the Lo River, near the confluence of the Wei and Yellow rivers. This failed. In general the experience of the Northwest Field Army until 1949 suggested that it could survive, swimming as a fish whose pond was the peasantry of the Shen–Kan–Ning area, but that it could not expand to either the Wei River valley where Hu Tsung-nan was in charge, or to the Kansu heartland of the Ma family generals.[38]

Elsewhere, meanwhile, between November 1948 and January 1949 the Nationalists evacuated Manchuria, lost the Huai–Hai campaign, and surrendered Peiping. Having destroyed the main Nationalist armies in battles fought within the communist heartland of north and northeast China, the communists were now able to expand and destroy other power holders whose power, though resting on a firm local base, remained merely local.

Yen Hsi-shan was the first such victim. In July 1948 the 30,000 men of Hsu Hsiang-ch'ien's Taiyuehshan military district, recently transferred from Liu Po-ch'eng's to Nieh Jung-chen's command, began to move on Taiyuan. The pressure exerted on Ho Lung's component of the Northwest Field Army by Hu Tsung-nan kept the Fen River line of communication in Shansi open until October, but

37 Ho Ping-ti, *Studies on the Population of China, 1368–1953* (Cambridge, MA, 1959), pp.94–5, for the 1953 census. Ho's discussion of civilian loss of life (pp.251–3) should be compared to Chalmers A. Johnson, *Peasant Nationalism and Communist Power: The Emergence of Revolutionary China, 1937–1945* (Stanford 1962), especially pp.51–9, which is based on Japanese sources.

38 Whitson, *High Command*, pp.112–13.

from then on the city was surrounded. Yen's army survived on existing stocks and airlifted supplies, and defeated five communist assaults between November 1948 and March 1949. Yen gave an interview to *Life* magazine in which he pointed to a pile of cyanide capsules on his desk and vowed to die rather than surrender. After the fall of Peiping and Tientsin, communist propaganda aimed at Yen's troops became much more effective, and thousands of them deserted. The Japanese who had entered Yen's service in 1945 remained loyal. In March Yen himself flew to Nanking, allegedly in search of reinforcements; in fact he never returned, having prudently taken the province's gold reserves with him. General Imamura Hosaku commanded Yen's troops in the last weeks of the siege, which ended with a general assault and bitter house-to-house battle (19–24 April), at the close of which 'about 500 senior figures' committed suicide.[39]

The fall of Taiyuan precipitated a rapid collapse of the Nationalist position in the northwest. By the end of September 1949 P'eng Te-huai's troops, by now redesignated the 1st Field Army, had conquered all of Kansu, Ninghsia and Chinghai. Hu Tsung-nan retreated from Shensi to Szechwan, where he was destroyed in December. In September, meanwhile, the Nationalist army in Sinkiang signed a 'truce' and then defected to the communists.[40]

COMMUNIST CONQUEST OF SOUTH CHINA

That the outcome of the Huai–Hai campaign meant the fall of Nationalist China was clear to all concerned, not least to the Nationalist leaders. Just as Chiang Kai-shek 'resigned' to construct his refuge on Taiwan, so did the lesser fry spend 1949 either making deals with the communists or transferring assets to safe havens abroad. The communist conquest of South China thus turned into a walkover, whose main significance is the sheer scale of the troop movements involved and the effect of the final deployments on the development of communist China.

After the Huai-Hai campaign Liu Po-ch'eng's Central China (now 2nd) Field Army lined up in western Anhwei and Hupei and Ch'en Yi's East China (now 3rd) Field Army did the same in eastern Anhwei and Kiangsu. Both prepared to cross the Yangtze. Lin Piao's Northeast (now 4th) Field Army, now reorganizing in Hopei after

39 Whitson, *High Command*, pp.352–3; Gillin, *Warlord*, p.287.
40 Whitson, *High Command*, pp.113–14.

the Peiping–Tientsin campaign, provided the reserve.

Chiang's resignation created new heights of disorganization on the Nationalist side. The hapless Liu Chih was made the scapegoat for the Huai–Hai defeat and was removed, but his patrons Ho Ying-ch'in and Ku Chu-t'ung remained in office in the War Ministry and the General Staff, respectively, and continued to take directions from private citizen Chiang Kai-shek. Li Tsung-jen, the new president, now had a new title but continued to be significant chiefly as head of the Kwangsi military clique. He appointed the other principal Kwangsi general, Pai Ch'ung-hsi, to command the critical Hupei area including Wuhan. His relations with the Cantonese generals Chang Fa-k'uei and Hsueh Yueh were friendly; after all, they had a history of cooperation against Chiang Kai-shek. All of these forces had been on the short end of Chiang's distribution of US equipment, which had gone to the Whampoa formations and was now being cared for and used effectively by the communists who had captured it. The stockpiles Chiang had built up on Taiwan were beyond Li's control. This applied also to the principal Whampoa formation remaining on the mainland, T'ang En-po's group at Shanghai. Li ordered T'ang to move up to defend Nanking, but in response to secret orders from Chiang, T'ang remained to supervise the continued looting of Shanghai. Li's appeals for more US aid were denied. Despite the subsequent allegations of the China Lobby and Li's apologists,[41] it is unlikely that additional US assistance at this time would have been of any use; there was not time to deliver new equipment and train the non-Whampoa troops in its use, and there were not enough of the latter anyway.

In late March elements of the 3rd Field Army crossed the Yangtze near Tungling in Anhwei. On the night of 20 April they drove the Nationalist 88th Army back on Fanchang. On the same night the Nationalist garrison commander at Kiangyin in Kiangsu defected, and the communists established a bridgehead there. Nanking now faced attack from both east and south. On 21–22 April the 2nd Field Army fought its way across the Yangtze in the Matang-Anking area. Nanking was 'hurriedly evacuated' and captured by the communists on 23 April. The 3rd Field Army units advanced on Shanghai, where T'ang En-po vowed to wage a 'second Stalingrad'; in fact fighting lasted there until 25 May, by which time

41 F.F. Liu, *A Military History of Modern China, 1924–1949* (Princeton, 1956), pp.264–7.

most of the Nationalist troops had been evacuated to Taiwan. The surviving Nationalist garrison at Tsingtao, Shantung, left for Taiwan on 26 May. Subsequent 3rd Field Army operations in inland Chekiang and Fukien were essentially mopping-up operations. Taking the coastal islands, however, required naval power, which remained mostly in Chiang Kai-shek's hands. Chiang decided to evacuate the 125,000 Nationalist troops on the Choushan Islands off the Chekiang coast, which was successfully accomplished during 13–17 May. But he decided to hold Quemoy (Chinmen) Island near Amoy on the Fukien coast. In October the Nationalist garrison destroyed an improvised communist landing force, and the Nationalists have held the island ever since.[42]

In the interior the communists confronted the efforts of Pai Ch'ung-hsi to organize a defence in Hupei, Hunan and Kiangsi. Pai had about 300,000 troops, with the usual Nationalist weaknesses. On 12 May elements of the 2nd Field Army captured Nanchang, Kiangsi's capital and principal city. Pai then decided to evacuate Wuhan and concentrate in Hunan.[43] Elements of the 4th Field Army approached Changsha in July, and Governor Ch'eng Ch'ien defected to the communists on 3 August. Ch'eng had commanded the Hunan contingent during the Northern Expedition. Despite his rumoured pro-communist sympathies he had supported Chiang during the 1927 crisis, and had been the principal figure in KMT politics in Hunan since then.[44]

Nationalist rule of a sort persisted in the provinces of Szechwan, Yunnan, Kweichow, Kwangsi and Kwangtung. President Li Tsung-jen had retired to Kwangsi after the fall of Nanking, while the government moved to Canton. Li blamed Chiang Kai-shek for the fall of Nanking, because of Chiang's interference in military affairs. Yen Hsi-shan visited Li with promises of full support from Chiang.[45] Li then returned to Canton, and appointed Yen his prime minister. The old problems resurfaced immediately. Pai Ch'ung-hsi was attempting to concentrate all surviving Nationalist units in Kwangtung and Kwangsi, so as to retain a beachhead on the mainland for the Nationalists. Not coincidentally, these formations would also all come under Kwangsi clique control. Chiang resorted to his usual policy of indirect sabotage, and Li and Yen fell out over

42 Whitson, *High Command*, pp.243–5; quotation on p.244.

43 Whitson, *High Command*, pp.186–7.

44 For Ch'eng Ch'ien, Boorman, *Biographical Dictionary*, I, p.283.

45 Gillin, *Warlord*, pp.289–90.

the issue of removing Chiang's supporters from the Canton regime. When elements of the 2nd Field Army took Canton on 26 October, some Nationalist units escaped to Hainan. The Nationalist government went by air to the Sino-Japanese War capital at Chungking.

After sustaining and inflicting heavy losses in a struggle for Hengyang in southern Hunan in September and October, Pai Ch'ung-hsi withdrew the main Nationalist force, still about 250,000 strong, to Kwangsi in November. Hu Tsung-nan, Chiang Kai-shek loyalist and former scourge of the communists in Shensi, still held on in Szechwan. The communists made some highly publicized troop rotations to give the impression that they would invade Szechwan from the north. In fact the main strength of the 2nd Field Army was held south of the Yangtze to invade Kweichow. Kweiyang fell on 15 November, Tsunyi on the 21st and the communists entered Szechwan from the south and took Chungking on the 30th. Simultaneously the 4th Field Army destroyed Pai Ch'ung-hsi in Kwangsi: after the fall of Kweilin and Liuchow by 26 November, Pai tried to regroup around Nanning, but his armies were soon afterwards forced to surrender or flee into Vietnam. Hu Tsung-nan in northern Szechwan now realized that the communist attacks from Shensi were merely diversionary, and concentrated his forces for a last-ditch defence of Chengtu with some 300,000 surviving troops. Chiang Kai-shek, whose personal courage was never in doubt despite his often disastrous military judgement, had flown into Canton and had accompanied the government move to Chungking. He was in Chengtu as the communist encirclement began to tighten on 1 December. On the 10th he said goodbye to his fellow Chekiangese Hu Tsung-nan and flew back to Taiwan over communist-held territory. Over the next two weeks Hu's army crumbled due to defections, and the communists marched into Chengtu on the 27th. The indomitable Hu escaped to Hainan, and later returned to the mainland in early 1950 to concentrate an army of 35,000 men in the Hsichang area of southeastern Sikang. This attempt to organize an anti-communist guerrilla resistance was destroyed in March 1950. Hu escaped once again and went to Taiwan. Some of the survivors, organized as the Nationalist 93rd Division under Li Mi, fled into the Shan regions of eastern Burma, where they entered the opium cultivation and export business.[46]

Other mopping-up operations in the southwest took place in

46 Whitson, *High Command*, pp.187–9.

1950. The same year saw the communist conquest of Tibet, which had remained free of Chinese interference for most of 1911–49, though it never secured international recognition of its independence.[47] However, the last military operation strictly assignable to the Chinese Civil War was the communist conquest of Hainan in April. Hainan should have been held; it was in principle less vulnerable than Quemoy to the kind of amphibious operation the communists were then capable of mounting, and the Nationalists inflicted serious casualties on the landing forces. But Nationalist resistance crumbled quickly once significant communist numbers were ashore.[48] Less than two months later the outbreak of the Korean War radically transformed the military situation in the Far East, ending the US policy of 'letting the dust settle' in China, and guaranteeing the survival of the Republic of China on Taiwan with US naval power.

47 Whitson, *High Command*, pp.192–3.

48 Barnett, *Eve*, pp.269–304, for the situation of the Nationalists on the eve of the communist attack.

CONCLUSION

PEOPLE'S WAR AND THE COMMUNIST VICTORY

Almost immediately afterwards, the communist victory in the Chinese Civil War was attributed, by Chinese as well as foreign analysts, to the specific strategy of the communists. This was sometimes called simply guerrilla warfare, but all of Mao Tse-tung's military writings note that guerrilla warfare is only part of the overall package, and the term 'People's War', popularized by Lin Piao during his years as Mao's heir apparent, has gained acceptance.[1] The main elements of People's War continued to be a politically motivated and organized peasantry, willing to suffer in order to deny both intelligence and supply to invading enemy columns, attrition by communist guerrilla units, and defeat in detail by communist regular forces. Since the campaigns recounted above typically ended with large Nationalist forces surrounded in cities, the strategy was often called 'surrounding the cities from the countryside'. Nationalist leaders were criticized for attaching too much value to the mere holding of cities, and the US theories of counter-insurgency that peaked during the Vietnam War stressed the value of getting out to the countryside and 'winning the hearts and minds' of the people. For Mao and his supporters, it remained important to stress the political, peasant-mobilization aspects of military strategy: doing so served the twin purposes of denying that non-Maoist regimes could ever imitate or defeat the strategy of People's War, and of claiming for Mao and for China a position of originality and leadership within the world communist movement.

1 Lin Piao, *Long Live the Victory of People's War, in Commemoration of the 20th Anniversary of Victory in the Chinese People's War of Resistance against Japan* (Peking, 1965), is the most fulsome exposition of this theory. It was published at the height of the Great Proletarian Cultural Revolution, one of whose themes was the repudiation of the steps toward military professionalization undertaken by Lin's rival P'eng Te-huai.

To appreciate the actual history of the Chinese civil wars, it is necessary to question the distinctiveness of this formulation, and to wonder if the communist triumph was not in fact rather the result of conventional military science and a united political leadership.

In his article 'Strategy for the second year of the war of liberation',[2] dated 1 September 1947 – after the Nationalist capture of Yenan but before the communist victories in Manchuria – Mao summarized the 'operational principles' of the communist army which were 'still the same as those laid down before':

> Attack dispersed, isolated enemy forces first . . .; attack concentrated, strong enemy forces later.
>
> Take medium and small cities and extensive rural areas first; take big cities later.
>
> Make wiping out the enemy's effective strength our main objective; do not make holding or seizing a place our main objective. Holding or seizing a place is the outcome of wiping out the enemy's effective strength, and often a place can be held or seized for good only after it has changed hands a number of times.
>
> In every battle, concentrate an absolutely superior force, encircle the enemy forces completely, strive to wipe them out thoroughly and do not let any escape from the net. In special circumstances, use the method of dealing crushing blows to the enemy, that is, concentrate all our strength to make a frontal attack and also to attack one or both of his flanks, with the aim of wiping out one part and routing the other so that our army can swiftly move its troops to smash other enemy forces.
>
> On the one hand, be sure to fight no battle unprepared, fight no battle you are not sure of winning; make every effort to be well prepared for each battle, make every effort to ensure victory in

2 Mao Tse-tung, *Selected Works of Mao Tse-tung* (4 vols, Peking, 1961–5), IV, pp.144–5; differently translated in F.F. Liu, *A Military History of Modern China, 1942–1949* (Princeton, 1956), pp.250–1, and analyzed in William W. Whitson, *The Chinese High Command: A History of Communist Military Politics, 1927–1971* (New York, 1973), p.89. In 'The present situation and our tasks' (December 1947) Mao summarized (*Selected Works*, IV, pp.161–2) ten principles essentially repeated from the earlier statement. Whitson's view that these principles 'blended the professionalism of the warlord and Russian models with the political imperatives of the peasant model' is close to mine.

> the given set of conditions as between the enemy and ourselves. On the other hand, give full play to our fine style of fighting – courage in battle, no fear of sacrifice, no fear of fatigue, and continuous fighting (that is, fighting successive battles in a short time).
>
> Strive to draw the enemy into mobile warfare, but at the same time lay great stress on learning the tactics of positional attack and on stepping up the building of the artillery and engineer corps in order to capture enemy fortified points and cities on a large scale.
>
> Resolutely attack and seize all fortified points and cities which are weakly defended. Attack and seize at opportune moments all fortified points and cities defended with moderate strength, provided circumstances permit. For the time being, leave alone all fortified points and cities which are strongly defended.
>
> Replenish our strength with all the arms and most of the soldiers captured from the enemy.

When this was written, the Nationalists had already occupied the cities in North China and Manchuria formerly held by the Japanese, while the communists still held their liberated areas in North China and had moved into, and begun to organize the peasantry, in Manchuria. The opposing forces, in other words, were positioned so that the communists could attempt against the Nationalists the 'surround the cities' strategy that had failed against the Japanese. Yet one may note the absence of the minimalist guerrilla strategy of attrition actually used, with minimal effect, against the Japanese during most of 1941–5. Instead the emphasis is on battle. The communist armies are engaged in 'wiping out the enemy's effective strength' through 'frontal attack', 'positional attack' and 'successive battles', in each of which they are to 'encircle the enemy completely' so that none escape. This does not mean that the communists had abandoned the mass-mobilization political techniques that were their trademark. Nor did the military annihilation of Nationalist forces always mean physical liquidation of Nationalist troops; on the contrary, most surrendered troops were expected, after being vetted and indoctrinated, to join the communists. Most did. 'China's wars are always civil', as the saying goes, so that, as in previous periods of dynastic change, communist victories had a snowballing effect, and the rank-and-file members of the old regime scrambled to get aboard the new.

Nevertheless, the central element in the communist military victory in the civil war was winning the major battles in the Manchurian, Huai–Hai and North China campaigns that together destroyed most of the Nationalist main force units that had been built up with US equipment in the latter stages of the Second World War. Without these battlefield victories the communists would have had little chance to spread politically beyond their North China base areas. Mao's September 1947 formulation is important because it foretells the essentially conventional strategy of regular armies destroying the enemy in sequential battles that the communist forces actually used in these decisive campaigns. The use of envelopments in these campaigns has nothing to do with guerrilla warfare, but is instead another example of the German theory of the decisive battle or 'battle of annihilation' (Vernichtungsschlacht), as applied by Count Helmuth von Moltke in the Austro-Prussian War of 1866 and the Franco-Prussian War of 1870–1, and as attempted by German forces in both world wars.

Training of staff officers in essentially German theory and procedures spread to all important armies, including the Japanese, by the late nineteenth century. As noted previously (pp.19–22, 27), these military doctrines entered the Chinese world, often through Japanese intermediaries, in the military academies founded as part of the Manchu reform movement and maintained during the warlord period. They were, in other words, part of the military science background available to educated officers in both communist and Nationalist camps. Mao himself had no formal military education, and derived his own doctrinal prescriptions from his own analysis of communist military experience and his interactions with other communist military leaders. He may not have perceived, and surely would have been indifferent to, the intellectual trail from himself to Moltke.

What is significant, however, is that Mao prescribed a strategy based on battles of encirclement and annihilation, and thereby rejected, for the decisive phase of the civil war, a substantial body of military wisdom and experience that also was held in common by communist and Nationalist leaders. This was the military practice of the warlord era and the military traditions of Chinese history, represented by the novels *Romance of the Three Kingdoms* and *Outlaws of the Marsh* and by the thought of Sun Tzu.[3] These

3 Andrew H. Plaks, *The Four Masterworks of the Ming Novel: Ssu Ta Ch'i Shu* (Princeton, 1987), and Samuel B. Griffith, *Sun Tzu: The Art of War* (Oxford, 1963), for discussion.

traditions are of considerable intellectual complexity and sophistication, but their overall tendency is to emphasize deception, surprise, and betrayal and other political moves, rather than fighting and winning battles. A warlord's army constituted his political capital; spending this in battle was to be avoided, and Sun Tzu could always be selectively quoted – 'those skilled in war subdue the enemy's army without battle' – to rationalize avoidance of action.[4]

If Mao was seeking a showdown in 1947, so too was Chiang. In fact, Chiang had been looking for a military solution to the communist problem since the end of the war with Japan, and had entered into negotiations and cease-fires only under US pressure. Chiang is sometimes caricatured as an archetypal warlord general, and indeed, down to his final departure from the mainland, he manoeuvred incessantly against his coalition rivals, even as he was fighting communists and Japanese. In fact, though, Chiang had considerable personal courage, and was willing to expend even his elite troops in fighting for his objectives. He demonstrated this against the northern warlords from 1926 and against the communists from 1927. As indicated previously (pp.181–5), he had good reasons for avoiding a showdown with the Japanese after 1931, but when it came in 1937 he risked and lost his elite troops. His reluctance to engage the Japanese during 1941–5 was, in retrospect, a mistake, since it permitted the communists to pose as the sole defenders of Chinese nationhood. But it was nevertheless a calculated mistake; Chiang was attempting during this period to reconstitute and preserve his elite forces for the final showdown with the communists, which he now welcomed.

Since both sides sought a decision through battle in the Chinese Civil War, and expected the war to be fought along the lines of contemporary (Western-derived) military science, it needs to be explained why the Nationalists, with their much greater numbers and higher standard of armament, lost the key battles. The political factor cannot be left out of even the most totally military context. For example, the Nationalist chain of command was badly disrupted by clique rivalries and backstabbing among the Nationalist generals, while the basic unity of purpose in the communist camp allowed their several field armies to cooperate on the battlefield even without detailed orders from above. The decisive campaigns were fought in North China, where existing communist control of much

4 Griffith, *Sun Tzu*, p.79.

of the rural population was not challenged by any serious Nationalist efforts to win popular support.

Nevertheless, the battles were what decided matters; the Nationalists could probably have reimposed their regime on the countryside from the cities, in the manner of Chinese imperial dynasties, had they defeated the communist regular forces. They lost because they underestimated the strength of the communist regular forces and their ability to undertake large-scale mobile operations and wage pitched battles even against powerful enemy formations. The Nationalists therefore overextended themselves in 1945, using their elite force units to occupy all of the Japanese-held cities in North China and Manchuria. The result was that, when the decisive phase of the civil war began, the best elements of the Nationalist army were already dispersed among a number of northern urban centres, each of which was connected to other Nationalist forces only by air, sea (a few cases only), or by railways that ran through territories inhabited by pro-communist peasants. Nationalist leaders were no doubt influenced by Japanese generals who assessed the communists as local bandits who posed no serious threat to their control of North China. To quote Sun Tzu again, 'when capable, feign incapacity'.[5] The communists had been lying low since the Hundred Regiments offensive and the Japanese mopping-up operations that followed in 1941. They could not outfight or subvert politically the Imperial Army, but in 1945 they were stronger than either the Japanese or Chiang realized, and they improved their relative position thanks to the entry to Manchuria given them by the Russians.

Communist victories were won by a well-organized regular army, fighting largely according to conventional military science, whose effectiveness was multiplied by communist political control of the peasantry in the theatres of operations. Understanding the Nationalist decision to risk the best elements of their army in the rapid reoccupation of North China and Manchuria requires further consideration of the state of the Nationalist leadership in 1945.

NATIONALIST POLITICAL AND MILITARY DEMORALIZATION

The conclusion that the communist victory in the civil war was due essentially to bad Nationalist generalship, within a conventional war

5 Griffith, *Sun Tzu*, p.66.

framework whose rules were understood by officers on both sides, may be hard to accept. It seeems to contradict not only various romantic conceptions of People's War, but also the argument that the communists triumphed because only they understood and solved China's rural problem. Four decades later calling collectivization and communist agricultural policy a success may seem overly generous, but in 1945–9 there is no doubting that peasant mobilization in North China greatly facilitated communist military operations. Peasant mobilization elsewhere, however, came in the wake of communist military victory, and did not contribute to it. Peasant mobilization in North China contributed to the Nationalist defeat because the Nationalists sent their armies there. Understanding why they did so requires further discussion of the Nationalist regime and its leadership.

Contemporary observers in the 1930s and 1940s, and scholars then and since, have emphasized corruption, hypocrisy and demoralization as features of Nationalist rule. Nationalist success in the Northern Expedition was followed immediately by conflict with the 'residual warlords' Feng Yü-hsiang and Yen Hsi-shan, the creation of communist-controlled Soviet areas in Kiangsi and elsewhere, and soon afterwards by the Japanese takeover of Manchuria. In 1926–7 the Northern Expedition was sustained by an idealism and nationalism that temporarily united Chinese across a broad spectrum of political beliefs, and fiscal probity played an important supporting role in the KMT's success. The political system that emerged in Nanking late in 1927, however, was depressingly reminiscent of the warlord system that the Northern Expedition was supposed to have overthrown. Chiang was hegemonial, but not all-powerful, and to maintain and increase his hegemony he used the same combination of violence and manipulation that other warlord leaders had employed. Keeping his coalition together increasingly became a matter of special deals, 'connections' (kuan-hsi), and Chiang's perception of personal loyalty to himself. The latter led Chiang to show to Whampoa graduates, even if corrupt or incompetent, a degree of favouritism that was excessive even by Chinese standards. With coalition maintenance the sole order of business, reform was hard to achieve. By turning so sharply to the right in 1927, even though he had excellent reasons for doing so, Chiang eliminated communists from his regime, but he also alienated democratic and Westernizing reformers whose support he needed to lift his regime beyond the constraints of warlord politics as usual. Obviously the 1930s were not propitious for reform in China, but the sense that the revolution embodied in the Northern Expedition had failed to accomplish even what it could was very strong throughout the Nanking decade.

Things got worse in the Sino-Japanese War and the Second World War. The fall of Nanking and the loss of the best Central Army units reduced Chiang's leverage and his ability to control other Chinese factions, and the prestige he supposedly gained as a national leader resisting Japan did not in fact make up for this. Furthermore, Nationalist China lost its customs revenues and most of its tax base. Serious US assistance had to wait until after 1941, and even then did not replace what had been lost. Meanwhile Chungking paid its bills by printing paper money, and let inflation take its course.[6] This led to the growth of a black market and barter economy, coupled with an essentially confiscatory ratio between official and black market rates of exchange for hard currency, which was of course noted by all US personnel in China. The latter also noted, and commented unfavourably upon, the way in which US supplies were pilfered and sold on the black market, or were hoarded for the exclusive use of units considered loyal to Chiang. Some apologists for Chiang claim that the generalissimo was not personally corrupt, but numerous anecdotes (Mme Chiang's rosewood furniture being flown to China over the Hump, for instance) suggest that his closest associates were at least extremely indifferent to wartime priorities. Chiang's expressed wish (related on pp.301–2) to route the US subsidies for certain X-Force divisions through Chungking was instantly interpreted by US personnel, correctly or not, as indicating his desire for a central government rakeoff. Since most US personnel saw plenty of evidence of corruption, demoralization, and unwillingness to prosecute the war seriously, on the Nationalist side, it is not surprising that some succumbed to the siren song of Yenan.[7]

The Japanese surrender did not improve the Nationalist regime. The inhabitants of the Chinese cities under Japanese occupation had been looking forward to liberation by their co-nationals. They were somewhat surprised when Japanese troops remained in charge after

6 Arthur N. Young, *China's Wartime Finance and Inflation, 1937–1945* (Cambridge, 1965) is the best discussion of this problem.

7 David D. Barrett, *Dixie Mission: The United States Army Observer Group in Yenan, 1944* (Berkeley, 1970); Joseph S. Esherick, *Lost Chance in China: The World War II Dispatches of John S. Service* (New York, 1974); and Mark Selden, *The Yenan Way in Revolutionary China* (Cambridge, 1971), are all good examples of the view from Yenan.

Japan's surrender, pending the arrival of designated Nationalist officers. The Nationalist authorities that eventually took over treated these Chinese civilians uniformly as collaborators and traitors. Initial waves of looting and violence were followed by more systematic confiscations under the cover of judicial procedures. No effort was made to win political support. Even the Nationalist constitutional convention at Nanking in 1947 was little more than stage-managed window-dressing to give a façade of legitimacy to Chiang's personal dictatorship. Here the point is that this was widely perceived by educated Chinese, while the equally anti-democratic tendencies of the communists were not.[8]

The island of Taiwan had reverted to Chinese rule on the Japanese surrender. While its Chinese inhabitants had been treated as second-class citizens under Japan's harsh and authoritarian colonial rule, the Japanese had nevertheless developed the island and educated its people. Chinese rule meant looting, violence and general arbitrariness. The Taiwanese rebelled against the Nationalist authorities, in the 2-28 (28 February 1947) Incident and its aftermath, and were suppressed with much brutality and killing, with consequences that continue to the present day.[9]

While inflation had been a serious problem since the start of the Sino-Japanese War, it also became much worse after 1945, and entered its 'runaway' phase while the Nationalist military position was collapsing in North China. It is worth noting that inflation impacted different segments of Chinese society differently. The Nationalist military supported itself by direct confiscation, in the warlord manner, and Nationalist government agencies were increasingly paid in kind as the inflation wrecked the money economy. The worst impact of the inflation, again, was on the people of the recently 'liberated' cities. Reimposition of Nationalist rule meant that their savings and incomes were at once subject to confiscatory devaluation, since the Chinese dollar had lost 90 per cent of its value between 1937 and 1943 alone, and the galloping inflation that followed was much more extreme. The victims of this chaos could contrast their situation with the communist areas, in which unbacked paper currency maintained its value, due to taxation policies that seemed both equitable and effective, and fiscal probity and general honesty seemed to reign.

8 Pepper, *Civil War*, especially chs II, IV, V, and VI for extended treatment of these issues.

9 George H. Kerr, *Formosa Betrayed* (Boston, 1965), for the 2-28 Incident and its background.

All of these factors contributed to the rapid disintegration of Nationalist rule on the mainland once the communists won the decisive battles in North China. Nationalist political and economic failures contributed to the sense that they had lost the 'Mandate of Heaven' in traditional terms, so that there was little chance of holding out south of the Yangtze, as had occurred in earlier periods of Chinese history. They are often cited as general explanations of why the Nationalists lost. But they do not explain the basic question posed at the start of this section: why did Chiang risk, and lose, his best forces in North China? Nationalist military histories are usually fairly harsh on Nationalist generalship during the crucial phase of the civil war. This is true even of those that do not share F.F. Liu's orientation toward the Kwangsi clique. They note in essence that the Nationalist armies committed all the errors made in the earlier encirclement campaigns. Separate columns entered communist areas without supporting one another. Nationalist armies concentrated in city garrisons, leaving large gaps through which communist regular formations could move.[10] But even these histories do not usually question the basic strategy of reoccupying North China as quickly as possible with elite Nationalist units. This was a decision of Chiang Kai-shek, who afterwards never accepted any responsibility for the loss of the mainland. His published works blame the débâcle on Soviet sponsorship of the Chinese communists, and on pro-communist Americans, including Stilwell and Marshall, whose efforts resulted in the cutting off of US aid.[11] These explanations are propaganda.

During the Northern Expedition and the 'residual warlordism' phase following it, Chiang had displayed effective military leadership, even though his forte was political manipulation. Chiang's position during the Nanking decade required him to defeat the armies of Ch'en Chiung-ming, Wu P'ei-fu, Sun Ch'uan-fang, Chang Tsung-ch'ang, Chang Tso-lin, Feng Yü-hsiang and Yen Hsi-shan, of which all but the first were impressive by warlord standards. He was sincerely interested in military reform then, and gave personal attention and support to the German military mission

10 Examples in Whitson, *High Command*, pp.235, 239 and passim.

11 Themes of Chiang Kai-shek, *Soviet Russia in China: A Summing Up at Seventy* (New York, 1957) and much other literature from the early Cold War period. For a critical view, whose publication in the USA the KMT tried to suppress, see Ross Y. Koen, *The China Lobby in American Politics* (New York, 1974). Also Lloyd E. Eastman, *Seeds of Destruction: Nationalist China in War and Revolution, 1937–1949* (Stanford, 1984), pp.203–15, for more of Chiang's views.

and the various efforts to create an air force. Despite defeats in the earlier campaigns of encirclement and annihilation, Chiang's generals devised an effective anti-communist strategy and uprooted not just Kiangsi but all the communist base areas. Since new communist base areas of similar size could be uprooted by the same means, Chiang is really not subject to criticism for his failure to destroy the communists during the Long March. It really made more sense to move against his warlord opposition first, and move against the communists later, as he was doing when Chang Hsueh-liang betrayed him at Sian.

From 1931 to 1937 Chiang was urged, especially by communists and warlords opposed to his rule, to give up civil war and fight the Japanese. While this also appealed to Chinese nationalistic sentiment, even a united China had no prospect of defeating Japan, and Chiang's policy of stalling, appealing for foreign support, and reluctant accommodation was in fact in China's interest. Full-scale war led to disaster, and also exposed Chiang's limitations as a military commander. He contributed to the Shanghai débâcle by trying to command through written orders from Nanking. He wasted troops in frontal assaults and in ordering units to fight to the last man. Such tactics, enforced by discipline based on mutual responsibility (lien-tso-fa), had given Whampoa-led armies a spiritual edge in the warlord wars, but were ineffective and wasteful against the even more dedicated and much more professionally commanded Imperial Army.

From 1938 on Chiang remained very aloof, being briefed by sycophants and cronies and losing touch with military realities on the ground. While his behaviour is easily documented and often described, it is hard to explain. War with Japan led to a vast outpouring of national feeling that the Chiang Kai-shek of the Northern Expedition might have channelled and exploited effectively. Whether he could have succeeded or not, Chiang made no efforts to win genuine loyalty from non-Whampoa generals, so the limited victories over the Japanese won by Li Tsung-jen and Hsueh Yueh only made them more dangerous in Chiang's eyes. Nor did he withdraw his confidence from Whampoa generals despite fairly egregious professional failings: Ku Chu-t'ung, T'ang En-po, Tu Yü-ming, Lo Cho-ying and Ho Ying-ch'in all come to mind, but they were not the only ones. What he wanted from the USA was all the arms he could get; he disregarded the arguments for army reform advanced by Stilwell and Wedemeyer, so that, ironically, the training programme that produced his elite units for the civil war really operated despite Chiang. He was always loyal to Chennault, but after Pearl Harbor Chennault was a US general, and the air force he created left China in 1945. The Chinese inherited a fair amount of equipment, but their air force was not a decisive factor in the civil war.

With awareness of all these factors, one may tentatively reconstruct Chiang's state of mind in the autumn of 1945. He overestimated the effectiveness of his own units, assuming that their monopoly of US equipment made up for any deficiencies in morale, and underestimated the Chinese communists, influenced no doubt by Japanese estimates after the Three All campaigns. He worried, especially after hearing about Yalta, about Soviet designs on Manchuria. At the same time, the United States had several times reaffirmed the official view that his government was the sole government of China, and had placed a lot of airlift and sealift at his disposal. A methodical anti-communist strategy based on the fifth campaign of encirclement and annihilation would have to start from the south, presenting the twin dangers of Russian absorption of a Manchuria unoccupied by Nationalist troops and combinations against Chiang by unreconciled non-Whampoa elements of the Nationalist elite, who would be given opportunities by the amount of time entailed by such a strategy. Against such clear and present dangers, the need for such a strategy is only clear in retrospect, if then, and would have required a better-trained military mind than Chiang's to discern in 1945. In the event, while Chiang failed to get to Manchuria before the communists, he did use the opportunity open in 1945 to move his armies into urban North China, including the cities of southern Manchuria. This decision guaranteed that, when the civil war expected by both sides began, it would be fought in communist territory and on communist terms.

PERIODS OF DIVISION IN CHINESE HISTORY

The civil wars beginning with the 1911 revolution essentially came to an end with Chiang's resignation in 1949, though derivative operations (Hainan, Tibet) continued into 1950. The reform movement beginning in 1901 preceded and contributed to the civil wars, by destroying the checks and balances characteristic of Manchu rule for over two centuries, and by creating the Peiyang and other new-style armies from which the warlords emerged. The persistence of the warlord pattern gives a conceptual unity to the entire period, and both the Nationalist and communist armies were very strongly influenced by what Whitson calls 'the warlord model'. In the end the Nationalists failed to transcend the divisiveness that had perpetuated warlordism. The communists remained united in allegiance to a common ideal throughout the civil war period, and even though factions based on the field armies have been important in subsequent PRC politics, civil war has yet to recur.

Educated Chinese who lived in the 1901–49 period could recognize it as comparable to previous inter-dynastic periods, in which the Mandate of Heaven had clearly departed from one ruling house but had not yet settled on another. Such periods were often quite short: Former Han (206 BC to AD 9) succeeded Ch'in, Later Han (23–220) succeeded Hsin, and T'ang (618–907) succeeded Sui with less than a decade of civil war. On the other hand, Ming (1368–1644) succeeded Yuan only after almost two decades (from 1352) of civil war, the period of the Five Dynasties and Ten Kingdoms (907–60) between the T'ang and the Sung lasted for over half a century, and the famous Three Kingdoms period (usually dated 220–65) preceding the Chin was actually a phase of an even longer period of division.[12] The collapse of the Chin in the fourth century led to a period of division between North and South China that lasted over two centuries. During these periods of division China in some respects resembled a multistate system, with the important caveat that the states lacked legitimacy. There could be only one sun in Heaven and only one emperor on earth. As with the warlords in the twentieth century, the rulers of the several states during such period of division paid an abstract homage to the ideal of unification, while fighting their rivals and betraying their allies in the hope of ultimately winning the big prize.

The inter-dynastic model applies to the 1901–49 period, but only with some significant modifications. Of greatest importance is the fact that the traditional, imperial mode of legitimation and the symbols associated with it lost their force rapidly after 1901.[13] Yuan

12 Representative studies are Hans Bielenstein, 'The restoration of the Han dynasty', in *Bulletin of the Museum of Far Eastern Antiquities* 26 (Stockholm, 1954), pp.1–210, 31 (1959), pp.1–287, 39 (1967), no. 2, pp.1–198, and 51 (1979), pp.3–300; Wang Gungwu, *The Structure of Power in North China during the Five Dynasties* (Kuala Lumpur, 1963); and Edward L. Dreyer, *Early Ming China: A Political History, 1352–1435* (Stanford, 1981).

13 See Joseph R. Levenson, *Modern China and its Confucian Past: The Problem of Intellectual Continuity* (New York, 1964), for a sensitive treatment of this theme.

Shih-k'ai's 1911–16 career illustrates both the speed and the degree of this collapse of the imperial mystique. Having used the major artifact of modernization – the Peiyang Army – to overthrow the Manchus, Yuan then destroyed his power base through his imperial project. Yuan's bewilderment on the eve of his death should not evoke any sympathy, but it is worth noting that even Yuan, one of the most capable promoters and exploiters of change in late Ch'ing China, was surprised and then destroyed by changes in political values that he failed to assess correctly. Chang Hsun's effort, the year after Yuan's death, to restore the Manchus could be treated as comedy because it aroused no support beyond Chang's own troops. The Japanese enthronement of P'u-yi as emperor of Manchukuo blackened what was left of the image of traditional monarchy still further.

The fall of Yuan Shih-k'ai proved that the Republic of China under the five-barred flag stood for more than rejection of the Manchus. It also stood for rejection of the imperial system under anyone. What it stood for in a positive sense was less clear. Sun Yat-sen and his US-derived political theory had been decisively marginalized at the beginning of the republic, and the appeal of Anglo-American political values diminished sharply when the Versailles Conference failed to pay attention to the grievances of Chinese and other non-white colonial peoples. Chinese intellectuals in these years engaged in the process usually called 'intellectual ferment' in which all foreign systems were eagerly debated and combined eclectically with elements from the Chinese tradition. These intellectuals came out of a Confucian tradition that stressed political participation, and many continued this effort at participation during the warlord period; Liang Ch'i-ch'ao and his Progressive Party come to mind. But such intellectuals could not serve warlords in the way that their ancestors had served the founders of imperial dynasties in China's past history.[14] Then, the adherence of intellectuals to a warlord was tangible evidence that the Mandate of Heaven was settling on him, that the warlord was

14 Levenson, *Liang Ch'i-ch'ao*; Benjamin Schwartz, *Chinese Communism and the Rise of Mao* (Cambridge, MA, 1958); Chow Tse-tsung, *The May Fourth Movement: Intellectual Revolution in Modern China* (Cambridge, MA, 1960); and John W. Israel, *Student Nationalism in China, 1927–1937* (Stanford, 1966), all are related to the issues raised in this paragraph. The best recent analysis of the traditional relationship of Confucian intellectuals to imperial power is John W. Dardess, *Confucianism and Autocracy: Professional Elites in the Founding of the Ming Dynasty* (Berkeley, 1983).

becoming a legitimate emperor in the context of a political theory understood and accepted by peasants and soldiers as well as by the intellectuals who articulated and interpreted it. Even though the northern warlords of the 1920s had the best armies in China, there was no Mandate of Heaven for them to win. This fact helped to prevent military victory from being conclusive. Warlords such as Wu P'ei-fu or Chang Tso-lin, who through skill or luck on the battlefield rose above their peers, faced coalitions of frightened rivals and betrayals by jealous subordinates.

Sun Yat-sen, often regarded as impractically idealistic and naive, nevertheless understood from the beginning of the warlord period the need for both a political doctrine to replace the Mandate of Heaven and an army loyal to this doctrine. The Canton Regime and the Whampoa Academy ended up incubating the party armies of both the KMT and the CCP. The two parties remained allies during the critical early stages of the Northern Expedition, and the amalgam of modern nationalism, rights recovery, democracy and development gave the National Revolutionary Army a degree of legitimacy comparable to that conferred by Mandate of Heaven symbolism on previous imperial armies. The ability of Chang Hsueh-liang and other northern warlords to adopt the red, white and blue KMT flag, often interpreted as a symptom of the failure of the Northern Expedition, is in fact a symbol of its partial success.

Chiang Kai-shek broke with the communists in 1927, fought afterwards with Yen Hsi-shan and Feng Yü-hsiang and with the communist-led rural insurrection, and continued the policy of civil war even after the Japanese takeover of Manchuria in 1931. In all of these policies Chiang followed the traditional statecraft of the imperial period, with which he was well familiar. Most Chinese dynastic founders had to destroy militarily over-powerful subjects even after being proclaimed emperor, and most dealt with rural insurrection by basing themselves on the cities and extending control networks from there. Even the Sung, who were notable in their effort to minimize violence and contain militarism during the founding process, nevertheless took care to end domestic opposition to their rule before turning (unsuccessfully) against the Liao invaders.[15] Chiang hurt his chances by always retaining the mentality of a faction leader, and by his loyalty to subordinates who

15 Edmund H. Worthy, 'The founding of Sung China, 950–1000: integrative changes in military and political institutions' (PhD diss., Princeton, 1976), for early Sung military policy.

were corrupt and/or incompetent. At the same time, it needs to be repeated that much of the agitation for a United Front against Japan after 1931 was orchestrated by Chiang's enemies for their own political purposes, and that Chiang had succeeded in his campaigns against his rival warlords and was on the verge of destroying the Chinese communists when Chang Hsueh-liang betrayed him at Sian in 1936.

The longest periods of division in Chinese dynastic history had been caused by the partial conquest of China by non-Chinese peoples who used their tribal cohesion as the basis of their military power, while using Mandate of Heaven theory to rule their Chinese subjects. The Japanese tried to carry on that tradition, but times had changed. While the Imperial Army retained its cohesion and military dominance within China to the end, the Japanese secured only grudging acceptance of their rule in Manchukuo and not even that in China proper. Chinese nationalism of the modern sort meant that Chinese who could not cooperate with each other still would not collaborate with the Japanese, while a Chinese state that could not expel the Japanese still could not come to terms with them without committing political suicide. The chief beneficiaries of these facts were the Chinese communists. Their past experience at rural insurrection and their United Front propaganda made it possible for them to organize effectively in the rural areas behind Japanese lines, away from the major cities and railways that sustained the Japanese occupying forces. Meanwhile, by destroying the best Nationalist formations and by remaining in occupation of North China, the Imperial Army protected the communists against the Nationalists, even as it inadvertently promoted the communists as defenders of Chinese nationalism by the brutality inherent in the Japanese Three All anti-guerrilla campaigns.

After Pearl Harbor the Sino-Japanese War merged with the Second World War, and the entire China theatre became a very stagnant sideshow in a war against Japan that would be won decisively by US sea power. US aid permitted the Nationalists, to a certain extent, to reconstitute their central military forces, which had largely been destroyed by the Japanese in 1937. These were to be used, however, in the civil war that both sides expected once the Japanese were removed. After 1945, or even 1941, Chinese imperial history was not a trustworthy guide to current events. For the Chinese communists, going to the country in 1927 had been a strategy of desperation. By 1945 they were a large, well-trained and skilled army who were hard to beat on ground of their choosing.

Any student of imperial history in 1945 would have concluded, as Chiang did, that the way to beat the communists was to occupy Peiping and the other cities and railways of North China. In fact this guaranteed that the decisive battles of the civil war would be fought under conditions advantageous to the communists. Even in the narrowest military sense, walled cities that were secure bases against insurrection in the dynastic period turned into death traps for Nationalist armies that had already surrendered their artillery to the communists.

1901–49 AND THE DEVELOPMENT OF MODERN CHINA

The decisive outcome of the period of military modernization, revolution, and civil and foreign war that began in 1901 was the creation of the People's Republic of China in 1949 and its continued rule of the mainland since then. The emergence of the PRC was welcomed by thousands of well-educated and patriotic Chinese who were not originally communists. These felt, in essence, that the CCP had gained the right to govern by triumphing over both internal divisions and foreign imperialism. Furthermore, in 1949 communism in its Stalinist form still had considerable economic credibility, and seemed to offer the means whereby China could develop her way rapidly out of the devastated state left by decades of war. Little is left of this optimism now. We shall conclude this account with some consideration of how the wars of the 1901–49 period affected the economic and social development of China in those years, and how the legacy of those wars affected CCP rule since 1949.

Prior to the Boxer Rebellion, Chinese reform efforts had been partial and sporadic, and had resulted in the creation of partially modernized armies (the so-called 'militia armies') and a limited industrial infrastructure (Foochow Shipyard, Kiangnan and Hanyang Arsenals) to support them. After 1901 the Manchu Reform Movement, as related, aimed at a thirty-six division modern army supported by military schools and arsenals on the necessary scale. Comprehensive educational reform and the building of a national railway network, including the buying back of lines that had been built with foreign capital, also were planned. The fate of the military reforms has already been treated in some detail. The history of the railways, which have been referred to frequently in the account of the wars, deserves a word or two, since the railways illustrate the way in which continuing civil war prevented economic growth.

Railway development of course was the cutting edge of economic modernization in the nineteenth century, in Europe, Russia and the USA as well as in China. There railways figured in the post-1895 partition schemes and in the creation of spheres of influence by the imperialist powers, of which the Chinese Eastern (Russian), South Manchurian (Japanese) and Tsingtao–Tsinan (German) railways were the most prominent examples. During the Manchu Reform period, the government actively promoted railway construction and railway recovery became a slogan of Chinese nationalism. Private investment in railway companies became briefly popular, and the Ch'ing government's takeover of these companies, on highly inequitable terms, contributed to the revolutionary situation of 1911. By then the Chinese railway system consisted of, besides the three lines mentioned, two major trunk lines (Peking–Hankow and Tientsin–Pukow, the latter connected by ferry with a Nanking–Shanghai–Hangchow line) plus connecting lines in the north (Mukden–Tientsin and Tientsin–Peking–Kalgan). The Shihchiachuang–Taiyuan line already existed, and the early republic saw further extensions (chiefly Kalgan–Tatung–Paotou in Inner Mongolia, and Wuchang–Changsha) as well as the completion of the east–west Lunghai line that intersected the two north–south lines at Chengchow and Hsuchow.

The outbreak of civil war halted railway development. The northern railway system was maintained, and was a key strategic prize for the Peiyang warlords and then the Japanese and Nationalist armies that successively occupied North China. The southern railways (principally Kunming–Hanoi and Canton–Hong Kong) built by 1911 were still not linked up to the main railway net by 1949. Railway construction in South China came to a halt in these decades, with right of way going back to paddy in some cases.[16] Sun Yat-sen's 'Railway Plan of China' and the dream of modernization and national integration that it represented remained a paper exercise. While China failed to enter the railway age fully, the developed countries meanwhile did fully enter the age of the internal combustion engine, with the air and highway transportation this made possible. China, in other words, in 1949 was relatively even further behind the advanced nations than she had been in 1911, in the critical matter of her transportation infrastructure.

16 Roy M. Stanley, II, *Prelude to Pearl Harbor* (New York, 1982), p.90, has a 1940 aerial photo illustrating this.

Similar observations hold regarding industry. The Chinese textile industry – much of it owned by Japanese or other foreigners – boomed during the First World War. Afterwards, its concentration in the treaty port concession areas shielded Chinese industry to some extent from the vicissitudes of warlord politics, though not from the post-First World War depression and the greater depression that began in 1929. The full-scale Sino-Japanese War that began in 1937 led to Japanese conquest of all the treaty ports, with obvious consequences for industries that depended on stable conditions and access to world markets. The same fate overtook warlord-sponsored industrial ventures. Feng Yü-hsiang and Yen Hsi-shan in particular gained more fame than they deserved as economic modernizers, yet in the end war wiped out their efforts. By 1949 Chinese industry, when not in ruins, was technologically backward and oriented toward a pre-1914 world economy that had vanished forever.

While Nationalist military mistakes permitted the communists to win in the way and time they did, it is also true that the communists were more successful than their rivals in constructing a 'modern' political ideology that could replace Mandate of Heaven theory as a source of legitimacy. Unfortunately for the Chinese people, the way the communists came to power corrupted their exercise of it, and made it difficult for them to pursue a rational strategy of development, even within the inefficient framework of Marxist economics.[17]

During the 1950s China implemented a Soviet model of communist-style economic growth. Agricultural landholding was first 'reformed' and then collectivized. Industry was to be concentrated under the control of central government ministries, each controlling a relatively small number of large enterprises. A state planning committee was responsible for the preparation of the five-year plans which, as in the USSR, were intended to provide detailed blueprints for coordinated economic growth.

Mao Tse-tung turned against this model in the late 1950s, launching instead the Great Leap Forward. While in some respects

17 Compare the concluding remarks of Dick Wilson, *China's Revolutionary War* (New York, 1991), p.188: 'civil war not only destroyed many human and material resources which should have gone into development, a destruction redoubled by the vicious Japanese attack, but it also delivered what remained of China into the hands of people espousing an ideology which was already out of date in its continent of origin, and who lacked the qualifications to bring their compatriots out of their semi-feudal state into the twentieth century'.

similar to the Stakhanovite movement and other speed-up drives in the USSR, the Great Leap also drew on CCP political practice: mass organization of the peasantry and orchestrated mass movements in support of CCP goals had been central to the CCP political style since the founding of the party. By trying to force overproduction in all economic categories during the Great Leap, Mao and his collaborators made nonsense of the planning process; by encouraging local and enterprise initiative in the absence of a market mechanism, they guaranteed that most output would be useless; and by denouncing statistical objectivity as 'bourgeois', they concealed the results even from themselves, until the roof fell in. From 1960 to well after Mao's death the PRC generally refused to publish comprehensive economic statistics of any sort, which made it difficult to assess exactly how dismal its situation was.

Temporarily eclipsed by the collapse of the Great Leap, Mao returned to the offensive in the mid-1960s with the Great Proletarian Cultural Revolution (GPCR). By then the PRC was engaged in polemics with the USSR, in which the real issue was which of the two major communist powers would lead the world communist movement. The last campaigns of the Chinese civil wars were a decade and a half away, and, in a manner reminiscent of the growth of the 'myth of the militia'[18] in the post-revolutionary war United States, official historiography had come to emphasize guerrilla warfare, peasant mobilization and the leadership role of the CCP at the expense of regular troops and standard military science. Lin Piao was then Mao's heir apparent, and the GPCR saw the publication in 1965 of Lin's *Long Live the Victory of the People's War*, which argued that, since People's War was an unbeatable formula by which all Third World countries could throw off the shackles of imperialism and colonialism, communist movements in such countries should look to Peking rather than Moscow for leadership.

Internally, the GPCR reflected Mao's unhappiness with the way in which CCP cadres had come to resemble KMT bureaucrats, and Mao supporters, often youthful, were organized in Red Guard units and ordered to 'seize the headquarters' of party and government organizations and 'snatch the handful' of 'rotten eggs and slippery backsliders' who were Mao's targets. The guerrilla warfare paradigms of these instructions harked back to the revolutionary

18 This term is from Marcus Cunliffe, *Soldiers and Civilians: The Martial Spirit in America, 1775–1865* (Boston, 1968).

heritage of the CCP, and, as in the Great Leap, local initiative was elevated and central planning and direction denigrated. Most PRC institutions collapsed during the GPCR, and roving bands of Red Guards clogged the railways, travelling around the country 'exchanging revolutionary experiences'. Few dared to suggest that this resembled the 'roving bandit mentality' which a much younger Mao had so strongly criticized.[19]

Mao's death (1976) and the eventual succession of Teng Hsiao-p'ing to the highest leadership led to the adoption of more pragmatic economic policies which have proved more successful. Within the Chinese military also, awareness of outside developments has stimulated interest in the practice of the advanced countries, and consequent devaluation of People's War. Meanwhile the world has witnessed a general collapse of faith in communism as a vehicle for economic growth. This has serious consequences for the PRC, since the example of Taiwan's wealthy capitalist economy is well known and envied within the mainland.

These are themes for the future, but they point to the conclusion that China's civil war period still casts a long, dark shadow over the present. For older Chinese, the massive demonstrations against the communist regime in the summer of 1989 held out, not the promise of a more humane new order, but the threat of a return to the anarchic warlordism of the 1920s. They were suppressed on 4 June 1989 by order of 2nd Field Army veteran Teng Hsiao-p'ing, himself a major player in CCP politics and military affairs since the 1920s. During the suppression Chinese armies from different field army groupings seemed, briefly, to be on the verge of fighting one another. After 1901 China achieved a very limited degree of military modernization at the price of political disunity, civil war and retardation of economic growth. The consequences still linger.

19 See Mao, 'On correcting mistaken ideas in the party'. *Selected Works*, I, pp.105–16.

CHRONOLOGY

1368–1644 Ming dynasty: last ruling house of Chinese extraction, whose system of civil service examinations and provincial administration was carried on by the Ch'ing. 'Restore the Ming' was a slogan of early anti-Manchu revolutionaries.

1644–1912 Ch'ing dynasty, established by the Manchu conquest. Manchus conquer much of Central Asia and create the Eight Banners and the Green Standard armies.

1839–42 Opium War and 1856–60 Arrow War. China is defeated by Britain and forced to accept the Unequal Treaties, under which tariff autonomy is lost and foreigners have extraterritorial jurisdiction in Shanghai and other designated treaty ports.

1851–66 Taiping rebellion devastates Nanking and much of Central China. Rise of the militia armies under Tseng Kuo-fan, Tso Tsung-t'ang, Li Hung-chang and others, who suppress subsequent rebellions and carry out piecemeal military and naval modernization in the provinces.

1862–1908 Empress Dowager Tz'u-hsi controls central government throughout this period, usually as regent for her son Emperor T'ung-chih (Tsai-shun, r. 1862–74) or her nephew Emperor Kuang-hsu (Tsai-t'ien, r. 1875–1908).

1884–5 Sino-French War. Naval defeat forces China to abandon role in Vietnam, despite victories on land.

1894–5 First Sino-Japanese War. China cedes Taiwan to Japan (Treaty of Shimonoseki) after unexpected defeat by land and sea, which sets off the Scramble for Concessions among Great Powers expecting imminent partition of China. Discredit of Li Hung-chang, whose apparently powerful Peiyang ('Northern Ocean') Fleet is easily destroyed by smaller Japanese fleet.

1898 Hundred Days of Reform (11 June to 16 September). Monarchist reform on the Japanese model, led by K'ang Yu-wei and Liang Ch'i-ch'ao, and terminated by Empress Dowager Tz'u-hsi with the military support of Yuan Shih-k'ai.

1900 Boxer Rebellion. Tz'u-hsi believes that Boxers can destroy foreigners with their magical powers. Her declaration of war on all foreign powers is ignored by most provincial governors, including Yuan Shih-k'ai in Shantung. Great Power expeditionary force captures Peking; China signs Boxer Protocol (7 September 1901) and Indemnity, which cripples her finances.

1901 Manchu reform movement begins. Yuan Shih-k'ai as governor-general of Chihli (1901–9) builds Peiyang Army into the most powerful modernized army in China. Other modernized armies in provinces, especially Hupei and Yunnan. Plans for constitutional government lead to creation of provincial assemblies in many provinces by 1911.

1905 Sun Yat-sen reorganizes his revolutionary movement as the Alliance Society (T'ung-meng hui), which appeals to Chinese students studying in Japan. Abolition of civil service examinations; traditional Chinese elite increasingly alienated from dynasty, and officers of the modernized armies increasingly attracted to the revolutionary cause.

1908 Death of Emperor Kuang-hsu and Empress Dowager Tz'u-hsi (14–15 November). Emperor Hsuan-t'ung ('Henry' P'u-yi, b. 1906, r. 1909–12) succeeds under regency of his father Prince Ch'un (Tsai-feng). Ascendancy of Manchu princes and nobles further alienates Chinese.

1911 Canton rising fails (April). Cabinet of Princes (May) and anger in Central and South China over railway nationalization on confiscatory terms. Unexpected success of Wuhan rising (9–10 October), nominally under Li Yuan-hung. Fleet defects to revolution, and many provinces secede. Yuan Shih-k'ai appointed prime minister (13 November), but revolutionaries elect Sun Yat-sen president of the United Provinces (later Republic) of China (ROC, 30 December 1911 to 1 April 1912).

1911 on: beginning of autonomous 'warlord' regimes in certain provinces. Chang Tso-lin (d. 1928) in the three Manchurian provinces, Yang Tseng-hsin (d. 1928) in Sinkiang, Yen Hsi-shan in Shansi (until 1949), the Yunnan Army under Ts'ai O and T'ang

Chi-yao, the 'Old' Kwangsi clique, and lesser forces in Szechwan and Kwangtung. All of these strive to escape control of Yuan Shih-k'ai's Peiyang Army, which remains the strongest army in China at this time.

1912 Ch'ing (Manchu) dynasty abdicates (12 February). Provisional constitution, under which Sun Yat-sen yields Presidency to Yuan Shih-k'ai (1 April), with Li Yuan-hung as vice-president, and Alliance Society reorganized as Nationalist Party (KMT).

1913 KMT wins elections to parliament. Reorganization Loan (April). Yuan repudiates KMT (May). Yuan crushes 'Second Revolution' (led by Li Lieh-chün in Kiangsi, July) and sends Peiyang Army units to occupy Yangtze provinces. Yuan formally elected president (6 October), and purges KMT from parliament (November).

1914 First World War begins (August); Japan takes Tsingtao from Germany (November).

1915 Japan presents Twenty-One Demands on China (18 January). Yuan proclaims himself emperor (12 December). Rebellion of Yunnan Army under Ts'ai O (25 December).

1916 Yuan repudiates monarchy (22 March) as other provinces secede and disaffection grows in Peiyang Army. After Yuan's death (6 June), Li Yuan-hung succeeds as president; he restores 1912 constitution and recalls parliament elected in 1913. Peiyang Army begins to split into Chihli clique (under Feng Kuo-chang and actually based on lower Yangtze region) and Anhwei clique (under Tuan Ch'i-jui and strongest in Peking area), with Chang Hsun as an independent force. Tuan appointed prime minister (1 August) with de facto control of Peking government; Feng elected vice-president (16 October).

1917 President Li Yuan-hung dismisses prime minister Tuan Ch'i-jui (23 May) and dissolves parliament (13 June). Chang Hsun seizes Peking and 'restores' Manchus (1–12 July). Tuan Ch'i-jui defeats Chang Hsun and resumes power as 'prime minister' (to 20 November), while Li Yuan-hung resigns presidency to Feng Kuo-chang. China declares war on Germany and Austria-Hungary (14 August). Sun Yat-sen's first Canton government (3 September 1917 to April 1918), supported by navy and Yunnan military clique.

1918 Tuan Ch'i-jui prime minister (23 March to 10 October). Nishihara loans and growth of War Participation Army under Hsu Shu-cheng. Ts'ao K'un abandons Feng Kuo-chang; Hsu Shih-ch'ang becomes president (10 October 1918 to June 1922).

1919 Shanghai peace conference (February). Tuan Ch'i-jui dominated government signs Treaty of Versailles; May Fourth Movement begins. Military government at Canton disintegrates (October onwards).

1920 An–Chih War (4–19 July): Chihli clique led by Ts'ao K'un and Wu P'ei-fu defeat Anhwei clique led by Tuan Ch'i-jui and Hsu Shu-cheng. Elimination of Anhwei clique except in Fukien and Chekiang; Fengtien Clique under Chang Tso-lin takes over Inner Mongolia. Ch'en Chiung-ming conquers Canton area (October) and is appointed governor thereof by Sun Yat-sen.

1921 Sun Yat-sen's second Canton government (May 1921 to August 1922). Chinese Communist Party (CCP) founded (July).

1922 Washington conference treaties (signed 4 February) all impact on China. Dismissal of Communications clique prime minister Liang Shih-yi (22 January) leads to First Chih–Feng War (April–May): Chihli clique forces under Wu P'ei-fu defeat Fengtien clique under Chang Tso-lin. President Hsu Shih-ch'ang resigns (2 June), and is replaced on an acting basis by ex-president Li Yuan-hung. Sun Yat-sen calls for a Northern Expedition against the warlords, but Ch'en Chiung-ming forces him out of Canton (June–August).

1923 Sun Yat-sen's third Canton government founded (March). Ts'ao K'un inaugurated president (10 October). Chang Tso-lin reorganizes Fengtien military.

1924 First KMT–CCP United Front (January). Whampoa Military Academy founded under Chiang Kai-shek (May). Canton Merchants Association strike (August) and failed coup (October). Second Chih–Feng War: Feng Yü-hsiang betrays Chihli leadership and seizes Peking (20 October). Ts'ao K'un and Wu P'ei-fu eliminated as military powers; Tuan Ch'i-jui becomes provisional chief executive (November) but Chang Tso-lin controls Peking area and Feng Yü-hsiang gets the northwest.

1925 Death of Sun Yat-sen (12 March). Ch'en Chiung-ming tries to seize Canton (January–February) but is defeated by KMT Eastern Expeditions (July, October). May 30th Incident in Shanghai and beginning (June) of Hong Kong and Canton strike. Assassination of Liao Chung-k'ai (20 August) leaves Wang Ching-wei leader of KMT left. Sun Ch'uan-fang consolidates control of five lower Yangtze provinces, and Wu P'ei-fu regains control of Hupei (October). Western Hills conference (November) of KMT right. Kuo Sung-ling rebellion against Chang Tso-lin (November–December).

1926 War between Chang Tso-lin and Feng Yü-hsiang, who is forced out of Peking and Inner Mongolia area into Shensi-Kansu (December 1925 to August 1926). *Chung-shan* incident at Canton (18–21 March). Chiang Kai-shek designated commander-in-chief (4 June) of the KMT National Revolutionary Army (NRA) for the Northern Expedition, which begins 1 July. NRA conquers Hunan–Hupei (July–August) and Fukien-Kiangsi (October–November) while moving toward Shanghai and Nanking. Hunan general T'ang Sheng-chih and many other warlord-affiliated units join NRA. Revolutionary activities and anti-foreign attacks in wake of Northern Expedition.

1927 Left-dominated KMT civil government at Wuhan, led from April by Wang Ching-wei. Shanghai and Nanking fall to NRA (March). Chang Tso-lin raids Soviet embassy in Peking (6 April); his troops push NRA back to Yangtze (3–11 April). Chiang Kai-shek launches massacre of communists and leftists at Shanghai (12 April). T'ang Sheng-chih moves on Chengchow while Chiang Kai-shek takes Hsuchow and confers with Feng Yü-hsiang (20 June). Feng and T'ang both turn against left. Chang Tso-lin and Sun Ch'uan-fang counter-offensive (July–August) leads to Chiang Kai-shek's resignation (12 August). Temporary capture of Nanchang marks birth of CCP People's Liberation Army (1 August). Chiang marries Soong Mayling (1 December). Ho Ying-ch'in and Kwangsi generals Li Tsung-jen and Pai Ch'ung-hsi defeat Chang Tso-lin and Sun Ch'uan-fang troops and expel them from Kiangsu (August–December). CCP-led Canton commune (December). Chiang resumes duties as commander-in-chief (20 December).

1928 NRA reorganized (February) into four army groups: 1st under Chiang, 2nd under Feng Yü-hsiang, 3rd under Yen Hsi-shan, 4th under Li Tsung-jen. Campaign against Chang Tso-lin (April–June). Tsinan Incident (3 May). Chang Tso-lin evacuates Peking and is assassinated (4 June). His son and successor Chang Hsueh-liang submits to KMT National government (December).

Temporary Organic Law (10 October) enacts Sun Yat-sen's

legacy of a Five Yuan constitution with the national capital at Nanking. Peking renamed Peiping; Chihli renamed Hopei. National government gains international recognition (July–December) and right to tariff autonomy. Generalissimo Chiang Kai-shek controls National government until 1949, sometimes under a figurehead president, but always as de facto commander-in-chief.

Chu Te joins Mao Tse-tung in the Chingkangshan area (May) and reorganizes communist military forces. Chu and Mao evacuate Chingkangshan (December).

1929 Chiang levers Kwangsi generals out of Hupei with Feng Yü-hsiang's help, then by bribery secures the defection of part of Feng's army. War between Chiang and Feng. Chang Fa-k'uei, supported by Kwangsi clique, fails to wrest Kwangtung from Li Chi-shen.

Main communist force under Chu and Mao in Kiangsi, while smaller communist areas in Oyuwan (Hupei–Anhwei border region) and Hunan survive.

1930 'Enlarged Conference' of KMT at Peiping, sponsored by Feng Yü-hsiang and Yen Hsi-shan, joined by Wang Ching-wei and Hu Han-min, calls for Chiang's resignation and proclaims new government (9 September). Chiang campaigns in Honan and Shantung while Chang Hsueh-liang, supporting him, takes Peiping and Tientsin. Defeat and exile for Feng and, temporarily, Yen.

Kiangsi communists win in first encirclement campaign (December 1930 to January 1931).

1931 Arrest of Hu Han-min (May) provokes anti-Chiang forces to create counter-government at Canton, supported by Kwangsi clique. Communists win second encirclement campaign (May) in Kiangsi; Oyuwan area also survives two Nationalist offensives. Provisional constitution adopted (5 May) by Nanking government. Chiang Kai-shek personally directs (from June) third encirclement campaign (August–September), which defeats Kiangsi communists. However, Mukden Incident (18 September) and subsequent Japanese takeover of Manchuria realigns Chinese politics: Chiang is forced to call off third encirclement campaign, permit Yen Hsi-shan to resume control of Shansi, and bring Canton opposition into Nanking government (Wang Ching-wei as chairman of the executive Yuan, December 1931 to December 1935).

1932 US Non-recognition doctrine proclaimed by Secretary of State Stimson (7 January). Shanghai Incident (28 January to May), in which Ts'ai T'ing-k'ai and the 19th Route Army hold out against Japanese. Chang Kuo-t'ao's Oyuwan communists defeat Nationalist third encirclement campaign (January). Japanese proclaim independence of 'Manchukuo' (18 February; Aisin Gioro P'u-yi as regent 9 March and later as emperor 1 March 1934 to September 1945); League of Nations appoints Lytton Commission. Nationalist fourth encirclement campaign (April–August) uproots Oyuwan communists, anticipating the blockhouse strategy later used in Kiangsi. But the fourth encirclement campaign in Kiangsi (June 1932 to April 1933) results in expansion of communist territory.

1933 Lytton Commission report condemning Japan is adopted by League of Nations, which Japan leaves. Japan occupies Jehol (January–March). Tangku Truce (31 May), signed by Huang Fu on behalf of five northern provinces, creates demilitarized zone in northern Hopei. Fukien rebellion (November 1933 to January 1934).

1934 Prince Te's Inner Mongolian movement at Pailingmiao, Suiyuan (from April). Fifth encirclement campaign (April–October): blockhouse strategy uproots communists, who break out (20 October) and begin Long March.

1935 Communists reach Tsunyi, Kweichow (5 January); Tsunyi Conference restores Mao Tse-tung's authority within CCP. Long March across western China to Yenan, Shensi (by October). Chang Kuo-t'ao's communists join forces with Mao's (June); Chang Kuo-t'ao's break with Mao (September). Hopei–Chahar Political Council created under Ch'in Te-ch'un (18 June); Ch'in-Doihara agreement (23 June). East Hopei Autonomous Council under Yin Ju-keng (24 November).

1936 Chiang Kai-shek establishes his own authority in Kweichow, Yunnan and Szechwan in wake of Long March; Chang Hsueh-liang resurfaces as one of Chiang's generals. Death of Hu Han-min (May); Ch'en Chi-t'ang's rebellion against Chiang (June–July), whose failure brings Kwangtung and Kwangsi under Chiang's control. Chiang orchestrates campaign in which Yen Hsi-shan and Chang Hsueh-liang are to crush Yenan communists. Fu Tso-yi defeats Prince Te at Pailingmiao (November). Sian Incident (12 December) leads to Second KMT–CCP United Front.

1937 Marco Polo Bridge Incident (7 July). Japanese decision to escalate fighting; they take Peiping (31 July). Fighting in Shanghai; Japanese expansion into Chahar and Suiyuan (Kalgan falls, 3

September; Kweisui, 14 October). Lin Piao's communists defeat Japanese at Pinghsingkuan (25 September). Japanese take Shihchiachuang (10 October) and invade Shansi; fall of Taiyuan (8–9 November). Japanese amphibious landing at Hangchow Bay (5 November) leads to collapse of Chinese army in Shanghai area; fall of Soochow (19 November) and Nanking (13 December). *Panay* Incident (12 December) and Rape of Nanking. Chiang moves his headquarters to Wuhan (December). Japanese create puppet 'Provisional Government of the Republic of China' at Peiping (14 December). Communist-dominated 'Base Areas' begin to evolve behind Japanese lines in North China.

1938 Japanese conquer Shantung; Chiang executes Governor Han Fu-chü (24 January). Japanese install 'Reformed Government of the Republic of China' at Nanking (28 March). Li Tsung-jen defeats Japanese at Taierhchuang (March–April). Japanese take coastal cities of Amoy, Foochow and Swatow (May). Japanese take Kaifeng (6 June), but Chiang 'saves' rest of Honan by blowing Yellow River dikes. Changkufeng conflict between Japanese and Soviet forces (11 July to 10 August). Japanese take Canton (12–21 October). Japanese take Wuhan (25 October); Chiang moves headquarters to Chungking.

1939 Burma Road opened to traffic (March). Japanese take Nanchang (27 March). Japan defeated by Soviet forces in Nomonhan battles, which Stalin breaks off because of outbreak of the Second World War in Europe (1 September). Japanese defeated in first effort to take Changsha (September–October). 'Cash and Carry' amendments to US neutrality laws (4 November) benefit Japan. Fiasco of the Chinese winter offensives (November–December). Japanese invade Kwangsi and eventually withdraw in defeat (November 1939 to October 1940).

1940 Wang Ching-wei inaugurates puppet government at Nanking (30 March). April–June: Japanese multi-division raid in Hupei sets pattern for Japanese operations in China until 1944. July–October: Britain closes Burma Road to traffic during the critical phase of the Battle of Britain. September: Japan occupies northern Vietnam after fall of France; partial US embargo on trade with Japan; Japan joins Germany and Italy in Tripartite Pact.

Communist Hundred Regiments campaign in North China (20 August to 10 September) is defeated, followed by extensive Japanese 'mopping-up operations' (October–December). Communists tacitly abandon the idea of operations against Japanese main force units for the rest of the war against Japan.

1941 USA begins Lend-Lease programme (March); beginnings of AVG. Hitler invades Soviet Union (22 June). Japan occupies southern Vietnam (July); US total embargo on trade with Japan. Hsueh Yueh defeats second Japanese attempt to take Changsha (September). Japanese take Chengchow, Honan (October). Japan attacks Pearl Harbor (7 December), Malaya, and other locations, bringing USA and Britain into the war.

New 4th Army Incident (4–17 January) in Anhwei effectively ends Second KMT–CCP United Front. KMT forces blockade communist areas for the rest of the war.

1942 Japanese conquer Philippines, Malaya and Dutch East Indies. Japanese invade Burma (11 December 1941); fall of Rangoon (7 March). Stilwell appointed to CBI (February). Japanese complete conquest of Burma; Stilwell's 'walkout' (to 15 May); his plan to train Chinese troops in India (X-Force), with a later echelon in Yunnan (Y-Force). Chennault rejoins US service; his air plan and the limitations of Hump tonnage. US victory at Midway (June), Guadalcanal campaign; Allied victories at Stalingrad, El Alamein, and the landings in North Africa (November) change direction of war, but British Burma offensive (winter 1942–3) is a failure; Wingate and the LRPG.

1943 Roosevelt tilts toward Chennault's air plan (3 May). Hupei campaign (May–June) falsely represented as a major Chinese victory. Quebec conference (August) creates SEAC under Mountbatten, but only limited US–British interest in the amphibious assault on Burma (BUCCANEER) that Chiang wants. Chinese X-Force troops invade northern Burma (October); Stilwell starts training a third echelon (Z-Force) at Kweilin. Chennault raids Taiwan (November), and Japanese start planning an offensive against his airfields. Cairo and Tehran conferences (November–December): BUCCANEER cancelled to free landing craft for operations in Europe.

1944 Advance of X-Force in northern Burma; siege (May–August) of Myitkyina. Japanese Arakan (February) and Imphal–Kohima (March) offensives against British forces, who win after heavy fighting. Roosevelt threatens to cut off Lend-Lease unless Y-Force supports Burma campaign, but Y-Force operations (from 11–12 May) fail to open Burma Road in 1944. Japanese Honan campaign

(April–May) is prelude to ICHIGO offensive (June): Changsha falls (18 June), followed (through September) by other airfield locations in Hunan and Kwangsi. 'Southern Opposition' plot against Chiang (July). September crisis: Stilwell recalled and replaced by Wedemeyer (October). Japanese phase out ICHIGO and open land link with their forces in northern Vietnam (December).

Philippine Sea naval battle and invasion of Marianas (June), Leyte landings and Leyte Gulf naval battle (October): with Japanese air and naval power gravely weakened, Japan can be invaded from the Pacific, ruling out a major US expeditionary force in China.

1945 Lashio taken, Burma Road reopened (by 4 February). Yalta Conference (7–12 February). Iwo Jima (19 February to 17 March) and Okinawa (1 April to 21 June) campaigns. Hiroshima (6 August), Soviet invasion of Manchuria (from 8 August), Nagasaki (9 August), Hirohito's surrender broadcast (15 August), Japan's formal surrender (2 September). Peiping, Nanking, Shanghai and other major cities reoccupied by Nationalist troops, aided by US airlift and sealift. Communists move into Manchuria, with Soviet assistance. Marshall named Truman's 'personal representative' in China (December).

1946 'Cease-fire' in Manchuria (10 January). Sixty Division plan for a unified Chinese army (February). Nationalist armies take Shenyang (15 January) and occupy central and southern Manchuria (May); they cross the Sungari and are stopped by cease-fire (6 June). Marshall asks to be recalled after Nationalists take Kalgan (10 October) in violation of cease-fire; this leads to Nationalist control of Peiping–Paotou railway line. National Assembly convened in Nanking (15 November) to create permanent Five Yuan constitution.

1947 Massacre of anti-KMT demonstrators on Taiwan (28 February). Nationalists take Yenan (19 March). Hopei: Nieh Jung-chen threatens railway lines to Peiping, briefly takes Shihchiachuang (19 October). Shantung: Communist gains, Tsinan–Tsingtao railway line cut, followed by communist victories at Taian and Mengliangku (April–May), and defeat at Nanma. Lin Piao's offensives in Manchuria (from January) and defeat in Szuping campaign (May–June), followed by September–November offensives aimed at cutting railway lines between Nationalist-held cities. Liu Po-ch'eng crosses Yellow River (30 June), and marches to former Oyuwan area.

1948 Chiang Kai-shek elected president (19 April) with Li Tsung-jen as vice-president. Ch'en Yi commands communist offensives in Shantung (from March), which cut railway lines and isolate Nationalists in cities; fall of Yenchou (13 July) and Tsinan (24 September). Further Communist offensives in Manchuria; capture of Szuping (13 March), after which Nationalists are isolated in Chinchou (surrenders 15 October), Changchun (surrenders 17 October), and Shenyang (surrenders 1 November). Huai–Hai campaign (November 1948 to January 1949): Ch'en Yi and Liu Po-ch'eng destroy main Nationalist force at Hsuchow. Fu Tso-yi isolated in Peiping (by 14 December) as Lin Piao moves to support Nieh Jung-chen.

1949 Communists take Tientsin (14–15 January). Fu Tso-yi surrenders Peiping (20 January). Chiang Kai-shek announces 'retirement' (21 January); Li Tsung-jen becomes acting president. Yen Hsi-shan flies to Canton (March); communists take Taiyuan (April); P'eng Te-huai's forces overrun northwest China. Communists cross Yangtze (March) and take Nanking (23 April) and Shanghai (25 May). Mao Tse-tung proclaims People's Republic of China (PRC, 1 October), and communists overrun the rest of mainland China by the end of the year, while Chiang Kai-shek consolidates his control of Taiwan.

1950 Communist conquest of Hainan and Tibet. On Taiwan, Chiang Kai-shek resumes presidency (1 March), while outbreak of Korean War (25 June) leads USA to defend Taiwan Straits; Communist forces poised to invade Taiwan are redeployed to Korea.

1950–76 PRC under Mao Tse-tung. Agricultural collectivization, the Great Leap Forward (1958–9), the Sino-Soviet Split, the Great Proletarian Cultural Revolution (from 1966). Nixon visit (1972) and beginnings of US–China rapprochement. Mao's death (1976).

1975 Death of Chiang Kai-shek. Slow beginnings of political liberalization in ROC/Taiwan, whose economy is already booming.

1976 Emergence of Teng Hsiao-p'ing as paramount leader of PRC and development of market and export-orientated semi-capitalist economy on mainland.

1989 Tiananmen: demands for democratization of PRC are suppressed.

BIBLIOGRAPHY

Allen, Louis, *Burma: The Longest War, 1941–1945* (New York, 1984).

Anders, Leslie, *The Ledo Road: General Joseph W. Stilwell's Highway to China* (Norman, 1965).

Ayers, William, *Chang Chih-tung and Educational Reform in China* (Cambridge, MA, 1971).

Bales, W.L., *Tso Tsung-t'ang: Soldier and Statesman of Old China* (Shanghai, 1937).

Barbey, Daniel E., *MacArthur's Amphibious Navy* (Annapolis, 1969).

Barnett, A. Doak, *China on the Eve of Communist Takeover* (New York, 1966).

Barrett, David D., *Dixie Mission: The United States Army Observer Group in Yenan, 1944* (Berkeley, 1970).

Bays, Daniel H, *China Enters the Twentieth Century: Chang Chih-tung and the Issues of a New Age, 1895–1909* (Ann Arbor, 1978).

Bergamini, David, *Japan's Imperial Conspiracy: How Emperor Hirohito Led Japan into War against the West* (New York, 1971).

Bielenstein, Hans. 'The restoration of the Han dynasty', *Bulletin of the Museum of Far Eastern Antiquities* 26 (Stockholm, 1954), pp.1–210; 31 (1959), pp.1–287; 39 (1967) 2, pp.1–198; 51 (1979), pp.3–300.

Boorman, Howard L., ed., *Biographical Dictionary of Republican China* (4 vols; New York, 1967–71).

Borg, Dorothy, *The United States and the Far Eastern Crisis of 1933–1938* (Cambridge, MA, 1968).

Boyle, John Hunter, *China and Japan at War, 1937–1945: The Politics of Collaboration* (Stanford, 1972).

Brandt, Conrad, *Stalin's Failure in China* (Cambridge, MA, 1958).

Brunnert, H.S. and V.V. Hagelstrom, *Present Day Political Organization of China* (English translation, Shanghai, 1912).

Burdick, Charles B., *The Japanese Siege of Tsingtau: World War I in Asia* (Hamden, 1976).

Butow, Robert J.C., *Tojo and the Coming of the War* (Princeton, 1961).

Byrd, Martha, *Chennault: Giving Wings to the Tiger* (Tuscaloosa, 1987).

Cameron, Meribeth E., *The Reform Movement in China, 1898–1912* (Stanford, 1931).

Chang, Carsun (Chang Chün-mai), *Third Force in China* (New York, 1952).

Chang, Ch'i-yun, *Chung-hua Min-kuo Ti-t'u Chi* (Atlas of the Republic of China) (Taipei, 1962).
Chang, Hao, *Liang Ch'i-ch'ao and Intellectual Transition in China, 1890–1907* (Cambridge, MA, 1964).
Chang, Hsin-pao, *Commissioner Lin and the Opium War* (Cambridge, MA, 1964).
Chang, Kia-ngau, *China's Struggle for Railway Development* (New York, 1943).
Ch'en, Jerome, 'Defining Chinese warlords and their factions', *Bulletin of the School of Oriental and African Studies* 31 (London, 1968), pp.563–600.
Ch'en, Jerome, *Mao and the Chinese Revolution* (New York, 1965).
Ch'en, Jerome, *Yuan Shih-k'ai (1858–1916): Brutus Assumes the Purple* (Stanford, 1961; 2nd edn, 1972).
Ch'i, Hsi-sheng, *Nationalist China at War: Military Defeats and Political Collapse, 1937–45* (Ann Arbor, 1982).
Ch'i, Hsi-sheng, *Warlord Politics in China, 1916–1928* (Stanford, 1976).
Chiang Chung-cheng (Chiang Kai-shek), *Soviet Russia in China: A Summing Up at Seventy* (New York, 1957).
Ch'ien, Tuan-sheng, *The Government and Politics of China* (Cambridge, MA, 1950).
China, Republic of: Kuo-fang pu, Shih-cheng chu, *History of the Sino-Japanese War (1937–1945)* (Taipei, 1971).
Chow, Tse-tsung, *The May Fourth Movement: Intellectual Revolution in Modern China* (Cambridge, MA, 1960).
Ch'ü, T'ung-tsu, *Local Government in China under the Ch'ing* (Cambridge, MA, 1962).
Coble, Parks M., *Facing Japan: Chinese Politics and Japanese Imperialism, 1931–1937* (Cambridge, MA, 1991).
Coox, Alvin D., *The Anatomy of a Small War: The Soviet–Japanese Struggle for Changkufeng/Khasan, 1938* (Westport, 1977).
Coox, Alvin D., *Nomonhan: Japan against Russia, 1939* (2 vols; Stanford, 1985).
Copp, DeWitt S., *A Few Great Captains: The Men and Events that Shaped the Development of U.S. Air Power* (Garden City, NY, 1980).
Craig, William, *The Fall of Japan* (New York, 1979).
Crowley, James B., *Japan's Quest for Autonomy: National Security and Foreign Policy, 1930–1938* (Princeton, 1966).
Cunliffe, Marcus, *Soldiers and Civilians: The Martial Spirit in America, 1775–1865* (Boston, 1968).
Dardess, John W., *Confucianism and Autocracy: Professional Elites in the Founding of the Ming Dynasty* (Berkeley, 1983).
Des Forges, Roger, *Hsi-liang and the Chinese National Revolution* (New Haven, 1973).
Dorn, Frank, *The Sino-Japanese War, 1937–41: From Marco Polo Bridge to Pearl Harbor* (New York, 1974).

Dreyer, Edward L., *Early Ming China: A Political History, 1352–1435* (Stanford, 1981).

Dreyer, Edward L., 'Military continuities: the PLA and Imperial China', in William W. Whitson, ed., *The Military and Political Power in China in the 1970s* (New York, 1972) pp.3–24.

Earle, Edward M., ed., *Makers of Modern Strategy: Military Thought from Machiavelli to Hitler* (Princeton, 1941).

Eastman, Lloyd E., *The Abortive Revolution: China under Nationalist Rule, 1927–1937* (Cambridge, MA, 1974).

Eastman, Lloyd E., *Seeds of Destruction: Nationalist China in War and Revolution, 1937–1949* (Stanford, 1984).

Eastman, Lloyd E., *Throne and Mandarins: China's Search for a Policy during the Sino-French Controversy, 1880–1885* (Cambridge, MA, 1967).

Esherick, Joseph S., *Lost Chance in China: The World War II Dispatches of John S. Service* (New York, 1974).

Fairbank, John K., and Ssu-yu Teng, *China's Response to the West: A Documentary Survey, 1839–1923* (Cambridge, MA, 1954).

Fairbank, John K., and Ssu-yu Teng, *Trade and Diplomacy on the China Coast: The Opening of the Treaty Ports, 1842–1854* (2 vols; Cambridge, MA, 1953).

Falk, Edwin A., *Togo and the Rise of Japanese Sea Power* (New York, 1936).

Fang, Chao-ying, 'A technique for estimating the numerical strength of the early Manchu military forces', *Harvard Journal of Asiatic Studies* 13 (Cambridge, MA, 1950), pp.192–215.

Feis, Herbert, *The China Tangle* (Princeton, 1953).

Feis, Herbert, *The Road to Pearl Harbor* (Princeton, 1950).

Feuerwerker, Albert, *China's Early Industrialization: Sheng Hsuan-huai (1845–1916) and Mandarin Enterprise* (Cambridge, MA, 1958).

Forbes, Andrew D.W., *Warlords and Muslims in Chinese Central Asia: A Political History of Republican Sinkiang, 1911–1949* (Cambridge, UK, 1986).

Ford, Daniel, *Flying Tigers: Claire Chennault and the American Volunteer Group* (Washington, 1991).

Franke, Wolfgang, *The Reform and Abolition of the Traditional Chinese Examination System* (Cambridge, MA, 1960).

Furuya, Keiji, *Chiang Kai-shek: His Life and Times* (New York, 1991).

Gillin, Donald G., *Warlord: Yen Hsi-shan in Shansi Province, 1911–1949* (Princeton, 1967).

Glantz, David M., *August Storm: The Soviet 1945 Strategic Offensive in Manchuria* (Leavenworth Paper no. 7; Leavenworth, KA: US Army Command and General Staff College, 1983).

Glantz, David M., *August Storm: Soviet Tactical and Operational Combat in Manchuria* (Leavenworth Paper no. 8; Leavenworth, KA: US Army Command and General Staff College, 1983).

Griffith, Samuel B., ed. and trans., *Sun Tzu: The Art of War* (Oxford, 1963).

Griswold, A. Whitney, *The Far Eastern Policy of the United States* (New York, 1938).

Hackett, Roger, *Yamagata Aritomo and the Rise of Modern Japan, 1838–1922* (Cambridge, MA, 1971).

Hail, William James, *Tseng Kuo-fan and the Taiping Rebellion* (New Haven, 1927).

Harries, Meirion and Susie Harries, *Soldiers of the Sun: The Rise and Fall of the Imperial Japanese Army* (New York, 1991).

Hattori, Takushirō, *Dai Tōa Sensō Zenshi* (The Complete History of the Greater East Asia War) (Tokyo, 1964).

Hayashi, Saburō, ed. and trans. by Alvin D. Coox, *Kōgun: The Japanese Army in the Pacific War* (Westport, 1959).

Heinrichs, Waldo H., jr, *American Ambassador: Joseph C. Grew and the Development of the U.S. Diplomatic Tradition* (Boston, 1966).

Ho, Ping-ti, *Studies on the Population of China, 1368–1963* (Cambridge, MA, 1959).

Hofheinz, Roy, *The Broken Wave: The Chinese Communist Peasant Movement, 1922–1928* (Cambridge, MA, 1977).

Hooton, E.R., *The Greatest Tumult: The Chinese Civil War, 1936–1949* (London, 1991).

Hou, Chi-ming, *Foreign Investment and Economic Development in China, 1840–1937* (Cambridge, MA, 1965).

Hsiao, Kung-ch'uan, *Rural China: Imperial Control in the Nineteenth Century* (Seattle, 1957).

Hsieh, Pao Chao, *The Government of China, 1644–1911* (Baltimore, 1925).

Hsueh, Chun-tu, *Huang Hsing and the Chinese Revolution* (Stanford, 1961).

Hu, Chi-hsi, 'Mao, Lin Biao and the Fifth Encirclement Campaign', *China Quarterly* 82 (June 1980), pp.250–80.

Huenemann, Ralph, *The Dragon and the Iron Horse: The Economics of Railroads in China, 1876–1937* (Cambridge, MA, 1984).

Hummel, Arthur W., and Fang Chao-ying, *Eminent Chinese of the Ch'ing Period* (2 vols; Washington, 1943–4).

Hutchings, Graham, 'A province at war: Guangxi during the Sino-Japanese Conflict, 1937–45', *China Quarterly* 108 (December 1986), pp.652–79.

Isaacs, Harold R., *The Tragedy of the Chinese Revolution* (2nd edn; Stanford, 1961).

Israel, John, *Student Nationalism in China, 1927–1937* (Stanford, 1966).

Jacobs, Dan, *Borodin: Stalin's Man in China* (Cambridge, MA, 1981).

Janowitz, Morris, *The Military in the Political Development of New Nations: An Essay in Comparative Analysis* (Chicago, 1964).

Jansen, Marius B., *The Japanese and Sun Yat-sen* (Cambridge, MA, 1954).

Jen, Yu-wen, *The Taiping Revolutionary Movement* (New Haven, 1973).

Johnson, Chalmers A., *Peasant Nationalism and Communist Power: The Emergence of Revolutionary China, 1937–1945* (Stanford, 1962).

Johnson, Chalmers A., 'Peasant nationalism revisited: the biography of a book', *China Quarterly* 72 (December 1977), pp.766–85.

Johnson, John J., *The Role of the Military in Underdeveloped Countries* (Princeton, 1962).
Johnston, Reginald F., *Twilight in the Forbidden City* (New York, 1934).
Jones, F.C., *Japan's New Order in East Asia: Its Rise and Fall, 1937–1945* (London, 1954).
Jordan, Donald A., *The Northern Expedition: China's National Revolution of 1926–1928* (Honolulu, 1976).
Kahn, B. Winston, *Doihara Kenji and the North China Autonomy Movement* (Temple, 1973).
Kapp, Robert A., *Szechwan and the Chinese Republic: Provincial Militarism and Central Power, 1911–1938* (New Haven, 1973).
Kennedy, Thomas L., 'Chang Chih-tung and the struggle for strategic industrialization: the establishment of the Hanyang Arsenal, 1884–1895', *Harvard Journal of Asiatic Studies* 33 (Cambridge, MA, 1973), pp.154–82.
Kerr, George H., *Formosa Betrayed* (London, 1966).
Kessler, Lawrence D., *K'ang-hsi and the Consolidation of Ch'ing Rule, 1661–1684* (Chicago, 1976).
Kinross, John Patrick Douglas Balfour, Baron, *The Ottoman Centuries: The Rise and Fall of the Turkish Empire* (New York, 1977).
Kirby, S. Woodburn, *The War against Japan* (5 vols; London, 1964–9).
Kirby, William C., *Germany and Republican China* (Stanford, 1984).
Koen, Ross Y., *The China Lobby in American Politics* (New York, 1974).
Kuhn, Philip A., *Rebellion and its Enemies in Late Imperial China: Militarization and the Social Structure, 1796–1864* (Cambridge, MA, 1970).
Langer, William L., *The Diplomacy of Imperialism, 1890–1902* (2nd edn, New York, 1951).
Lary, Diana, *Region and Nation: The Kwangsi Clique in Chinese Politics, 1925–1937* (New York and London, 1974).
Lary, Diana, *Warlord Soldiers: Chinese Common Soldiers, 1911–1937* (New York and London, 1985).
Lee, Robert H.G., *The Manchurian Frontier in Ch'ing History* (Cambridge, MA, 1970).
Levenson, Joseph W., *Liang Ch'i-ch'ao and the Mind of Modern China* (2nd. edn; London, 1959).
Levenson, Joseph W., *Modern China and its Confucian Past: The Problem of Intellectual Continuity* (New York, 1964).
Lewis, Bernard, *The Emergence of Modern Turkey* (Oxford, 1958).
Li Chien-nung (ed. and trans. by Ssu-yu Teng and Jeremy Ingalls), *The Political History of China, 1840–1928* (Princeton, 1956).
Li, Lincoln, *The Japanese Army in North China, 1937–1941: Problems of Political and Economic Control* (Tokyo, 1975).
Lin Piao, *Long Live the Victory of the People's War: In Commemoration of the 20th Anniversary of the Victory in the Chinese People's War of Resistance against Japan* (Peking, 1965).

Lindsay, Michael (Lord Lindsay of Birker), *The Unknown War: North China 1937–1945* (London, 1975).
Liu, F.F., *A Military History of Modern China, 1924–1949* (Princeton, 1956).
Lo, Jung-pang, ed., *K'ang Yu-wei: A Biography and a Symposium* (Tucson, 1967).
Lu, David J., *From the Marco Polo Bridge to Pearl Harbor* (Washington, 1961).
McCormack, Gavan, *Chang Tso-lin in Northeast China, 1911–1928: China, Japan and the Manchurian Idea* (Stanford, 1977).
MacKinnon, Stephen R., *Power and Politics in Late Imperial China: Yuan Shi-kai in Beijing and Tianjin, 1901–1908* (Berkeley, 1980).
Mao Tse-tung (Mao Zedong), *Selected Works of Mao Tse-tung, vols I–IV* (Peking, 1961–5).
Marder, Arthur, *Old Friends, New Enemies: The Royal Navy and the Imperial Japanese Navy. Volume I: Strategic Illusions, 1936–1941* (Oxford, 1981).
Marder, Arthur, *Old Friends, New Enemies: The Royal Navy and the Imperial Japanese Navy. Volume II: The Pacific War, 1942–1945* (Oxford, 1990).
Meisner, Maurice, *Li Ta-chao and the Origins of Chinese Marxism* (Cambridge, MA, 1967).
Metzger, Thomas A., *The Internal Organization of Ch'ing Bureaucracy: Legal, Normative and Communication Aspects* (Cambridge, MA, 1973).
Michael, Franz, *The Origins of Manchu Rule in China* (Baltimore, 1942).
Michael, Franz and Chung-li Chang, *The Taiping Rebellion: History and Documents* (3 vols; Seattle, 1966–7).
Morley, James W., ed., *Japan's Road to the Pacific War. Volume I: Japan Erupts: The London Naval Conference and the Manchurian Incident, 1928–1932* (New York, 1984).
Morley, James W., ed., *Japan's Road to the Pacific War. Volume II: The China Quagmire: Japan's Expansion on the Asian Continent, 1933–1941* (New York, 1983).
Neidpath, James, *The Singapore Naval Base and the Defense of Britain's Eastern Empire, 1919–1941* (Oxford, 1981).
Nish, Ian H., *The Anglo-Japanese Alliance: The Diplomacy of Two Island Empires, 1884–1907* (London, 1966).
Nish Ian H., *Alliance in Decline: A Study in Anglo-Japanese Relations, 1908–1923* (London, 1972).
Ogata, Sadako K., *Defiance in Manchuria: The Making of Japanese Foreign Policy, 1931–1932* (Berkeley, 1964).
Oxnam, Robert B., *Ruling from Horseback: Manchu Politics in the Oboi Regency, 1661–1669* (Chicago, 1975).
Pepper, Suzanne, *Civil War in China: The Political Struggle, 1945–1949* (Berkeley, 1978).

Plaks, Andrew H., *The Four Masterworks of the Ming Novel: Ssu Ta Ch'i Shu* (Princeton, 1987).
Pogue, Forrest C., *George C. Marshall* (4 vols; New York, 1963–87).
Powell, Ralph L., *The Rise of Chinese Military Power, 1895–1912* (Princeton, 1955).
Purcell, Victor, *The Boxer Uprising: A Background Study* (Cambridge, MA, 1963).
Pye, Lucien, *Warlord Politics: Conflict and Coalition in the Modernization of Republican China* (New York, 1971).
Rawlinson, John L., *China's Struggle for Naval Development, 1839–1895* (Cambridge, MA, 1967).
Romanus, Charles F., and Riley Sunderland, *Stilwell's Mission to China* (United States Army in World War II, Series 9: China–Burma–India Theater, vol. 1) (Washington, 1953).
Romanus, Charles F., and Riley Sunderland, *Stilwell's Command Problems* (United States Army in World War II, Series 9: China–Burma–India Theater, vol. 2) (Washington, 1956).
Romanus, Charles F., and Riley Sunderland, *Time Runs Out in CBI* (United States Army in World War II, Series 9: China–Burma–India Theater, vol. 3) (Washington, 1959).
Schafer, Edward H., *The Empire of Min* (Rutland, 1954).
Schiffrin, Harold Z., *Sun Yat-sen and the Origins of the Chinese Revolution* (Berkeley, 1968).
Schram, Stuart, *Mao Tse-tung* (Harmondsworth, 1966).
Schrecker, John E., *Imperialism and Chinese Nationalism: Germany in Shantung* (Cambridge, MA, 1971).
Schwartz, Benjamin, *Chinese Communism and the Rise of Mao* (Cambridge, MA, 1958).
Selden, Mark, *The Yenan Way in Revolutionary China* (Cambridge, MA, 1971).
Sharman, Lyon, *Sun Yat-sen: His Life and its Meaning* (Stanford, 1934).
Sheridan, James E., *Chinese Warlord: The Career of Feng Yü-hsiang* (Stanford, 1966).
Slim, William, 1st Viscount, *Defeat into Victory* (New York, 1961).
Snow, Edgar, *Red Star over China* (New York, 1938).
Spector, Ronald H., *Eagle against the Sun: The American War against Japan* (New York, 1985).
Spector, Stanley, *Li Hung-chang and the Huai Army: A Study in Nineteenth Century Chinese Regionalism* (Seattle, 1964).
Spence, Jonathan D., *The Gate of Heavenly Peace: The Chinese and their Revolution, 1895–1980* (New York, 1981).
Spence, Jonathan D., *The Search for Modern China* (New York, 1990).
Spence, Jonathan D., *Ts'ao Yin and the K'ang-hsi Emperor: Bondservant and Master* (New Haven, 1966).
Stanley, Roy M., II, *Prelude to Pearl Harbor* (New York, 1982).
Struve, Lynn A., *The Southern Ming, 1644–1662* (New Haven, 1984).

Sutton, Donald S., *Provincial Militarism and the Chinese Republic: The Yunnan Army, 1905–1925* (Ann Arbor, 1980).
Swanson, Bruce, *Eighth Voyage of the Dragon: A History of China's Quest for Seapower* (Annapolis, 1982).
Tan, Chester, *The Boxer Catastrophe* (New York, 1955).
Thomson, James C., jr, *While China Faced West: American Reformers in Nationalist China, 1928–1937* (Cambridge, MA, 1969).
Tien, Hung-mao, *Government and Politics in Kuomintang China, 1927–1937* (Stanford, 1972).
Toland, John, *The Rising Sun: The Decline and Fall of the Japanese Empire, 1936–1945* (New York, 1970).
Tsou, Tang, *America's Failure in China, 1941–1950* (Chicago, 1963).
Tuchman, Barbara, *Stilwell and the American Experience in China, 1911–1945* (New York, 1970).
US War Department, Military Intelligence Division, *The Chinese Communist Movement*, (2 vols, mimeographed; Washington, DC, July 1945). Col. Alfred McCormack was the author of this study, which was classified 'Confidential' and of which 114 copies were distributed.
Van Slyke, Lyman P., *Enemies and Friends: The United Front in Chinese Communist History* (Stanford, 1967).
Vatikiotis, P.J., *The Egyptian Army in Politics: Pattern for New Nations* (Bloomington, 1961).
Wade, Thomas F. 'The Army of the Chinese Empire: its two great divisions, the Bannermen or National Guard, and the Green Standard or Provincial Troops', *Chinese Repository*, vol. 20 (May, June and July 1851), pp.250–80, 300–40 and 362–422.
Wakeman, Frederic, jr., *The Fall of Imperial China* (New York, 1975).
Wang Gungwu, *The Structure of Power in North China during the Five Dynasties* (Kuala Lumpur, 1963).
Wang, Yeh-chien, *Land Taxation in Imperial China, 1750–1911* (Cambridge, MA, 1973).
Wei, William, *Counterrevolution in China: The Nationalists in Jiangxi during the Soviet Period* (Ann Arbor, 1985).
White, Theodore H., *The Stilwell Papers* (New York, 1948).
Whitson, William W., *The Chinese High Command: A History of Chinese Communist Military Politics, 1927–71* (New York, 1973).
Willmott, H.P., *The Great Crusade: A New Complete History of the Second World War* (New York, 1989).
Wilson, Dick, *The Long March, 1935: The Epic of Chinese Communism's Survival* (New York, 1982).
Wilson, Dick, *China's Revolutionary War* (New York, 1991).
Wilson, Herbert Wrigley, *Ironclads in Action* (2 vols; Boston, 1898).
Wilson, Herbert Wrigley, *Battleships in Action* (2 vols; Boston, 1926).
Worthy, Edmund H., 'The founding of Sung China, 950–1000: integrative changes in military and political institutions' (PhD diss., Princeton, 1976).

Wou, Odoric Y.K., *Militarism in Modern China: The Career of Wu P'ei-fu, 1916–1939* (Canberra, 1978).
Wright, Mary Clabaugh, ed., *China in Revolution: The First Phase, 1900–1913* (New Haven and London, 1968).
Wright, Mary Clabaugh, ed., *The Last Stand of Chinese Conservatism: The T'ung-chih Restoration, 1862–1874* (Stanford, 1957).
Wright, Stanley F., *Hart and Chinese Customs* (Belfast, 1950).
Wu, Tien-wei, *The Sian Incident: A Pivotal Point in Modern Chinese History* (Ann Arbor, 1976).
Yoshihashi, Takehiko, *Conspiracy at Mukden: The Rise of the Japanese Military* (New Haven, 1963).
Young, Arthur N., *China and the Helping Hand, 1937–1945* (Cambridge, MA, 1963).
Young, Arthur N., *China's Wartime Finance and Inflation, 1937–1945* (Cambridge, MA, 1965).
Young, Ernest B., *The Presidency of Yuan Shih-k'ai: Liberalism and Dictatorship in Early Republican China* (Ann Arbor, 1977).

INDEX

AD Saunders 2/97

> COOX, p. 383

> Mao, starting at p. 155.
> Overall Assessment at p. 260.
> Conclusion, at p. 350.
> 1. Nationalism (Unity)
2. Anti Foreign, incl. Japanese
3. No unequal Treaties
Sun/Chiang/Mao
No Feeling

> 3 anti: Kill All, Burn All, Destroy All

Circumstance of peasant

The spark for the dry prairie and strong wind (CO)